I0100660

ADVANCED PRAISE

"It has been pointed out that more can be learned about a society from the way it treats its prisoners than the way it treats those on the outside. The cruelty and inhumanity of death row can easily be described to those who will never directly experience it—what is far more difficult is to enable it to be *felt*, and that is what these stories achieve. This book poses a deep and unsettling question to each of us: What would we lose by treating even the worst offenders as human beings? The answer that emerges from *The Darkest Hour* is shocking and profound: it is our ability to silence our own compassion, to blind ourselves to what we are doing to others, and to pretend that we have acted morally and justly. Yet in doing so, we cause untold suffering not only to prisoners but also to the victims and families, to the entire legal system, to our capacity for justice, and to the culture and society in which we live. This book opens our hearts and changes the way we think." —Kenneth Cloke, former judge, mediator and author of *Dance of Opposites: Explorations in Mediation, Dialogue and Conflict Resolution Systems Design* and *Conflict Revolution: Mediating Evil, War, Injustice and Terrorism*

"Psychologist Betty Gilmore and Nanon Williams, a former death row inmate, bridge academic expertise and personal experience to bring awareness to the extreme psychological, emotional, physical and spiritual impact of isolation and living under a death sentence in Texas prisons. The inclusion of narratives from individuals who have survived death row, as well as those who have not, bring the readers into the story, touching a place deep within the human spirit that will most certainly foster a sense of compassion, while inspiring them to make an informed decision and to initiate meaningful discourse about human rights issues." —Sister Helen PreJean, author of *The Death of Innocents: An Eyewitness Account of Wrongful Executions* and the national best-seller *Dead Man Walking: An Eyewitness Account of the Death Penalty in the United States* which was nominated for a Pulitzer Prize and spawned an Oscar-winning movie and an internationally-acclaimed opera

"In *The Darkest Hour*, Betty Gilmore and Nanon Williams take us into the depths of the darkest part of the darkest institution in our country—the death rows and solitary confinement units of our nation's penitentiaries. They bring us the personal stories of those whose lives have led them to this horror, and they help us experience, just a little bit, what it is like to be there. They also explore the social policies and socio-economic factors that create this experience. Gilmore and Williams face the systemic inhumanity that only humans seem to exhibit, and they challenge us to do better by the people we cast out, reject and often murder. They do this without sentimentality, anger or righteousness. They leave the reader to find their own reactions without prescribing for us what they should be. This is a beautiful, moving, clear-headed and important book that is easy to read, but not easy to accept. It was an act of courage to write this book, and it behooves all of us to read it." —Bernie Mayer, Ph.D., professor of Dispute Resolution, The Werner Institute, Creighton University

"*The Darkest Hour* brings to light the unspeakable abuses that occur in the stark solitary confinement of Texas' death row. The stories of these men expose the inhumanity of a justice system that places them in conditions well known to cause immense pain, mental illness and suicide. *The Darkest Hour* reminds us of our humanity and the urgent need to reconsider the punishments meted in our name." —Terry A. Kupers, M.D., M.S.P., psychiatrist and author of *Prison Madness: The Mental Health Crisis Behind Bars and What We Must Do About It*

"Relegated to remote locations, surrounded by thick windowless walls and abysmal living conditions, America's 3,200 death row inmates are the easiest group of people to think and care nothing about. But major human rights violations are being committed against them daily. Even worse, it's being done in silence. Except in this case. Thankfully, this work sheds light on the fact that all people are entitled to protection and dignity, regardless of whatever terrible, even horrific, things they may have done—or, sometimes, not done. This work also underscores the one essential truth of all human rights work: that there is no such thing as a lesser person." —Dr. Rick Halperin, director of the Embrey Human Rights Program at Southern Methodist University and three-time board chair of Amnesty International USA

"Dr. Betty Gilmore of Southern Methodist University and Nanon Williams, a former death row inmate, have combined their expertise and personal knowledge to produce a most important book on solitary confinement in American prisons. This book provides valuable insights as we strive to bring systemic change to the prison industrial complex so that it is not only more humane in its treatment of incarcerated individuals, but also more effective in its efforts of rehabilitation so that these individuals may become productive members of society." —David Atwood, founder of the Texas Coalition to Abolish the Death Penalty of author of *Detour to Death Row* and *My Search for the Beloved Community*

"People in our prisons are often the most overlooked members of our society. They are hidden away from view, and we know little about what they are thinking and doing. This book is a revealing examination of the experience of death row and offers surprising insights into the attempts of these inmates to live meaningful lives under desperate circumstances. Readers will come away from this book thinking of the possibilities of redemption in this population." —Richard Tedeschi, Ph.D., Professor of Psychology, University of North Carolina, Charlotte

The Darkest Hour is a must-read for all who are concerned about the effects extreme isolation in Texas prisons has on those who are incarcerated. The focus on the death penalty highlights the particular horrors for those who are incarcerated as they await execution, shedding light on the inhumanity that impacts the inmates, guards and the families of all involved. This book will change the way you think about crime and punishment." —Dr. Roger C. Barnes, professor of Sociology, University of the Incarnate Word

"*The Darkest Hour: Shedding Light on the Impact of Isolation and Death Row in Texas Prisons* by Dr. Betty Gilmore and Nanon M. Williams provides a much needed, critical examination of the impact of solitary confinement on human lives. In a unique and scholarly presentation, the authors have tackled the complexity of ascribing linkages between the isolation of a human being in restricted space under conditions of cognitive, sensory and physical deprivation and severe psychological outcomes. As the authors rightfully emphasize, the frequency and severity of isolation-linked trauma must be understood within the context of a constellation of developmental history, socio-economic, psychosocial and neurocognitive factors in order to understand, in detail, the excruciating proximal and distal outcomes of solitary confinement. This work holds promise in adding to the extant knowledge base relevant to PTSD and its various manifestations across different traumatic events." —G. Reid Lyon, Ph.D., Distinguished Scientist in Cognition and Neuroscience, University of Texas, Dallas, and emeritus professor, Southern Methodist University

"This book is essential reading for every American and for anyone who wants to understand how the death penalty really works in the U.S. today. Nanon Williams and Betty Gilmore share powerful insights into the lives of people on death row, the interlocking systems that put them there and the urgency of finding more effective and meaningful ways of responding to violent crime." —Dr. Lisa Guenther, associate professor of Philosophy, Vanderbilt University and author of *Solitary Confinement: Social Death and Its Afterlives*

THE DARKEST HOUR

ALSO BY NANON M. WILLIAMS

The Ties That Bind Us

The Darkest Hour: Stories and Interviews from Death Row

Still Surviving

Peace People

THE DARKEST HOUR

SHEDDING LIGHT ON THE IMPACT OF ISOLATION AND DEATH ROW IN TEXAS PRISONS

Betty Gilmore
Nanon M. Williams

GoodMedia Press
Dallas, Texas

GoodMedia Press
25 Highland Park Village, 100-810
Dallas, Texas 75205
www.GoodMediaPress.com

No part of this book may be reproduced or transmitted in any form or by any means, electronic or mechanical, including photocopying, recording or by any information storage and retrieval system, without written permission from the publisher, except for the inclusion of brief quotations in a review.

Copyright© 2014 Betty Gilmore and Nanon M. Williams. All rights reserved.

Cover design and book layout by Lindsey Bailey.

The text in this book is set in Gotham and Georgia.

Manufactured in the United States of America

Gilmore, Betty Iglesias.
    The Darkest hour : shedding light on the impact of isolation and death row in Texas prisons / Betty Gilmore , Nanon M. Williams.
    p. cm.
    ISBN 978-0-9883237-6-6

1. Prisons--Texas. 2. Prisoners --Texas. 3. Death row inmates --Texas. 4. Death row --Texas. 5. Solitary confinement --Texas. 6. Punishment --Texas. I. Williams, Nanon McKewn. II. Title.

HV9475.T4 G55 2014
364.1/523 --dc23
2012952845

CONTENTS

Foreword   11

Introduction   13

Preface   17

PART I: ISOLATION   23

Life in Isolation   25

Life and Death on the Row   35

The Inside   47

Rights, Ethics and Human Decency in the Face of Isolation   61

PART II: THE IMPACT   69

The Continuum of Grief and Loss   71

The Limits of the Human Psyche   77

Protecting the Vulnerable and Oppressed   105

PART III: INVISIBLE VICTIMS   119

Victim Survivors   121

Stay Strong   129

Unintended Causalities   147

PART IV: ADJUSTING TO THE DARK   165

The Battle to Maintain Self   167

PART V: CALL TO ACTION   191
Ways Forward   193

PART VI: RESOURCES   211
Texas Resources   213
National Resources   215
International Resource   217

PART VII: LAST STATEMENTS   221
The Last Words   223
Acknowledgments   371
About the Authors   375
Bibliography   379
Explore Other Books by Nanon M. Williams   390

FOREWORD

By Susan Sarandon

A S OF MAY 1, 2014, the state of Texas has executed 515 individuals since 1982.[1] Some of these individuals, like my friend James Allridge, were very creative people. Most were hurting, suffering individuals seeking redemption, forgiveness and the basic human craving of unconditional love from a parent, a friend or even a stranger. When James was executed, his final words indicated that he hoped his death would bring peace to the family of the victim. He regretted that he could not make a contribution that would be able to pay back what he had done.

The death penalty robs society of people who are ready to try to give back in some way within the prison system. James wanted to atone for what he did by spending his lifetime in prison.

While the human spirit is strong, life is fragile. Those who have had the horrible experience of witnessing a precious life fade away right before their eyes know well the fragility of this human experience. When society deems the execution of a human being as an appropriate punishment for murder, we overlook the good in that person as well as the suffering that will undoubtedly be experienced by others: the family and friends of the person executed, the warden and correctional officers who carry out the execution, the prison chaplain and the citizens of the state that approved the execution.

Several studies demonstrate that a death sentence is not a deterrent to crime. So what is a deterrent? I would suggest early childhood education and intervention as well as community services that hold the emotional, spiritual and psychological well-being of the child as the core focus. What the world needs is more compassion and empathy.

My hope is that this book will inspire you to view all people through the lens of empathy and compassion for that is how we save lives, heal our nation and save our collective soul.

INTRODUCTION

By Frans Douw, Governor of Prisons, Holland

I FIRST BECAME INVOLVED in working with incarcerated individuals in 1975. I worked as an attendant in a correctional facility for juveniles in the Netherlands. For the past 15 years, I have gained international knowledge through exchange projects with prisons in Russia, Lithuania and Georgia. Today, I hold the position of governor of four prisons in North Holland—a position similar to that of a regional director for Texas Department of Criminal Justice.

Throughout my career working in correctional facilities, I have personally turned the key of prison cells more times than I can count. I am responsible for assigning men and women to isolation, separating them from general population and forcing them to take medication, whether they chose to take it or not. I have had my share of violent incidents, prison riots and hostage situations. I believe it is inherent to the human experience to be compassionate and empathetic to the suffering of others, and yet working in a prison I have often felt like a surgeon putting his knife in the body of another human being who violently opposes the surgery I must conduct. Professionally, I have learned to manage my natural inclination toward empathy. I have become a more hardened individual.

Prison is a closed community that directs itself inward. It is a small, isolated cellar, closed off from society. At times, it feels as though the institution itself is suffocating. The smell in every prison is similar and self-contained. Within these surroundings, one group has all the power and another group has no power at all. Prison is a repressive organization that forces people to not only remain physically enclosed but emotionally and psychologically enclosed as well. The goal of prison administrators and correctional officers is to maintain an environment of cooperation and order. Incarcerated individuals are treated as though they are incapable of managing responsibilities, as though they are children incapable of making the most basic decisions for themselves.

In this self-contained, institutional environment, prison staff and inmates often do not communicate with each other. They speak in the presence of one another about one another as though neither can hear what the other is saying. They stop perceiving each other as human beings—human beings with families, children and personal characteristics. The staff often treat the inmates in the same manner they feel treated by their boss; in other words, the culture of the prison is top-down. Prison is highly hierarchical, and as it is at the highest level, so it will be at the lowest. How the director or warden treats his or her subordinates is how those subordinates will treat theirs. When there is an abuse of power in a hierarchical culture, that abuse of power trickles down all the way to the lowest power member. In prison, this often results in inmate-to-inmate abuse. Prison is a classic example of the survival of the fittest, but in prison, the weak cannot escape. Instead, the weak are bullied, beaten, raped, and at times, murdered. The existence of corruption and unauthorized violence by staff strengthens this mechanism. Staff and inmates tend to create their own set of rules and regulations, which the warden often does not know about. All these tendencies together create a very unsafe environment.

As the governor of prisons, I consciously seek strategies to circumvent these destructive tendencies within the prisons. Incarcerated individuals are people too; they are our fellow human beings. A prisoner is not a different breed of human; they do not derive from another planet. These are individuals who once were our neighbors. They are our brothers. They are children of our friends and friends of our children. They are different from us in that they made severely bad choices that brought severe consequences.

The Darkest Hour: Stories and Interviews from Death Row, the prequel to this book, touched me deeply.[2] Every day I meet young men whom society has deemed as less than human. These men are deeply wounded people whose actions derived from a place within themselves that is scarred and often calloused from years of suffering. And yet, they have feelings just like our own. They are sons, brothers and fathers. I was filled with horror as I read the life histories of the young men depicted in *The Darkest Hour: Stories and Interviews from Death Row*—the violent acts of abuse they suffered as children and committed as young men, their perspectives of themselves and their childhood families and especially the concern they felt for their own children's futures. The interviews, conducted by Nanon Williams, demonstrate the intelligence and empathy of a young man, who despite his own incarceration grew into a wise and respectful person. Although Nanon is no longer on death row due to changes in federal law, the original interviews were conducted from death row at a time in his own life when he had every reason to believe the state of Texas would eventually take his life. His understanding of each man's personal journey on death row brought forth a pure, honest and unique document that could only have derived from an individual with intimate knowledge of such a severe, desperate and inhumane environment.

The Darkest Hour: Shedding Light on Isolation and Death Row in Texas Prisons, the sequel to the above mentioned book, revisits these men more than a decade later. Psychologist Betty Gilmore joins forces with Nanon Williams to examine the impact these prison conditions have on the lives of all it touches— the incarcerated individuals and their families, the prison administration and correctional officers and their families, the victims' families and ultimately society as a whole. Readers experience the story through the lives of men who lived on death row and survived to tell about it. The book demonstrates the impact of prolonged isolation on all those whose lives it touches directly and indirectly.

The quality of the short time we live is the most precious thing any human being has, whether that human being is incarcerated or an individual living in the free world. The question is, "How important is the quality of life of those who are incarcerated?" This book helped me to realize that the answer to this question says a lot about the quality of my own life.

PREFACE I

Betty Gilmore

THROUGHOUT THE COURSE of writing this book, several of the same men who granted interviews to Nanon Williams for the prequel to this book, *The Darkest Hour: Stories and Interviews from Death Row*, discussed in great detail with me the decades of incarceration that they have lived, both on death row and later in the general prison population.[3] Even though all of these men were eventually scattered geographically throughout the Texas prison system after the original interviews, they never forgot Nanon. With the exception of two men— Christopher Coleman and Michael Richard, both of whom were executed after the first interview— the others opened up to me about their current lives, as they will to all of you through these pages, with the hope that their experiences would help to create some desperately needed awareness and action in our communities. There were many other men and their families who shared their stories with us who chose to remain anonymous. They all expressed the same vision—that their voice would serve as a catalyst for change in the outside world.

You will notice that the scope of this book focuses on the experiences of men specifically. The stories in *The Darkest Hour: Stories and Interviews from Death Row* were based on a collection of interviews conducted by Nanon. As an individual living on death row, he only had access to the men with whom he was housed. The specific needs and experiences unique to women are very important, and we chose not to generalize those needs for the sake of including women in this work. Although many of the experiences, statistics and housing conditions are the same or similar to that of men, we believe that a separate piece of work, dedicated to looking at these factors with women as well as other diverse groups, is needed.

Several of the men who chronicled their life experiences to us were minors when they were convicted. In 2005, the U.S. Supreme Court decision in *Roper v. Simmons* concluded that sentencing minors to capital punishment was unconstitutional.[4] As a result, 29 men who were juveniles at the time of the crime for which they were convicted had their death sentences commuted to life in prison. The men were removed from death row and relocated to the general population. Between 1976 and 2005, the United States executed 22 individuals who were juveniles at the time of their alleged crimes. Thirteen of those executions were individuals incarcerated in Texas—the state that executed more juveniles than any other state in the United States. At the time of the *Roper v. Simmons* ruling, Texas also had the highest number of juvenile offenders on death row, more than any other state in the United States.[5] Among the men that were affected by this Supreme Court ruling were Gabriel Gonzales, Oswaldo Soriano, Son Vu Khai Tran and Nanon Williams. They share their narratives in this book.

In 1999, seven men living on death row attempted unsuccessfully to gain their freedom. As a result, the men on Texas' death row were moved from the Ellis Unit to the super-max Terrell Unit in Livingston, Texas, which was later renamed Polunsky Unit. Prior to this time, the men were housed in confinement cells, but their lives were very different than life in a super-max prison. They had the opportunity to leave the barred jail cells during the day, recreate in small groups and participate in work programs that provided them with the opportunity to be productive and interact with others. Following the move to the Polunsky Unit, the men's world got much smaller. They were all placed in complete isolation. In place of the bars that allowed them to see and communicate with those around them, they now lived in complete isolation. Soundproof steel doors prevented the men from seeing and hearing one another. They were no longer able to experience group recreation or the ability to participate in meaningful programming. Many of the narratives told by Martin, Gabriel, Nanon, Oswaldo, Son Vu and Christopher include their experiences and descriptions of death row prior to this move. All of the men were awaiting their executions when the original interviews were conducted.

This body of work is not attempting to justify the criminal actions of any of the individuals who have committed crimes. The suffering that the families and community members of victims have endured has been devastating and have changed their lives forever. I have spoken to survivors and have heard their heartbreaking stories of despair and survival. Every human being has a right to live without fear and feel safe in the communities in which they live. Unfortunately, no one can reverse the crimes that have already been done, and everyone touched by violence deserves to be heard, to heal and to have their needs respected. What we do as a society to move forward after violent acts have occurred, however, is up to us.

In an effort to present as many perspectives and viewpoints as possible, I spoke with many people whose lives have been touched by the criminal justice system. I was both amazed and humbled by how many people, representing multiple walks of life and diverse perspectives, were interested in telling me their stories. Although their positions differed, every one of them had one common interest— they wanted change. Writing this book has been a life-changing journey for all those involved. The spirit of who we are has been forever changed. Due to the subject matter of my study for this book, some people have made assumptions about my personal beliefs. It is a common misgiving that those who choose to take a humanitarian approach to justice are unsympathetic to the plight of the victim and are often accused of being "soft on crime." I caution the readers about the tendency to look at things dichotomously and make conclusions. This type of thinking limits opportunities to consider various viewpoints and prevents people from reaching their own independent conclusions. These matters are much too complex to analyze with "all or nothing" thinking. There is no perfect answer.

The current institutions and practices in the state of Texas that are designed to protect citizens are actually perpetuating a dangerous cycle that is steering us in the opposite direction of the goal to make communities safer for its citizens. Legislators, experts, agencies and community members are asking some important questions right now. For example, what impact does releasing more than 800 Texans from prison in one year directly from spending months, and in many instances years, in solitary confinement with no rehabilitation or adequate treatment back on the streets have on the safety of our communities? Did the years of isolation and insult on their physical wellness, mind and human dignity promote in any way their rehabilitation and prepare them for release? Or, did it make them less likely to be successful? Is it possible that the strategies that are currently being used inside of prisons to keep those who are incarcerated and the staff safe by isolating them are actually putting a temporary bandage on a problem that has great fiscal and public health consequences? Is mental illness being created prior to these men's release? Our hope is that readers will wrestle with these questions and consider the implications that the current practices have on the bigger societal picture and what they say about the values of the state of Texas.

Removing the layers of these multi-faceted and complex social and human rights issues allows us to uncover the grim realities that reside underneath. Many people feel powerless regarding issues that threaten humanity and seem beyond their control. These are truths that not everyone wants to accept or integrate into their belief systems, making it more likely to turn away from mass injustices and ignore the impact that this has on a mass scale. This type of apathy can have dangerous ramifications.

As we peel back the layers and look underneath, we find many invisible casualties. We also find a culture in which incarcerated individuals and correctional officers alike often view each other as subhuman, creating a breeding ground for conflict and violence that are held together by the very systems that bind them. When I asked one of the prison guards what it was like to overhear an interview with one of the men, there was a blank stare, followed by a sullen response, "I see him as a person now." The correctional officer seemed to snap into reality when

I asked, "And what if everyone saw these individuals as people?" The immediate response was, "We simply are not allowed to do that." The officer then turned and walked away, seemingly stunned by the realization.

We know that there are various perspectives and strong opinions surrounding the issues that will be raised by the contents of this book. We invite them all. Conflict can be a catalyst for change and growth. Our desire is that this work creates awareness and provokes deeper questions so that productive dialogue can ensue, allowing readers the opportunity to find answers for themselves and be moved to be a part of solutions that create foundations for safer and more humane communities for us all. As Nanon Williams continues to tell me, "We have work to do." Nanon and the strength of his spirit propelled me forward. He gave me, and so many others, the confidence to keep on writing and the belief that we can make a difference in the lives of those whose voices are silenced.

PREFACE II

Nanon M. Williams

THE JOURNEY OF WRITING this book, for me, has spanned more than a decade. Capturing the lives, thoughts and perspectives of the men has not been easy. Telling their personal narratives without experiencing a tidal wave of emotions has been equally challenging. The men who shared their stories in this book have been judged to be the very worst of men, yet they attempt to give their best. Many of them did not expect to be alive to see the prequel to this book, *The Darkest Hour: Stories and Interviews from Death Row*, to completion.[6] They never imagined a sequel would be written more than 10 years later. Of these men, some have long since been executed. Only their words remain.

Some of their stories are heartbreaking, and the men involved were highly aware of the fact that their words, when taken public, might run the risk of negative repercussions. The personal narratives I provided in this book are given only from the perspective of the incarcerated man. They do not represent the perspectives of all of the others involved or affected by their actions, including the victims and their loved ones. I believe the perspectives of victims and those who commit crimes and hurt others should be shared and merged together to look at the whole. All of the perspectives matter greatly. Everyone has an important story to tell. As a former death row prisoner, my intent has never been to ignore those who have been victimized by others. Individuals who have been harmed by the actions of others need to be heard and understood, and they need healing in order to move forward with their lives.

Although I always told my co-author Betty Gilmore that I may not be around to see this body of work move forward, time has taught me that change occurs on both societal and individual levels. This book will primarily be used as a tool to educate others, raise awareness about the prolonged effects of isolation and allow us to reexamine old issues in creative new ways. I know each story has the potential to tear away the group ideologies that repeat historical patterns of inequality. The individual can rise above and beyond the web that catches some and learn to form their own views based on the knowledge that they had the courage to obtain themselves. I hope the information that we have provided in this book helps us all to take steps toward promoting institutional change and the eradication of extreme forms of punishment.

While researching the material required for this book, Dr. Gilmore faced insurmountable hurdles as she went through appropriate channels to seek information. I experienced personal attacks for daring to reach beyond the confines of the prison cell. Individuals close to me were removed from my visitation list in an effort to cause enough pain and pressure to make me stop this work. Much suffering was caused as a result of this work. We often had to ask ourselves: "Is this worth it?" And ultimately, the answer lies in the fact that the struggles we faced as individuals in this journey pale in comparison to the internal struggle one faces when presented with the opportunity to do what is right yet unpopular and chooses to do what is easy and without controversy. When people have the courage to advocate for social justice and be agents for change, we create new lenses for us all to see through. A tremendous amount of courage was required of Dr. Gilmore and of our friend and publisher Robyn Short, who has been integral to the process to see this book through to its fruition.

PART I
ISOLATION

CHAPTER ONE
LIFE IN ISOLATION

To deprive a gregarious creature of companionship is to maim it, to outrage its nature. The prisoner and the cenobite are aware that the herd exists beyond their exile; they are an aspect of it. But when the herd no longer exists, there is, for the herd creature, no longer entity, a part of no whole; a freak without a place. If he cannot hold on to his reason, then he is lost indeed; most utterly, most fearfully lost, so that he becomes no more than the twitch in the limb of a corpse.

—John Wyndham, The Day of Triffids

WHEN THE CELL DOOR closes the first time, it seems final. Steel slamming against steel creates a solid, final, unbreakable sound that would make anyone want to jump out of his skin. The sliding steel door instantly steals away the sight of the world, separating everything within from the rest of civilization. The sense of being buried alive is overwhelming. The cell becomes its own microcosm, a concrete tomb; separate from humanity, separate from society, separate even from the lowest caste that exists at the bottom of the human quagmire.

The visual appetite remains hungry with the need to feel connected to something, anything, but there is nothing. In just a few seconds, one can scan the whole of the enclosure, yet the need to see something new cannot be quenched. The "nothingness" is all-consuming; it is suffocating. There is nothing on the concrete walls; nothing on the concrete floor; nothing on the ceiling. There is nothing to examine but the same six by 10 feet enclosure of absolute nothingness.

There is a steel slab that protrudes from the wall with a blue plastic, sweat-ridden mattress that other men, many of whom are now long dead, have slept on. Built more like an oversized shelf than an actual bed, the steel frame bites into a person's skin. The water from the sink and toilet, which are combined into a single unit, are the only link to the outside world. As the water flows in and back out, a sense of envy is born—the water can leave; it is only here until the next flush. But even the water has a miserable existence amid the feces caked onto the toilet bowl by the many men who have lived and possibly died in this godforsaken nothingness.

Hours pass, and then days. The months turn into years. The nothingness has become an armor worn on the hottest of days. The solitary cell and the body seem to become one. There is no fresh air and no circulation, and temperatures can creep as high as 120 degrees Fahrenheit. The heat is a heaviness that accompanies the solitude. The men pour water on the concrete floor to lie in, or they wet their clothes in an attempt to cool their body temperature. The sound of other men screaming, trying desperately to prove that they are indeed alive, becomes the voice of solitary. Solitary itself seems to be its own living breathing entity—it is alive. The person living in solitary, however, often feels dead.

Three times a day a lukewarm food tray is thrust through a slot in the door, a practice that is used to feed animals in captivity. The captors must feed the solitary monster. "Sit down on your bunk, Inmate, if you want to eat;" "Stand up and face the wall, or you will not get a tray;" or, even worse, "Get on your hands and knees and face the wall." Orders are barked into the cell three times a day as officers walk cell by cell pushing child-sized portions of barely edible food into the belly of the solitary beast. Anyone who refuses to comply with the orders will not be fed. More often than not, the food is not worth the self-degradation required to receive it. What is sometimes worth the degradation is the few seconds of connection to something outside the smothering solitude, even if it is just a voice. For two or three seconds, a brief scent from outside the cell wafts in and the sounds of something other than one's own heartbeat and deafening breath can be heard. Those two seconds are the reward, not the food that is barely fit for human consumption. Some officers seem to have lost the ability to realize they are feeding human beings; they seem to be feeding the cell itself and not the human inside it.

A walk-in closet, a bathroom, a non-climate control storage unit—there is nothing that feels like home in a 60-square foot concrete box. Contrary to the popular image that media portrays of steel bars slamming shut with the incarcerated individual looking out through the bars, the door of a confinement cell is solid steel. There is a small window that is of questionable size. When questioned about the exact size of the window, TDCJ public information officer replied via email, "I don't know exactly, but probably ten inches high and maybe 2 feet long."[7] This is approximately the size of a piece of notebook paper. To gain access to it, the individual must climb on the bunk to reach it. The window is the only source of natural light; it is the only connection to the outdoors.

There is little stimulation, and the tiny, porous holes in the wall can only be counted so many times. Cleaning the stench from the walls, sink and toilet can become an obsessive compulsion. Since the cell and the body become one, cleanliness can take on a new meaning. Movement is the only thing that can push back the solitude, but it never gives. The solitude is relentless. The solitude never lessens, and it never offers even the slightest moment of reprieve. Eventually the senses begin to lose the battle. Sight, smell and sound all begin to wave little white flags, surrendering to the solitude and accepting defeat. The solitude, however, is a mighty beast that never gives up. The solitude never surrenders.

Sleep becomes the great escape. Dreams are vacations where the mind can travel and escape the unending nightmare of the waking hours. Waking from these dreams is as heart-wrenching as the escape was life-saving, as the solitude dutifully greets the break of each dream getaway. Sleep never lasts more than a couple of hours at a time. Just as the sweet, nocturnal dreams begin to overcome the beast of solitude, an officer switches on a bright light or bangs on the cell door, and the "fight or flight" mechanism of the brain swiftly puts an end to the great, sleep escape. Adrenaline pumping, heart pounding, all chances of sleep have disappeared.

Count time. "Stand up Inmate. What's your name? What's your number?" Orders are once again commanded. Seven times a day officers walk the row taking count of the state's human property—12:00 a.m., 2 a.m., 5 a.m., 8 a.m., 1 p.m., 3 p.m., 7 p.m., 10 p.m., and then the never-ending cycle repeats itself. There is never more than a two-hour period without someone banging on the door. Sleep, the only escape, is as crushingly unattainable as human contact itself.

The lack of human contact is more painful than a blow to the abdomen would be with a baseball bat; physical violence becomes desirable because at least then there would be human contact. The idea of touching a blade of grass, feeling the wind blow, experiencing any skin on skin contact, or even watching other human beings have these experiences on television, are thoughts that become so painful, it is impossible to even consider them. One constant thought begins to run like a ticker across the mind, "Is death the only way out?"

Solitary, confinement, isolation, the hole, the box, management cell, blackout cell, administrative segregation—all the different terms equate to one word that is a perfect description ... hell.

ALTHOUGH IT CAN BE DIFFICULT to even imagine the misery of what an hour, a week or a lifetime of deprivation can be like, thousands of human beings live this deplorable existence every day. The United States houses far more people in solitary confinement than any other democratic nation.[8] The state of Texas alone houses thousands of individuals who are forced to live in isolation cells. As of March 2014, there were 7,433 adult individuals deemed by the state of Texas as "the worst of the worst" and placed in extreme isolation within the walls of the Texas Department of Criminal Justice system (TDCJ). This includes individuals classified by the terminology of TDCJ as being in solitary confinement, protective custody, administrative segregation and those individuals living on death row who also live in solitary confinement.[9] All of them are living in the same conditions of isolation. Of those individuals, 273 are awaiting their executions on death row.[10] Other than some individuals in protective custody, individuals in isolation do not have telephone privileges, making any opportunity for connection with other individuals an abnormality.[11]

Prison environments must be safe for the staff, the correctional officers and the incarcerated individuals. This responsibility to safety presents a tremendous challenge to the prison community. There are violent individuals who pose a serious threat to others and the highest level of vigilance is required. Texas prisons are severely understaffed, which makes maintaining this level of vigilance difficult.[12] Texas Department of Criminal Justice offers recruitment bonuses to full-time employees in an effort to address these concerns.[13] Insufficient staffing increases the threat risk to others, a situation that would ordinarily require heightened levels of security. This problem creates a dangerous vacuum. Solitary confinement serves as a resource to address the repercussions of under staffing in Texas prisons. Although the long-term consequences and threats to safety related to complete isolation can be severe, prison staff find it to be "easier," at times, to manage individuals who are locked in solitary cells 23 hours per day rather than in large groups where violence is often more difficult to control.

Texas Department of Criminal Justice uses different terminology than what is used in this book for describing conditions of solitary confinement. There are three different types of isolation housing utilized by the Texas Department of Criminal Justice. Each of these designations has several different levels for which incarcerated individuals may be assigned according to their perceived level of threat to themselves and others. In the Texas system, individuals who live in isolation are assigned to one of the following: 1) administrative segregation, 2) solitary confinement, or 3) death row.

Administrative Segregation

According to the Texas Department of Criminal Justice's *Administrative Segregation Plan (2012)* Administrative Segregation is defined as:

> ... a non-punitive, maximum custody status involving the separation of an offender from general population for the purpose of maintaining safety,

security, and order among general population offenders and correctional officers within the prison and the public.

An offender shall be considered to be in administrative segregation anytime the offender is separated from the general population in a cell for 20 hours or more without disciplinary hearing.

At no time shall administrative segregation be used as a punishment for misconduct.

There are three levels of administrative segregation—all reportedly based on the offender's behavior. Although the previous statements indicate that segregation shall not be used as punishment, the same document asserts that offenders can be assigned on a level due to being a "chronic rule-violator."[14]

There are a few reasons cited by TDCJ as to why an incarcerated individual would be assigned administrative segregation:

If an individual is identified by TDCJ as a gang member in one of the 12 identified Security Threat Groups upon arrival, they are immediately assigned to administrative segregation. They are not entitled to any vocational or academic opportunities. Their status remains permanent while incarcerated unless they apply and are selected to the GRAD program.[15]

Individuals can also be placed in administrative segregation or solitary confinement as defined by TDCJ for a rule violation. These violations can range anywhere from horrific acts of violence, escape and sexual misconduct, to using obscene language or talking too loud. "Protective custody" is another type of administrative segregation that is used to provide protection to vulnerable incarcerated individuals. These individuals are placed in isolation on a permanent or temporary basis. Individuals who may be placed in protective custody include: those who have been preyed on by people in general population; some members of law enforcement, judges and public officials; someone who has been sexually assaulted; a gang member who is trying to remove himself from a gang.[16]

In essence, being a victim of a traumatic event during incarceration, such as rape or another violent crime, can lead a person to be placed in harsh isolation conditions, for their "safety and protection." Although it is not considered to be a punitive status by TDCJ, this practice can also further marginalize a victim in some situations. In one example, a man of small stature was brought in on a non-violent, drug-related charge. Within a few days of his stay in general population, he was sexually assaulted by multiple unidentified men. After receiving appropriate medical care, the sexual assault victim was placed in protective custody to ensure his protection from the men who had violated him. "Protective custody" is complete isolation. While this person may at first feel a sense of relief, his protective custody will become a nightmare, as he will now be forced to serve the remainder of his sentence in complete isolation. Some individuals have expressed a preference to live in isolation, as their fear of being killed in general population is so great. Given the fact that the prison system is too ill-equipped and understaffed to control its violent offenders, vulnerable populations, including juveniles, must be isolated "for their own protection." Although the term "punishment" is not used, an individual who is placed in this custody level loses a significant amount of mobility and human contact, and the isolation subjects them to a new level of deprivation while they simultaneously attempt to cope with the traumatic impact of their recent victimization. The walls have literally closed in on them.

Protective custody is defined as "an Administrative Segregation status designed to provide the ultimate protection to offenders."[17] According to data obtained from the public information office of TDCJ on May 1, 2014, there were 73 individuals in protective custody at TDCJ.[18] These individuals are segregated from general population, but they have different privileges than other administrative segregation offenders. For example, according to the *Administrative Segregation Manual*, individuals in protective custody are: (a) allowed to group recreate, which is different from all other administrative segregation statuses; b) able to view television programs; (c) provided opportunity to shower seven days a week.[19] The idea being that they are not in protective custody because they are a risk to others but because they are in need of special protection, so a greater degree of freedom is permitted.

In a phone interview with the director of the public information office for TDCJ by which the conversation was confirmed over email, he reported that although the policy allows for individuals within this level of administrative segregation to group recreate, the current practice is currently that they do not recreate in groups. Instead, they recreate individually—i.e., in complete isolation. The reason, as described by John Hurt, is that "it is easier that way, as a general rule."[20] Doing what is "easier," may help temporarily, but individuals whose behavioral health declines may pose a greater threat upon release, creating yet another management issue. In addition, it is a violation of the rights of the individuals who are entitled to group recreation.

Every six months, each administrative segregation case is reviewed to determine whether the individuals should return to administrative segregation or if they should be re-integrated into the general prison population.

Solitary Confinement

On its website, the Texas Department of Criminal Justice defines Solitary Confinement as, "The separation of an offender from the general population as punishment assessed during the disciplinary process."[21] The *Offender Orientation Handbook* further defines the housing status:

> ... a segregated housing status, which may be imposed as the result of a major disciplinary hearing or a State Jail offender disciplinary hearing. Solitary confinement is ordinarily used when all other levels of discipline have been tried; where the safety of other offenders or staff is concerned; or when the serious nature of the offense makes it necessary. Offenders in solitary will be allowed out of their cell only one (1) time each day to shower. Offenders may be placed in solitary for up to 15 days. Consecutive terms will be separated by 72 hours.[22]

Death Row

Death Row is different from solitary confinement and administrative segregation. Death row is not considered a designated status in the prison, but it has its own area of housing. The living conditions for all of the described isolation statuses, including death row, are very similar but may vary slightly depending on the individual unit within the Texas prison system. All individuals living on death row are held in solitary confinement cells that are on average 60 square feet. They live in their cells 23 hours per day with one hour of individual recreation and no opportunities for physical interaction other than the interaction required for shackling their ankles and wrists when being transported from one location to another.

GIVEN THAT LOCKING INDIVIDUALS in confinement, as referred to when describing protective custody privileges by the public information director, can make the environment easier for the correctional officers and other prison staff to manage, many question if the practice is overused. Steve J. Martin, former General Counsel for the Texas prison system stated, "It is easier to get into segregation than to get out."[23]

Overuse of Isolation Conditions

In an effort to gain the perspective of correctional officers on these matters, a qualitative research study was conducted with participation from thebackgate. org, a Texas-based criminal justice and personnel- and employee-based website.[24] The response rate was low due to multiple factors including an expressed fear of retaliation and distrust of the true intentions of the survey. After the survey was posted, readers and forum members of thebackgate.org posted comments cautioning TDCJ employees to not participate in the survey. One individual warned, "Be careful boys and girls, be VERY careful." Another comment read, "This could go real bad. Smells like a story that could turn on you, be careful."[25]

The responses that were gained, however, seemed to confirm the views that were expressed by others. One participant, for example, who posted on thebackgate.org,[26] shared a similar concern to Steve Martin's by explaining, "I saw many offenders that were either put into isolation, or mistreated when it was uncalled for. Many of the officers I worked with took advantage of their position and used it to mistreat the offenders." Another officer stated, "I have seen inmates that are in population who need to be locked in solitary, and some in solitary that could make it in general population. The TDCJ classification system of placing these inmates where they need to be has been broken and ineffective for years."

Although many people are placed in solitary confinement due to a serious threat to themselves or others, there are individuals assigned to isolation who are not a physical threat and are not incarcerated for violent crimes. Individuals can be sent to solitary confinement for a broad range of issues including rule violations and non-violent acts. The overuse of isolation conditions is raising the same old questions on a new level and on a national scale. On June 19, 2012, the Senate Committee on the Judiciary held the first ever congressional hearing of the Subcommittee on the Constitution, Civil Rights and Human Rights entitled, "Reassessing Solitary Confinement: The Human Rights, Fiscal and Public Safety Consequences." During the hearing, Senator Dick Durbin expressed concerns about what this practice implies about our nation's values. He also reported his concerns that confinement was not only being used for "the worst of the worst," but also for individuals who do not need to be there.[27]

Due to the fact that all of the individuals described above live in almost complete isolation and have very similar housing conditions and maximum security status whereby they are confined for weeks, years or a lifetime, all of these living conditions will be referred to as solitary confinement from this point forward in this book, a deviation from the various terms used by the Texas Department of Criminal Justice to describe individuals who live in isolation cells. The official language adopted by the Texas Department of Criminal Justice and other prison systems across the United States used to describe confinement, such as "administrative segregation" and "protective custody," add a layer of sanitization or a cleaner way to frame the harsh conditions that present isolation in a light of protection and separation. This can ultimately minimize the negative connotation and associations of cruelty that are often used to describe solitary confinement.

Regardless of the various terminologies and their respective connotations, they are all mechanisms that describe the immobilization and complete control of human beings. Historically, these mechanisms of control have their roots in, among other factors, a lack understanding and a need to exert power to gain control.

CHAPTER TWO

LIFE AND DEATH ON THE ROW

He saw either death or the approach of it everywhere. But his undertaking now occupied him all the more. He had to live his life to the end, until death came. Darkness covered everything for him; but precisely because of this darkness he felt that his undertaking was the only guiding thread in this darkness, and he seized it and held on to it with all his remaining strength.

— Leo Tolstoy, Anna Karenina

DEATH ROW IS A long stretch of solitary confinement that begins the day a person enters and continues until the last breath of life that occurs strapped down on the table with people watching from all angles. Back and forth they pace—sometimes for miles at a time. The only destination is to escape deep into the recesses of one's mind in hopes of never returning to this small space. Nothing prepares a person for life on death row. The isolation, lack of human contact, idleness and the harsh conditions all have a devastating impact on the psychological health of a person, but it is the slow and painful wait for one's own death that can be the most psychologically traumatizing.

SON VU KHAI TRAN was born in Vietnam and waited three years in the Harris County jail for his trial. A jury, most likely not of his peers, sentenced him to death when he was 20 years old for crimes committed when he was a teenager. Son's first interview for *The Darkest Hour: Stories and Interviews from Death Row*, the prequel to this book, was conducted in the county jail in the late 1990s.[28] At the time, he was anxiously awaiting his transfer to death row. In his initial interview, Son was reluctant to share too much about himself, and he spoke very little about his childhood. After getting to know Nanon Williams—who was at the Harris County jail on bench warrant—Son and Nanon developed a friendly relationship.

When Son first entered the cell block, he wore a mask of anger. He quickly took off his shirt to display the tattoos that covered his upper torso. Displaying an image of toughness was an effort to disguise his fear. In a sense, Son's tattoos were a coat of armor to ward off potential prison predators.

Son wasn't just going to prison; he was going to death row. His imagination was running wild with curiosity about his new environment and fear of the unknown. The realization that he would be living amongst 500 convicted killers gave him reason to be on guard. Son knew he would not have anyone to relate to culturally on death row. Most prisoners could find comfort in relating to someone of the same background. Son grew up in gang-infested environments in which gang affiliation was a means of survival. Having a gang affiliation also meant having a social network, a group in which Son felt he belonged. Because of his ethnicity, Son knew Texas death row was not a place where he would fit in. Being one of the few Vietnamese in the entire country on death row, Son was trying to adjust to the realization that soon he would be more alone than ever before. He rarely, if ever, had the chance to use his native language while incarcerated in Harris County, unless he was speaking to his parents. Son would soon learn just how blessed he was it to have such loving parents who supported him.

Son's parents came to the United States when the communists took over South Vietnam and drove them out of their country. "To be suddenly uprooted from the country my father fought for was very hard. Think about it, when the place you call 'home' is taken from you, many can't imagine what that is like," he shared. Throughout his childhood and teenage years, Son's family moved frequently from state to state, making it hard for him to develop and keep friendships.

With respect to education, Son completed the eighth grade. Although his parents tried their best to instill the importance of obtaining an education, Son did not find school to be a place that he fit in. He pretended to go to school, but he was actually skipping it altogether. His mom was physically disabled, and his father worked at night. Speaking only their native tongue, Son's parents had a very difficult time keeping up with his academics. They could not communicate with his teachers or school administrators. Ethnic discrimination had been a thread that had woven itself around Son ever since he could remember. It was a constant part of his life. Son described the impact that discrimination had on his life: "I've had to deal with racism from blacks, whites and Hispanics. For some reason, people always think most Asians are Chinese, that we know karate and that my family owns some kind of store."

During his incarceration in the Harris County jail, Son's teenage playful side came out at times. He would often engage in a trash-talking game of dominoes and shared a genuine smile with others. Those were memories he could hold onto as he developed friendships—friendships he would most certainly lose through a constant onslaught of executions.

While awaiting his transfer to death row, fears of being an open target for others invaded his thoughts. The daunting reality that those around him would die made him determined not to form any relationships when he arrived. "I want to protect myself from any more pain," he explained.

Although he knew he had to protect himself from the pain, he was ill-prepared for what he would find. Years later, he recalled what his experience was like when he arrived to death row. The way that he spoke made it clear that it was a memory that he would have preferred to keep buried.

> I was butt-naked with guards standing around with a baton; they were joking and thought that it was funny that I was standing there naked. I didn't like that. When I walked through the gate, everything was shut off, dark. They turn off the lights so you sleep and don't bother them. A lady puts me in the cell, closed it and walked off. They didn't tell me anything. These people don't give a damn about you.

Arrival on Death Row

When the newly arrived are assigned their cells, many of them wonder about all of the men who died there before them, wondering if they are next, and knowing there will be more after them. They contemplate the fact that many men had slept on their very same mattresses, looked out the same small window and put their drawings on the same walls. Other men lived their last years in the same minuscule space, waiting to be executed. Their ghosts are always present. Death is ever present.

Among those living on death row, there is often a sense of solidarity that has been described in a manner that is rarely seen in the general inmate population. Since they cannot see each other through the steel doors and can only hear each other if they shout, they form complex methods of communication in desperate attempts to have some form of human connection.

Homemade "fishing lines," which are strictly prohibited, are used to pass items back and forth between cells. Death row is a community complete with values, norms and communication systems. Several men have described arriving to death row feeling mortified to be living amongst a group of "monsters" that reputedly inhabit "the row," only to receive a welcome bag that is passed down the row on a fishing line containing coveted commissary items. Son recalls his experience, "I got a bag when I got there; gym shorts, soap, legal pads, stamps. We help each other out when we get on death row."

Christopher Coleman, who was interviewed by Nanon Williams in *The Darkest Hour: Stories and Interviews from Death Row* and who has since been executed, had a difficult time describing his arrival to death row.[29] Upon his arrival at Ellis Unit, he got off the bus at the back gate and was handcuffed and shackled from head to toe, feeling as though he was being looked at as if he was a wild beast. When placed in a dirty and soiled cell, the sound of his neighbor screaming over and over again pierced his soul. In his interview he recalls thinking, "I have to do what I have to do, and I meant that in regards to many things. ... I had to preserve my sanity and to survive at all costs." Christopher defined death row as a place that was designed for psychological torture as well as a breeding ground for anxiety.

Martin Draughon, a former death row inmate also interviewed for the prequel of this book, detailed the sense of palatable anxiety of living on death row, "If you *could* go to sleep, right after, they wake you up to pick up your tray, shower, recreation; they wake you up for whatever reason—count, turn the cell light on, angry, beating on the doors, counts, beat and bang on the door, just checking to make sure you are OK and still alive." The inability to ever get more than an hour or two of sleep felt like a form of mental torture on death row.

The Darkest Hour

Upon receiving a death sentence, a person is not given an execution date, usually for years, even a decade. Once convicted, individuals are allowed to appeal their convictions, but it is not likely any type of relief will be granted, even for those with strong evidence pointing to their innocence as well as those who did not receive a fair trial. Once condemned to death row, the solitary confinement cage becomes a living graveyard, and everyone on the row knows that. Execution dates are typically set several months in advance, with seemingly no rhyme or reason to the appointed date. Some counties seemingly forget prisoners, and they are there for years prior to getting a date. Other counties seem more expedient in the process. For months at a time, the person to be executed and all those on death row count down the days. The person being executed will write farewell letters because there is no access to phones and many are not fortunate enough to receive visits. And, when a visit does occur, there is the barrier of thick Plexiglas and a black telephone. Those on death row will never again have the ability to touch or hug their loved ones. From the moment they are sentenced until after their death, their loved ones are denied the ability to hug or touch their own child, friend or family member. Those who do have visits from loved ones watch helplessly as their loved ones' mouths tremble, eyes widen and then begin blinking fast, trying to force back the tears. Their voices crack, as the battle against the tears is quickly lost and salty drops begin streaming down their faces, and then the floods come. Words of hope are given, Bible scriptures are quoted and the feeling of loss is immediate. Laugher keeps some from crying, but the laughter is only a skeleton with no life whatsoever. Grief is evident, and the fear is often palatable. Pregnant with emotion, the condemned men return to their isolated cells. The solitude, the concrete walls and all the pain give birth to a new feeling of desperation and helplessness.

Eventually, the condemned individual receives a notice of execution date and has a meeting with the supervisor to go over details of the execution procedure. There are forms to fill out that require the individual to choose what size clothing he will wear to the execution, what witnesses he would like present, what he would like to happen with his body and possessions following the execution. Once he receives his execution date, according to TDCJ's *Execution Procedure,* "The condemned offender may be moved to a designated cell."[30] The incarcerated individuals often refer to this cell as a "deathwatch cell" because they are closely monitored for suicidal behavior.

Arnold Prieto, who received his execution date for January 2015, provides his account of the experience in the following letter.

> May 12, 2014
> As the mist of my early morning dream of walking down the ling corridors of a futuristic warehouse dissipated, I heard my name being called from far away. It was 6:32 a.m., and the far away voice was that of a female mail room staff member: "Prieto! 999149?! Show me your ID! You have a certified letter."
>
> As I was walking to my cell door in a morning fog, I instantly realized what was actually waiting for me at my door … death.
>
> After getting my ID back from the mail room lady, she opened my legal letter before me and inspected its contents without reading the actual legal papers. She passed it to me after she saw it was cleared of any contraband. She walked off to continue her work day, her life, not knowing she was the messenger of death. I fault her not, of course, for she was only doing her job.
>
> Sure enough, the letter contained an order to set an execution date and the warrant of execution. As I read the order, I heard clear as a bell the ticking hand very loudly … click, and it started to tick. I'll be quite honest with you, while I read my legal papers and how my life had an expiration date, my heart sank to the pit of my stomach. As you can see from the order of execution and warrant, my number is to be punched January 21, 2015. My ticket has been called.

"149! 149!" calls out the Angel of Death. So I step forward and out of the formation of "normal" ... and onto the conveyor belt toward the Texas killing machine behind four other men. So the process starts now ...

May 15, 2014
Today is Thursday night, and I have been moved to death watch. Death watch is a section of 14 cells that have 24/7 surveillance. In each cell is a camera that has night vision as well. It took three days to be moved because TDCJ had to process the death warrant which validated my execution date.

I was already waiting for the move, so I had all my property backed and ready to go. After lunch, I was escorted to the captain's office for the interview with her. The captain proceeded to tell me that I was given an execution date for January 21, 2015 and basically what I needed to know and gave me a copy of the execution summary and notification of execution date.

Captain Tamez did her job very well and professionally, she answered all my questions with short and precise answers. During my interview with the captain, my property was being packed into a laundry buggy to be X-rayed and shaked down for any pills and any other contraband. I am not allowed to keep my "KOPs" (keep on person) medications. In my case, it was my blood pressure meds. I now have to depend on a pill tech to bring me my medication twice a day. After my talk with Captain Tamez, I was escorted straight to A-Pod 12 cell in the death watch section. As I walked in, I heard my name called from all those guys that know me, but as I walked into the death watch section, I heard four guys call out to me. The loudest saying: "Prieto!! Man I got a cold bucket of water!"

He made that comment because we were living on the same pod before he was moved to death watch. He was not given any kind of legal notice as I had. On Wednesday, May 14, he was called to the captain's office and was told that he had an execution date set for October. He actually thought he was confused with me because his name is similar: Paderes. He was living in seven cell while I was living in 17 cell. Thus the statement, "I got a cold bucket of water." I feel for my young friend for that is one hell of a rude awakening indeed. The guards packed all his property while I had my property all packed up. Now we are but one cell apart from one another. He is holding on strong ...

As I now sit on death watch, in this cold cell, penning you this entry, I cannot help but to think of the opening of an Iron Maiden song called "Hallowed Be Thy Name." It opens like this: "I'm waiting in my cold cell, when the bells begin to chime ..." Unfortunately, the song is about a condemned man sentenced to the gallows pole. I will be right back ...

I just *had* to stare up into the camera for a minute or so! I needed to stare back at it for a while to let it know that I too can stare back at it! And yes, I did blink first!

Yeah, I can now see that it is going to take me a while before I'll get used to it! I have no choice but to get used to it somehow ...

Soon, everyone on the row knows who has an execution date. Sometimes that person is a neighbor, the guy a couple of cells away or the guy below on the first tier. As a person's execution date draws closer, all the men watch the shift in his behavior—his heightened quest for redemption; the sense of loss being felt deeper than ever before; the need to be forgiven and understood; the change in his tone of voice as memories are recalled from prisoners talking from cell to cell; and the outburst of emotion from being overly sensitive.

As the months go by some of the men become sensitive toward those with pending execution dates. Talk of the future is intentionally avoided. The men attempt to sidestep the expression of anger, sadness or even laughter in consideration of others whose days are numbered. In some cases, it almost feels like visiting a dying friend in the hospital, only through vent shafts. Attempts at comforting the person are overshadowed by the fact that his fate is totally out of anyone's hands. There's nothing anyone on death row can do to really help him except listen and perhaps honor a dying wish or two. Listening is what feels best, but some men do not want to talk at all. Most everyone tries to respect that space as well.

There are also those who simply are not able to cope with their pending executions. They cry, lose control, cut themselves, swallow razorblades, attempt suicide and lash out at anyone within earshot. No matter how the person behaves, most of the men make a conscious effort to be considerate of the soon to be executed man. Everyone knows that his own days are numbered.

Seven days before the execution date the individual scheduled to be executed has his activities logged every 30 minutes. This is referred to as the "Execution Watch Log." In the last 36 hours, activities are logged every 15 minutes.[31]

Before being moved to the Huntsville Unit, the man's personal property is packed up to be mailed to a person of his choice or picked up. Sometimes someone will ask an officer to break the rules and give his property to men on the row with whom he has become close. The items to be dispensed could be a radio, book, fan, writing paper, pictures or commissary items. Some officers are sensitive to this gesture and will pass the items to the men nearby while others remain committed to the rules and fail to honor the dying man's wish. As the man is moved from death row, some men will yell through the doors to say their final goodbyes, while some choose to say nothing, honoring the last few moments of seeing that man alive. Every moment is emotional. For many, the tears do not stop running. Salt lines run down their faces even when there are no more tears and at some point, the night disappears. For those getting visits on the day of their execution, the final goodbyes are said.

Men comb their hair for the last time, perhaps shave, make their jumpsuit as neat as possible to say goodbye to their mother, father, wife, children or friends for the last time. "Now, keep up your head," they may say. "I love you brothers. I'm going home," another will say. While others may offer support by stating, "Keep the faith, be strong, I'm going home," some remain completely silent. Their head may be down in sorrow or lifted with a sense of dignity they feel they owe everyone. They enter visitation for the last time.

For the other incarcerated men who are also at visitation, watching the soon to be executed say their final goodbyes is an emotional experience. They are not allowed a contact visit. They will not touch anyone for the last time. They must communicate with the barrier of the telephone and thick, scratched and smudged Plexiglas that never provides a clear image of the loved one on the other side. There is no privacy for anyone, and all the men in visitation can hear the man's intimate goodbyes on the caged side of the glass, as each man sits in his own cage next to each other.

Then you see it. Mothers crying, begging and pleading, praying out loud and some literally falling out of the stool and laying on the floor. Everyone suffers as they witness children crying, telling their daddy goodbye for the last time. Some understand it is the last time they will ever see their father. Some don't realize that this really is goodbye. The last visitation is orchestrated chaos, and everyone's emotions are like a time bomb, even for the men's families who do not have an execution date. Everyone can imagine this scenario playing out eventually in his or her own lives in the not too distant future. All the men on death row attempt to script in their minds what this scene will be like when it is their turn; but is impossible to truly imagine.

Those moments hurt. They hurt so badly and so deeply that there is no pretense in acting as though everything is all right, because no one is all right. Each man is watching his own experience through the lives of someone else first. No one ever gets used to it. No one ever grows calloused to it. Families try to help each other, needing to connect with other families who carry the same pain and shame of having a loved one executed. Witnessing someone being dragged from the visitation area, whether it is the man's family or the incarcerated man himself, is a very painful sight. Everyone knows that when he leaves his death is not far away. Execution, murder, premeditated and orchestrated killing ... whatever you want to call it, the intentional extermination of a person's life will soon occur. This is the only situation that exists in which a person and his family know the exact time and date of his own or his loved one's death.

Soon after visitation, the individual is transported. According to Robert Hurst, TDCJ public information officer, "After an offender has been transported from the Polunsky Unit to the Huntsville Unit for an execution, they are kept in a holding cell inside the 'death house' where they are closely monitored by correctional officers until they are moved to the 'death chamber.'"[32] This holding cell is similar to the regular solitary confinement cell except for its history. Just a few days, weeks or months prior, another man may have sat in the same cell occupying his last few hours of life in the same way: writing final letters, consuming the last meal, drinking his last drink of water or experiencing the last few moments of life without shackles and handcuffs. This is perhaps one of the few times a man wants to experience solitude, but the last moments are not spent alone. The public information officer comes in to find out if the individual has any statements that they would like issued to the media. A chaplain is permitted to visit as well. A correctional officer sits in a chair outside the cell and monitors and documents every move that is made as a precaution so that the soon to be executed man cannot take his own life. There is a strong sense of irony that accompanies the practice of suicide watch for the soon to be executed. Suicide will be prevented at all cost, because the manner of death must be controlled. If suicide is attempted, the condemned man could be gassed with pepper spray, beaten and restrained by an extraction team of officers in riot gear and then placed back in the deathwatch cell. Suicide attempts are met with severe punishment.

When the time comes to go to "the death chamber," some men are at peace while others are in shambles. Some men are actually dragged from their cells weeping and begging, and some simply refuse to walk. There is a belief on death row that if you walk to your death, then the state is committing an execution, but if you refuse to participate and must be carried, then it is a murder. Some men want to make it very clear that they are being murdered. If they refuse to come out of their cells in their final protest of their lives, they are warned to come out. Nanon recalls the scenario that often resulted from the warning.

"Inmate, are you refusing to come out?" The warden might ask.

No response.

"I'm giving you a direct response to be handcuffed."

No response.

This is repeated, and then pepper spray is shot into the cell from a canister. The spray hits the condemned man in the eyes, mouth, ears, back, legs, face—anywhere with exposed skin. The pepper spray feels like liquid fire on the skin and causes a burning and gouging pain when it hits the eyes. Once the spray has been inhaled into the lungs, the person cannot breathe, and before he can really adjust to what is going on, guards rush the cell. Their helmets and shields crash in on the person and various moves are applied all over his body to subdue him. At times, the condemned men are put in headlocks until they are restrained while all the other staff observe the attack.

Back on death row, reactions vary. Cell blocks can explode in protest. Fires are set, toilets flooded, screaming and shouting is heard throughout death row. The pain, fear and anger are like an open wound, but it is not over yet. It is only mid-afternoon. The actual execution is still hours away and one cannot help but count down the hours. No one knows what this is like except those who have received a stay of execution and have actually gone through this process again and again. For a couple of hours prior to his execution, all the men left behind on death row reminisce about the man they knew. While he became a number to the state of Texas many years prior, he is a man to everyone who knew him on the row. Everyone reminisces as if he is already gone, because although everyone hopes he will receive a stay of execution, it is not likely. In a show of unity, so everyone can be aware that an execution is taking place, men often refuse their last meal of the day which is served around 3:30 or 4 p.m. When officers open the bean slots from the door to slide the tray in, many refuse. Solidarity is the order of the day.

Around 5 p.m., most everyone participates in a moment of silence. The cell block is painfully quiet. Deep down, all the men are desperate for the distraction of talking, but silence rules. Every person is aware of his own fate at this moment, and the harshness of death row is all too real. It is a moment of torture for some, prayer for others, and the realization that every person there is a "dead man walking." The men who have radios will listen to the news in hopes of learning that the condemned man received a stay of execution, but usually it is the time of death that is reported. At 6 p.m., the execution begins.

Each execution drastically affects the environment. Those living on death row get to know one another. Their characteristics, good qualities and bad, the individual challenges, hopes and achievements of each other, and of course, the crimes committed and how each person has processed his actions and the affects they have had on the lives of others. Like most people, they share stories of the past and a corny joke or two. They meet each other's family and friends at visitation and encourage each other to forge on despite terrifying odds that they will likely die.

Without fail, around 6:45 p.m., someone will yell out, "They got him. They got him, y'all." Most of the time the same words are said. Silence resumes for the remainder of the night. For everyone on death row, the darkest hour is the silence, the crushing hope that a man's life will be spared as the day is slowly erased by the night. The night wins. The light is gone, but in more ways than one. The 6 p.m. hour is the darkest hour for all. It is the hour of death.

Each man knows that it may one day be his hour of death as well. Every man knows that he will also become just a memory, and life will move on without him. For the families of the executed, they must struggle on without their loved one. For the victims' families, many do not receive the closure the execution is supposed to offer. For those still on death row, they will continue to repeat this process and these very hours hundreds of times. Over the course of a decade—the average time to await an execution on death row—a person living on death row may have experienced the loss of one hundred or more people to executions.

Most people living on death row spend years preparing for the last hour of their lives. Many search for a spiritual pathway to find peace. Some will strive to become kind and compassionate people in an attempt to make amends for the wrongs they have done in life. Some embrace anger, lashing out at others because the pain they feel refuses to leave them. Some seek justice for being wrongly convicted and become a statistic for a future newspaper article. And many see the world through a blind eye, a coping mechanism for the preservation of their sanity, until finally the illusions they see are ripped away, and they are reminded of whom they are. All come closer to the final hour of their existence. Some feel everything crashing down at once, and others find peace in their belief that they have been forgiven and are going to a better place—somewhere other than the hell they have lived for a decade or more.

Texas Death Row

Texas has one of the largest death row populations in the nation and executes more individuals than any other state. As of May 1, 2014 there were 273 men and women awaiting their execution dates on death row. These individuals will spend an average of 10.74 years in isolation waiting for their execution and have a few months warning of their impending execution. Although the time between convictions and executions fluctuates, the shortest amount of time spent on death row has been 252 days and the longest has been 31 years.[33] With respect to privileges, those awaiting execution are allowed one general visit per week. They are not allowed telephone calls, except from their attorneys. Contact visits are not permitted.[34]

There is an overwhelming representation of people of color on Texas death row. As of May 20, 2014, 71.3 percent of individuals on death row are people of color.[35] This statistic does not mirror the rates of capital crimes committed by whites and non-whites in Texas and is a gross demonstration of bias and discrimination against the people of color in the criminal justice system and capital punishment. Texas has more non-white individuals on death row than the national average, which as of October 2013 was 56.76 percent.[36]

CHAPTER THREE
THE INSIDE

A CLIMATE OF CRUELTY, DESPERATION AND CONTROL

There's an internal culture in place to turn inmates in solitary confinement into a "conquered people" at the whim of punitive measures and inhuman conditioning.

—Anonymous

AMONG THE TIERS OF confinement cells, the sounds of slamming metal doors and resounding voices are a constant. Correctional officers continuously shout orders; some men ramble to themselves while pacing back and forth in their small cells in utter boredom and frustration, and others, yell in a desperate attempt to connect to those they cannot see or to release a mind-numbing sense of desperation. One man describes his experience in an anonymous letter:

> The noise levels are deafening most of the time. In solitary confinement, the avenues of communicating with other people are terrible and very uncivilized. Hollering from cell to cell is the order of the day, as well as having to holler distances to get an officer's attention. Hollering is the norm and most common form of communication in the culture of solitary confinement that I experienced.

Sometimes the men escalate their voices and become verbally combative to prevent being controlled or demeaned by orders. The officers, in turn, get louder and exert their power in order to maintain control. The adrenaline pumps through everyone's veins, and fear is almost visible. The vicious cycle continues all day, and sometimes, all night. From a distance, it all sounds like loud rambled voices talking over each other, rattling the minds of the incarcerated men and officers alike. A cacophony of chaos—the incarcerated men and the correctional officers are united by the same culture of captivity, each with their respective roles, but all immersed in a dangerous and oppressive environment where dehumanizing behaviors are commonplace.

The dehumanization of individuals within the prison system extends to both sides of the cell doors. The incarcerated often routinely refer to correctional officers as "pigs." Likewise, correctional officers frequently use dehumanizing language when referring to the incarcerated. The dynamic goes on, and the power differential fuels the fire. Both correctional officers and the incarcerated individuals speak about one another in the presence of the other as though they cannot hear one another, depersonalizing the other. At some point, the dehumanization of individuals within the prison system begins to reshape all the individuals involved into being anything other than what they are ... *human beings.*

Prison is a microcosm of society, a fascinating study into human behavior in the face of captivity and despair. Media often depict prison environments as extraordinarily violent places, fraught with corruption. In particular, employee behavior is usually portrayed as cruel and dehumanizing toward those who are incarcerated, who are often portrayed as violent monsters. The relationship between the officers and the incarcerated for example, can be reminiscent of the master-slave relationship. Reality shows have captured the curiosity of the public by taking camera crews into jails and prisons to capture "the inside." Images of cell extractions, aggressive behavior and power struggles are prominently featured.

There is a long history of research into the dynamics and culture of prison environments. One leading researcher, Craig Haney, described prisons as, "... psychologically powerful places, ones that are capable of shaping and transforming the thoughts and actions of the persons who enter them, often in unintended and adverse ways."[37] Environmental factors play a powerful role in shaping and modifying the behavior of individuals and groups. There is a tendency to underplay the impact that social context can have on individual and collective behavior. Many historical events have been put under a magnifying glass in an attempt to understand how seemingly ordinary people can engage in collective torturous acts against humanity. In 1994, the world was shocked by images that were released of war prisoners in Abu Ghraib, also known as the Baghdad Correctional Facility, being physically, sexually and psychologically tortured by government agents, including men and women from United States Army. The photos led to intense public scrutiny. Some of the horrific images displayed agents laughing and giving a thumbs-up hand gesture as they taunted and abused the Iraqi detainees.

In prepared testimony before the U.S. Senate and House Armed Services committees May 7, 2004, Secretary of Defense, Donald Rumsfeld, provided an apology and acknowledged the impact of such horrific acts of violence, "I feel terrible about what happened to these Iraqi detainees. They are human beings. They were in U.S. custody. Our country had an obligation to treat them right. We didn't do that. That was wrong. To those Iraqis who were mistreated by members of U.S. armed forces, I offer my deepest apology. It was un-American. And it was inconsistent with the values of our nation."[38]

Although images of this and other historical events are forever etched in the memories of those who bore witness, these types of events are not uncommon and continue to persist in many forms, all with similar underlying behavioral dynamics and justifications. Susan Fiske, a researcher on the abuse of those who are incarcerated reviewed more than 25,000 studies inclusive of 8 million participants and found that this was not a rare event. In her opinion, anyone is capable of these atrocities.[39] The ongoing question is: How can so many people collectively engage in acts of cruelty that they may not otherwise engage in on their own? Obedience was offered as a defense by the accused in such mass atrocities such as the genocide in World War II at the Nuremberg War Criminal trials.

In 1963, Stanley Milgram, a social psychologist, conducted an experiment to look at the dynamics of obedience[40] His leading research questioned whether or not Adolf Eichmann and his millions of accomplices in the Holocaust conducted horrific acts because they were just following orders. He also questioned whether or not they could actually be called accomplices to the crimes.[41] What he found gave credence to the power of obedience to authority figures as the leading influence of their behavior. For Milgram's study, he recruited male volunteers and paid them for their participation. Everyone would like to think that with such extreme acts, they could never participate. The experiment showed otherwise. In Milgram's experiment, the participants were told that the study focused on obedience and learning. Although the recruits were told that they would be given either the role of the teacher or the role of the student, they were all given the role of the teacher, and actors played the role of the students. Actors were connected to electrodes that administered shock. The individuals who acted in the role of the teacher were asked by the experimenter to shock the students at increasingly higher intervals if they answered the question wrong. The students answered incorrectly in most of their responses. Of course, the actors were not actually being shocked, but as the level of shock increased over time, they grunted, screamed and pleaded for help. The teachers thought that they were administering severe levels of electric shock by the time the experiment was nearing completion. When the teachers expressed concern to the experimenter, he would prompt them to continue providing high levels of shock. What Milgram found in several variations of his experiment, was that all individuals administered up to 300 volts to the actors. Sixty-five percent administered 450 volts.[42] In his article, "The Perils of Obedience," Milgram summed up his conclusion with the following:

> The legal and philosophic aspects of obedience are of enormous import, but they say very little about how most people behave in concrete situations. I set up a simple experiment at Yale University to test how much pain an ordinary citizen would inflict on another person simply because he

was ordered to by an experimental scientist. Stark authority was pitted against the subjects' [participants'] strongest moral imperatives against hurting others, and, with the subjects' [participants'] ears ringing with the screams of the victims, authority won more often than not. The extreme willingness of adults to go to almost any lengths on the command of an authority constitutes the chief finding of the study and the fact most urgently demanding explanation.[43]

Although there were methodological and potential ethical issues related to his study, its implications are far-reaching and have been replicated in many settings with similar results.[44]

Philip Zimbardo, who was also curious about the relationship between good men and evil situations, conducted the infamous Stanford prison experiment in 1971. A professor of psychology at Stanford University at the time of the experiment, Zimbardo selected what he deemed to be 24 physically and mentally healthy male participants for his study. None of the participants had criminal or violent backgrounds and were each paid $15 per day to participate.

Each man was randomly assigned to either the prisoner or guard group. Prisoners experienced a mock arrest, booking, were provided smocks to wear and were given an identity number. The guards, on the other hand, were assigned uniforms. By the second day of the experiment, the prisoners rebelled and barricaded themselves inside their cells, refusing to follow orders. A power struggle was suddenly evident, and the guards began punishing the so-called inmates, even though it was not part of their assigned role. Zimbardo, who played the prison superintendent, noted that the guards initially punished due to disobedience; however, as the days progressed, some seemed to be delighted to enforce punishment. In his writings during the experiment, Zimbardo notes the psychological abuse and the "zombie-like attitude" of the prisoners and their total obedience of the guards. Although the experiment was intended to be 14 days, Zimbardo was forced to end it after only six days due to the extreme emotional abuse that was occurring toward the prisoners. Ultimately, Zimbardo concluded, "The situation won; humanity lost."[45] The experiment was terminated due to the escalating dynamics of violent behavior.

Zimbardo argued that if good people are put in a bad environment, the dynamics will take over and the person will do bad things. "That line between good and evil is permeable," Zimbardo said, "any of us can move across it. I argue that we all have the capacity for love and evil—to be Mother Theresa, to be Hitler or Saddam Hussein. It's the situation that brings that out."[46] The Stanford experiment demonstrates that leadership and oversight play a significant role in how people behave in any environment, especially high conflict and high stress environments.

In some ways, the cruel behavior of the student prison guards in the Stanford experiment was allowed to develop due to the ground rules and culture established at the outset.

Although this was just an experiment, real prison environments can mimic this same dynamic, and they often do. Yet the cruel dynamics are either ignored, or they become so insidious that the desire to control and overpower can infiltrate the prison environment. In so doing, they legitimize the actions and staff neglect personal responsibility and social accountability. They are willing to leave behind their own values and beliefs in order to comply with the demands placed on them by leadership. Not only are prison staff heavily influenced by the leadership, but in some instances, staff are fearful if they do not use harsh means to control the incarcerated population, they will be treated harshly themselves. The controllers become the controlled, and the dynamic infiltrates the prison, often serving as a platform for unconscionable behavior.

In comments delivered at a congressional science briefing about the atrocities at Abu Ghraib, Steven J. Breckler, executive director of American Psychological Association stated the following:

> We consider it inappropriate, even reprehensible, to harm others. Yet, here we are faced with the undeniable fact that harm has just been caused. How do we explain that? This is where social behavior gets very interesting. What the research shows is that people in these cases tend to deflect personal responsibility. Perhaps they blame the authority who ordered them to do it. Perhaps they blame the situation, which offered them no choice. Perhaps they even blame the victim, claiming that the harm was deserved. Whatever the explanation, people tend to shift the responsibility for their own harmful actions away from themselves.
>
> Science also reveals that although social context is remarkably powerful, it is not the only factor in a person's choice to participate in collective undesirable behavior. Individual characteristics and ethical imperatives play an important role in these situations as well. Analytic thinkers and independent personality styles tend to be the ones who are less likely to follow authority who command them to engage in harmful acts.[47]

In an interplay between individual personalities and collective behavior, some officers witness violent acts committed toward those who are incarcerated and feel powerless to intervene for fear of retaliation by the system. The choice of doing nothing is made in self-preservation, but at high cost to others. Correctional officers are constantly receiving mixed messages. They may be issued consequences if they do report retaliative behavior, and consequences if they do not. Several officers have reported feeling traumatized and helpless by this dilemma. Texas Department of Criminal Justice past and present correctional officers who responded to the survey posted on thebackgate.org disclosed their comfort level in reporting excessive force, one person responded as follows:

> Officers don't report these types of things or any other agency corruption for that matter. They would be singled out and harassed by their peers and the agency. You have to have help in a prison setting. If you went outside of the lines on reporting issues, you would be left alone to fend for yourself and that could become deadly. Employees have been fired for not reporting out of fear. Although the agency publicly expects it, it punishes if you actually do.

Another guard shared a similar concern:

> I may not feel comfortable reporting it because I know there would be backlash from the people I worked with, but I would report it nonetheless. Of course, this would be depending on who the individual is that used excessive force because if it was an officer or ranking officer well-known within the unit, they would all come together and try to drive you out for reporting it. When I say, "drive you out," this would be by means such as spreading gossip that you are doing something wrong such as bringing things in to inmates or that you are inmate friendly.

Correctional officers are placed in a situation in which their work environment can be even more hostile by attempting to do what they believe is the right and/or humane action to take. The culture of fear is pervasive throughout all levels of the system.

There are many who ascribe the conditions and treatment of the incarcerated men as necessary, or understandable, because of the behavior and the "type of people" who are housed there. Although most are not incarcerated for violent crimes, the perception is that all of those who are incarcerated are a physical threat to the safety of others, and oftentimes, this is one of the assumptions that is used to justify their mistreatment and is a misnomer that is well-known within the walls. While some people may be a severe threat to others, it is not the case for all. Yet, there is a dynamic inherent to this ecology. Being forced to live in a setting in which basic needs are not met has consequences both on the individual and the collective environment. Violation of needs not only occurs with the men who are incarcerated, but to some extent, with the staff as well. This is often expressed in the form of internal and/or external conflict, which is constantly present inside the walls and can occur between those who are incarcerated and staff, staff and staff, and incarcerated person on incarcerated person.

In his book, *Dynamics of Conflict,* Bernard Mayer describes a set of human needs that drives people's behavior in conflict. These include survival needs, identity needs and interests.[48] Needs differ from comforts in that survival needs are fundamental; they include food, shelter and security. These basic human needs are not adequately met for people who are incarcerated in Texas, and particularly those in isolation. Adequate nutrition is necessary for survival and health. Clean drinking water is part of that nutritional requirement. This is not always provided to those who are incarcerated in Texas. There have been time periods in which signs were posted indicating that the water is not safe to drink and that the water must be boiled in order to drink it. Of course those that are incarcerated do not have access to a stove or hot plate that heats to an adequate degree to boil water. Media have reported water shortages within the prison system in Texas citing various reasons for the shortage such as contaminated well water and speculations of staff shortages. During these shortages, the incarcerated men are rationed water: they are not allowed to shower regularly, if at all, until the problem is rectified; they are not allowed to flush toilets in their 60 square-foot confinement cells, which results in an accumulation of urine, feces and toilet paper.[49] The men are locked in cages 23 hours a day, sitting only 6 feet way, at best, from this human waste. With little ventilation, this environment is a breeding ground for bacteria. In the scorching hot Texas summer heat, these unsanitary living conditions pose several challenges to the health and safety of those who are incarcerated. Prison officers and other staff are also surrounded by the putrid conditions. Inevitably, the frustration, on all fronts, escalates, adding fuel to an existing flame and making it a ripe environment for aggression and conflict.

Adequate shelter is also a survival need. Although the incarcerated men have a roof over their heads, the conditions have proven to be detrimental to psychological and physical well-being. The minuscule size of the cell, the above 100-degree temperatures with inadequate ventilation, the lack of air conditioning and inadequate sanitation make the cells uninhabitable as compared to all other public housing or commercial properties.

The incarcerated men are responsible for cleaning their own cells, yet they are not afforded any cleaning supplies with which to do so. The only cleaning agent provided to them is the lye soap that is intended for personal hygiene and a weekly distribution of a toilet paper roll. The lye soap is often handed to the men inside of the toilet paper roll; therefore, it is not a significant enough quantity for all the purposes it must be used for. The same lye soap that is intended for use on the person's face, body and genitals is also the same small bar of soap used to wash their cell walls, floors, toilets and sinks. Many men report that it is not enough to maintain proper hygiene while keeping their cells sanitary. Those with access to money can purchase a washcloth in commissary or use a shirt or other clothing item to clean with; of course, he will also have to wear that shirt again or someone else will wear it when the shirt is turned into laundry. When an individual arrives to a new cell, there may be blood, feces, semen, sweat, vomit and urine on the walls, beds, mattresses and floors. In an effort to obtain hygienic cells, the men will often acquire bleach from someone who works in an area in which he would have access. This constitutes contraband and is a violation of the rules and subject to punishment. This is one of many examples of the risks that the incarcerated men will take in order to get their basic needs met.

Mayer also asserts that security is a basic survival need. Unless the brain perceives that the individual is secure, the brain will remain in a chronic state of hyper vigilance, ready for self-protection at any moment.[50] People who are incarcerated live in constant fear and perceive that they are in constant danger. They are always protecting the possessions they do have, worried that correctional officers will steal or destroy their property. Items such as photos, letters or drawings can serve as lifelines to the outside world, and the loss of such items is devastating. Neglect is also a concern for these individuals. The men are reliant on others to meet almost every basic need that they have. It has been disclosed by many that they have witnessed their food being spit in or officers threatening or joking with them about the possibility of their food being spit in. Other thoughts that race through their mind include, "What if I am dying and nobody knows, nobody believes me or nobody cares enough to call for help?" Their fears are not unfounded. Lawsuits resulting from deaths related to medical neglect and asthma, including heat exhaustion have been brought upon the system.[51]

Violence and control are part of the daily lives of the men who are incarcerated and undermine the very sense of security that is needed for the brain to perceive that the body is safe and not under attack. Due to having experienced, heard about or directly witnessed abusive behavior, the men live under the fear that any day they may have to fend for their life or their dignity. Several men have reported that they are afraid to close their eyes at night. Scott Medlock of Texas Civil Rights Project described the case of *Doe v. Richard Carter*. The case serves as only one of many examples of a violation of security needs as well as an attack on fundamental human dignity and basic sense of self. Richard, a gay man, shorter in stature than some men, was considered to be a "vulnerable population" and placed in administrative segregation for his protection. While he was housed in solitary confinement "for his protection," an officer forced him to perform oral sex. Because of the way the cells are constructed none of the officers could see what was occurring. The officer was ultimately convicted of violating civil rights.

The Memorandum Opinion and Order for *Doe v. Richard Carter* reads, "Officer Carter's employment with the TDCJ was terminated May 31, 2010 [see doc. 46, Ex. A, Affidavit of Human Resources Director Lawrence Meyers], and he has since pleaded guilty to the crime of Improper Sexual Activity with a person in Custody against John Doe, and is currently incarcerated as a result."[52]

Though security is a basic human need, those confined in Texas prisons are routinely denied access to this basic need. Instead, they are frequently subjected to excessive use of force. Many of these instances are not reported but are well-known as part of the culture as the system of power and control. According to open records data, there were 932 disciplinary actions taken on TDCJ employees for "Use of Excessive/Unnecessary Force" between the years 2008 to Oct. 1, 2012.[53] The "General Rules of Conduct and Disciplinary Action Guidelines for Employees" lists the definition of "Use of Force" as "a controlling measure taken during a confrontational situation in an effort to cause an offender to do anything involuntarily." According to the same manual, "excessive force" is defined as the "use of more force than is objectively reasonable to accomplish a lawful purpose." "Unnecessary Force" is defined as "the use of force when none is required or appropriate."[54] In those five years, and nearly 1000 actions taken, eight criminal cases were opened, and only one employee was criminally sentenced for assault.[55] In essence, although TDCJ deemed that the egregious behavior fit their definition enough to issue a consequence for the 932 known violations, only one of those violations resulted in a criminal charge.

One criminal charge among 932 violations sends a message not only to the staff, but to the men who are incarcerated as well. The incarcerated men are harshly punished for rule violations, yet staff can engage in violence toward the incarcerated without the appropriate criminal charges or loss of jobs. The number of disciplinary actions taken are likely nowhere close to what violations actually are, given what is known about the fear of whistle-blowing and concerns of retaliation. The covert, and sometimes overt, message is that everyone is to keep their mouth shut, or they could be a victim in one form or another. Many staff are put in the position of choosing whether or not to be a victim, being a victimizer or turning a blind eye, which is a passive form of victimization. Doing nothing is, indeed, doing something. In order to adapt to constant feelings of witnessing violent acts and feeling powerless to stop it, adaptive mechanisms are often adopted in order to continue doing the work. When describing the impact of being a witness, one correctional officer who was a participant in the survey placed on thebackgate.org website stated: "This messed with my mind because I could not understand why the ranking officer felt the need to use the force that was put on the offender. I once saw a team (this is at least five men) go into a cell and beat a man because he refused to come out and take a shower." Some cast external blame, "They deserve it, because they are horrible people anyways." Most often in those cases, dehumanization and demonization is the end product. It is much easier to mistreat someone who is perceived to be evil or non-human. Others, in an attempt to rationalize their behavior, will blame the environment, "This is a powerful system that is much greater than me, and there is no way that I could make an impact. If I just look away, I will be OK." Others question the legitimacy of their concerns in the first place. "Everyone else is witnessing it and are not doing anything about it; therefore, something is wrong with me." Nonetheless, in order to cope with the realities of the situation, a person must distance himself, rationalize or justify his or her role and participation in order to adapt. The incarcerated men are not alone in their insecure state. Many prison staff, including correctional officers, report feeling unsafe. Many have witnessed or personally experienced a broad range of violent acts committed by an offender. Due to serious under staffing concerns at TDCJ, the officer's ability to monitor and ensure the safety of both the incarcerated men and the staff is compromised. Although the men are locked in isolation 23 hours per day, violent acts continue to occur, requiring officers to be in a constant state of physiological hyper vigilance. One correctional officer participant reported his concern in the survey stating, "I have not seen adequate staffing numbers since about 2000. It's common to see one officer doing the job of three. Literally. If we can't watch each other and be safe there is no way we can safely monitor the inmates to keep them from victimizing each other. It's like putting your finger in the dike to stop the leak that just keeps growing."

Identity needs, which consist of meaning, community, intimacy and autonomy, are among Mayer's list of basic human needs. Identity needs consist of living a purposeful life and having the ability to contribute meaningfully to one's only life as well as to the lives of others. Individuals living in isolation are deprived of all aspects of life that would help them to develop a sense of purpose. Intimacy, another aspect of identity, is impossible to achieve. The only physical touch that a person in isolation experiences is being handcuffed, strip searched, medically evaluated or being physical disciplined. Incarcerated men living in isolation have no channels for developing autonomy. Every aspect of their lives including environmental temperature, mealtime, when and how often they can shower, how far they can walk around, the temperature of the shower water and when and for how long they can sleep are all controlled by hostile, outside forces. The ability to control one's own time or temporal sequences is non-existent.

Just as there are basic needs common to all human beings, there are also basic interests that all people will go to great lengths to accommodate. The three most notable basic human interests, that if not met, can also cause both internal and external conflict. These have been referred to by Chris Moore as substantive, procedural and psychological.[56] Substantive interests refer to the material things that are necessary to help ensure the basic human needs are met. In the prison environment, like in most environments, individuals need money to purchase their essentials. Stamps and paper are necessary to meet their basic human needs of intimacy (e.g., connection with loved ones in the free world). Procedural needs are necessary to ensure predictability and consistency. In the prison environment, procedural needs are not often met due to the lack of adherence to the rules and laws from both the correctional officers and the incarcerated population. The process of decision-making is unclear, arbitrary and unpredictable. Consequences can be completely unrelated to anything that has actually happened. Realistic guarantees of safety are not provided by the staff or the incarcerated population. Individuals who do not speak English, speak English as a second language or who cannot read or write in English often do not know their rights, creating an intensely unpredictable environment. Basic psychological interests—how a person is treated, respected and acknowledged—are routinely denied. Basic needs for attachment, respect, dignity and privacy are denied and frequently insulted, to all individuals in prison, especially those in isolation.[57]

While many people may argue that those who have committed crimes have forfeited their rights of having their basic human needs met or basic interests met, how can society or prison authorities expect individuals to behave optimally and within the institution's policies when all their basic human needs are either denied or severely violated on a daily basis? Prison rules and policies are so severe and restrictive, yet the expectation of the behavior from those who are incarcerated is that they "tow the line" without faltering in severely stressful and exceptionally conflicting environments while simultaneously having their basic human needs denied. When they try to circumvent the rules in order to meet their basic human needs, they are deemed as manipulative and noncompliant. When a person's basic human needs are not met, a state of chronic deprivation takes over, as does the innate drive to survive.

Individuals housed in harsh environments are not set up for success. In fact, their environment is a perfect recipe for failure. In her book, *Solitary Confinement: Social death and its afterlives,* the author, Lisa Guenther describes this phenomenon:

> In short, super-max prisons are set up to fail. They are told to conduct themselves as autonomous subjects while under near-total control. They are told to reflect on the consequences of their actions in a situation that typically produces cognitive impairment and mental illness. They are told to accomplish a social and ethical transformation in a situation that blocks

social and ethical relationships to others. They are *told* this in a way that both uses language and abuses it: by demanding accountability while excluding in advance the possibility of an interlocutor to whom one may give an account of oneself."[58]

Innate to the human experience and common to all humans is the will to achieve basic human needs. In prison, an economy forms around the meeting of these needs. People who do not have outside resources will often go to extreme measures, selling their bodies for something as simple as a book of stamps, stealing from the prison in order to obtain soap to trade for other necessities, finding a "tradable" commodity in order to pay to have cell phones smuggled in to the prison so that they can speak with their children since those in isolation are denied the use of a phone and those in general population must pay exceptionally high phone rates in order to use the offender telephone system. Although the incarcerated men know the consequence is great, they are willing to sacrifice what little they do have in order to maintain an attachment to the voices of loved ones on the outside. To many, there is nothing more valuable than hearing an outside voice of someone who actually cares for them. For this reason, cell phones are one of the hottest commodities in prison. Some men are willing to do anything in order to obtain them, for even an hour of use. When humans are forced into desperate situations, they will resort to desperate measures.[59]

These underground economies could not exist without some level of cooperation, reliance and participation between the officers and the incarcerated population. Each of them has what the other wants or needs. Some of the incarcerated men have given highly underpaid officers hundreds of dollars for minutes on their cell phones. It has also been reported that incarcerated men have provided sexual favors to officers in order to gain additional privileges or items that they may not be able to afford. A complex underground barter system is highly present in the prison environment and is often a vehicle for people, on both sides of the cell door, to get their needs met, despite the potential for heavy consequences. Behavior that may be deemed irrational in the free world may be perceived as rational in a world of severe deprivation. People will go to great lengths to feel safe, to feel needed, to get a stamp or minutes to communicate with a loved one. When survival is at stake, seemingly irrational behavior can actually be adaptive behavior. These are also examples of how far people will go to preserve whatever little bits of intimacy is available to them.

Prison is an entire society in quarantine, replete with morals, values, power hierarchies, economies and mechanisms of control. Confinement has a subculture of its own. As one man anonymously describes it: "Solitary confinement is jail inside of jail, prison inside of prison, isolation inside of isolation, confinement inside of confinement, and the depths of its chambers go deeper." For individuals living in isolation on death row, they have their impending death added to the existing list of cruel realities of isolation. In this environment, everyone is a victim, trapped in the same hell, but in different cages for different lengths of time. Some get to leave for the comforts of home away from prison, but will forever be changed, and for others, there is no respite other than death.

CHAPTER FOUR

RIGHTS, ETHICS AND HUMAN DECENCY IN THE FACE OF ISOLATION

What's good about America is that we are supposed to protect all people's rights, not just the ones we like.

—*Scott Medlock, Texas Civil Rights Project*

CORRECTIONAL OFFICERS, MEDIA AND other entities and individuals within the prison industrial complex often refer to prison cells as "cages," which contribute to a zoo type of mentality where there are animals and zookeepers. Much like dog kennels are lined up at the dog pound, so are the rows of cells in prison, except in prison, most cell doors are now electronically opened. When an officer needs to transport an individual, he or she screams out, "Open cage number three," the incarcerated person—even nonviolent individuals—is often handcuffed to cell bars or to other inanimate objects to prevent freedom of movement within the cell. Once handcuffed, and sometimes shackled, a leash is attached to the handcuffs. When being escorted anywhere, the leash is clamped on the chain of the handcuffs, an officer holds onto the leash behind the person's back and pressure is applied to pull or stop the forward movement of the person. When the person is returned to his cell, the steel door is slammed shut behind him. He must back up and squat down to a small square hole in the door where the officer unleashes him and removes the handcuffs.

Meals are served on old plastic trays that are either slid through a square hole on the door, or if the officer does not want to take the time to unlock the square hole, he or she may slide the tray under the door. The bottom of the door, which is filthy from lack of cleaning, often scrapes the top portion of the meal. Like a caged animal, those who are incarcerated receive their meals—which are often referred to as "slop"—without any sign of an actual human being. The "slop" is almost inedible and smells like something more fitting for a farm animal than a human. Cell by cell the guards slide food into the human cages, yelling "chow time" as they go. As though every person receiving food is unaware of the rank-smelling slop that was just slid under his cell door.

The degradation of incarcerated individuals is so extreme that even their most private body parts are poked and prodded. Incarcerated people are constantly strip searched by male and female officers several times per day. Incarcerated individuals, many of whom have suffered a childhood rife with sexual abuse, are told to strip naked, bend over and spread their buttocks for inspection. These individuals are routinely commanded to lift or open their genitals, and then herded together like animals with other naked people only inches apart. Privacy is nonexistent. Male and female guards are able to view all aspects of private acts, and if anyone attempts to hang a sheet to create a sense of privacy, including for the purposes of masturbating, a disciplinary case can be given for obstruction of view.

Sex is a natural occurrence amongst all mammals, and humans are of course no exception. Some state prison systems within the United States allow family reunification visits, or conjugal visits as they are more commonly known as, for married couples, allowing the incarcerated person to experience sex as a natural occurrence and to remain bonded to his family. Texas does not allow family reunification visits. Without a private outlet for sexual expression and family bonding, incarcerated people are denied a natural human need.

With the eyes of guards viewing intimate and private moments, and with the constant strip searches and spreading of buttocks, the incarcerated person often experiences these acts as sexual violence—over and over again, day after day, month after month, year after year and decade after decade. When entering the prison for a media visit and awaiting the interview, one of the guards stated in the presence of all, "Make sure that he is strip searched." The degrading language is so commonplace that the incarcerated person is not allowed to have dignity in these situations. Dignity is not even a consideration for many of the staff, and the policies that are created.

Demeaning language and behavior, such as hollering about strip searches within earshot of all of the visitors and staff, occurred at several media visits throughout the duration of writing this book. There is no legitimate excuse for engaging in this type of humiliating behavior. In fact, this demeaning behavior was so commonplace that no one outwardly expressed surprise.

Although some of the policies created are designed to prevent violent activity, there are many instances in which dignity is threatened or taken without a legitimate reason. The dehumanization of individuals within the prison system is embedded in all aspects of prison policy. There are other ways to achieve safety goals as well as prevent and address conflicts rather than make them worse. One

TDCJ correctional officer who participated in the survey posted on thebackgate.org explained: "The agency makes it hard to use common sense to deal with inmates as people. They would rather employees treat them like cows. Numbers without names. The training now preaches being hard and not asking any questions or allowing any common sense in dealing with inmates. Sometimes a calm approach works wonders where as now days they teach my way or the highway."

AS PREVIOUSLY REFERENCED, SUPER-MAX prisons are often described in the same manner used to describe zoo settings that house animals in captivity. Craig Haney describes the similarities by analogizing confinement cells to "places where exotic, presumably dangerous species are caged in so completely, far from their natural environment, kept separate from one another and largely apart, even from their keepers."[60] In fact, in both of these environments, the caged begin to pace, experience restlessness, have violent outbursts and demonstrate unpredictable behavior toward the caregivers—or jailers.

Human beings are currently being housed in conditions that are unsuitable, by several standards, for animals to live in. For example, the United States Department of Agriculture (USDA) as well as the Animal Welfare Act, a federal law, mandate physical environments that promote the psychological well-being of many animals, including primates. In the lawsuit *Animal Legal Defense Fund (ALDF) v. Glickerman* it was found that a chimpanzee in a roadside zoo was housed in solitary confinement and deprived of companionship and care. The chimp was displaying signs of severe psychological distress when he escaped and was subsequently killed by an employee. The lawsuit was based on the caregivers' failure to protect the primates under the Federal Animal Welfare Act (AWA). The U.S. district court judge found the USDA in violation of the Animal Welfare Act and mandated that stricter standards be adopted by the agency. The judge emphasized the need to maintain the psychological well-being of primates in captivity, calling this failure of care "egregious."[61] There are several other laws, policies and guidelines that include specifications for animal care and use, but all refer to the Animal Welfare Act as the minimum acceptable standard.

Incarcerated human beings locked in solitary confinement cells are not protected by the same standards that animal caregivers are mandated to uphold. In one account, a correctional officer participant reported in the thebackgate.org survey: "TDCJ trains employees to feel no sympathy or to have any feelings of understanding for inmates. They are to be treated as less than human. I think they train us that way to try to steer employees away from having relationships with inmates later on down the road."

A former correctional officer from TDCJ who participated in the survey offers a slightly different opinion about the training of officers' inhumane treatment, but claims that the training does not often translate to practice. "It (The Academy) does teach us to treat them as human beings, but for the majority of officers within TDCJ, this just does not happen."

In the landmark case, *Ruiz v. Johnson,* that resulted in 30 years of litigation that cast a spotlight on the practices of the Texas prison system, the presiding federal judge stated, "The federal court that critically examined the plight of vulnerable prisoners who were suffering inside the Texas super-max units concluded that whether because of a lack of resources, a misconception of the reality of psychological pain, the inherent callousness of bureaucracy, or officials' blind faith in their own policies, [the state prison system] has knowingly turned its back on the most needy segment of its population."[62]

Human rights activists have long maintained that solitary confinement is a violation of the Eighth Amendment to the Constitution of the United States, a part of the Bill of Rights, "that limits the sanctions that may be imposed by the criminal justice system on those accused or convicted of criminal behavior." Under the Amendment, "excessive bail shall not be required, nor excessive fines imposed, nor cruel and unusual punishments inflicted." The Constitution does not precisely define what constitutes "cruel and unusual punishment;" therefore, the interpretation of this clause has been left up to the courts. Due to the subjective nature of the terms, there have been widespread challenges to the statues.[63] The Eighth Amendment of the Constitution of the United States requires prison officials to provide all incarcerated people with adequate medical care, including mental health and dental care. Since many incarcerated people experience mental and medical health consequences associated with extreme isolation, access to care that meets the treatment needs can be compromised and less than adequate. In addition, many incarcerated individuals have pre-existing conditions that can be exacerbated under extreme stress. When there is a lack of connectivity to the world or any meaningful communication, more resources are necessary to compensate for the additional stress that often accompanies the multiple states of unyielding deprivation.

When an individual is in solitary confinement, screenings for physical and mental health are often conducted through the slot on the door where other officers, staff and neighboring individuals can hear, preventing privacy to the individual and reducing the likelihood of the person initiating care, disclosing symptoms or getting an "adequate" psychiatric or health evaluation. Incarcerated people are denied the right to patient confidentiality—a cornerstone to ethical mental health treatment—making mental health treatment less likely to occur and be effective.

As mentioned previously, the extreme heat experienced by those incarcerated in Texas prisons has been the cause of lawsuits against TDCJ. The Texas Civil Rights Project and Austin attorney Jeff Edwards filed a lawsuit against Texas prison officials after Larry Gene McCollum died of heat related injuries. When he reached the hospital, he had a core body temperature of 109 degrees.[64] According to Scott Medlock of the Texas Civil Rights Project, this is not an isolated incident. Incarcerated individuals and correctional staff have suffered from heat-related injuries.

Texas Civil Rights Projects' attorneys also represented the family of 25-year-old Michah Burrell in a federal wrongful death lawsuit against TDCJ that settled for $140,000.[65] TDCJ denied responsibility and reported that the treatment provided met the required standards. According to the family's attorneys, Michah, who was asthmatic, was having an asthma attack, and rather than coming to his aid, the staff, including a nurse and several officers allegedly made jokes directed at him and accused him of faking his symptoms while watching him struggle to breathe for one hour, significantly delaying proper treatment that could have saved his life. By the time he was taken to the hospital, it was too late. According to TDCJ policy, asthmatic individuals are not permitted to be housed in isolation, and yet, Michah was housed alone in solitary confinement without an inhaler. Metlock reports that in the McConnel Unit, there have been at least 16 other cases of TDCJ-alleged negligence resulting in death.

One correctional officer at TDCJ, who was a participant in the survey distributed on thebackgate.org, gave an account of a situation in which an incarcerated person was witnessed being medically neglected:

> While I was gone on my break, they had to call out for insulin patients to go to medical for their shots. When I returned to my post, an offender had not been let out of his cell to go for his shot. So, I went to the building desk boss and explained that one of the offenders has not been let out, and I was told, "He should have came out of his cell when they opened the doors, he will just have to be stuck out." This man is a diabetic! You cannot refuse him of medication that he must have to live. Yet, she tried in every way that she could to do so. Of course, I chose to take the initiative and go over her head by calling the medical department and asking the nurse to call to the desk and ask for him to be sent there. This is the only reason that man got his shot that afternoon.

Because of confidentiality and health care privacy regulations, evaluating medical care and neglect can pose a serious challenge. In seeking data to clarify this matter for this book, all attempts at accessing public information about medical data was denied. Although identifying information was not requested, officials cited concerns regarding violations of confidentiality. Several concerns related to solitary confinement and human rights were heard in front of the United States Congress June 19, 2012. The Senate Committee on the Judiciary held the first ever congressional hearing of the Subcommittee on the Constitution, Civil Rights and Human Rights entitled "Reassessing Solitary Confinement: The Human Rights, Fiscal and Public Safety Consequences." The congressional panel heard testimony on psychological and human rights issues that are often coupled with the use of solitary confinement in the United States. During the hearing, Senator Dick Durbin expressed concerns about the current practices of isolation. "(There are) more prisoners in segregation than any other democratic nation on Earth," he explained.

Senator Lindsey Graham, also provided testimony, stating the following:

> American values are on display when you have the power to confine someone. It says a lot about who we are as a nation. You know, the individual conduct has to be balanced against who we want to be as a nation. And I understand the need to protect prisons from people who are acting out and doing—doing things that are disruptive to the prison environment. At the same time, I want to make sure our detention policies live within the values that we are and that is try to turn people around, not just protect them, keep them off the streets, but try to be constructive in changing people's behavior and lives."[66]

Dr. James Scully, the medical director and CEO of the American Psychiatric Association provided testimony expressing his concerns regarding mental health issues and solitary confinement and a lack of adequate care stating, "Many prison systems often lack adequate health care facilities to provide mental health services in an ethically appropriate fashion, and the APA recommended necessary investments be made in both physician workforce and physician workspace."[67]

Several health care professionals have raised concerns about the ethics behind providing care in conditions in which they feel people are being mistreated. Jeffrey L. Metzner, M.D. and Jamie Fellner, Esq. examined these ethical challenges and reported, "Physicians who work in U.S. prison facilities face ethically difficult challenges arising from substandard working conditions, dual loyalties to patients and employers, and the tension between reasonable medical practices and the prison rules and culture. In recent years, physicians have increasingly confronted a new challenge: the prolonged solitary confinement of prisoners with serious mental illness, a corrections practice that has become prevalent despite the psychological harm it can cause."[68]

From a global perspective, there have been several organizations that have made regulations or recommendations about solitary confinement, as well as capital punishment. Some of these entities, for example, encompass international treaty bodies and human rights experts that include the Human Rights Committee, the Committee against Torture and the U.N. Special Rapporteur on Torture. All of these entities have reached a conclusion that the practice of solitary confinement may amount to cruel, inhuman or degrading treatment in violation of the International Covenant on Civil and Political Rights and the Convention against Torture and other Cruel, Inhuman, and Degrading Treatment or Punishment.

In December 1948, the United Nations General Assembly adopted the Universal Declaration of Human Rights in response to the horrific atrocities that occurred during World War II. Article 5 of the declaration stipulates that, "No one shall be subjected to torture or to cruel, inhuman or degrading treatment or punishment." Representing the United States, Eleanor Roosevelt was one of the drafters of the Declaration. This declaration has served as a platform that has led to legally binding international human rights treaties and serves to ensure justice and dignity for all people, based on rights that are inalienable to all human beings.[69] Super-max facilities have been a particular focus in the United States because of the documented psychological consequences of confinement and isolation. The National Commission on Correctional Health Care (NCCHC) issued a position statement that correctional health care professionals, "should not condone or participate in cruel, inhumane or degrading treatment of inmates."[70]

In 2011, U.N. Special Rapporteur Juan E. Méndez, an expert on torture called for a ban on solitary confinement in all but extraordinary circumstances, completely banning its use in juveniles and individuals with mental disabilities because it can amount to torture. "Segregation, isolation, separation, cellular, lockdown, super-max, the hole, Secure Housing Unit … whatever the name, solitary confinement should be banned by states as a punishment or extortion technique." He also expressed that confinement in excess of 15 days should be forbidden due to its lasting psychological effects.[71]

Although national and international bodies have determined that solitary confinement is, or may be considered to be, "cruel and unusual punishment" in and of itself and have banned or strictly limited its use due to concerns, it has been the subject of debate among the courts for years and continues to be a widespread practice despite the many documented consequences to psychological, physical and public health. The violation of these international laws and treaties indicates that the use of extreme isolation has been outwardly justified in many ways—a primary one being safety.

The crux of the matter remains finding a manner by which maintaining safety and allowing people to be treated humanely can occur at the same time. There is also a belief that people who have harmed others should not have rights at all and taking away someone's humanity is an acceptable form of punishment for their crime. In addition, some individuals make an internal decision on whether humane treatment is warranted based on the severity of the crime committed, from their individual perspectives. None of the international laws, treaties or standards relates the type or severity of the crime to a person's right to receive humane treatment. Punishment, in the form of imprisonment, has been rendered by a judge and jury, and some of these individuals spend years of their lives imprisoned for their crimes. In fact, some will die there facing the consequences of their actions. In addition to receiving a sentence, individuals in confinement are often treated like animals in cages, completely relying on another human being for basic needs—many of which will never be met. We must ask the questions: How far is too far? And, is there rational logic behind people and institutions committing crimes against those who commit crimes with the goal of reducing crime? Putting rational decision-making aside, there is a heavy emotional component, including fear, that determines individual and collective perceptions of justice.

PART II
THE IMPACT

CHAPTER FIVE

THE CONTINUUM OF GRIEF AND LOSS

Death row can be compared to being locked in your neighborhood and one by one you see your neighbors, many of whom you have known for years, walk out of their doors, and you know they are going to die. You know they are leaving to be killed. At that moment, you see and experience so much suffering. You don't know how to deal with it.

—Nanon M. Williams

WHEN INITIALLY ARRIVING TO death row, the experience itself is overwhelming. The realization that your loved ones are also experiencing an immense loss is an unbearable pain. The father loses his son, and the son loses his father. The imprisoned father knows he is helpless. He will not be there to give his daughter a hug when she is hurt or help her feel protected when she is scared. He will not be there to walk her down the aisle on her wedding day. When his children are sick—perhaps even facing a terminal illness—the sense of helplessness, guilt and inadequacy will consume him because a simple written letter is the only thing he can offer. Each individual experiences the loss of his family in different degrees: one man will lose his wife; another will learn a parent has died and will not attend the funeral; and many will never see the grandchildren that will always wonder where their grandfather is, because it can be difficult to explain the complexity of the situation in a way that a young child can understand. The sense of loss is a tortuous existence for the family who needs their loved one and for the individual who has lost everything and everyone.

Life in prison is consumed with enormous sense of loss. Prison and loss always coexist. Not only does an individual live through a loss of identity, future dreams, sense of control, liberty, dignity, integrity and choice, but he loses the sense of connection to everything that matters most to him, including family, community and friends. The loss of relationships is extraordinarily painful. The loss is experienced upon arrival when everything and everyone is left behind, and it continues to pervasively follow the incarcerated men through every day of their lives.

The individual's identity, privacy and sense of independence and control are destroyed, and sometimes completely lost. Whatever roles or characteristics once defined that person are stripped away, and in their place is a file and an offender number or death number that will be used more frequently than his name. Any perception of having control over one's life has also been stripped away. Those condemned to prison feel powerless over their fate, and their entire existence is planned for them. This involuntary relinquishing of control is not without consequence.

In the publication *Dying Twice*, the author describes the potential impact of this dynamic: "Much of a person's identity is grounded in its relationships with other people and their environment. Their existence relies entirely on being reliant on the system. A highly controlled environment by which they depend on others for their most basic needs dictates their life and death. As a result, inmates may lose their ability to control their own behavior."[72]

In addition to grieving the loss of what was left behind, new forms of loss become ever present and can knock a man down again and again. As former relationships wither away, new relationships are sought. Connections are vital to survival. Relationships are formed without seeing faces. Talking through vents and connecting via fishing lines allow the sharing of their most painful moments with each other.

Watching neighbors on death row be led or dragged away to be executed one by one is a constant reminder of mortality. Death row is a place that is in constant countdown mode, as each of its inhabitants is marked for death. When each execution day arrives, the clock is reset and a new countdown begins. Not only are the men grieving their lost neighbors, but they also know that one day, they will be the ones taken away to their death. Nanon recalls his experience of living on death row.

> I lived on death row 10 years. In that time, I witnessed hundreds of men be taken to their death. When you know someone for a couple of years, you get to know them well. If you and I could talk to only each other for the next 10 years, I would know everything about you: what makes you angry; what makes you laugh; the crime you committed; the hopes you once had; all of the things you lost. When you can count 100 people you have known who died, it becomes very hard. I knew 300 men who died while I was on death row. When you know them personally and speak to them about their families, their fears and hopes, their crimes, and when you live with them every day, it is impossible to overcome the loss of that many people.

Despite having been away from death row for more than a decade, Martin Draughon still remembers the horrors of the place. The memories are seared in his mind. "While I was on death row, 288 men were executed. It is easy to not think about when you leave, but when you do start thinking about it, you see their faces."

Every individual experiences the pain associated with loss in a highly individualized manner. Grief, which accompanies loss, is a normal process that is experienced by everyone in his or her lifetime and is not indicative of pathology. Elizabeth Kubler Ross, in her groundbreaking and widely read book, *On Death and Dying,* identifies five stages of grief.[73] She identifies these stages as being sequential. They include denial, anger, bargaining, depression and, finally, acceptance.

The majority of individuals in the free world are able to cope with what may seem to be an insurmountable stressor at the time and resume to a normal level of functioning without developing a psychological or physical disorder. A wide variation of cognitive, behavioral, emotional, physical and spiritual manifestations of grief is commonly experienced. However, there are many factors that make incarcerated individuals more prone to disorders and maladaptive behavior.

Most individuals come to prison having already experienced multiple traumatic losses in their lifetime. Some have even lost their childhood. Kevin (name changed for privacy) knows that story all too well. Kevin was born in Los Angeles, California to a white, poor, single-parent household that lived off the land. Sugar cane fields were in abundance, and the crop sustained his seven sisters and two brothers. Having another child was too much for his mother to bear. At the age of two, he moved away from his mother to live with his aunt who volunteered to take care of him. He felt loved with his aunt and finally had some stability in his life. He became attached. Unfortunately, this did not last. When he was 5 years old, he moved back in with his mother who had recently married a man that Kevin had never met. Kevin was excited that he finally had the father figure that he had longed for. Sadly, his stepfather was an alcoholic and engaged in violent arguments with his mother. The children were helpless witnesses to this abuse. When Kevin was 8 years old, his mother took all of the children out of the home that they knew, and went to a shelter out of desperation and a fear for her life. His family no longer had a home or a plan for the next meal. After two years of barely surviving, his mother felt that her only option was to move back in with her abusive husband, this time in the inner city where prostitutes, drugs and gangs infiltrated the neighborhood. Once again, his sense of safety was lost. After a few more moves motivated by breakups and poverty, it became increasingly difficult to get settled into a school routine. As his mother had more children and some of the older ones went to live with other family members, change and loss became routine, and life remained unpredictable and cruel. Different men came in and out of his mother's life—none of them were the father that Kevin needed and deserved. Many were abusive. The only thing that became predictable was his mother's physical and emotional absence.

As a young 12-year-old boy, Kevin lost hope in having the mother that he wanted and came to the harsh realization that his mother would never show up at any of his school events. Eventually he stopped looking for her in the stands at his sporting events, which became increasingly less important to him. No one cared if he hit a home run or not. In many ways, Kevin grew up very fast. He became a father figure to his sisters at home while his older brothers scattered about. He knew that if he did not clean the house and provide the meals for his siblings, then it would not get done. Combing his sister's hair became a part of the morning routine that he became proud of; it gave him a sense of self-worth. "Someone had to step up," he explained.

Eventually, Kevin no longer minded his mother's absence. When she was home, he got the brunt of the physical abuse. He was often beaten with extension cords, rods and belts. He felt anger growing inside his body and mind, and he did not know how to process all the abuse and instability. His home life significantly interfered with his connection to school and ability to make good grades. No one noticed the marks and bruises on his body, or maybe they did notice and chose to look away. Sadly, many of the children Kevin knew showed signs of abuse. He began skipping class and let his curiosity get the better of him.

Kevin started smoking marijuana at the age 12 and had several occurrences of school suspension. Each day he spent away from school made him question the whole reason why he was there. "My greatest aspiration was to be a good man, husband and father. I didn't have anyone to guide me into being a man," he said tearfully. By the age of 20, he finally quit trying to make people proud. His addiction washed away the pain and led to a downward spiral into a world of drugs and violence that would cost him a life sentence.

Kevin's story is one of many that are illustrative of a child who experienced many traumatic losses during his life. Throughout his childhood, he experienced a chronic loss of hope, stability, trust and attachment to friends, family, schools and homes. Looking back at his life, one has to wonder how things may have been different if children like Kevin would have had at least one healthy, constant attachment with another human being who believed in him. His past traumas were compounded by his newfound traumas when he came to prison.

Arriving to death row with histories of traumatic loss and maladaptive coping, in addition to being thrust into an environment where ongoing multiple traumatic losses will continue, make any type of a normal grief process unlikely. New losses that occur inside or outside of prison can serve as psychological triggers for past traumatic events. Individuals are in a situation in which they are not adequately permitted to grieve in a manner conducive to healthy coping, sending many individuals on a trajectory that steers far away from resiliency. This is often referred to as "disenfranchised grief."[74] The term is used to describe grief that is experienced in situations in which loss cannot be fully mourned due to certain impeding factors. These include the inability to adequately have the loss recognized, acknowledged, mourned publicly and supported socially.[75] Normal cultural rituals that allow for closure such as social support, funerals, visitations and congregating with loved ones are not permitted in the living environments of solitary confinement and death row. Expected outward expressions of emotion are often limited, and mental health outlets can be, or are perceived to be, inadequate to deal with the issues. The consequences of disenfranchised guilt are a suppression of emotion that may amplify reactions and lead to complicated grief.[76] Grief can be referred to as complicated when reactions impair daily functioning in several areas and usual coping mechanisms no longer serve them. Individuals may become clinically depressed, develop post traumatic stress disorder (PTSD) and other psychological disorders. Pre-existing mental health and physical conditions can also be exacerbated. In an extensive literature review of the subject, examples of these complications are described.

> Complications also lead to dysfunctional thoughts, maladaptive behaviors and emotion dysregulation such as troubling ruminations about circumstances or consequences of the death, persistent feelings of shock, disbelief or anger about the death, feelings of estrangement from other people and changes in behavior focused on excessive avoidance of reminders of the loss or the opposite, excessive proximity seeking to try to feel closer to the deceased, sometimes focused on wishes to die or suicidal behavior.[77]

Many research studies have examined various facets of complicated grief and have been fairly consistent in describing their predictors. Findings indicate that people are more susceptible to complicated grief if the manner of death was violent, the relationship was close and the death was unexpected.[78] There are few research studies that look at these issues with respect to individuals living in prison isolation, including death row. The majority of the studies that do focus on prison populations relate to the grief experiences of the family members whose loved ones are in prison and on death row.

Individuals in isolation sit in their cells, reflecting on a life ridden with trauma and unending loss. They hear of people in neighboring cells crying out for help without answer, committing suicide, being murdered or dying of unknown causes. Without warning, a family member or friend back at home may die, and the pain of not being able to say goodbye is suffered in silence and becomes all encompassing. Many people in prison know no other life, and yet, they never get accustomed to the loss.

CHAPTER SIX

THE LIMITS OF THE HUMAN PSYCHE

THE BIOPSYCHOSOCIAL CONSEQUENCE OF ISOLATION

*The person who tries to live alone will not succeed as
a human being. His heart withers if it does not answer
another heart. His mind shrinks away if he hears only
the echoes of his own thoughts and finds no
other inspiration.*

—Pearl Buck

THE HUMAN BRAIN IS wired for connectivity. Without the ability to make meaningful connections with others, a person experiences tremendous stress physically, emotionally and mentally. The following narrative, written by an incarcerated man who chose to remain anonymous, describes the despair many experience in solitary confinement.

I felt utterly alone in segregation. My cell was in the shape of a steel box. The floor was scarred concrete. The walls were decorated with illicit gang imagery and graffiti. I missed my daughters. They were two and four at the time of my incarceration, so I thought of them often. As I sit and write this, my body still feels the numbing isolation that is the soul of segregation.

Every day I would hear a symphony of dark sounds. Sounds that I used in segregation to identify the time of day and the events in my surroundings. The clanging of keys calculated the closeness of a guard. The opening and closing of doors signified the opportunity for recreation or showers. I can remember lying on my bunk, thinking about my children and worrying about my family. I felt powerless over my life and the lives of my daughters.

Oftentimes, the kicking of metal doors, and the yelling of inmates would interrupt my thoughts. Maybe they had mental health issues; maybe I had mental health issues. I can remember being huddled in the fetal position on the cold concrete floor, pounding my own skull with a closed fist, trying to shake the stabbing pain in my head. Everyday felt the same. No one could hear my inner screams. My mother had drug abuse issues. My father was not a part of my life. In this cell, I was reminded of my situation. No mail. No money. I felt as if I had no value, and I sat in a place where I was treated like an animal. I dealt with so many issues, shame, regret, anger and depression.

I was a 22-year-old man, trying to figure out life's questions while living in a cage. But I made it out sane and alive. Some men do not. I remember one evening it rained real hard; the thunder was so loud that it vibrated through the whole building. The lights flickered, and the backup generators kicked in. At about 4:30 a.m., the nurse was making her rounds before breakfast, and I heard a scream. I looked out the small window in the front of my cell, and I saw guards and nurses running up the stairs with a stretcher. They were in an upstairs cell for about 45 minutes. Eventually, they came down with a young man strapped to the gurney. The whole time they were doing chest compressions and blowing into his mouth, but no response. It got real quiet after they left. For a few hours, everybody was quiet. No screaming, no kicking—even the guards looked somber.

The next morning I was pulled out of my cell and told that I would be leaving in a couple of hours to go to another unit. I packed my meager belongings and was placed into a holding cell until the bus arrived. Once the bus arrived, I was told that there was no room for me, so I was taken back to segregation. After I left, another prisoner was placed in my old cell, and the only cell left was the one the guy had just died in. I arrived at the front of his cell amid a bunch of whooping and hollering, "Watch out! You'll die next," was the chatter.

I entered my new cell, and I put my belongings on the floor in front of the bunk. The man in the next cell called me over to the vent. He told me that the guy hung himself from the light fixture and his legs kept kicking the wall, but the thunder drowned the pounding out. He also told me that the guy was my age, and he was only serving a four-year sentence. By this point, I was tired. I had been up all night and my body was exhausted. I laid down on the mattress and taped to the bottom of the top bunk was a picture of a guy leaning down and kissing a little girl. The little girl was my daughter's age. I realized this guy had laid there, just like me, and thought about his family, just like me. He thought about his children, just like me, but unlike me, he didn't make it. To this day, that picture is burned into my mind.

Segregation ... yea, I remember it. (Anonymous)

THIS IS ONE IN AN estimated 8,000 stories of people housed in isolation in Texas prisons. Each of the other thousands of confinement cells holds lone individuals. They share cells only with the ghosts that used to sleep miserably in their beds. These men stare at concrete walls, sometimes, as if they are dead. They writhe in pain, and no one sees them. They scream, and no one cares. Unless one has lived and breathed a person's existence in confinement, there are no written or spoken words to describe the experience or impact. Those who have experienced solitary confinement consistently describe it in one word—hell.

The stress on the brain that results from what is so often referred to as hell, and the ability to cope in isolation environments, can vary from individual to individual. All individuals experience some level of anguish and distress. Whether or not the individual's trajectory leads to pathology and functional impairment often depends on the interplay between the individual's brain characteristics, genetics, current environmental factors and biopsychosocial history. When examining pre-existing (pre-morbid) histories of mental health diagnoses, there are a great number of incarcerated individuals who meet these diagnostic criteria prior to incarceration. For example, prior to arriving to TDCJ, in fiscal year 2012, 17,008 people out of the entire prison population had a prior primary diagnosis of a mental health disorder. During the fiscal year 2013, there were 18,089. There are significant limitations to the accuracy of these statistics when trying to identify the numbers of individuals with pre-morbid conditions, particularly those housed in isolation. First, these statistics are not specific to isolation environments—although requested, that data was not provided. Second, these numbers only reflect individuals who have had prior contact with Mental Health Mental Retardation (MHMR) agencies, which are divided by counties. The only individuals who have been reported by MHMR are ones who have been diagnosed with major depression, bipolar disorder or schizophrenia.[79] Therefore, the individuals who meet any other diagnostic criteria, such as post-traumatic stress disorder (PTSD), general anxiety disorder (GAD) or substance abuse, to name a few, are not counted. It is important to recognize that there are many people with pre-existing mental health conditions who have not been diagnosed, so the number of people entering prison with a mental health condition is undoubtedly significantly greater.

When analyzing historical factors, many of the men living in solitary confinement have lived through traumatic events, oppressive environments and have had pre-existing issues that have already had a profound impact on their brains, bodies and spirits. What awaits them when entering confinement is an environment that will likely worsen previous conditions and have deeper life-altering consequences. In order to understand the complexities that play a role in the impact of solitary confinement, it is important to examine some of the common background variables of those who are confined. After interviewing several men, some who are named in this book and some who chose to remain anonymous, as well as reviewing many case examples, it is remarkable how common their histories are. Most of them have been plagued with childhood histories of oppression, discrimination, extreme poverty, horrific trauma, poor education, substance abuse and extensive caregiving of siblings and/or parents at a young age. In addition, many of these individuals committed crimes while under the influence of drugs and/or alcohol.

Martin Draughon was one of them.

BORN AUG. 31, 1963, little Martin became the Draughons' pride and joy. As a boy, Martin spent a lot of time with his grandfather, who he affectionately referred to as "Paw-Paw." His father worked for a cable television network in a small town in central Florida, and he was often very busy. Martin's mom was a stay-at-home mother, but she also stayed quite busy. So, whenever Paw-Paw came by in his big, long Cadillac, little 4-year-old Martin jumped in without a seconds' hesitation.

Paw-Paw was an alcoholic but to a child that held no significance. Whenever Paw-Paw came cruising by the house, he and Martin made their way to what was referred to as the "colored" part of town to a bar named Bubba Lester's. Bubba was a big, jolly man with a big heart. While Paw-Paw got drunk and talked shop with Bubba, little Martin sat at the bar drinking soda as Bubba winked at him and tossed him candy. Because there were not many children Martin's age in his neighborhood, Bubba Lester's bar was his playground, while Paw-Paw, a regular at the bar, made everyone laugh.

A few years later on May 7, 1970, Martin's sister Felicia was born. Shortly after his sister's birth, Martin's parents separated and eventually divorced. Martin had no way of understanding why the family broke up, but he later learned that his father had abandoned the family in order to have a relationship with his administrative assistant. Life did not go smoothly after his father left. Having left with all the family's money, Martin's mother was now jobless and alone with two little children. "I still remember the day very well. I was outside catching fireflies at dusk. I came into the house and found my mother crying. I did not understand why she was crying at that time. I remember tagging along with her the next day trudging up and down the dirt road going from house to house with my baby sister in her arms. Again mom was crying and literally begging people for food, money and diapers," Martin remembers. As an adult, Martin was able to fully realize the magnitude of an event such as that. As a child, Martin had no way of knowing exactly how hard the times were, or how difficult it was for his mother to raise his sister and him.

Eventually, the family ended up on welfare. Once or twice a month the welfare office passed out canned goods, rice, chicken and a block of cheese. This relieved some of his mother's financial pressure. During the next several years, his mother brought the family some stability. They had a place of their own, but his mother had to work more than one job, and so when Martin came home from school, he took care of Felicia. It was up to him to pitch in. He didn't mind. As an elementary student, he was responsible for getting himself out of bed, preparing his breakfast and lunch and getting himself to school because his mother left for work very early.

In the early 1970s, Martin's uncle returned from the Vietnam War after serving in the Marines. He moved in with them. Now there was company in the house along with a lot of parties, pot, booze and lava lamps. As a young woman in her twenties, Martin's mother found enjoyment in having her brother live with her and the children. After Martin once got a "contact high" from being in the room with so much marijuana smoke, he banished himself outside more often. He eventually built a fort in a big oak tree deep in the woods and escaped there often.

Martin's mother started dating again when he was in the fourth grade. She remarried for security and love, giving Martin and Felicia a stepfather. Initially their family life improved, but after moving from place to place, the family was uprooted and moved to Texas. The uncle stayed behind in Florida. Soon after arriving to Texas, Martin's mother and stepfather had a new baby girl.

The family environment became increasingly stressful. His stepfather was very volatile. His emotions shifted quickly, causing confusion and fear when anything went wrong. After a while, Martin was given stern warnings not to do anything that would upset his stepfather. Martin understood that to mean that he should stay completely out of his stepfather's way. Every day he wore the same faint smile around his stepfather until he could escape his eyesight and find refuge outside.

The summer after Martin's seventh grade and Felicia's first grade years, they both went to Florida to spend the summer with their father. By this time, their father was divorced from his second wife. So it was just the three of them whenever his father was not working. Felicia got bored very quickly and went back to Texas. Martin stayed with his father and enjoyed his time, now that it was just the two of them. His father's ex-wife and her sons lived in the same town. Martin found himself spending time with his stepbrothers who were in their late teens. Martin wanted to hang out with the boys since they were so much older than him. It was not long before Martin found himself "cruising" in the van with his stepbrothers. He was exposed to marijuana and started getting drunk by the age of 12.

By the time Martin entered the eighth grade, he was coming home in the afternoons stoned from smoking weed all day. His father, finally taking notice of this, sent Martin back to Texas to live with his mother, sisters and stepfather. Martin dreaded seeing his stepfather again and did not care how he spent his time. Martin's father was not the only one upset with him. He just had to look sideways at his mother, who was having problems with his drunken stepfather, and an intense beating would ensue. He was so depressed over his tense, fear-filled family environment that he escaped into LSD, mushrooms, more pot and even cocaine. He eventually became so depressed that he could not stay awake in class without popping pills or smoking a joint between classes. Without much surprise to anyone, toward the end of his sophomore year, he was expelled from school. He was again sent to live with his father in Florida. Of course, nothing changed for Martin. He was like a Ping-Pong ball, bouncing back and forth between two parents.

Martin's uncle welcomed him into his home, but this was not a move in a positive direction for Martin. He and his uncle often got high together. As Martin grew older, he wanted to change his life. He decided that in order to have a future, he needed to do something with himself. He started to talk to military recruiters, and he decided to join the military. He was almost 18 years old and only had minor offenses as a juvenile, so he thought the military would be more than happy to provide him with the discipline he so desperately needed. Martin was a strong young man. He had sobered up for a few months and wanted to change his life by offering it to his country. His country rejected him due to his criminal past. He was shocked, but he refused to give up. He spent the next few weeks looking for a job.

He eventually found employment with a tree trimming company. Martin was now paying rent to his mom and stepfather and taking responsibility for his life. He was a hard worker, and the company quickly promoted him to new positions. In fact, he eventually became the company's youngest foreman.

Martin was earning good money, so he decided to make roots in Houston. He got an apartment and eventually his girlfriend moved in with him. Other than smoking marijuana from time to time, like Paw-Paw, he found himself at bars similar to Bubba Lester's. He was in his early twenties, and he felt that he was leaving life's misery behind and enjoying a normal life.

One day, Martin was having a particularly hard day at work. Martin's boss noticed, and sent him home. They argued a bit, but Martin did end up leaving work. He decided to go to the bar around the corner and have a few beers and then later return to collect his paycheck. He went back at the end of the shift and waited in line for his check. He had some time to wait, so he climbed up on a tall pallet rack and guided the guy with the forklift load. Being drunk, Martin slipped off the rack and fell 20 feet to the concrete below, fracturing his wrist. He was fired on the spot. Having been fired for trying to be helpful was something Martin could not understand. From that day, Martin sought refuge in drugs. He bought some cocaine and took too much. He passed out on the kitchen floor. His girlfriend and friends dragged him into the bathroom and into the tub and coached him to breathe.

After being fired and turning to drugs, Martin's life became a blur. He was arrested for drugs, assaults and other crimes. Although he never completely got off drugs, he found jobs at construction sites, other tree companies, fast food restaurants and other odd jobs.

He sank deeper into debt and trouble. Sleeping at his girlfriend's apartment for a long while brought him closer to her children. Soon her children began calling him "daddy." This both touched and angered him. He knew that he was in no position to play stepdad to two little children, but he did not want to reject their affections. He knew what being rejected by a parent figure felt like. He did not want to impose those feelings on these children.

When his girlfriend got evicted from her apartment, Martin did not want to just leave her with no money and two children. The situation was a painful reminder of how his own father left his mother penniless. With no job and his girlfriend sneaking off with the last of the money to buy drugs instead of groceries, a bad situation was made worse. He wanted to do what was right for the children, and their mother was too strung out to care what happened to them.

In an effort to help his makeshift family, Martin made a bad decision. He robbed a restaurant, armed only with a steak knife. He got away with it and was able to keep a roof over the children's heads and put food on the table. He felt rewarded by the satisfaction of seeing the children's smiles. Drugs would erase the memory of the wrong he had done, so his conscience felt clear. When he loaded up the needle, nothing else mattered.

Of course, the money quickly ran out. He bought a cheap pistol to do another robbery. He said a prayer and promised God that this would be the last one if he got enough money to buy a car, move them to Florida, and get the support from his family. Surely, someone would help them. He just had to get enough money to get them there.

Getting enough drugs into his system to build up his nerve, he and the brother of his girlfriend robbed the same restaurant. Robbing the same restaurant twice was not very smart, but drugs helped him to go through the motions. The robbery took a bad turn, and shots were fired in the air as they were chased out of the building and into the street. Unbeknownst to Martin, bullets ricocheted off the ceiling and killed a bystander in the restaurant.

The very next day, after an accidental overdose, Martin was arrested. The charge was capital murder. Martin was convicted and sentenced to die by lethal injection.

During his first few years of being on death row, Martin was still naive about prison life. He was still learning and maturing, searching for the good in all the bad. In each new experience, he tried to soak up as much as he could learn.

After almost a decade in prison, Martin had experienced all there was to experience on death row. The first few years refined Martin and made him better person through all the hardships. The last few years seemed to erode all the good that could be squeezed out of the miserable existence. The longer he was there, the more spiritually, socially and mentally disconnected he became. Seemingly, as time went by, the only thing that seemed to grow in him was anger and hatred—two of prison's most consistent commodities.[80]

AS DEPICTED IN MARTIN'S story, life in poverty is another common historical thread among individuals in the prison population. Living in poverty exposes individuals and families to many ongoing traumatic stressors.[81] These stressors, such as ongoing exposure to violence, discrimination, substance use and abuse as well as a lack of safety, security and basic needs, among a few, can interfere with the ability to access resources to cope effectively.

In one thorough examination of pre-morbid factors, Cunningon and Viegen conducted an extensive literature review examining the histories of people living on death row. The studies concluded those on death row are often intellectually and academically challenged. High rates of mental illness, histories of substance abuse, dysfunctional families, neurological damage and developmental histories of trauma were prevalent with these individuals. These pre-morbid conditions are shown to get worse in confinement.[82] Throughout his extensive work with individuals in confinement, psychiatrist Terry Kupers noticed that many of the incarcerated men were victims of severe trauma in childhood and as adults. He pointed out that these individuals "are more prone to stress response syndromes, decompensation, suicide and other forms of psychiatric co-morbidity while incarcerated."[83] These findings are prevalent throughout the literature. When referring to the characteristics of people on death row, Michael Mushlin, professor of law at Pace Law School, also found that:

> Many have mental illnesses often undiagnosed and untreated. Trauma histories are almost universal. Substance abuse has a very high prevalence, often secondary to trauma or untreated psychiatric disorders. There is often poor intellectual functioning, sometimes even illiteracy. Brain damage is common. Suicidal histories are also frequently present, and

often are unrecognized as such, as well as long histories of self-destructive behaviors. Many clients in this population have suffered at the hands of their caretakers historically, or have been abandoned by them."[84]

In an interview with Reid Lyon, from the Center for Brain Health at University of Texas at Dallas, he conveyed that trauma histories have resulted in brain chemistry alterations that often occur as a result of childhood trauma. These effects lay down a platform for how later experiences are processed. These alterations are not a pattern of neurochemistry typical in developing brains that have not been exposed to trauma. Adding the extreme stressors of isolation and deprivation can produce newly formed emotional, behavioral and neuro-chemical effects, particularly in those who experienced isolation or neglect as a child.

Every individual who told their stories for the purpose of this book reported a history wrought with severe childhood abuse and/or neglect. Gabriel Gonzales relays his childhood experience, "I know what it is like as a child to walk around with this all-consuming hurt; this confusing hurt that makes a child live self-destructively, attempting to escape the pain only to destroy our lives because we didn't have the knowledge conducive to healing and overcoming it."

The life of Oswaldo Soriano is illustrative of many of the factors outlined above. Sadly, the undercurrents of his story are common among this population of inmates.

OSWALDO WAS BORN IN Mexico in 1975 but has no memory of what life was like there. When he was 3 years old, his mother and one of his brothers came to the United States in search of a better life. Oswaldo and his family made a home in Pama, Texas. His mother eventually married, giving him the father he never had and a provider for the family. Oswaldo never knew his biological father. His father abandoned the family before Oswaldo was born. When his mother married, Oswaldo was proud to have someone to call "father." Life was good for while, but the good times did not last very long.

When his stepfather lost his job, Oswaldo suddenly found their relationship turning sour. His stepfather, as a way to relieve his frustrations, began to use Oswaldo as a punching bag. When his mother protested, the beatings became more frequent and more intense. As time went on, his mother began to pay scant attention to Oswaldo or the beatings Oswaldo suffered. By the time Oswaldo was 10 years old, he had become a tough little kid who suffered abuse without shedding a tear. On the inside, however, his spirit was breaking. Oswaldo's voice became flat and void of all emotions when he described the abuse he suffered as a child, "If I did cry or my mom cried, I would get hit harder. It got to the point where I conditioned myself to feel nothing at all." At a very early age, Oswaldo learned how to numb his pain.

Oswaldo did not do well in school, and he frequently got into fights. He was eventually transferred to another school for his behavioral problems. As he entered fifth grade, he noticed that he was one of the few Mexicans in a predominantly African-American school. His schoolmates did not accept him and trouble came in bundles. Soon school became a battleground for Oswaldo, and he began to hate going. One day a few children jumped him and beat him badly, causing the teacher to notice his bruises. When questioned, he kept silent. He was sent to the principal's office and still kept silent. He would not tell on the children who beat him, so his parents were called in. Oswaldo's stepfather, fearing that Oswaldo told the principal of the home beatings and that the bruises were from him, came to the school outraged. When they got home, without fail, the beating began again. Oswaldo closed his eyes and ignored the pain from the lashes. He felt nothing.

A few weeks later, a child named Lamar thanked Oswaldo for not snitching on him and the others. They became best friends. As an act of friendship, Lamar gave Oswaldo a pit bull puppy. Oswaldo was allowed to keep the dog since his stepfather liked pit bulls too. Oswaldo promised he would care for the dog and keep it away from the chickens that roamed the backyard. Oswaldo named the dog Pancho. Sometimes Pancho gave Oswaldo more trouble than he was worth by chasing his stepfather's chickens, inciting his stepfather's anger.

Early one morning as Oswaldo was getting ready for school, he heard his stepfather calling him to the backyard. He went outside smiling. "What's up, Papa?" As he looked around, he saw that Pancho killed a few chickens. He recalls staring into his stepfather's twisted enraged face. "It felt like a snake bit me in the leg when he hit me with the water hose. I stood there like a warrior trying to take the beating, but the hose was tearing my skin. I heard my mom screaming as I saw the blood rush from my wounds. For the first time in a long time, I started to scream and cry. When another blow hit me in the neck, I reached up in rage and snatched the hose from Papa. Soon after this incident I left home." Oswaldo had no choice but to leave his beloved dog behind. He never returned to school.

Reported to the police as a runaway, Oswaldo stayed at Lamar's house for a few weeks and later found refuge on the streets of Amarillo with a gang called Vario 13. Due to his young age, the gang members gave him the name Junior. From that point forward, Oswaldo took the name Junior, leaving his birth name in the backyard with the blood-soaked hose and abandoned puppy. "Oswaldo was the part of me that went unloved and accepted those beatings that my stepfather gave me. Although I was still a boy, Junior became the part of me that no longer accepted those beatings," Oswaldo explained.

Crack cocaine flooded the streets of urban America in the 1980s, and gangs controlled this lucrative drug trade. Junior joined the ranks and started running the streets. In its early years, Vario 13 was just another bunch of children who were sought to distribute drugs. So at 12 years old, Junior got involved in drug distribution. Junior was like a young pup in a den of wild dogs. By the time he was 15 years old, he had been in and out of the state's juvenile reformatories. The reformatories were a second home to him.

While Junior was in these institutions, he was described by juvenile authorities and probation officers as a "child in need of supervision … a follower." The resident psychiatrist said that most children who were like Junior were regarded as a hero when they are morally impoverished, have no remorse and are expected to lead other juveniles in the segregated institutions.

When Oswaldo was in state school, he found a way to express himself. He could not read or write at the time, so when he communicated with people, he expressed how he felt through art. Art was his way of coping, as well as sharing his fears, hopes and dreams. One staff member at the reformatory encouraged him to draw and recognized his talent. His art later became a way for him to express himself and take his focus off the daily life on death row.

Subsequently, Junior unconsciously destroyed the boy within him and took the role of "wolf" in the eyes of the neighbors who knew him. Like the tale of so many other abandoned and abused children, they clung to others with whom they could self-identify. Although he could not read or write, his counselors did notice that he had great artistic talent. When spoken to about his talent, Junior became defensive. Emotional preservation required that he close himself off from feeling anything. Oftentimes, people become a reflection of those around them and a product of their childhood experiences. Sadly, Junior was never embraced nor did he ever feel loved.

On Nov. 18, 1992, Junior was arrested again, this time for capital murder. Subsequently, many people's lives were changed forever. One of those lives was needlessly taken and another one thrown away. Oswaldo was deemed a threat to society, and he was sentenced to death at the age of 17.

Junior arrived to death row as a juvenile, prior to when men on death row were forced to live in total isolation. The other men on death row offered him the support he never received in school, and through their mentoring and tutoring, Oswaldo finally learned to read and write. They also encouraged him to become closer to God. Fears of getting raped, stabbed to death or beaten savagely remained largely on his mind. As a 25-year-old man, he was still very aware that each passing day brought him closer to his last. He woke up every day missing his family, even his stepfather. He often reflected on how his life could have been different, and what his world would be like if he did not have to struggle every day of it.[85]

Examining the correlation between psychosocial histories and the violent behavior that landed the men on death row, as well as the lives of other incarcerated men, does not imply that all people who have experienced various forms of trauma will perpetrate crimes. This in fact, is not true. Many people with severe histories of trauma go on to lead productive lives. There are many factors that come into play. What cannot be ignored, however, is that most people who end up on death row have highly predictable histories. Dismissing these factors denies opportunities to provide tailored prevention and early intervention strategies at various stages in the life span that can mitigate the consequences of these oppressive histories. Analyzing the backgrounds of the men raises questions about how lives may have turned out differently if an adult would have intervened and provided an opportunity by which the delicate needs of the young children and adolescents were met, and they were protected from harm during the critical periods of development.

Deprivation and Isolation

In his book, *Still Surviving,* Nanon wrote, "In 1997, 37 inmates were executed in Texas. Amongst them were my closest friends. Afterward, the days ahead looked lonely and cold. *I don't need anyone else*, I often thought to myself. I still had me, myself and I. When I first came to prison, I didn't think I would need anybody. I came to realize that we all need someone. No matter who we are or how tough we think we are, no man is truly an island." As illustrated in this quote and in Oswaldo's story, childhood trauma can affect a person's ability to fully experience emotion. The impact of this trauma worsens, however, when individuals are void of any meaningful connections on the inside as well. There is an implied personal connection among the men on death row. When referring to another man on death row, Oswaldo stated, "You are [all] on the same boat, there is only one boat. You are on the same mission, and you are both going to die." Having this sense of connection and relatedness can be better than none at all.[86]

In the world outside of prison, or even within the main prison population, a person has the ability to choose to process an ongoing traumatic stressor or event with another human being. They have opportunities to obtain support, solicit advice, obtain resources or, at the very least, to be heard. Individuals in social isolation are deprived of this. Instead, the pain, the exasperation and the grief have no place to go, except to circulate energetically in the mind, body and the cell. The mounting anguish has to be dealt with alone, without many constructive outlets or adequate venues for seeking support or treatment.

Son Tran recalls how he coped during his time in isolation, "[It was] not until years later that I could think about how [I was] feeling. It's not a time to be scared. They are going to throw you with the dogs, and you are going to be with dogs. There is no choice. You have to deal with every emotion on your own. My family and friends can't help me, and the system surely is not going to help me."

Much of the human experience is defined through relationships with others within a broad social context. Connections with family, friends, co-workers, acquaintances and even strangers provide a continuous feedback loop of verbal and non-verbal messages that are received, interpreted, internalized and sent back. When separated from others, there is no way of knowing how others perceive you, and how to respond or adjust behavior accordingly.[87] An individual normally exchanges thousands of messages per day with others. Messages are consciously and unconsciously utilized to exchange ideas, to solve problems, to convey acceptance or disapproval and to connect. In some ways, feedback from others can provide a mirror for a person and can help to shape and regulate behavior.

In the absence of this social stimulation, this feedback loop is almost non-existent. The only mirror looking back is one that is usually harsh, restrictive and punitive. The lack of social context can create detachment from reality, which is a common experience in isolation. There is little to attach to. Losing social contact leads to a distorted view of the self and a disconnection from a sense of meaning.[88] Many of the men on death row are alone in the world. Some do not have any family or friends and others have never received a letter or seen the inside of the visiting room. The sense of disconnection to other humans is pervasive.

Not only are the men alone, but also their stimulation is extremely limited, causing deprivation. Every day a person proceeds about his life in non-confined settings, he experiences multiple stimulations of all of the senses. Some of the experiences are routine, but there are many opportunities to introduce novel stimuli to the brain on a daily basis. No two days are ever the same: alternate music is played; new environments and climates are experienced through the various senses either in person or through media; new ground is walked on; people are introduced; new images, art, and textures are felt and seen; new stories told and heard; novel mental challenges arise and choices are made; and new smells are ever-present. Inherent to everyday life is the ability to experience a broad array of novel stimuli that promotes healthy circuitry of the brain and body. A person in confinement endures the same mind-numbing experiences every single day of his existence with very little variation. Identical colors, textures, smells and lighting of the cell surround the individual for 23 hours per day. The food that is brought in through the slot has very little assortment of taste, smell, consistency and temperature. The only departure from the cell is the walk to the shower, while wearing shackles, and the one-hour of "recreation" in a small enclosure that may or may not be outdoors. The same stress-inducing noises of metal doors crashing and people shouting continue all day, every day. There are no bars to see out of, there are no opportunities to interact with other living entities in the environment, such as stepping on grass, smelling fresh air and interacting with animals. The monotony of these experiences does not provide the brain an opportunity to gain the novel stimulus required. Stimulation is not a luxury; it is something the brain requires in order to function correctly.

One of the experiences that used to provide the men on death row with occasion to get some of these needs met was a work program. The program provided a chance for the men to experience self-efficacy and obtain social and sensory stimulation. The men worked in a garment factory (though some men resisted this program since the garment factory produced uniforms for TDCJ correctional officers) and were able to recreate in groups. They were only isolated in the evening. In addition, they were able to participate in educational programming. These programs were completely cut when the men were moved to the Polunsky Unit and were placed in isolation as the result of the death row prison escape of seven men that severely changed the lives of those on death row. Steve J. Martin, former General Counsel of the Texas prison system, reported that he believed the work program was successful and felt that it was a shame that things changed when the men were moved into segregation in an environment that fostered severe deprivation. This drastic change of environment had some serious repercussions and deprived the men of some of the needs that were actually being met by the agency. According to agency figures obtained by *The Texas Observer*, suicides on death row increased after Texas placed the men in solitary confinement following the move. Between 2004 and the time the article was written in November 2010, five men had committed suicide on death row—more suicides than in the previous 25 years.[89] Deprivation and isolation feed on each other, creating negative outcomes.

All people have the need to experience meaning in their lives and to be able to influence their environment—to feel efficacious. Knowing that what you do in your world, no matter how small, makes a difference, can propel a person forward in life through goal-oriented behavior. Most people need something to live for. Lacking a mission, a goal or a meaning in life can have devastating consequences on a person's sense of self-worth and consequently impact his behavior.

Another powerful form of social connectedness that is nonexistent in solitary confinement is the ability to experience human touch. In his memoir, *Still Surviving,* Nanon describes this painful realization when arriving on death row, "There would never be contact with another being's skin again, in any fashion, unless a guard's hand brushed against your own while being handcuffed through the metal slot in the door. Otherwise, we were further separated from other people, as though our being human was finally erased completely."[90] Individuals on death row are not permitted to have contact visits. Their families are not able to touch their loved ones until after they have been executed, at which point, they may touch their bodies. Dr. Hal Barclay, a licensed professional counselor and professor at Southern Methodist University, commented about the deprivation of touch for people in confinement.

> The purpose of prison, in the eyes of the law, is punishment. As it turns out, one of the subtlest forms of punishment is to deny these prisoners the opportunity to touch and be touched. Carl Rogers noted that, "We all have a need to be touched, both literally and figuratively." Rarely does either happen in confinement. As a result, prisoners are prevented from experiencing what the renowned sociologist, Ashley Montagu, coined the "significance of skin." Touching others or being touched is one of the most powerful forms of communication between humans. Research throughout the 20th century repeatedly demonstrated the importance of human contact in terms of psychological and physical health and the long-lasting negative impact of deficiencies. The positive chemical realities derived from human touch become next to non-existent in these conditions.

The brain is wired to be in connection with others throughout a person's life span. When a human, or animal, is placed in isolation, the environment goes against one of the most primary needs. According to Dr. Bonnie Badnoch, co-founder of Nurturing the Heart with the Brain in Mind, the circuitry of the brain needs to be refreshed constantly with attachment. She explained, "If the brain is deprived from this, what is generated is an activation of the limbic system, which brings about pain and fear."

She also discussed that in absence of any form of meaningful connection, isolated people will find any manner they can by which to experience connection. If you take a person with attachment wounds, for example, and cut them off from attachment, further union occurs. Unpleasant interaction is more pleasant than an absence of interaction. An example of this concept is the manner by which interactions with correctional officers occur. Sometimes, an incarcerated person may evoke a conflict with a correctional officer, for seemingly no reason. Craig Haney explains this concept, "Some prisoners, for example, act out literally as a way of getting a reaction from their environment, proving to themselves that they are still alive and capable of eliciting a genuine response—however hostile—from other human beings."[91]

Oswaldo Soriano shared his experience observing this type of behavior, "I have seen an officer who is a nice respectable person and an inmate will kick [the] officer for no reason." Several men who have spent time in solitary confinement have described this behavior as a manner of creating a link with the outside world. Any link is celebrated. Some have described feeling joy when an outdoor creature—such as a rat, cockroach or spider—entered their cell. They describe catching and keeping rodents, transforming them into their own pets. These animal relationships can serve as a meaningful connection to the outside environment as well as to another living being. It can also create a sense of self-efficacy. Finally, in the person's own eyes, he has an important role—to sustain and take care of another. The person is afforded the opportunity to have the mutual exchange of needing and giving back—of touching and of being touched.

Brain and Behavior: Adverse Effects

Describing his experience on death row, Nanon recalls, "You listen to people talk to themselves and bang on the walls all day, and it becomes normal to hear it. And at some point you realize that none of this is normal, and you wonder when you are going to become one of them." The adverse effects of living in isolation are well documented. A plethora of research studies confirm the damaging overarching effects and, in some cases, severe irreversible harm.

The effects of deprivation on brain functioning in adults have been informed by numerous studies using animal models as well as neuro-imaging brain and behavior studies that include incarcerated individuals. Previous data derived from animal studies have been effective in assessing these variables because their research designs are highly controlled. Conclusions drawn from these studies have been replicated in human models, indicating that specific neuro-chemical systems are impacted.

The consequences of sensory and social deprivation have been heavily examined in different contexts, leading to similar results. The National Aeronautics and Space Administration (NASA), for example, has conducted research evaluating experiences that astronauts face in a sensory and socially deprived environment. Findings report that, "The presence of new stimuli in our environment is important to healthy psychological functioning and well-being." In addition, "Lack of sensory stimuli has deleterious effects on our cognition. Visual monotony, for example, comes from the lack of new and interesting things to see and limited information to gain from in the environment." The findings also indicate a significant decline to cognitive and affective states in social isolation.[92] Cognition, which is the manner by which new information is learned, is a mental state that describes the brain's capacity to reason, perceive and make decisions. When cognition is impaired, a person experiences difficulties with memory and judgment as well as irritability, depression, confusion and anxiety.[93] Individuals can also distort their perceptions and experience things differently than they are, causing an additional layer of confusion.

In his book, *Still Surviving*, Nanon describes the living reality of perceptual distortions, "If we weren't careful, our imagination could swallow our perception of reality, and we would just sit in the cell like a babbling fool uttering things that weren't even comprehensible anymore. I've heard some men talking so casually when you walked by their cells, that you would have sworn they had a cell mate. Sometimes when guards did a count, they checked some prisoners' cells to make sure they were alone." [94]

Studies also indicate that the brain, even after a short time in confinement, will show changes in pattern. Stuart Grassian, a psychiatrist who served on the Harvard Medical School faculty for more than 25 years and has been cited in numerous federal court decisions, stated: "This literature, as well as my own observations, has demonstrated that, deprived of a sufficient level of environmental and social stimulation, individuals will soon become incapable of maintaining an adequate state of alertness and attention to the environment. Indeed, even a few days of solitary confinement will predictably shift the electroencephalogram (EEG) pattern toward an abnormal pattern characteristic of stupor and delirium."[95]

In addition to changes in cognitive functioning, sensory deprivation and the related stress and anxiety that comes from it has been shown to impact language as well as social and emotional functioning. Individuals in isolation may experience paranoia, delusions and hallucinations, disorientation and other types of psychosis and alternative perceptions of reality. A former psychiatrist at TDCJ who worked on death row and who chose to remain anonymous, recalls, "[I] have seen a lot of people on death row that were psychotic. [They] weren't trying to manipulate the system with it; it was not something that they came with."

Anger and Fear

Oswaldo Soriano was one of the 29 mean on death row whose death sentence was commuted to a life sentence. Nine years after his removal from death row to general population, he described what it was like living in isolation. The emotion immediately surfaced, followed by a conscious attempt to suppress it, inside and out. "I am trying to close that world out because there is so much anger, bitterness and rage that exists in that type of environment. I try to close it out as much as I can." He vividly recalled living in complete fear. "I don't think there are any words to describe that fear until you lived it. Every night you are going to sleep with something on you. You are going to sleep with a weapon on you or you can get killed. These guards get paid to open doors. It's the only way to survive. A lot of officers get paid because they make so little money at TDCJ. In a place like death row, money runs freely. If I need a favor, and you give me one to two thousand dollars to pop this door so someone can kill this inmate—things happen like that whether you want to believe it or not. I have seen it and witnessed it with my own eyes."

The emotional states that lie hidden under a tough outer shell often percolate and can eventually overwhelm a person's ability to cope in conditions of extreme stress and isolation. Craig Haney describes the external manifestations that can occur as a result of these emotions, "The deprivations, restrictions, the totality of control and the prolonged absence of any real opportunity for happiness or joy fills many prisoners with intolerable levels of frustration that, for some, turns to anger and then even to uncontrollable and sudden outbursts of rage."[96]

Martin Draughon described an experience that would cause him and the others on death row a great deal of frustration. "You are already locked up in a concrete tomb with no socialization with others, all you do is read, write, sleep and try to stand up and holler at someone you can't see. Why would you [correctional officer] go out of your way to antagonize folks? Made people crazy. [It is like being in a] big metal dumpster and at random, every few minutes, someone comes along with a hammer and hits the metal dumpster. BANG. BANG. BANG."

Misdirected emotions occur frequently outside of the prison environment, in conditions where people have access to basic needs and have various resources for coping and learning. In solitary confinement, where one lives in a constant state of trauma and has extremely limited access to resources or opportunities to learn how to constructively manage emotion and deal with conflict, explosive behavior is almost inevitable.

Traumatic Stress

The same brain structures that are negatively impacted as a result of combat-related post-traumatic stress disorder (PTSD), torture and trauma victimization are the brain systems that are impacted by solitary confinement. Some of the structures that are negatively impacted include the following:

• Hypothalamus, which has many functions, among which are to produce hormones in charge of the regulation of sex drive, emotional responses and sleep.[97]
• Adrenal glands, which keep stress response hormones in balance. [98]
• Amygdala, which is the emotional center implicated in fear, aggression, rage and pleasure responses.[99]
• Hippocampus, which has been implicated in memory.

Reid Lyon of University of Texas at Dallas Center for Brain Health explains that damage to these structures including a decrease in hippocampal volume, have been found in traumatic environments such as solitary confinement. Structural or functional impairments to these regions can have a detrimental impact on mood, stress response, cognition, memory, coping and behavior.

A person may experience these changes as a constant hyper-vigilance, paranoia, extreme anxiety and constant activation of the "fight or flight" response. Living in constant survival mode has direct implications on one's ability to regulate mood, behavior and make decisions. It has frequently been described by those living in isolation as, "needing to always be ready for battle" and "sleeping with one eye-open." This continuous activation can eventually lead to fatigue in regions of the brain and can cause depression.

Even when the men are removed from these conditions, they can still experience lasting effects, such as PTSD, which can be debilitating. Expert Craig Haney remarks, "Taking prisoners out of these places often goes a long way in reducing or eliminating the negative effects. But there is good reason to believe that some prisoners—we do not yet know how many or, in advance precisely who—cannot and will not overcome these social pathologies; their extreme adaptations to super-max confinement become too ingrained to relinquish."[100]

At the time of the interview for this book, Son Tran had been off death row for more than a decade, and yet he still walked with his hands in a cuffed position, even though he was not cuffed. "It's a habit to put my hands down because you used to be restrained all the time," he explained. Martin still gets flashbacks when he hears the banging noises from inside the prison, "Internally, stress rises up another notch, and I feel tension building. Living here [in prison] is a trigger and reminds me of being on death row," he described. After describing a traumatic memory from death row, Oswaldo had a rough time continuing his train of thought, almost as if he was going to someplace else in his mind. As he was recalling the events from years ago, he relayed, "I think [of] memories, that was just one. There is more memories that … ." He then changed the direction of the conversation.

Many of the men who were interviewed during the writing of this book, seemed to, at times, minimize the impact that living on death row or solitary confinement had on them. There appeared to be incongruent information between what happened and their emotional response. It was very common for them to describe how other people coped and expressed their trauma, but they almost seemed to hit a wall when asked about their own experiences. Almost all of them directly or indirectly changed the subject, some appeared to be at a loss for words that could express the experience. Others seemed to have a sense of disconnection from the events from an emotional level but could recall the events and facts. Many factors can be looked at to explain these observations. Trust and personal attributes of the interviewers, such as gender could have played a role. Feelings of shame or embarrassment could have also been present. Cognitive impairments, including memory, language, processing and perceptual deficits were noticed in some of the men and may also have also played a role. Disconnection and detachment in response to emotionally difficult material may be coping responses that were adopted years ago. In his research, psychiatrist Stuart Grassian noticed that the people he interviewed appeared to rationalize, deny or distort their symptoms and would often become defensive about their psychiatric issues.[101]

Self-Mutilation

Craig Haney has been studying the psychological effects of solitary confinement for more than 30 years. In a Senate Judiciary Subcommittee on the Constitution, Civil Rights and Human Rights Hearing on Solitary Confinement June 19, 2012, he provided the following testimony:

> It is not uncommon in these units to encounter prisoners who have smeared themselves with feces, sit catatonic in puddles of their own urine on the floors of their cells, or shriek wildly and band their fists or their heads against the walls that contain them. In some cases, these reactions are even more tragic and bizarre, including grotesque forms of self-harm and mutilation—prisoners who have amputated parts of their own bodies or inserted tubes and other objects into their penises—and are often met with an institutional matter-of-factness that is equally disturbing.

Dr. Haney also described a situation in which, "a prisoner sewed his mouth shut and one who amputated one of his pinkie fingers and chewed the other off, removed one of his testicles and scrotum, sliced off his ear lobes, and severed his Achilles tendon with a sharp piece of metal."[102]

In the same hearing death row exoneree Anthony Graves reported an experience he witnessed that he will never forget. "I know a guy who would sit in the middle of the floor, rip his sheet up, wrap it around himself and light it on fire." These extremely violent forms of self-mutilation are highly infrequent among the general prison population. In general, "Prisoners in solitary confinement have been found to engage in self-mutilation at rates higher than the general population."[103] One study explained self-mutilation as a means to "liberate the self from the unbearable tension—the physical pain becomes a compensatory substitute for psychic pain or shame."[104] The level of all-encompassing exasperation that these individuals experience that would lend them to injure themselves in this fashion is incomprehensible. Individuals who work in the corrections environment often claim that this type of behavior is simply attention seeking and manipulative. In an interview with Craig Haney, he described the depth of this ideology, "How many people in corrections operate is that they begin with a presumption that the prisoner's motivation is always bad and that everything they do emanates from that."

Suicide

Idle chatter—guys yelling from cell to cell. The idle chatter keeps the loneliness at bay. The constant bantering back and forth is a chaotic symphony with periodic bursts of conversation so rapid and loud it reminds one of machine-gunfire. Amid all the noise, the absolute silence of a few eventually becomes as apparent as all the screaming going on through vents and through the door cracks. There is no doubt that those who remain silent find a small bit of comfort in the noise, assurance that they are not alone in their solitude. Bryan (name changed for privacy) was one of the quiet ones.

Bryan was so quiet that it was easy to forget he was even there. He rarely acknowledged anyone. Even when the officers came by for count, Bryan held his silence. "Bryan! Bryan! What is your ID number?" Whether he was asleep, catatonic or simply unwilling to be acknowledged by a number, no one ever knew. He simply never spoke. Although his silence was a definite indicator that something was truly wrong with him, no one ever interfered. Prison has so many unwritten rules, but the one most adhered to is the "mind your own business" rule.

One morning a loud scream broke through the idle chatter. It was count time, and the officer counting all the men began running down the tier in a panic. Several minutes later, more officers rushed up the stairs and down the tier. "Inmate, respond! Inmate, respond!" the officers yelled over and over again. There was no response. A ranking officer arrived, and the door was rolled open. About 30 minutes later a stretcher arrived. Bryan was placed on it and slowly carried out of the solitary confinement cell. His face was very white. His eyes were closed. All he wore was his boxer shorts. He was dead. Bryan escaped the executioner. He was free.

The idle chatter ceased for a while. Everyone worried they might too succumb to the same fate. Solitary confinement is a brutal existence, and everyone wonders if he too will one day lose the will to live. Officers arrived back on the scene to take photos of the cell for an investigation into Bryan's death. He had somehow hung himself with a sheet.

Over the course of the next several weeks, I contemplated what I could have done to help Bryan. Perhaps I should have ignored the "mind your own business" rule and sparked up conversations with him. Maybe if he had been able to talk with someone, he would still be alive. For a long time, as I passed by his cell, I looked inside, contemplating his death. We lived in such extreme isolation. The prison administration expected us to behave normally while living in the most extraordinarily abnormal conditions. Isolation is torture. It is cruel and unusual punishment.

On death row, those four concrete walls are all anyone can see ... day in and day out for years on end. Bryan wanted to move on. He wanted to experience what was next to come. Death was his only way out.

BEHAVING "NORMALLY" IN SEVERELY abnormal conditions is a perpetual challenge that is seemingly impossible to accomplish. Current and past TDCJ prison staff have described the relative impossibility of being able to follow the rules and stay away from the consequences that often lead to more time in confinement. Jack Henry Abbott, in his book, *Belly of the Beast*, writes about his experience in solitary confinement, "Any sane man would wonder: what grievous crime would a man have to commit to be thus treated? The answer: In prison, anything at all ... A contraband book. A murder."[105]

Steve Martin, former general counsel of TDCJ, reflects on the challenges of the system, "[It is] easier to get into segregation than get out. In a situation where mental decompensation is common, being able cope internally in the conditions and not feeling any control on what one needs to do to get out of confinement, can prove to be a futile effort for someone who has no one." Feeling like they have no other escape, some resort to suicide.

In general, suicide risks are higher in correctional settings such as prisons and jails at an increased rate than in the outside community.[106] Studies also suggest that suicides are more prevalent in maximum security prisons, where deprivation levels are higher.[107] The risk factors of suicide in isolation can include a history of previous trauma, including abuse and neglect, as well as a history of suicide attempts by family members.[108] Other studies have indicated that it is a combination of institutional conditions, such as deprivation, coupled with characteristics of the incarcerated men, which were predictive of suicide.[109] In *Death Before Dying*, it was noted that there is an absence of national statistics that examine suicide rates that are specific to those incarcerated on death row in solitary confinement. What has been identified, however, is that about half of all suicides occur in isolation cells.[110] According to data obtained from an open records request, individuals who live in prison isolation cells in TDCJ were nine times more likely to commit suicide than those living in general population (see table on next page). Between 2006 and 2013, there have been 89 completed suicides of individuals housed in TDCJ's safekeeping, administrative segregation and death row combined, which are all what this book refers to as solitary confinement. Four of these suicides occurred among those living on death row.[111]

OFFENDER POPULATION [1]	CY2006	CY2007	CY2008	CY2009	CY2010	CY2011	CY2012	CY2013	
	156,760	157,424	157,865	158,068	157,466	158,792	156,305	153,294	

CUSTODY STATUS [2] (included in the total population above)	CY2006	CY2007	CY2008	CY2009	CY2010	CY2011	CY2012	CY2013	
ADMINISTRATIVE SEGREGATION	9,542	9,186	8,807	8,492	8,547	8,784	8,060	7,597	
DEATH ROW	379	360	346	324	302	292	287	270	

GENERAL POPULATION	CY2006	CY2007	CY2008	CY2009	CY2010	CY2011	CY2012	CY2013	8-YEAR AVG. SUICIDE RATE
POPULATION COUNT	146,839	147,878	148,712	149,252	148,617	149,716	149,716	145,427	
SUICIDES COUNT	18	19	15	21	18	16	14	11	
SUICIDE % RATE	0.01%	0.01%	0.01%	0.01%	0.01%	0.01%	0.01%	0.01%	0.01%

ADMINISTRATIVE SEGREGATION	CY2006	CY2007	CY2008	CY2009	CY2010	CY2011	CY2012	CY2013	8-YEAR AVG. SUICIDE RATE
POPULATION COUNT	9,542	9,186	8,807	8,492	8,547	8,784	8,060	7,597	
SUICIDES COUNT	5	15	4	12	6	11	13	5	
SUICIDE % RATE	0.05%	0.16%	0.05%	0.14%	0.07%	0.13%	0.16%	0.07%	0.10%*

Comparison Results: * This eight-year trend shows the Ad Seg suicide rate to be 9x greater than the general population suicide rate.

DEATH ROW	CY2006	CY2007	CY2008	CY2009	CY2010	CY2011	CY2012	CY2013	8-YEAR AVG. SUICIDE RATE
POPULATION COUNT	379	360	346	324	302	292	287	270	
SUICIDES COUNT	1	1	0	2	0	0	0	0	
SUICIDE % RATE	0.26%	0.28%	0.00%	0.62%	0.00%	0.00%	0.00%	0.00%	0.14%**

Comparison Results:** This eight-year trend shows the death row suicide rate to be 13x greater than the general population suicide rate.

GENERAL POP SAFEKEEPING [3]	CY2006	CY2007	CY2008	CY2009	CY2010	CY2011	CY2012	CY2013	
SUICIDES COUNT	2	2	2	2	2	3	1	0	

ISOLATION ALL TYPES	CY2006	CY2007	CY2008	CY2009	CY2010	CY2011	CY2012	CY2013	8-YEAR AVG. SUICIDE RATE
POPULATION COUNT	9,921	9,546	9,153	8,816	8,849	9,076	8,347	7,867	
SUICIDES COUNT	8	18	6	16	8	14	14	5	
SUICIDE % RATE	0.08%	0.19%	0.07%	0.18%	0.09%	0.15%	0.17%	0.06%	0.12%***

Comparison Results:*** This eight-year trend shows the death row suicide rate to be 11x greater than the general population suicide rate.

[1] All data represents a count of individuals within the categories shown
[2] Included in the total offender population; Data does not include suicides which occurred in TDCJ's disciplinary housing status ("Solitary Confinement")
[3] Data for safekeeping included in total Isolation figures below

Physiological Effects

In addition to the psychosocial implications of isolation, physical health is also impacted. A person's environment has a strong influence on their physical health, mental health, spiritual health and mortality. One of the manners by which solitary confinement can have a detrimental effect on individuals is through exposure to chronic stress. An abundance of evidence supports the effect that stress has on health and health behaviors.[112]

Individuals in solitary confinement experience high levels of ongoing stress that produces changes to multiple systems in the body. Chronic stress can alter the immune system response as well as cause changes in heart rate and blood pressure. In addition, it can lead to gastrointestinal problems, skin problems, sleep and memory difficulties, anxiety, depression and PTSD. Stress has been connected to heart disease in men, particularly in situations where there is a loss of control.[113]

An Amnesty International report on solitary confinement described the wide reaching health consequence that individuals living in isolation face, "Devastating physical problems include vitamin D deficiency because prisoners are deprived of exercise and sunlight for so many years. Prisoners' eyesight deteriorates, and they develop photophobia and vision loss. In addition, prisoners develop balance problems, chronic asthma, severe insomnia and memory loss, all of which are permanent afflictions that will follow them for the rest of their lives."[114]

Exercise and nutrition are also critical components of health and wellness. People living in confinement are not afforded the opportunity to exercise adequately, as movement is severely restricted. The one hour of recreation time allows them to have space that is approximately double the size of their cell. Some individuals pace or run in place in their cells, do sit-ups and other forms of stationary exercise. Although TDCJ maintains that incarcerated individuals receive proper nutrition, many feel otherwise. Former death row exoneree Anthony Graves testified about his concerns about nutrition, "The food lacks proper nutrition, because it is either dehydrated when served to you or perhaps you'll find things like rat feces or a small piece of broken glass. When escorted to the infirmary, I would walk by the kitchen and see inmates cooking the food and sweating into it."[115]

The lack of social relationships has also been found to cause a detrimental effect on health and mortality. In a meta-analysis that involved 148 research studies that looked at social relationships and mortality risk, the findings indicated, "The influence of social relationships on the risk of death are comparable with well-established risk factors for mortality such as smoking and alcohol consumption and exceed the influence of other risk factors such as physical inactivity and obesity."[116] Loneliness has also been implicated in a large body of research, demonstrating a strong association between loneliness and worse health.[117]

As previously mentioned in the Amnesty International Report, vision can be impaired for individuals living in solitary confinement. When locked in a confinement cell that does not contain bars, 23 hours per day, the opportunity to see at long distances is virtually non-existent. In an interview with Dr. David Goss, professor of Optometry from Indiana University who specializes in myopia, he described that the restriction of visual space on vision has been studied extensively and has been found to cause myopia, or near-sidedness. Other physical outcomes that can be associated with the environmental conditions experienced in confinement are related to sleep deprivation. Various forms of sleep deprivation have been used among prisoners of war as a technique to gain information. It is considered by some to be a form of torture. Many of the incarcerated men who were interviewed described many factors that would interfere with their ability to sleep on a daily basis. One factor is the loud screaming and "animal type noises" that comes from the isolation cells 24 hours per day. A former TDCJ psychiatrist, who chose to remain anonymous, described his experience, "I could not stand the screaming and hollering; it was deafening. It was sad that they were in a situation that was so desperate. [It was] sad for the guards that had to endure that. I don't see how you could stand it. For some of the guards, it was intolerable. They [incarcerated individuals] weren't saying words. [It was the] desperation and frustration of being in that confinement. Some personalities could take it, some couldn't."

Another factor interrupting sleep is the frequent count times that occur every three hours, preventing the individual from ever achieving all the necessary sleep cycles. Some men in confinement report symptoms of anxiety, chronic fear, nightmares, hallucinations and environmental conditions such as extreme heat, impacting their ability to sleep. Numerous studies have pointed to the fact that sleep deprivation can cause serious impairments in brain functioning, performance, health, memory, cognition and mental status.

Death row exoneree Anthony Graves testified, "I was subjected to sleep deprivation. I would hear the clanging of metal doors throughout the night, an officer walking the runs and shining his flashlight in your eyes, or an inmate kicking and screaming because he's losing his mind. Guys become paranoid and schizophrenic and can't sleep because they are hearing voices."[118] Chronic partial sleep loss, which is experienced by these individuals, has also been found to have dynamic changes in physiology and behavior.[119] The full extent of the public health consequences is currently unknown. It is impossible to measure, because no country has ever incarcerated people at this rate. The full extent of the impact will not be known for many years.[120]

So What?

A mountain of research dating hundreds of years confirms the devastating impacts of solitary confinement, yet it is still widely practiced. Some individuals think that providing opportunities for social connectedness, as well as other basic needs, including an environment where sleep can occur and very basic needs to be met are luxuries that are not deserved by people who committed crimes. In fact, many believe that they should pay for what they did for the rest of their lives. A common view is that criminals should not be rewarded for their criminal behavior by providing them with an environment that provides safety and comfort. There is a fundamental difference, however, between basic human needs and luxury. When basic human needs are not met, the body, mind and behavior will often respond in ways that are not only detrimental to the self but also to others around them.

Some people will call the subjugation of incarcerated individuals to the cruel and degrading isolation conditions a well-deserved form of "justice." Definitions of justice are often molded to fit individual, social and emotional needs, morals, ethics, values and specific situations. Retributive justice is often implicated to rationalize the abuse and neglect of prisoners, often using the "eye for an eye" mentality that can be viewed as a form of legalized vengeance. A person does not need to be an advocate for incarcerated individuals to be concerned about the serious risk to public health and safety inherent in caging individuals that nobody knows how to deal with and subjecting them to well-documented damaging effects, and in most cases, releasing them to the public once their sentence has been served or keeping them incarcerated and putting the prison staff and other incarcerated people in more danger. In addition, the cost implications for providing on-going health care to address these damaging results are severe and are costing the system, i.e., the taxpayers, an enormous amount of money. The logic that has been used as a justification for solitary confinement is that it provides greater safety for the institution and public. It is unreasonable to expect people to follow all of the rules perfectly, when placing them in isolation conditions alters brain chemistry as well as impairs their ability to think, feel, relate to others, cope and regulate their mood and behavior. If rules are violated, more isolation will occur and the cycle continues. This flawed logic is not informed by evidence, fails to promote rehabilitation and poses a safety risk to us all. More research studies analyzing the long-term effects of solitary confinement, including recidivism rates need to be conducted to fully understand the ramifications to the individual and community.

When speaking to a member of executive management from TDCJ regarding concerns about the impact of isolation on those who are incarcerated, the response given indicated that he was "not aware" of any damage that was caused by the conditions. He pointed to a lone study that negated the negative effects of confinement. Turning a blind eye to the cruelty that is occurring, the problem that it has created or denying its magnitude does not absolve people from taking responsibility and accountability for making things better. This negligent approach has been documented throughout history with oppressed groups and has had devastating consequences to all of humanity.

CHAPTER SEVEN

PROTECTING THE VULNERABLE AND OPPRESSED

Each year I have lived behind these brick walls has been a year of watching others being destroyed. I have watched kids grow to be men inside this place. I have seen developmentally and intellectually disabled prisoners suffer confusion and torment, as well as abuse, because they did not have the mental capability to understand why they were there.

—Nanon M. Williams, Still Surviving

AS REINFORCED BY PREVIOUS chapters, there is more than enough research evidence and clinical observations made by qualified professionals to raise serious concerns about the dangers associated with solitary confinement. One does not need to be an experienced health care professional or researcher to infer the devastating consequences that can occur by placing especially vulnerable individuals in severely isolated conditions. Placing people who are more susceptible to the damage of confinement goes against strong recommendations from multiple experts and leading health care organizations.

Solitary confinement exposes vulnerable individuals to an elevated risk of harm, a lesser chance of rehabilitation and what many would argue to be cruel and unusual punishment. Despite all of these contraindications and a strong consensus of professional opinions, thousands of vulnerable citizens are housed in inhumane conditions and held up to the same expectations as those who lack these vulnerabilities. Vulnerable populations, for example, can include juveniles and historically oppressed groups such as immigrants, LGBT individuals and individuals with cognitive, emotional and physical impairments. Rather than provide an additional layer of protection to ensure the safety of these individuals, they are exposed to even harsher conditions.

Protecting the Vulnerable Through Isolation

Other vulnerable individuals in prison can also include victims of sexual assault as well as victims of other forms of violence. For their own protection, these individuals may be placed, based on these factors alone, in a TDCJ housing status known as "protective custody," so that they are safe from the potential violence that other incarcerated individuals may inflict on them. Although protective custody status offers more privileges, these individuals are still in the same solitary confinement cells 23 hours per day.[121]

The concern that grave harm may be inflicted upon vulnerable individuals if they were to reside in the general prison population, and additional need for protection, is a well justified one, as many of these individuals are at a much higher risk of victimization, dehumanization, discrimination and exploitation. Housing the vulnerable individuals in solitary confinement for their protection, however, is not solving the problem in its entirety. It may, in fact, increase the level of protection from other incarcerated people, but it makes them more susceptible from victimization from prison staff.

The case of *Doe v. Richard Carter*, whereby the plaintiff, John Doe, described as a gay man who was small in stature, was allegedly forced by an officer to perform oral sex is one example.[122]

Due to the fact that solitary confinement cells do not have bars, there is limited visibility as to what occurs inside the cell. Opportunities for exploitation and mistreatment, therefore, are increased and accountability decreases. This creates an environment that is ripe for mistreatment. Individuals with mental illnesses are at an increased risk for victimization. One study that looked at the dangers faced by incarcerated individuals who are mentally ill, for example found that, "The physical victimization rates of male prisoners with a serious mental illness were 1.6 times higher for inmate-on-inmate violence and 1.2 times higher for staff-on-inmate violence than those of male prisoners with no major mental disorder."[123] Other studies have found similar conclusions.

Nanon recalls his experience witnessing this type of abuse on death row.

I was scheduled to be reviewed by the Unit Classification Committee. They questioned me about the previous night when several prison guards antagonized and provoked a mentally disabled prisoner. The guards were spitting on the prisoner, calling him "nigger" and physically assaulting him for their own entertainment ... simply because they were bored. Two other prisoners and I refused to sit quietly and accept such behavior by the guards, so we yelled and requested that ranking officials remove the guards who were harassing this prisoner on J-21. These were cowardly guards who would not harass a prisoner capable of fighting back, yet they took ungodly pleasure in tormenting and brutalizing the mentally ill prisoners who were incapable of defending themselves. Many other prisoners, tired of such inhumane cruelty, set fires, flooded their cells, screamed and used what means they possessed to protest the abuse.

INCARCERATED PEOPLE WITH INTELLECTUAL and developmental disabilities are often the subject of ridicule, discriminatory treatment and neglect. In his book, *Still Surviving*, Nanon recounts witnessing this type of egregious behavior while he was living on death row.

All morning long the prisoner who had cried out had not been given his psychiatric medication. At last, in insane desperation, he had broken open a shaving razor to cut his wrists. Although the man wasn't dead, as we thought, he passed out because his blood pressure dropped dangerously low. Of course, this would not have happened if guards on duty were doing their job and checked on him when he began screaming.

"Did you see his cell?" the guard laughed as he walked by my cell. "The blood is even on the ceiling and the walls, and it looks like he slung it everywhere, like he enjoyed it. That stupid retard even wrote his name in blood on the wall," the guard spoke excitedly, obviously enjoying the diversion from his usual routine duty shift. I felt as if this sadistic guard must also be in need of psychiatric treatment.[124]

Dehumanization and stereotyping of persons with intellectual and developmental disabilities, as well as mental illness, has been evidenced for centuries. This population of individuals is highly stigmatized, largely misunderstood, their needs are minimized and they are feared by others and heavily persecuted. With the exception of health personnel, which are lacking in numbers to adequately meet the overwhelming needs, prison staff are ill prepared to communicate with and recognize specific behavioral health care needs as well as be able to identify warning signs that are vital to the health, security and rehabilitation.

Solitary confinement has the capacity to cause even high-functioning individuals intense suffering and mental illness over time. For those who have pre-existing vulnerabilities, as many do entering the system, the damage is compounded and their conditions are likely to worsen, having a wide reaching impact.

One federal judge addressed the suitability of putting mentally ill people in confinement, he remarked, "It is the mental equivalent of putting an asthmatic in a place with little air."[125] Mental health research describes the effects of extended solitary confinement as especially harmful for incarcerated individuals with mental illness. Research by Stuart Grassian, for example, showed that in one sample of 200 people in administrative segregation, one-third became psychotic as a result of their solitary confinement.[126] Testimony by psychiatrist Terry Kupers, in a court case from Wisconsin, supports the assertion that confining incarcerated people with mental illness is harmful, reporting that, "It is an extreme hazard to their mental health and well-being. It causes irreparable emotional damage and psychiatric disability as well as extreme mental anguish and suffering, and in some cases, presents a risk of death by suicide."[127]

The American Psychiatric Association compiled research, devised practice guidelines and informed the community that clinicians, "generally agree that placement of inmates with serious mental illnesses in settings with extreme isolation is contraindicated because many of these inmates' psychiatric conditions will clinically deteriorate or not improve."[128] As a consequence, an increasing number of states are making it illegal to house mentally ill individuals in administrative segregation.[129] TDCJ currently houses individuals in solitary confinement who have been diagnosed with a mental disorder. The following data were gleaned from an open records request.[130]

DESCRIPTION	CODE	FY2010		FY2011		FY2012	
		DEATH ROW	AD SEG	DEATH ROW	AD SEG	DEATH ROW	AD SEG
No diagnosis of mental disorder or history of mental illness	1A/1AP	183	4,971	177	4,831	165	4,172
History of mental disorder, resolved; no history of serious mental illness	1AH	49	1,599	49	1,872	48	1,790
Currently receiving ongoing counseling or monitoring for a mental disorder, behavior problem or emotional condition; not on psychotropic medications	2BR	7	248	8	282	6	276
Currently receiving psychotropic medication for a mental disorder or emotional condition	2BT	16	489	17	584	22	709
Currently receiving ongoing counseling or monitoring for a serious mental illness or history of serious mental illness; not on psychotropic medications	3NR	5	148	5	164	5	173
Currently receiving psychotropic medication for a serious mental illness	3NT	31	1,066	28	1,023	30	931
Currently admitted to inpatient mental health care	4PT	7	9	8	7	6	5
Unclassified		4	17	0	21	0	9
TOTAL		302	8,547	292	8,784	282	8,065

Note: The table above does not include individuals on bench warrant.

As with any other medical disorders, individuals with mental illnesses and intellectual or developmental disabilities require a regimented treatment plan, that if not followed could cause regression and deterioration. Given what is known about the risk of suicide and the mental deterioration that occurs by putting mentally ill individuals and those with histories of mental illnesses in solitary confinement, a prison system should ensure that close monitoring, counseling and behavioral health care treatment is provided.

An open records request revealed that during the Fiscal years of 2010–2012, an average of 40 percent of individuals on death row and 45 percent of those in administrative segregation in TDCJ are classified as having a "history of current mental illness or mental health diagnosis."[131]

Yet 17 percent of these individuals on death row, or approximately 50 individuals, were not receiving counseling, monitoring, psychotropic medication, inpatient care for "mental disorder, behavior problem, emotional condition, serious illness."[132]

Although every disability and impairment will manifest differently, some of the behavioral problems that may be displayed include physical and verbal aggressiveness, withdrawal and refusal to cooperate, throwing things, screaming, refusing food, self-injuriousness, property destruction, non-compliance with rules and poor hygiene. Difficulties with impulse control, mood regulation, social and coping skills and cognitive processing can leave the individuals with impairments ill-equipped to cope with the frustrations resulting from constantly breaking, misunderstanding or forgetting the rules, being mistreated by others and not having opportunities for much needed social interaction.

Prison systems are not well equipped to provide a spectrum of adequate behavioral health care services to the volume of people that are imprisoned in this age of mass incarceration. Therapy or evaluation, for example, services are often conducted through a meal slot, as more of a "check in" with no privacy or confidentiality. Interventions such as psycho-education, group therapy and consistent individual sessions are almost non-existent.

Staff are not well trained to manage disordered types of behavior and are often not able to adequately assess the difference between what they perceive to be manipulation and signs of decompensation. Individuals who are perceived as being manipulative are often dismissed or punished, and they do not get the treatment that they need. People will manipulate to get fundamental needs met with whatever tools they have. Therefore, to disallow treatment because someone is manipulative is not reasonable. Under the circumstances, manipulation is a survival skill. Behavior management and conflict de-escalation skills are not competencies that most staff develop during routine training, but such skills are crucial when dealing with this population. This lack of skill, coupled with existing stereotypes and the prison environment can lead to escalation of violent conflict, mismanagement of behaviors and use of force that may have been prevented if adequate de-escalation skills, monitoring and treatment were provided. Refusing to leave the cell, for example, is a violation of rules that can result in drastic consequences. The behavior can have various etiologies and motivations. Some incarcerated individuals may feel like their cell is their only safe place and have an intense fear of leaving it. In turn, they will do anything they can to not be removed.[133] Increased paranoia and other psychotic symptoms can cause individuals to perceive themselves in a grave level of danger and are willing to protect themselves at all costs. This may, in turn lead to refusal to cooperate and violent behavior. Failure to comply with a request to leave a cell will result in an extraction. This involves multiple correctional staff entering the cell with chemical agents to manually extract the individual through physical violence and chemical spray. Nanon recalls a description of a cell extraction that occurred when he refused to go to a "blackout cell," an especially severe form of solitary confinement that existed when Nanon was on death row.

> As I was speaking, the warden sprayed me with pepper spray, directly into my eyes and mouth. I could not breathe or see, so I panicked until I could regain control of my respiration. I withstood the assault as he continued to spray the pepper gas, but then explosive tear gas packets began exploding in my cell, and I lost consciousness. This went on, over and over, for more than an hour. I thought I was going to die as I continued to drift in and out of consciousness. I forgot where I was, but after a while I realized what was happening. I tried to stand but couldn't, and in my efforts to do so, I was sprayed again.

> When the cell opened, I made an attempt to exit the gas-filled cell, but an extraction team entered. An extraction team normally consists of five or more guards, each dressed in a vest, shield, helmet and boots and carrying a baton. As the extraction team entered, I was hit with vicious blows to my head and abdomen. I fought back as best I could and gave them hell all the way through. I was eventually dragged to the ground and shackled. The guards kept yelling, "Inmate, quit resisting!" But I wasn't resisting anymore, because I was being beaten into unconsciousness again.

> I awoke with pain searing through the left side of my head from being repeatedly kicked with their heavy boots, while I was still restrained. My head was slammed against the concrete floor, and batons steadily pounded my ribs and back. When I was dragged down the tier by the extraction team, a close friend of mine, Emerson Rudd, known as the Young Lion, dashed the warden with scalding hot water, causing him to scream. I was later told that the warden was still wearing that oily smirk on his face as

I was being dragged down the hall, until Rudd wiped it off his face. I was deeply touched by this act of courage to help a fellow prisoner and by his protest of such inhumane conditions. However, I feared for Rudd's safety as well.

I was dragged to the end of the tier and thrown head first down two flights of stairs (that was standard practice)—a puddle of my blood quickly formed around me. I had cuts everywhere, and it felt as if my head was split open. I was then put onto a stretcher and carted down the hall toward solitary. I felt someone squirting liquid into my eyes so I could see, but soon after blood rushed over my face again, obscuring my vision. Of course, I didn't know all of this at the time, as I drifted in and out of consciousness, I was told later by a sympathetic guard who witnessed the whole act of violence but was not brave enough to intervene and thereby lose his job.

I was rolled into solitary on a stretcher, then pulled to my feet and pushed into the shower to wash off the gas. Scalding hot water was turned on, hitting me directly in the face. I jumped back so quickly that I could feel the shackles tear into my flesh, cutting my ankles. I banged on the bars loudly to indicate to one of the guards that the water was too hot (as if they didn't already know), and they turned it to completely cold water. After the water ran on me for a few minutes, I was taken to the last cell in solitary, and the shackles were removed. Then I had to move toward the slot in the door so they could take off the handcuffs. They told me to remove my wet clothes, but I refused, so they took photos of my face. After they left my cell door, I took off the wet clothing.

It was very, very cold. I couldn't see anything at all because there was still pepper gas and tear gas in my eyes. So I was temporarily without sight, freezing, sitting naked on the steel bunk. As I surveyed the parts of my body that I could see, I realized that I had deep cuts around my ankles from the shackles and my left wrist had a cut so deep that it needed stitches. Every time I blinked, blood dripped from my left eye. At first I thought I might have had a cut under it, but I later learned that a few blood vessels were broken in my eye because of the tear gas, and it permanently destroyed much of my vision. I also saw bruises covering my rib cage, and I knew from the terrible pain as I breathed, that some ribs were broken. At that time, I could not say I had ever been battered so badly, but I was alive, and that is what mattered.[134]

Not everyone who resists a cell extraction is mentally ill and not all reasons are due to mental illness. The cell extraction that was described above did not involve a person with a mental illness, and does not represent the manner by which all cell extractions occur. One can only imagine how a person with any type of intellectual, mental or developmental impairment might experience the situation and possibly resist a cell extraction.

It is possible that an individual may not understand what is happening and why. Many behaviors associated with rule infractions can be symptoms of mental illness. People with mental health issues often have a difficult time regulating their behaviors and adapting effectively to their environments. Some, for example, may show a decline in self-care and their personal hygiene suffers. This can be a symptom of many illnesses, such as depression or psychosis. Self-injurious behaviors, such as cutting and other forms of self-mutilation, can also be symptoms of severe mental disorders. All of these are rule violations and are subject to disciplinary action. One study found that individuals in prison who engaged in three or more different types of self-injurious behaviors while incarcerated were twice as likely to be housed in segregation. [135]

A number of studies have found that mentally ill individuals are more likely to violate prison rules than those without mental illnesses.[136] People with severe post-traumatic stress disorder, whose symptoms have been worsened by the isolation, may perceive the environment outside of their cell as a type of unsafe war zone. They would avoid coming out of their cell at all cost for fear of their life. The parts of their brain that deal with fear and self-preservation are telling them to fight or flee. Many systems of the body, such as hormones, become engaged to accomplish this goal. A person who is severely psychotic and is experiencing paranoia, may feel that he is being taken out of his cell to be part of an experiment and his actions will reflect this intense fear that is his reality. Clearly, this type of behavior creates a serious safety risk not only to the individual, but also to the prison personnel who may be violently attacked, spit on and/or have feces and other bodily fluids thrown at them. The more resistance given by the incarcerated person, the more force that staff will use to remove him out of his cell and protect themselves and those around them. All of these actions may stem from a request for the incarcerated person to take a shower. In his testimony, former director of the Wisconsin Department of Corrections Michael Sullivan addressed the dangers of this vicious cycle, "When [the mentally ill are] in segregation, if they're not appropriately engaged, they continue exhibiting the behaviors that got them there in the first place. If anything, they heighten that activity, which then puts them back before a disciplinary committee, and they get more [segregation] time. So instead of getting out, they wind up staying longer and longer and longer, and they deteriorate."[137]

Successfully steering individuals to rehabilitation becomes almost impossible when an individual's mental condition and cognitive abilities deteriorate due to isolation and consequently, the amount of disciplinary infractions increase as does the amount of time spent in confinement. A result of rule infractions is most often extended time and/or the loss or restriction of the few privileges they already have such as recreation time and social connectivity or phone privileges for those in administrative segregation. The longer the time spent in isolation without necessary social supports, treatment and programming, the more mental deterioration and poor coping can occur, resulting in a higher number of behavioral issues. It is a cycle that is difficult to break if adequate treatment and non-isolative housing conditions are not provided.

Steve Martin, former General Counsel of TDCJ, relates his experiences on this dangerous dynamic, "It [confinement] has a large effect on the mentally impaired. [There is] a vicious cycle with the mentally ill. They decompensate, which makes them more likely to make an additional infraction. They were more prone to be handled physically by staff than the non-mentally ill." This cycle often ends with solitary confinement.

An incarcerated man, who chose to remain anonymous, describes his own deterioration as well as that of those around him.

> I recognized a slippage in myself after a few years. My personal hygiene began to suffer, and I quit caring about my environment. I spent the majority of my time inside my head, fantasizing about living a real life. I ate out of boredom and depression, ballooning from my "entry" weight of 155 pounds to 210 pounds in about five years. I stopped interacting completely. Everyone I wanted to associate with I created in my head, including myself.

> I knew a guy I called "Braveheart" who lived on the wing full of crazies with me. He was full blown mad. He'd stopped bathing, shaving, trimming his nails and all other forms of hygiene. He walked around in dirty boxer shorts everywhere when he left his cell, which was not often. I called him Braveheart because he would get in his door and scream out at the top of his lungs angry rants against African-Americans, police and doctors and wouldn't let any African-American person, officer or member of the medical staff walk by without spitting, cussing and screaming racial epithets at them. He would get gassed and still not bathe to wash the gas off. When I met him in 1999, he wasn't like that at all. He was quiet and in solitary confinement just like me.

His story is not unusual and can be illustrative of the many symptoms that can emerge with the deterioration for the mind, spirit and body. Braveheart's behavior reflects an increased level of desperation. It is the type of behavior that will land more disciplinary action and increase the likelihood of prolonged time spent in confinement. The Bureau of Justice Statistics found that on average, incarcerated people with mental illnesses spend five months longer in prisons than those without mental illnesses. This extra time may be spent in isolation, potentially making illnesses worse.[138]

The prison system and contracted medical providers face real economic and staffing challenges to adequately meet the needs of these vulnerable individuals. They are also faced with the reality of housing some extremely violent people that are a real threat to the lives of staff and other incarcerated individuals. These are real challenges without easy solutions. There are highly complex systemic issues that include underlying belief systems that support these conditions. Solutions, therefore, are not simple ones. Antidotes must be humane and meet the psychological and medical needs of the individuals, which is their right. In the absence of these, it is highly likely that conditions will worsen and threats to safety will increase. Both of these issues will require even more resources. This cycle is perpetuating both a financial and resource drain to the system, as well as neglecting the human rights of the individuals in what many would believe to amount to nothing short of torture. Safety should be paramount for all.

How can prison administration protect those individuals in prison who are lesbian/gay/bisexual/transgender, those who have been raped, those who may be raped and those who are at risk for violence, although they have not violated any rules? Further victimizing them by subjecting them to inhumane conditions should not be an option much less the solution. How can prison administration care for people with psychiatric disorders who are screaming, throwing toilet paper, cutting themselves and hallucinating? Housing them in six by 10 cells with little human contact that knowingly makes conditions worse followed by neglect of their behavioral health care needs should not be an option. How can prison administration care for those who have intellectual or developmentally disabled individuals since they are more likely to be victimized in general population? Subjecting them to 23 hours per day of confinement and punishing them for violating rules that they have little to no control over should not be an option. What about the juveniles? Abusing them should not be an option.

Regarding the lack of logic and institutional wisdom this system poses, Craig Haney commented in an interview that the system, "removes everything that allows people to be human, and then in some type of correctional leap of faith expects people to get better." Yet all evidence shows that these cruel and inhumane conditions only perpetuate existing behavior problems and create behavior problems that did not exist prior to isolation.

Physical Impairments

Texas Department of Criminal Justice also houses individuals with physical impairments in solitary confinement. According to an open records request asking for the number of individuals housed in administrative segregation and death row who have physical impairments TDCJ provided the following information: "An offender who is physically handicapped is recognized by TDCJ as being an offender with a special need and is referred to the Assistive Disability Services (ADS) for further evaluation and treatment. For physical disabilities, we are only able to provide current data, as past data are not available. As of Oct. 1, 2013, the following ADS data are responsive.[139] (This data does not reflect those categorized by TDCJ as being in "solitary confinement.")

INDIVIDUALS WITH DISABILITIES HOUSED IN CONFINEMENT (COUNT)

ADMINISTRATIVE SEGREGATION	
Hearing Impaired	5
Mobility Impaired	18
Vision Impaired	16
DEATH ROW	
Mobility Impaired	1

Youth in Confinement

"Our children are our greatest treasure. They are our future. Those who abuse them tear at the fabric of our society and weaken our nation." This quote from Nelson Mandela is especially poignant when considering that many youth in Texas and throughout the United States are caged in confinement. When people think of youth in solitary confinement, they often think of children who display violent behavior and are a danger to others—children who are contained when all attempts for less restrictive measures have failed. In some instances, this is the case. However, many adolescents who are placed in confinement are not incarcerated for violent offenses and are not a threat to others. To those that do present a safety risk, there are other proven and effective methods to assess, modify and treat behavioral issues, rather than use strategies that are known to exacerbate their issues.

Children and adolescents can be placed in solitary confinement for a multitude of reasons. Youth may be placed in confinement for the same reason as adults, as a disciplinary measure and as a "protective" measure. Some are in county jails awaiting trials and may be innocent, housed in the same facility as adults, but are "isolated" for "their own safety." The ACLU of Texas describes their concerns associated with this issue: "Under Texas law, children as young as 14 can be tried as an adult and held in solitary confinement, even before they have their day in court.

Many are found innocent, yet have spent a year or more of their lives in solitary confinement. This is inhumane treatment that also undermines the rehabilitative purpose of incarceration."[140]

According to Jennifer Carreon, policy analyst with the Texas Criminal Justice Coalition, juveniles in Texas are placed in solitary confinement in various correctional facilities, many of which do not release data on the numbers of youth placed in confinement and the average length of time served. These facilities include:

- Adult county jails, where minors cannot be placed with adults. Therefore, they are placed in isolation "for their protection."
- State run juvenile facilities.
- County run juvenile facilities.
- State prison facilities, where juveniles have been certified as adults.[141]

TDCJ released data that conveys the use of juvenile segregation in their facilities. An open records request revealed, "During Fiscal Year 2013, 23 offenders (age 18 and under) entered administrative segregation for an average of six months."[142] This data does not include county jail facilities. When questioned about the minimum age requirements for a juvenile to be placed in administrative segregation, the TDCJ public information officer replied: "I'm not aware of any minimum age for a person to be placed in administrative segregation."[143]

Previous chapters have highlighted the risks associated with the use of solitary confinement with adults. Children and juveniles, who are at critical stages in development, are even more vulnerable. Adolescence is a period in which prominent changes in the brain, hormones and body occur. Neuroscientists and developmental psychologists have found that fundamental reorganization of the brain occurs during this time period.

The adolescent brain is highly plastic, meaning that as a result of experience and environmental influence, it can change. This neuroplasticity allows for intellectual and emotional development to occur, but it also makes the brain more susceptible to damage.[144] Research indicates that placing children in solitary confinement can harm them psychologically, physically, socially and developmentally. In addition, these practices increase their risk of suicide significantly.[145]

Despite the countless number of research studies on the developmental needs of children and adolescents, as well as the potential effects of solitary confinement and associated trauma, these practices continue and do not lend themselves to rehabilitation. Not only does confinement housing violate their critical needs, but provides an environment that causes known harm.

In an effort to protect the most vulnerable of citizens, states have laws in place to ensure that children are protected from harm. In addition, consequences are implemented for those who violate these laws that were specifically designed to prevent and protect against abuse and neglect of minors. Chapter 261, Title 5 of the Texas Family Code, for example, defines child abuse as including, "(A) mental or emotional injury to a child that results in an observable and material impairment in the child's growth, development, or psychological functioning; (B) causing or permitting the child to be in a situation in which the child sustains a mental or emotional injury that results in an observable and material impairment in the child's growth, development, or psychological functioning."[146]

Prison and jail facilities are not equipped to assess short- and long-term damage to brain development that may be occurring while a child is in isolation. This damage may not be evident or "observable" until later. In settings outside of correctional facilities, placing children in solitary confinement for prolonged periods of time would constitute abuse and/or neglect, and it could result in criminal prosecution of those who placed the child in that situation. The very laws that are designed to protect children seemingly do not apply in correctional settings, despite the research that demonstrates the potential for injury. National and international agencies and reputable professional organizations stress the importance of protecting the health, well-being, and rights of children, but their recommendations are ignored. The United Nations, for example, established rules and minimum standards for juveniles in correctional facilities. This resolution gained approval from the General Assembly in 1990 and was supported by the United States. Section 67 of the Rules, reads, "All disciplinary measures constituting cruel, inhuman or degrading treatment shall be strictly prohibited, including corporal punishment, placement in a dark cell, closed or solitary confinement or any other punishment that may compromise the physical or mental health of the juvenile concerned."[147]

The American Academy of Child and Adolescent Psychiatry wrote a policy statement demonstrating its strong opposition to the practice of solitary confinement with juveniles, "The American Academy of Child and Adolescent Psychiatry agrees with the position of the United Nations and strongly opposes the practice of solitary confinement for juveniles in correctional settings. The rule also states that any young person that is in confinement for greater than 24 hours must receive an evaluation by a mental health professional."[148]

Correctional settings have the responsibly of integrating the recommendations that are based on evidence and consensus data from the experts and are making a conscious choice to disregard them, thereby placing children at risk for harm. By the time children and juveniles have reached the criminal justice system, many of them have already experienced extreme stress and have been failed by those individuals and systems who were supposed to protect them and safeguard their rights. They are in desperate need of rehabilitative practices to steer them in a positive trajectory rather than those that will keep them in the criminal justice system. Children are among the most vulnerable citizens in society. They are highly reliant on adults to meet their needs. Without proper care, protection, social support, nurturance, resources, attachments and dedication by adults to meet their developmental needs, children are at great risk of psychological, physiological and behavioral consequence. The responsibility for the proper care, protection and well-being of minors, therefore, lies in the hands of parents, community members, caregivers, institutions and policymakers.

PART III
INVISIBLE VICTIMS

CHAPTER EIGHT

VICTIM SURVIVORS

*Concerning the claim of justice for the victim's family,
I say there is no amount of retaliatory deaths that
would compensate to me the inestimable value of my
daughter's life, nor would they restore her to my arms.
To say that the death of any other person would be just
retribution is to insult the immeasurable worth of our
loved ones who are victims. We cannot put a price on
their lives. That kind of justice would only dehumanize
and degrade us because it legitimates an animal instinct
for gut-level blood thirsty revenge. ... In my case, my
own daughter was such a gift of joy and sweetness and
beauty that to kill someone in her name would have
been to violate and profane the goodness of her life; the
idea is offensive and repulsive to me.*

—*Marietta Jaeger*

*Marietta Jaeger's 7-year-old daughter Susie
was kidnapped and murdered in 1973.*

EVERY INDIVIDUAL, FAMILY AND community responds differently to losing a loved one to a violent crime. Grief is a highly individualized, dynamic and fluid process. Victim survivors, who can include any surviving victim or impacted persons such as loved ones, often feel powerless throughout the process and need safety, information, empowerment and, many times, an opportunity to tell their story. Not only are reactions unique, but they can change over time. The emotion and types of questions that are often present in the immediate aftermath of a devastating incident may take on different forms months and years later. Oftentimes, the needs of the impacted individuals may change, and the need for closure may take various forms. Every individual and family who is impacted by trauma can have varying needs, but they all have the same thing in common: their lives are forever altered, and the loss is always present.

When it comes to the healing process, many believe that closure can be met through the execution of the accused. Executions are often thought to be "for the victims." Although some survivors report feeling a sense of closure and a sense of finality after an execution, some do not. One of the challenges in assessing the issue of closure is a lack of empirical data that can shed light on the subject. Individual stories, media reports and case studies have been a utilized resource to make inferences about the closure process. Helene Burnes, the daughter of Maxine, a murder victim, expressed her feelings about closure. "There is no closure after a loved one is murdered. The criminal who is executed leaves behind relatives/friends of their own. These families not only have to live with the anguish of knowing their loved one was a murderer, but they then live a lifetime of grief after the execution. Tragedy begets tragedy, like a snowball rolling downhill."[149]

Although there is much discussion about closure, the subjective use of the word "closure" does not seem to be consistently well defined in the psychological literature and has been used as a legal term. In addition, "closure" may hold varied meanings to different people. To rely on the legal system to provide much needed healing from emotional pain, grief and trauma neglects some serious needs that the victim survivors may have. This reliance and expectation of healing or finality associated with it may actually disrupt the healing process.

Capital murder trials allow for victims to tell their story at sentencing hearings through victim impact statements. Having the opportunity to tell the story can be empowering and can allow victims to be heard. On the other hand, unless the fullest punishment is handed down, even if the family does not want it, it can leave a victim feeling like their story wasn't heard, or wasn't enough to warrant the maximum penalty. If experienced in that manner, it can also interfere with the healing process.

Capital punishment sentences can address a need for vindication, as some have reported, but they can also bring false hope that can often lead to disappointing outcomes and prolonged complicated grief that can last for years.

Some victims, and victim survivors, report feelings of relief associated with death penalty verdicts and executions and report feeling a finality following a long and arduous process. Some research studies indicate that executions help some co-victims of murder victims "move on" from the experience.[150] For some, a death penalty verdict is not about revenge or closure, but about justice. For others, an execution or a death sentence does not provide needed closure and fails to address the real needs of victims. With some victim survivors, an execution can actually lead to disappointment caused by the unmet expectation of emotional relief that would follow.

A death sentence is often followed by post-conviction appeals, a painfully arduous process that can extend through the course of many years. At times, victim survivors feel that their needs are not met by the system throughout this process. Much of the initial support received following the traumatic events, in fact, may have decreased over the years and desperately needed information about the process wanes. Information and education helps reduce the anxiety associated with an unpredictable process that they have no control over.

Lengthy trials can create additional feelings of powerlessness, a lack of control over outcome, chronic recollections of the traumatic events through testimony and a prolonged connection with the perpetrator. During trials, survivors often have to be in the same room as the person who is accused of having killed their loved one, which can prove to be traumatic. Miriam Thimm Kelle, whose brother Jim was brutally tortured to death, shared her own experience of the process:

> When my brother was murdered, I thought I was supposed to support the death penalty. Little did me and my family know then that when Michael Ryan was sentenced to death, we were sentenced too. Our sentence has been going on for 20 years, and there has been no execution. For 20 years, it has been all about Michael Ryan. He is all my family and I ever hear about. Jim is never mentioned. Having seen what the death penalty has done to my family, I have since changed my mind, and now think it should be abolished.[151]

The execution itself has the potential of causing emotional harm for the witnesses in the room, as well. Physically watching a person take their last breaths can be highly impactful. In addition, it may prove to be difficult for some to hear the last words of the individual being executed, as they are unpredictable. These words can have various effects on those hearing them. They can be harmful, healing, or they can be inconsequential. Some of the individuals being executed will ask for forgiveness or provide an apology such as in Bobby Lee Hine's last statement:

> To the victim's family, I am sure I know that I took somebody special from y'all. I know it wasn't right; it was wrong. I wish I could give it back, but I know I can't. If giving my life in return makes it right, so be it. I ask that y'all forgive me. I know God forgave me. I know He has forgiven me for what I did. I don't believe that taking my life will solve anything. I believe that if I was locked up for the rest of my life that would be more of a punishment. To do this is setting me free. God bless y'all. I wish there was something I could do.
> Bernard, thank you. Bill, thanks for being there for me and showing me to the Lord. I give glory to God, I believe I am going home. I love my family. I love everybody. I have love in my heart for y'all and for my family, we're

all victims behind what I did. I wish there was some other way to show I'm sorry. I have a prayer that me and my wife have come up with that I'd like to say. God, hear our prayer. We want to give thanks for this day. I can't do that prayer ... that prayer is not right for y'alls family or my family. Please forgive me. I love y'all. OK Warden, I am ready. I'm going home. I love y'all. I'm feeling it. [152]

Some individuals declare their innocence. For example, Preston Hughes stated:

Yes, Warden. Mom, Celeste: Please know I'm innocent, and I love you both. Please continue to fight for my innocence even though I'm gone. John, Cort, Allen, Barbara, Louis and Anna: Thank you for helping me and trying to save my life. I love you. Give everybody my love. Jason, thank you for your friendship. Thank Laura, too. I love all of you. Bye. OK, Warden."[153]

Keith Thurmond, in his last statement, proclaimed his innocence as well:

All I want to say is I'm innocent. I didn't kill my wife. Jack Leary shot my wife then her dope dealer Guy Fernandez. Don't hold it against me, Bill. I swear to God I didn't kill her. Go ahead and finish it off. You can taste it. [154]

Some victim survivors may be waiting for a final admission of guilt and get the opposite, creating disappointment and the lack of emotional closure that they were looking for. Many of the men being executed direct part of their statements to the families of the survivors. A portion of Donnie Lee Roberts, Jr.'s last statement reads:

To all of y'all over here: Mr. Bivins, Allen, Joey, all of y'all back there, I am truly sorry. I never meant to cause y'all so much pain. Not one day has passed that I wish I could take it back. After today, I hope you can go on. I hope this brings you closure. God knows I didn't want to do what I did. I loved your daughter. I hope to God, He lets me see her in heaven, so I can apologize to her. I'm sorry. I'm glad y'all came. Joey, I am really sorry, Joe.[155]

Other last words may be a display of incoherence, anger, fear or resentment. Thomas Barefoot was convicted of capital murder of 31-year-old police officer Carl Levin. He was evading arrest from charges of the rape of a 3-year-old child from another state. In his last words, he directed a portion of his comment toward the wife of the victim.

I hope that one day we can look back on the evil that we're doing right now like the witches we burned at the stake. I want everybody to know that I hold nothing against them. I forgive them all. I hope everybody I've done anything to will forgive me. I've been praying all day for Carl Levin's wife to drive the bitterness from her heart because that bitterness that's in her heart will send her to hell just as surely as any other sin. I'm sorry for everything I've ever done to anybody. I hope they'll forgive me. Sharon, tell all my friends goodbye. You know who they are: Charles Bass, David Powell. ... [156]

One need not be present to know the last statements. Texas is one of two states that makes these statements available on their website. Texas is the only state that catalogs and lists each statement.[157] Witnesses, however, may have a different reaction watching the words leave the mouth of the person who changed their lives forever. (See the Part VII of this book for a full list of last statements.)

No matter how much a person is prepared for the execution process, the impact of watching is unpredictable. Whether or not an execution goes forward can also be unpredictable. Condemned men have been granted stays of execution that have occurred even minutes before the scheduled execution time, which can be exasperating for victim survivors who will have to wait for a process that will determine if or when the execution will move forward. The anxiety that this causes can be devastating to loved ones as they are victimized by the system.

The TDCJ website contains a section that is used to describe the execution process to the victims' families and victim advocates. It states, "For some witnesses, this process is very traumatic because it allows old wounds to be reopened."[158] The wounds, that may have never healed, continue to be poked, opened and closed. This process can hinder the healing process that victims need to be able to move forward. It often fosters a lack of empowerment and high levels of uncertainty, which are contrary to the needs of the survivors and their loved ones. Some witnesses may need ongoing support services for the very reasons that TDCJ described.

There is a belief that surviving victims would also want their perpetrators to receive the death penalty. This is not always the case. Several victim survivors have requested that their alleged perpetrators not to be executed, but rather, have life sentences. In their eyes, any other death that occurs as a result of the tragedy can make matters worse. Some victims will go through intensive measures to ensure that this does not happen. One such example is the case of Rais Bhuiyan.

Two weeks after the terrorist attacks of Sept. 11, 2001 on the World Trade Center and the Pentagon, Mark Stroman, a white supremacist, went on a hate crime spree targeting innocent people of Middle Eastern decent, seeking vengeance. During his rampage, he killed two men and seriously injured one survivor. Rais Bhuiyan was that survivor. In the horrific attack, he was shot in the face at close range with a shotgun and left to die while working at a gas station in Dallas, Texas. Mark Stroman, the man who shot him, was sentenced to be executed by lethal injection. Rais requested that Mark's death penalty be commuted to life without parole. His hope was that he would begin a new narrative in his life. Strong in his Muslim faith, Rais believes in forgiveness and that all human lives are precious and that no one has the right to take another person's life. He also recognizes the multiple victims in this tragedy. After repeated actions and pleas made by Rais and his attorneys to save Mark's life, they were unable to halt the execution. The state of Texas executed Mark Stroman July 20, 2011. This experience taught him that hate does not bring a peaceful solution to any situation. Rather, "It creates obstacles to healthy human growth, which in turn diminishes society as a whole. Mark Stroman's hate only brought more pain and suffering to an already mourning nation," he proclaimed. Rais Bhuiyan has formed an organization called World Without Hate. The mission is to provide much needed education about forgiveness, peace and compassion in order to end the cycle of hate and violence.[159] Rais's story generated worldwide attention and dialogue about the power of forgiveness.

In another example, Ronald Carlson's sister was brutally murdered by Karla Faye Tucker while she was engaged in a drug binge. Ronald came to the determination that his sister's murderer, a former prostitute and drug user, had transformed into an entirely different person while in prison on Texas' death row. Ronald not only forgave her, but strongly opposed her execution. Many others noted Karla's transformation since her conversion to Christianity and believed that she could make a positive difference in the lives of other people who were also incarcerated. They made attempts to have her sentence commuted to life imprisonment. Her case also inspired international attention. Despite ongoing attempts to spare her life, Karla Faye Tucker was executed in 1998.[160]

There are several organizations comprised of loved ones of murder victims who oppose the death penalty. Some encourage forgiveness and reconciliation. A few of these organizations include Murder Victims Families for Reconciliation, Murder Victims Families for Human Rights and Journey of Hope.

The criminal justice system should be more committed toward meeting the needs of the victims. It is not equipped to make assumptions and decisions on what victims need; only the victims are. Being "tough on crime," may in fact be making matters worse for some. Victims deserve to have a system that makes it less likely for their accused perpetrators to re-offend. Individuals who live through the damage of solitary confinement and the inhumane treatment in which they are subjected in Texas prisons and who are later released directly into communities often pose a continued danger to society.

Scott Bass, director for the Murder Victim's Families for Reconciliation, claimed in an interview, "Many victims have a vested interest in how the offenders are treated so that they are better people when they come out. It raises some important questions. What is best for our communities and our victims of crime? Don't victims deserve to have a system that releases an ex-offender who is less likely to re-victimize? The reality is that most of these incarcerated individuals who have served time in solitary confinement are coming home. Is how we are treating people in prison going to be a better scenario for the victims?"

Victim survivors face unimaginable trauma and grief that can impact them for the rest of their lives. The needs of the survivors vary, and there is no recipe for healing that applies to all. What is considered healing for some may be exacerbating the harmful impact for others. It is important to recognize that the survivors themselves, rather than the legal system must have voices in their own healing and deserve to have systems in place that utilize interventions and preventative efforts built upon proven methods of keeping communities safe, so that these tragedies can be prevented, as much as possible from happening in the future.

CHAPTER NINE
STAY STRONG

My little brother would ask my mom, "Where is Nanon?"
That was hard for him. People would judge him like
they would judge me. If people knew his brother was
on death row, people would look at him, like what the
hell did he do, and what is he capable of? That went
for my sisters and my mom as well. They always had to
explain why I was on death row. It was a cloud that was
over my family's life. And every day, it was a struggle to
try to remove that cloud to show that I was more than
what they said I was ... to overcome the odds, to make a
difference in other people's lives.

—Nanon M. Williams

THE CONDEMNED PERSON'S FAMILY becomes incarcerated with them, suffering the pain and the shame associated with a death sentence. Nanon shares a story that demonstrates the family sentence.

George Cordova was in his forties. He was rail thin, about 5 feet 7 inches tall and had sleepy eyes. He shaved his head bald repeatedly during the day to chase away the gray hairs, but even that could not hide how the many years on death row had aged him. After almost two decades on Texas' death row, his tattoos told more about him than his own words would reveal. Cordova was known throughout the prison system by his chosen moniker "Spider" that linked him to the notorious Mexican Mafia—a prison gang that dominated the black market in Texas for decades. Spider was the leader, the spokesman, the shot killer—a rotating figurehead that had the last call on any decisions.

Confined to a cell 23 hours a day, Spider often paced the concrete floor barefoot until blisters appeared on his feet. This was not uncommon amongst the men confined to a cell all day. Some paced and read books or magazines. Some walked a couple of steps, turned around and did a few pushups. And others, well, they walked for miles in a closet-sized space as though it was a stretch of endless highway. Holes were worn into their shoes. Some of the incarcerated men's feet had so much dead skin it looked like rusted metal. And some, like Spider, only stopped when the blisters burst and blood smeared the floor. For many, the pain—the blood, however it leaked out—let them know that they were still alive. Trapped in such small cells for months, years and even decades caused some men to look for any sign to help them realize they were still alive. Pain was one of those signs—pain and love. The pain had to be physical to snap a person out of the dazed mental state that made days and weeks merge together. And love, it came in the form of letters or visits from family members, girlfriends, wives, uncles and aunts, brothers and sisters, parents or even kids. That love was a lifeline thrown to a person drowning in the sea.

Though Spider was once prideful, soft-spoken and very thoughtful, he, at times, became a chatterbox, saying anything that came to his mind without thought and was even aggressive in his demeanor. Other times, he would say absolutely nothing at all and withdraw, ignoring any response directed to him.

No matter what he said, he would forever be seen as a killer. He was the head of the most feared gang in Texas, and his name invoked more fear than his size. Who he once was remains a mystery to most, but who he became was a broken man, tired and ready to meet the executioner to escape the living hell of Texas death row. We often walked on the yard in separate single-man cages. Spider expressed to me that he had begun to see his own death as a release from the constant state of suffering.

He had once been a muscular man weighing 160 pounds, but his thin frame became a mere 140 pounds. He no longer did pushups; he just paced his cell and the small cage we walked in that was considered a "recreation yard." While outside one morning, we talked about the suicide of James Gunter weeks before, and I'll never forget his words: "That vato had cojonas! He had enough courage to end this fuckin' ride, eh?"

We weren't friends by any means, but we always felt that we understood one another. We were judged to be the monsters of the world, but beneath the judgment and the descriptions of who we were, whether it was just or unjust, we were still people. We still heard the screams at night, people talking to themselves, the crack in someone's voice who was on edge, or just witnessed the madness creeping on others without being able to help. And depression was always king. We were all its subjects, whether we admitted it or not.

A week prior to his execution, Spider was granted daily visits with his family. That was rare, but somehow I think Spider was the exception. Perhaps the administration did not want him to cause problems before he was executed. Day in and day out he went to visit. One day, I heard him over the run describing his visits to his homeboys. The following day would be his last visit, and it was going to be his last day on Earth. It would also be the first time Spider would meet his daughter. I don't know how old she was when he was locked up, or if he really had any contact with her, but I could hear him talk about the last pending visit.

The following morning, off Spider went to visit. Shortly after, I was called to visit with my grandparents. I sat side by side with Spider as he visited with his mother and daughter. There was only thin mesh wire that separated us from each other. My grandmother kept trying to console Spider's mother who was crying and speaking in Spanish. My grandmother couldn't understand anything Spider's mother said, but she kept leaning over to hold her as she spoke louder and louder and then retreated to a restroom to wipe her face as Spider spoke with his daughter.

Finally I explained to my grandparents that the guy next to me was going to be executed today and this was his last visit. My grandfather's mind seemed to reject what I was saying, so I had to make it clear. "He'll be executed today, Papa," I said. When they finally accepted what I was saying, my grandmother said they needed to trust in God and everything would be OK. Spider didn't much believe in God, but at this point I think my grandmother needed to hold on to her own faith. His pending execution made my own situation even more real to her. I told her that I still recited Psalms 23 every day, said my rosary, and believed all would be well. At that moment, Spider's mother returned and went into a loud wail that shook every visitor. Other families and friends came to her aid, and I watched tears pour down Spider's face. Even I wrestled with my own emotions.

Spider's mother returned to talk with her son in Spanish, and my grandparents wished me well. They were visibly shaken as they left. I knew my grandmother would pray for the family, but what shook me the most was when Spider asked me to talk to his daughter. "Make her lift her head up, eh," he said, as though it was a command. I didn't speak Spanish, but she slid over into the next chair and asked me in clear English, "Why won't they let me at least hug my dad before they kill him?"

"I don't know," I said. "No one is allowed contact visits."

"Oh, so it's not just my dad they denied contact visits to?" she asked.

"No," I replied. "None of us are allowed to have any human contact whatsoever." And with that reply, somehow, she seemed to find comfort in that. I guess it made her feel a little better knowing that it was not just her, but rather no one on death row could have contact with their loved ones. Then the tears came down her face, and she whispered to her grandmother who was still crying while talking to her father, "We'll take him home. That's all he wants."

"You can hug him then," I said. Yet, as soon as the words left my mouth, I regretted it.

"Maybe he'll get a stay. Maybe we'll be here to see him tomorrow," she said.

"Maybe," I said. But I knew Spider wouldn't receive a stay. He was a dead man walking and everyone knew it, even Spider. At that moment the guards arrived, told me to turn around and put my hands through the slot to be handcuffed, and then the metal door opened.

"Your father loves you," I told her. I didn't know their relationship. I didn't know how Spider felt. Those words just seemed appropriate. "Be strong for your grandmother," I said, nodded at Spider for the last time and walked away. I walked away with a vision of his mother's hands on the window, talking through the small screen and crying. I could barely move my legs, but I was relieved to leave the visitation area. I wanted to escape. We all did.

Later that day, Spider was executed. Some would say he was caught up in his own web of destruction. I never knew the crime he committed. I wonder about his family. I wonder if he would have become a grandfather. I wonder if he was alive today, if his family would have been spared the suffering. I wonder if he has a grave instead of being placed in an unmarked grave at the prison cemetery in Huntsville.

Years later, I would come to know hundreds of men who would eventually be executed. I have seen mothers fall on the floor and kids sobbing as they say goodbye to their dads. I have seen wives become widows. I know there are many victims whose lives were taken by the many of the people on death row. I know their family's lives were tragically changed. I also know the death penalty creates many more victims who also suffer and grieve the loss of their loves ones along the way.

Not only was Spider trapped in his own web of destruction, his friends and family became entangled as well.

ALTHOUGH A DEATH SENTENCE is designed to punish perpetrators of crimes and remove them from society, there are multiple generations of innocent casualties left behind that often live with unimaginable pain.[161] The family of the accused have been largely ignored historically, and at times, shunned by their own communities. Individuals like Spider had parents, grandparents, aunts, uncles, children, cousins, brothers, sisters, friends and other extended family members who will suffer a lifetime of consequences inherent with the judicial process. This process begins following the alleged crime and carries on with multiple hearings, sentencing, incarceration, appeals and finally, the execution. The number of lives that are devastated by one death sentence can be far reaching, and for the most part, the lives of these survivors and the distress they face goes unrecognized.

The Crime

It is human nature to try to make sense of the tragedy. If people can understand why a tragic event, such as a murder occurred, there is hope that such a crime can be prevented from happening again, thus establishing some sense of control over future tragedies. Without having a person to blame or a reason for the tragedy, individuals and communities feel helpless with the idea that these horrific events can happen anywhere and anytime. There is tremendous value in analyzing the origins of such crimes so that early intervention and other preventative strategies can be implemented. As people try to make sense of senseless tragedies, parents and family members of the alleged perpetrators are often blamed and targeted directly or indirectly for the crime. Media frenzy ignites as a spotlight focuses on friends, neighbors and families involved, and make their shock, grief and anguish a public spectacle. Family histories are placed under intense scrutiny, and private lives become public for years to come—all searching for reasons why. Understanding the etiologies of criminal behavior can be very complex. Historically, researchers have debated between nature and nurture as pre-cursors to criminal behavior. Current research, however points to an interaction between biology, environment and genetics as influences of behavior. Focusing solely on the parents of the accused neglects other possible systemic factors such as poverty, widespread oppression, lack of resources, quality of education and many other factors that may be significant. Parenting can play a role in a child's behavior, in that it can precipitate, exacerbate or ameliorate certain conditions, but it is not alone a predictor of criminal behavior.

Although there is no one absolute predictor of violent behavior, researchers and clinicians have noted many parallels in the backgrounds of those who end up committing violent crimes. It is important to mention that the authors are not implying that these factors are excuses for the crimes committed. There are many individuals who may have had similar experiences and backgrounds that do not end up committing these crimes. Nor are their biographies being used to minimize the tragic losses that the victims endured. Telling the stories of the men in this book is not an attempt to justify or condone criminal behavior. The commonalities in their histories are so predictable that they cannot be ignored. Rather, they should be examined in order to find avenues by which interventions can be implemented in an effort to thwart the violence. One can look at any of these life stories and point to many intersections by where a community member, professional, program or educational setting could have intervened and, in certain circumstances, altered the trajectory of that person's life. It is vital to look backward in order to change things moving forward.

Many of the men who end up on death row have been reared in environments ridden with poverty, discrimination, violence, abuse and neglect, drugs and alcohol and minimal education. The vast majority of people incarcerated and on death row are people of color. Data obtained May 1, 2014 indicates that 71.1 percent of individuals on death row are persons of color.[162] Many of these individuals arrive to death row not knowing how to read or write and often have low intelligent quotients. Although it is easier to blame individuals and ignore the big picture, the big picture must be examined in order to understand the nature and cycles of violence in society.

Vicarious Offenders

It is not uncommon for all members of the family of the accused to be punished, as though they were the ones who committed the crime. These "vicarious offenders" are often shunned from their communities. As described in the book *Hidden Victims,* "They must live with the humiliation and stigma of being related to a person deemed so vile that he had to be exterminated."[163]

The day after 13 people were killed in a shooting spree in Fort Hood, Texas in 2009, Nadar Hasan's life changed in many ways. Mr. Hasan, a criminal defense attorney and the cousin of the accused gunman, experienced immediate repercussions to his business, as others associated him with his cousin. In addition, his personal life was also impacted. In a child custody dispute that he was involved in, for example, a petition stated that he should no longer be a guardian to his children because of his connection to the alleged gunman. In addition, he was told that he was unable to continue his volunteer position at a local school.[164] In other examples, families have had to change identities and move frequently to escape from harassment and physical threats that can last for years. In addition to having to cope with the crippling guilt and shame of having a family member commit a heinous crime, families face significant psychological, social and economic strain associated with frequent relocation and disruption of the family unit.

The children of these families can suffer greatly from having to readjust to new environments and fearing future losses, discovery and judgment. At times, parents make the excruciating decision to leave their children with other family members so that they do not have to experience the frequent relocation. As a result, the family is no longer an intact unit. Attachment bonds are weakened, which can have ongoing psychological and relational consequences. Parents can suffer from intense distress and can develop depression, post-traumatic stress disorder and other physical and emotional ailments that result from the isolation, powerlessness and grief associated with the overwhelming process. Families can experience what is known as "disenfranchised grief," in which they are not able to properly grieve publicly or acknowledge their loss.[165] When this level of shame is experienced, families may be less likely to involve outside support resources.

Not only do families feel like they are treated like perpetrators by members of the community, but many have reported feeling treated this way by the prison system itself. In one example, to add insult to an incredibly painful process for loved ones, TDCJ uses tactless language to describe the execution process of somebody's family member. On the Victim Services portion of the TDCJ website, there is a section titled "Victim Witnesses Viewing Executions: The Texas Experience." This section aims to prepare victim witnesses for observing the execution process.[166] Although this comes from Victim Services, do the victims actually consider this a "Texas experience"? Although the phrase can have different connotations to different people, it can be incredibly minimizing of the seriousness of whole process for everyone involved. The impact that this language can have on the families of the individuals being executed, as well as the victims' families can be devastating. It can be insulting for a child, parent, friend or other loved one of the person being executed to hear that their loved one's death was part of the "Texas experience" for witnesses, as if the occasion was a cultural event. In addition, it degrades Texas as a community for using such language to describe such a painful process. This use of terminology equates an execution process with strong sense of state pride and cultural identity, ensuring that everyone knows that in Texas, we are "tough on crime."

The Hearing

Napoleon Beazley was executed in 2002 for the murder of John Luttig. Napoleon admittedly committed this murder when he was 17 years old. Ireland Beazley, the father of Napoleon, and his wife Rena had three children, Maria, Napoleon and Jamaal. The Texas After Violence Project interviewed Napoleon, and he described his family's experience during the trial process.

> And so—and basically the little court-appointed attorney, the state court-appointed attorney, he come running down to the jailhouse talking to us— tried to convince us that he was the right way to go and stuff like that. Since we didn't have the money, we went with the court-appointed attorney, you know? But when we did see him—you got— he was still our kid. I didn't see it in him before, and I didn't see it in him that day. Shucks, he was still my kid. That's all I can tell you: he was just still my kid. But anyway, that's when—like I said, we just went day by day after that. We never had any good days. Just continued to go down, down, down. And the trial ... the trial was ... it wasn't ... I don't know how to say it ... well it's the only trial I ever been in ... and I guess I don't know if I was expecting it'd be like the trials on TV when Perry Mason at the end jumps up and fools everything. But it didn't ... it didn't come out like that, which is what we were hoping for. But it didn't come out like that. And things that we thought they shouldn't be doing, we saw them doing it. A lot of the statements that couldn't be proven being introduced as facts and all that kinda stuff. And just taking incidents to make it look like Napoleon was the worst thing that could live, you know? The prosecutor even described him as "an animal hiding in the jungle that was hunting somebody to kill." And he was allowed to say that kind of stuff. I mean ... and the judge sat there and listened to him. Let the jury hear all that kind of stuff. I don't know. I don't know what to tell you.[167]

Part of the powerlessness that families experience reflects an absence of needed resources available to them coupled with the underlying biases, marginalization and racism that plays a major role throughout every step of this arduous process. The families are often economically disadvantaged and are rarely educated in the legal process. The accused are also disproportionally black or people of color. Racial bias runs rampant in capital trials, making it extremely difficult for the alleged to obtain the fair trial that they are entitled to by law. Experts agree that individuals who are more economically advantaged and white have better outcomes in capital trials. The families are forced to endure these unjust realities, which can be exasperating. It is impossible to have trust for a system and process that is, and has historically has been, biased.

Sentenced to Death By Lethal Injection

After lengthy trials that take a devastating physical and emotional toll on everyone involved, sentences are read and a person's family member or friend is sentenced to death by lethal injection by the state of Texas. As loved ones hear the reading of the sentence, hope is drained, and the realization that unless the appeals process yields positive results, the person they love will live the rest of their days in a confinement cell until they are taken to their death. There will never be an opportunity to touch their loved one again while they are alive. How families cope with this reality varies by individual and family.

Lee Greenwood, the mother of Joseph Nichols who was executed in 2007 for the 1980 murder of Claude Shaffer, Jr., shared a glimpse of her experience with Texas After Violence Project during an interview of how her family coped with having a son sentenced to death and living on death row.

> When he was moved to death row, which was in Huntsville at the time, it's now in Livingston, you could only go once a week. So, someone would go every week. As years went on and on and on, most times, you will find that it's the mothers that keep going every week. I don't know why it is, I guess it may be a man thing, but most times dads get really, really—I don't want to say it gets to a point where they just can't stand it. They have to find a way to deal with it in their own way and usually you will see, if you ever have the occasion to visit death row, it's usually a lot of mothers and sisters and girlfriends and wives. And dads and brothers come sometime, because they deal with it in a different way. And that's OK.[168]

The Execution

Enduring the death of a child is the worst nightmare for any parent. In most cases, the deaths of children are unexpected. There is no other occasion, other than an execution, in which a person knows the exact time and date their child will die. In addition, they know the exact manner of death. The parent knows that their child will be strapped to a table and killed. The intentional death will be witnessed by the media as well as other individuals. This pain can be incomprehensible to those who will never experience it. On some occasions, individuals and groups outside the walls cheer and celebrate the execution. Someone's child, sibling, parent, spouse, relative or other loved one is being executed and people outside are cheering. This adds an indescribable insult to the trauma. The years of anticipatory grief leading up to this date and the life afterward is crippling. The execution of one's child is an occasion that will be replayed in the minds of these parents over and over again—from the moment of the sentencing through the rest of their lives.

In an interview with the Texas After Violence Project, Lee Greenwood described the experience of her son's execution.

The day of the execution, or prior to the execution, we were allowed to visit him each day up until 12 o'clock on the day of the execution. That day, one of the guards refused to—tried to turn his daughter away the day before the execution, saying that she was not on the visiting list. That was not so. She was always on the visiting list, because after all, she was just a little girl when he went to death row. Well, this ranking officer and I had words, and Joseph had already told us, instructed us what we were to do if we had a problem. So we followed what he said, and the problem was taken care of. She was allowed to come in and visit. On the day of the execution, as a lot of the inmates do, they won't go peaceably. They won't just say, "OK, here I am. Take me." As it was, they kind of knocked him around a bit. They disrobed him. Finally gave him a pair of boxer shorts to put on, and that's how they transported him from Livingston to Huntsville, in a pair of boxers, no shoes, no nothing. Shackled. When he got to the Walls Unit he was given clothing to put on. We made the caravan from Livingston to Huntsville and along the way they had, I guess there were sheriffs' cars stationed along the way because it was about six or seven cars, and we could not follow him because evidently they took a different route than we did. So when we got to Livingston, of course they had me wait at the hospitality house. And it was about, I guess maybe 75 of us that day, family members and friends, and we were all piled in there. The hospitality house seemed to get a bit uneasy, so one of my niece's said, "Oh don't worry, when we leave, we will leave you a substantial donation." Then they allowed him to call the hospitality house and talk to us on the phone. And he could talk to us until five o'clock. And he and I were the last persons on the phone. After a while, he didn't want to speak to anyone else. He just wanted he and I to talk. And there was still a brief in the Supreme Court waiting to be ruled on, and I guess around four o'clock they called and said that the Supreme Court had turned it down. They had also told him, so we didn't speak about that very much.

His concern was that everyone be OK, and that everyone know that whichever manner it happens everyone has to travel that same road and to be assured as he said, "I got this." No, he would rather have not lived. He once said if they had offered him a life sentence, he was of the mind that he did not want that. Already he had done two life sentences as far as the prison system was concerned and had begun a third. He assured me he was OK and wanted to be sure that I was going to be OK and that his sister and his brothers were going to be OK, and his daughter, and just how everyone was going to be and to let them know that as he always told me, "Stand on your faith and be at peace because I got this." And just let him be a part of the abolishment of the death penalty. And I think that this is happening without any, really without a lot of effort of mind, because periodically his case comes up in the most unexpected way. Out of all the cases that have been mishandled and all of the injustice that has gone on, his case keeps coming to the forefront. So, I've been pleased about that. It's kind of hard on the heart, because when you get in a place that you can kind of deal with it, it comes up again. So, that's his wish and it is kind of going on without a lot of effort on my part, and I believe that's because it was such a gross miscarriage of justice. And it's not his—it's plain to be seen. If you just read a few lines of the case, you know, "What happened here?" When you have a question mark in your mind, on your face, and I know a lot of people that have said to me, "After reading your son's case, I became a fighter for the abolishment of the death penalty." And that's as he wanted it.[169]

Jamal, the brother of Napoleon Beazley describes his experience of the execution process in an interview with Texas After Violence Project.

I can remember like it was yesterday. That day I can remember like it was yesterday. I just remember ... I remember we was staying ... we didn't go to the actual room where they executed him at. We stayed at the Hospitality House, which is two streets over. I mean it was stressful for us too, because we were sitting, we were all sitting in the room. It was, I think, my immediate family: my mom, my dad, my sister, me. No, I don't think my sister was there. I can't remember. My aunt, my cousin, Arthur J.R. Johnson, he's one of my friends, we're real good friends, Anthony Turner, my cousin, Cynthia Turner. I think she was there if I'm not mistaken. I can't remember who else was there, but those are the main people that I remember. It was ... I mean the building was packed full of people. And we're just sitting around waiting. Waiting, waiting, waiting. Just waiting. Six o'clock came. We still waiting, waiting, waiting. Still no answer. 6:05 came, and I think, I think Walter called at like 6:02 or something. He was telling us ... I mean like there was nothing else he could do. He had already did everything else, and then I think at like 6:07 or something like that, they had called us and told us that he was dead. All I remember was I went outside. Everybody was crying, and I went outside. Soon as I went outside, I saw my dad. He gave me a hug, and that's all I remember there. How I got home? I have no idea. I don't even know if I drove. I can't remember. I don't know. Everything else is a blur. Can't remember too much of nothing, nothing else. It's been almost six years in a couple more months, but it's all right, though. I can't think of anything else.[170]

In the immediate aftermath of an execution, family and friends are able to finally touch their loved one for the first time in a bittersweet moment. The child, father, sibling, wife or other loved ones of the executed person finally has the opportunity to touch the still warm body. For some, it has been 10, 20 and 30 years of visiting through cloudy, scratched Plexiglas, but never touching, never smelling, never seeing clearly enough to see all of the scars, tattoos and wrinkles that have branded their loved one. For the first time in years, they share a free space together, reunited as a family, with no cages in between. They would have given anything to have had that opportunity just one hour earlier.

A New Normal

For those families that can afford a funeral, a ceremony is conducted and last goodbyes are rendered. Some believe that their loved one is finally free from chains and have gone to a different place. The newfound grief, however, is just beginning Jamal, Napoleon Beazley's brother describes his brother's funeral:

Actually he was cremated. We had a funeral. Everybody, some ... I think one of his classmates, Teal Morphea, was trying to get me to get it to be an open casket, but I mean that ain't it. Nobody really have ... because he, my brother, he really didn't want a funeral. He just wanted it to be over with it like it was ... because he didn't want to invite a crowd or anything. If I had that poem here, you would ...He wrote a poem, and it's on the back of his tombstone that we made. We actually got a tombstone out at the church house, Mount Zion Baptist Church in Grapeland, Texas. We got a picture, a tombstone, his tombstone with a picture on it and his poem on the back. But at the funeral, man, I don't even know. I was ... my family's so big, man, I was sitting by my own grandfather, and I ain't even know who he was. I ain't ... I've only seen him like three or four times, but I was sitting right by him, and I didn't even know who he was. But other than that I don't remember anybody else. Something like that. I don't know. God's just blessed me, man. Wiped everything out for me like a disk cleanup on a laptop or something. He just took everything out and was like, "You'll be all right." I didn't ride in the limousine, though. I know that part. I remember that part. I drove my own car there. I think I drove by myself. I don't think anybody rode with me, but I don't really remember anything. I don't even think that anybody cried at the funeral, because he told them

... we was like, "Man, if you cry, we're going to escort you out of there." I mean because my mom, she was already having a hard enough time as it was, so I don't know.[171]

What Happens to the Children?

OK, to start I have been affected by my dad in jail. Feeling that I was left on purpose. I didn't have a father figure so I fell into a bad crowd. It feels bad not having a father to wake up to every morning and I think about that and it makes me feel bad. Makes me feel like I am missing something. It makes you feel like you lost the important part of your life. When you know he is on death row it makes you think about the "what ifs" that could happen.

The poignant words of this 16-year-old-boy reflect years of formidable challenges that children face by having a parent on death row. Every child experiences these hurdles in disparate ways, and, likewise, they will manifest a wide range of reactions and coping mechanisms. There are, however, some notable commonalties to their struggles. The impact on a child and his or her ability to cope is dependent on many factors including, age, developmental stage, genetics, availability of resources, the manner by which they are told, social support system, history of trauma and oppression, level of involvement in the process, education, personality variables and the manner by which their community responds to them.[172]

Some children experience denial that their parent committed the crime that they are accused of. They can struggle to adequately process the reality that someone they love and admire is capable of taking a life. Hanging on to the believed innocence of that parent can become a vital way by which to cope. When their father is executed, the state is murdering an innocent man in their eyes. Others fully acknowledge that their parent committed the crime and as a result, end up distancing themselves from that parent. On the contrary, some children will support their parent and even forgive him. Children are taught from an early age that killing is wrong both morally and legally. Many children, therefore, have a difficult time understanding why their parent will be killed by the state if killing is wrong. Children experience this as cognitive dissonance, which can cause confusion, anger, distrust and even feelings of vengeance toward the system that is not carrying out what it teaches. For younger children who are not yet capable of full abstract thinking, this concept can be particularly challenging and damaging. In their minds, as well as in the minds of others, the system is murdering their daddy, and murder is wrong.

A child has to live with the fact that his father is going to be permanently taken away one day, and that he will never be able to touch or have his dad home again and be a part of his everyday life. Regardless of the level of involvement that the father had in his children's life, young children often see their fathers as heroes and look up to them, no matter what crime they committed. The loss is forever present and having the knowledge that they will never have a father who is physically present in their lives and in their homes is very painful. Losing a father, and more specifically, losing a father in this manner, can cause significant distress and changes in psychological, physical, cognitive and behavioral health. Adolescent boys, for example, who do not have a father in their lives are three to four times more likely to be arrested for juvenile offenses.[173]

The Texas Department of Criminal Justice acknowledges the importance of maintaining family ties on its website.

> In keeping with its mission of providing public safety, promoting positive changes in offender behavior, and assisting offenders in their transition to the community, the Texas Department of Criminal Justice recognizes the importance of maintaining familial ties, particularly that of offenders and their children. To that end, the TDCJ is committed to providing opportunities for visitation as well as incorporating programs which, in respect to maintaining public safety, include children of offenders or impact the children of offenders.

> Without intervention, children of incarcerated parents are six to eight times more likely to become involved in a criminal lifestyle. According to a recent National Institute of Corrections (NIC) solicitation, "Parental arrest and confinement lead to stress, trauma, stigmatization and separation problems for their children. These problems are coupled with existing problems that include poverty, violence, parental substance abuse, high crime environments, intrafamily abuse, abuse and neglect, multiple caregivers and/or prior separations. As a result, these children often exhibit a broad variety of behavioral, emotional, health, and educational problems that are compounded by the pain of separation." Over half of the juveniles confined in a secure institution had a parent that has been or is incarcerated.[174]

Although TDCJ acknowledges the potential harm to the child, family and community of not maintaining familial bonds, the system does not allow children to have contact visits with their parent on death row. Individuals on death row are also not allowed to call their children on the telephone.[175]

Despite the multiple and ongoing devastations that these children face, they receive little to no attention and support through the entire process. In fact, Texas Department of Criminal Justice does not keep data on the number of children that are affected by having a parent sentenced to death, including the number of children of incarcerated individuals that visit their parent.[176] There is an absence of this type of data nationally as well. Consequently, the children are not counted.[177] It is critical that this data be collected so that the children can be acknowledged and outreach efforts can be designed and provided accordingly.

Children have to deal with a multitude of problems on top of the normal stressors that they have to deal with growing up. Many already live in poverty and are immersed in environments where drugs, trauma, gangs, violence and oppression are commonplace. They have to live with the identity of having a father who allegedly committed a heinous crime and is in prison on death row. For many children, this causes a great deal of shame. Eventually, the children will have to manage the identity of having a deceased parent and will have to explain the loss. The emotional state and well-being of involved family members directly impacts the well-being of the children and the care that they receive as well. These adults are going through a complicated and anticipatory grief process, and they may be coping with depression, anxiety and trauma that are often associated with the capital punishment process. The trial process often takes significant time and energy away from the family unit and other caregivers, creating a disruption in the family dynamic. Children often feel neglected by other family members who are physically and emotionally consumed by the process and less available to meet the entirety of their needs.

Ireland Beazley, the father of Napoleon Beazley, described what he had to do to protect Jamaal, Napoleon's little brother who was only 10 years old when his brother was arrested.

> And that … automatically you don't want to air no dirty laundry, but he accused us of not paying attention to him, cause of all the things that we went through with Napoleon. He had trouble in school because of it. And he even said to me one time, "You don't love me." And basically, I don't know how to tell you, it was a couple of times I would walk into the house and call him Napoleon instead of Jamaal. And you know that kind of stuff hurt him. And hurt me to think that he thought that I didn't even care about him. And it was tough. But he's doing all right now. He's doing all right now. He knows I love him, and I'll do anything for him just like I would do anything for Napoleon.[178]

Regardless of age, a child has to go through a disruption in attachment and the loss of a present parental figure if that parent was active in his life. Tearing apart attachment bonds may be more detrimental at different stages of the developmental process and can create long-term physical, psychological and social impairments. It is important that children maintain attachments with their parent who has been incarcerated when it is appropriate. Yet, the system makes it virtually impossible to maintain proper attachment bonds. In Texas, as well as in other states, individuals incarcerated on death row are not allowed to have contact visits or speak on the telephone with their loved ones. Many families have geographical limitations that do not afford them the opportunity to visit their loved ones on a regular basis. In those instances, communication is limited to writing. Not all children are capable of writing and articulating themselves in written form other than through drawing. It is not reasonable to expect a child to experience a healthy attachment with their parent when they are limited to this medium. And, not all people who are incarcerated are capable of reading and writing. When children are able to visit their fathers, they are not able to touch them. Many younger children are unable to comprehend this, and it can be excruciatingly painful for them to not be able to hug or be held by their dad. It is not just the absence of the father that is harmful. Rather, it is a combination of factors as described previously, including the reason that father is absent, that can prove to be harmful to their psychosocial development.

Socially, the children and their families carry the stigma and embarrassment of having a parent who is serving time on death row. Children are often victims of vindictive behavior and ridicule, just like their families. Although not always the case, their ability to process and cope with it, however, may prove to be more difficult than it may be for an adult. Children can suffer from depression and/or anxiety; they may isolate, internalize or blame themselves; and academic and social performance can suffer. Many view themselves as being in a different category from their peers and find it highly challenging to relate to others. In a report published by the Quaker United Nations Office entitled, *Lightening the Load of the Parental Death Penalty,* research on the implications of having a parent sentenced to death or executed on children's psychological and emotional reactions, found some commonalities in the children studied: "Low self-esteem; embarrassment about oneself or others; inability to explain the situation to others; anger, loss of appetite; loss of interest in playing; loss of interest in school; loss of concentration; loss of sleep; dreams and nightmares; bed wetting; halt in menstruation and psychosomatic pains. Behavioral issues may include a use of violence, vandalism, intentional self-isolation, starting or increasing time spent in paid work and increased frequency and dedication to religious practice."[179] Post-traumatic stress disorder can also be diagnosed at various stages of the process.

Children begin a new grief process as soon as their parent is sentenced. Some have been experiencing anticipatory grief for an extended period of time already. These children experience a wide range of emotional upheavals and traumas through the different stages of the process including, the arrest, pre-trial, trial, sentencing, imprisonment, final visits, execution and life post execution. With a lack of services provided to these children that can assist in meeting their needs, they are at higher risk for developing psychological impairments and maladaptive behaviors.

Parents who are sentenced to death are often well aware of the harm that this process has had on their children and families, and they recognize their children and families in their last words. These are the last words they will ever hear from their dad, but the memories, good and bad, will never end.

> I want to thank all of my family and friends for supporting me. I love you and I'm glad that y'all are by my side through this whole thing. I know it's hard for y'all. I love you Jennifer, mom, Jaime, Cory, David. Thank God for you being there for me. It's not easy, this is a release. Y'all finally get to move on with your lives. Take care of my kids and stay strong, life has to go on. We've all lost grandpas, brothers, and sisters. Support and love each other. Don't fight with each other. I love you. —Robert Garza

> Bohannon, Peg and Kim, I love y'all. Son, get your life right with Christ, also your mother. Give mom a hug for me and tell her that I love her. Y'all do understand that I came here a sinner and leaving a saint. Take me home Jesus, take me home Lord, take me home Lord. I ain't left yet, must be a miracle. I am a miracle. I see you, Rich. Don't cry son, don't cry baby. I love y'all. I'm ready. ~ Marvin Wilson

> I love my family. Thank you for all of your support. Stay strong. I am at peace. I love you and my kids. See you[180]. —Ortiz, Ricardo

Many of the last words spoken from the execution table include directives to family members to "be strong." Some of the roles that the father, son, uncle, grandson, husband, friend or boyfriend had changed when they were incarcerated, others, however, stays the same. The role of protector, encourager, disciplinarian, lover, supporter and others, continues as a function of this family while they are living. Many people underestimate the positive influences and roles that these individuals can have in the lives of others, even behind bars. It is a common belief that someone who is in prison has nothing to offer, in particular, to children. This is an erroneous belief that, if supported, can be damaging to a child. Even in prison, parents can have an important and constructive role to play in their children's lives.

Individuals who have been impacted by the criminal actions of another person are punished for crimes that they did not commit. Following the execution, the role that their loved one played in their lives is gone, leaving a hole that will never be filled.

CHAPTER TEN
UNINTENDED CAUSALITIES
SUFFERING IN SILENCE

Living with the nightmares is something that we know from experience. No one has the right to ask a public servant to take on a life-long sentence of nagging doubt, and for some of us, shame and guilt. Should our justice system be causing so much harm to so many people when there is an alternative?

—Open letter by Georgia corrections officials [181]

WHEN A PERSON ARRIVES to death row for the first time, he or she leaves behind dozens of individuals and families who were affected by the process. Years, and sometimes decades later, even more individuals will participate in the actual execution process. Some individuals report relatively little impact from the process, describing their participation merely as necessary parts of their job, carrying out the wishes of the state. Others, however, tell a different story of pain and enduring effects.

Capital Trial Process: Juries, Judges and Attorneys

Regardless of the type of trial, these processes can bring intense stress and tend to be overwhelming, both during and after the trial. Multiple variables are interjected into the daily lives of jurors that can be extremely traumatic. Jurors are required to repeatedly hear, at times, extremely gruesome details of crimes, hear from victims and view horrific crime-scene photos that most jurors have probably never seen in their lives. Jurors are required to sift through evidence and look closely at gruesome details repeatedly as they deliberate. They hear and see details that may be forever etched in their minds. How these experiences impact each individual juror is highly dependent on many factors. This issue has been the subject of psychological studies. In addition to having the ordinary stressors of the trial process, capital trials produce a new layer of variables that can produce intense suffering on the part of the jurors. Unique to capital trials is the fact that the outcome of their decision determines the defendant's future to live or die, as well as the damage the outcome will have on the family members and loved ones of the defendant. Many jurors, for example, feel like they are playing God. When a juror is faced with the possibility of a death penalty sentence, there is an increased risk for emotional suffering and significant stress.[182] When comparing post-traumatic stress disorder symptoms between jurors who rendered a death sentence as opposed to a life sentence, those who imposed a life sentence displayed less symptoms.[183]

Research conducted by Michael Antonio revealed that both men and women alike experienced upsetting emotions related to crime-scene evidence. Participants reported sleep related problems, loss of appetite and a sense of loneliness and isolation. In addition to these findings, women reported more generalized fear, isolation and use of prescription drugs and even illicit substances.[184] Janvier Slick, a licensed clinical social worker who has counseled juries after capital punishment trials, shares her experience with jurors, "When called on to decide not only guilt, but also whether the death penalty is warranted, jurors are faced with what for many is a distressing decision. For some jurors, this experience results in a variety of symptoms related to post-traumatic stress, and the problems may remain with them for a long time. Further, the trauma is not mitigated and may even be exacerbated when the defendant's execution occurs."[185]

Despite the known mental health consequences that can occur with jurors, vital post-trial counseling that could mitigate long-term effects is not adequately available. An article in the *Texas Bar Journal* reported that despite 70 percent of jurors in any type of trial experiencing stress, few states offer post-trial services for jurors. The author noted a few exceptions including Arizona, California, Florida, Minnesota, Ohio, Oregon and Wisconsin. One of the earliest post-trial counseling services organizations in the United States began in Seattle, Washington in 1998. The organization provides group therapy for jurors post-verdict and has since become a model for other states that have adopted post-trial juror services. In 2007, a Texas murder victim's mother desired to help jurors serving on traumatic murder trials. She championed Texas House Bill 608 that allows up to 10 hours of counseling for jurors who report being traumatized by graphic evidence from murder, child sexual assault and other trials. Due to the bill not being mandatory, it appears that only few counties offer the services.[186]

Like jurors, judges in capital trials can also feel like they influence the decision, if not decide, whether someone lives or dies. Although judges are in their positions by choice, unlike jurors, they can also suffer both psychologically and physically. However, it may be more challenging for them to discuss the impact and obtain support.

One Texas capital trial judge, who chose to remain anonymous, described her thoughts and experiences regarding the impact of issuing death penalty verdicts.

> The thing about the death penalty is that it is not the judge that decides; it is the jury. When you sentence someone to the death penalty, it is almost surreal. You tell them the date, time, place and how they are going to die. When else does that happen? There is nothing you can compare that to. It is overpowering; it does get to you. It does not matter what they did, and you are still telling them that. It does not matter if you do or do not believe in the death penalty. Judges don't sit around and talk about this. They want to file it away. The system did what the system is going to do, and you move on. The hardest thing is to sit there and listen to the pain. Only God is supposed to tell someone where and when and why. It is not a position that I relish or enjoy or ever want to do again, but if the situation calls for it, I would. It is the job I have chosen."

Law school leaves capital defense attorneys ill-prepared for the human consequence that this work carries. For many, the work was not anything they could have imagined. Defending capital cases requires lawyers to work countless hours and expend extensive emotional energy and commitment to fight for the lives of others. This carries an enormous sense of responsibility. In many cases, the capital defense attorney is the only person fighting to preserve the defendant's life when hundreds of people are fighting against it. The connection that can form because of this is one of many factors that make this a unique client-attorney relationship.

In the book *Fighting for Their Lives: Inside the Experience of Capital Defense Attorneys,* Susannah Sheffer presents the stories of 20 attorneys and highlights the human element in their careers. She found that many of them feel the burden of having to manage and, at times, conceal their own feelings of guilt, fear, anger, grief and pain in order to be most effective for their client, while at the same time appear calm and professionally competent. Susannah describes this seemingly impossible challenge, "Through the shakiness, the panic reactions, the numbness and the disorientation, their bodies are saying that it is impossible to insulate oneself from the pain and sadness that this work engenders. It's impossible not to take it in and be changed by it in ways that never entirely subside."[187]

Once all options have been exhausted, according to Susannah, the attorney must deliver the daunting news to the client and to the family that nothing more can be done to save his life. The family, with whom they have oftentimes formed a unique bond, is devastated. After the client is executed, attorneys often go through a vast array of intense emotions and physical reactions including grief, sadness and guilt. Caseloads are often so overwhelming that there can be little time to properly grieve one execution, and another one comes on its heels. This can result in secondary trauma, a continuous re-opening of the wound.[188]

Witnessing an Execution

"Every execution requires a team of workers who watch the inmate in his or her final days, who strap the inmate to the gurney, who insert and reinsert the needles, and who remove the inmate's body from the gurney after the execution. They are the ones who deal with botched executions, who struggle with inmates fighting to stay alive, and who pull inmates away from their families when it is time for their final goodbye." This quote obtained by Equal Justice USA highlights the behind-scenes efforts involved in bringing a man to his death.[189] Despite the public intrigue surrounding capital punishment, relatively little attention has been directed toward understanding the experiences of those who are part of the execution process itself. Rick Halperin, Ph.D., director of the Embrey Human Rights Program at Southern Methodist University and member of Amnesty International and the Texas Coalition to Abolish the Death Penalty, wrote an open letter describing his experience witnessing an execution in 1998.

Dear Friends,
On Wednesday, April 29, I witnessed the execution of Frank McFarland, in Huntsville. The following is an attempt to convey to you what I saw and experienced:

BACKGROUND:
Frank McFarland was condemned for the Feb. 1, 1988, death of Terri Lynn Hokanson; before she died, she told police she had been raped and stabbed by two men. When he was sentenced to death, Frank was 24.

Frank first wrote to me two years ago, and we had a steady correspondence. He steadfastly maintained his innocence.

His family lives in the Dallas metroplex area, and in 1997, he asked me to contact his sister, Dawn, to introduce her to people in the abolition effort in the Dallas area.

In February and March of this year, when it looked as though Frank's April 29 execution date would indeed be a serious one, he requested a meeting with me, and had me added to his visitor's list.

On Saturday, Dawn and I made the (three hour) trip from Dallas to Huntsville, and had a four-hour meeting with Frank, from 5:30–9:30 p.m.

Frank and I discussed many things, mostly centering on his impending execution. He was, at that time, awaiting news on whether or not he would be granted an evidentiary hearing which he and his attorney felt would cast serious doubts upon his conviction.

Frank was [not] in very high spirits, and was not overly optimistic about getting his hearing. He was, instead, focused upon getting his affairs in order and planning for his execution and the things he wanted done afterward.

He said numerous times during our conversation that he was ready for death, and that it would be a release from the psychological and physical torture, which he had endured for 10 years on death row. He said he was tired, for example, of returning to his cell after family members had visited him, only to find that guards had destroyed his belongings and damaged his property. He said it was common to be handcuffed and to then have as many as five or six guards beat, kick and punch him (and others), stating that "we are the condemned ... no one cares about us ... we have no one to complain to ... they look at us like we are animals, and they treat us worse. If they kill me Wednesday night, it will only mean that I am going home, going to the land of my ancestors. I will be free from here."

It was very sobering to hear these comments.

Frank then told me that he was not asking, and would not ask, for clemency on his own behalf. He said he would make no apology for a crime he did not commit, and he talked at length about his case. He explained that he was well aware of my involvement in the anti-death penalty movement as a human rights educator and activist, and that was precisely the reason he wanted to speak with me.

We had, in fact, briefly chatted in late 1997, when I was a member of the Amnesty International delegation that toured the death row facility in Huntsville. We met (very briefly) with several inmates in a variety of locations, and had longer talks with three men who were awaiting execution dates which were scheduled after our visit.

Frank asked me if I would be willing to witness his execution, so that I could talk firsthand about it in my discussions, lectures, travels, etc. He wanted me to use his death in a constructive and educational way.

I was initially startled by his request, but I consented to indeed witness his death if, in fact, his final appeals were denied.

He said that his witnesses list would include his mother, his spiritual adviser, and myself.

**Note: A brief mention about his family.

Frank's father was a career military man who, once retired, worked in law enforcement in the Fort Worth area. He had been hounded mercilessly after Frank was sentenced to death, and was eventually forced to leave his job.

Frank has two sisters, Theresa and Dawn. Dawn is married and currently five and half months pregnant with her first child. Frank would not let her witness his death because of her pregnancy. In the 10 years that Frank was on death row, Dawn's husband never once made the visit to Huntsville with her to see Frank, his brother-in-law.

Frank said that he was luckier than most death row inmates in Huntsville, in that he had the love and support of/from his family. His mother and Dawn were the two who came to visit him on a regular basis.

At 9:30 p.m., the guards came and said our time was finished—I told Frank that I hoped he got a stay, but that if he did not, I would see him Wednesday evening. I left a bit ahead of Dawn, who stayed behind for a few moments to have her goodbyes with Frank in private.

She told me on the drive back to Dallas how happy Frank was with the meeting, and that she too was resigned to his fate, not expecting any relief from the courts. She added that she would be returning to Huntsville on the next night, Sunday, to remain there until she heard that either Frank had received a stay or until after his impending execution. She was coordinating the family plans, as she had three aunts flying to Houston from Maryland, Delaware and Georgia.

On Tuesday afternoon, April 28, Dawn telephoned me at work, from Huntsville, to inform me that the courts had rejected Frank's request for an evidentiary hearing, and that it now appeared certain that his execution would proceed the following day. I finalized my travel plans to Huntsville, as Dawn told me that the witnesses to the execution had to be in Huntsville for a meeting with the prison chaplain at 3 p.m.

The Final Day, Wednesday, April 29, 1998
Wednesday, April 29, was a physically beautiful day in Dallas. It was quite sunny, a very warm 85 degrees, and the type of day which allows one to bring back pleasant memories of spring. However, I found myself during my drive to Huntsville fixated on the reasons for my journey, namely, that in a few hours' time, I would see a human being put to death.

I arrived in Huntsville at 3 p.m., and went to the designated meeting room in a motel in the center of town, only a few blocks from the prison where the execution would be carried out. I met Frank's mother, Diana, his spiritual adviser, Camille (from Houston), and two chaplains: one male and one female.

Our meeting lasted about one hour, in which the male chaplain discussed the scenario of what was going to occur prior to, during and after Frank's execution.

He asked Diana several times if she was emotionally ready to see her son die, and her answer was always the same … "yes, I'm ready." He reminded each of us that we could still change our minds and decide not to participate as a witness if we chose, but we each said that this was not an option; we would indeed witness this execution.

Frank's mother told me several times that she was very bitter. She was very angry that the judicial process had led to this conclusion for her son and her family. She said she knew her son was innocent, and that their lack of financial resources had helped lead to his demise through ineffective court-appointed counsel at his original trial.

She said her husband had initially, but reluctantly, agreed to be a witness to this execution, but after the family had their final (four-hour) visit with Frank Wednesday morning, her husband had broken down and decided to return home. He was not going to witness the death of his son.

She added that Dawn's husband, Scott, who made his first and only visit to Huntsville to see Frank that (Wednesday) morning, had also left, to follow Frank's father back to Fort Worth to make sure he got home safely.
The only two male members of the McFarland extended family who had been present were thus gone.

Diana also said she was very bitter at her (Baptist) church. She said that as soon as Frank received his death sentence, no one in the congregation, nor the minister, ever spoke to the family, nor ever made any gestures to comfort the McFarland family in their times of grief and hurt and suffering. She said that, "For 10 years, we have been treated like lepers. What kind of Christians are these people?"

At approximately 4:15 p.m., we drove from the motel to the prison, The Walls Unit, where we were escorted into a large waiting room.

Already there were Diana's three sisters (Frank's aunts), and both Theresa and Dawn. There were also two members of the church in Houston to which Frank and his spiritual adviser belonged. This was the first time I had met any of these folks except, of course, for Dawn.

The family members were speaking about the morning's final visit with Frank, and were telling stories about him and the family as they remembered aspects of his life as it intersected their own. Frank had requested, and had been granted, the chance to listen to Scottish bagpipe music on a tape in his holding cell prior to his journey to the death chamber, and his family was trying to imagine what he was listening to as they waited in the room.

About 5 p.m., three male prison staff members, and one female prison guard, came and escorted the three witnesses to separate rooms to be searched. I was frisked by one guard while another went through my wallet. I had already given them my photo identification, but they never told me what they were looking for.

At 5:15 p.m., we were led back into the large room, but were told we could have no contact, either physical or verbal, with any of the other family members. We went to one far end of the room, and a prison staff member came over to us and told us he would be escorting us to another part of the building prior to execution. We then waited until almost 5:50 p.m., sitting in silence by ourselves, while the other family members huddled at the other end of the room, chatting about Frank and their remembrances.

At almost 5:50 p.m., three guards came in the room and immediately the family members fell silent. One guard then said: "Will the three witnesses please come with us?" It was a very difficult parting from the other family members; Frank's mom hugged Theresa and Dawn, and we then left the room, and were escorted into a different wing of the building, having to actually walk across the street to another waiting room.

We entered a very large room at 5:58 p.m., and were asked to sit on a couch. There were six prison staff members, two guards, and a reporter from The Associated Press in the room.

No one looked at or spoke to any of us. We sat on the couch for 17 minutes, until 6:15 p.m., and not once did anyone acknowledge our presence or existence. No one made eye contact with us, and certainly no one spoke a word to us. Frank's mom was very quiet, very pensive. Camille, Frank's spiritual adviser, told me that this was the second time she was witnessing an execution, and asked me if I had done this before.

I had just finished saying "no" when a man came into the room at the opposite end to where we were located, looked at us, and said simply, "It's time. Please follow me."

We walked outside and around a corner. It was still very sunny and very warm. We walked past a tall fence with a triple row of razored barbed wire on the top, and two guards stood outside the room we were about to enter.

We were led into the viewing room. My first impression was that it was quite small for everyone: there were the three witnesses, five newspaper reporters (they were already in the room), the female chaplain, and four prison staff members.

The witnesses walked up to the window, looking into the death chamber. I was on the left side of the viewing window, with Frank's mother next to me, and Camille next to her on Diana's right.

Frank was strapped in the gurney, with his head turned to his right, looking at us as we entered the viewing room. There were no victims' family members present. (They would have been in their own separate viewing room, and they would not have come into contact with us at all.)

Frank gave us a brief smile to acknowledge our presence. He was dressed in a navy prison one-piece jumpsuit, wearing white socks and his Reebok running shoes. He had an individual ankle restraint around each ankle. He also had a large, leather strap around his shins, another over his thighs, another over his waist and still another over his chest. He was very tightly secured to the gurney. He had ace bandages across both his hands, so we could not see his hands or fingers at all.

The chaplain had told us in our afternoon meeting we would in fact see this, but had no explanation as to why prison officials do this.

Still, it was a strange sight.

The death chamber itself is very small. If there had not been glass in the window frame, it appeared that one could have leaned through the opening and touched his right arm on the gurney.

He had a needle inserted into each forearm, and the connected tubing for the solution was plainly visible. He had a towel folded in thirds under his head which acted as his pillow.

The male chaplain stood at the foot of the gurney, and stared only at the floor. He never looked at Frank, nor did he ever look at anyone in the viewing room.

The prison warden stood at the head of the gurney, behind Frank's head, and he too never looked at anything except the floor.

A large microphone came out of the ceiling and was only a few inches from Frank's mouth.

It was very quiet, both in the viewing room and in the death chamber. Frank closed his eyes, and turned his head away from the viewing room so that he could speak directly into the microphone.

The warden then said to Frank, "Proceed with your final comments, if you have any." The warden kept his eyes focused on the floor, and it was amazing, at least to myself, that the warden still did not look at the condemned individual, who was no more than a few inches from him.

In his final statement, Frank, with his eyes still closed, repeated his claim of innocence, stating that, "I owe no apology for a crime I did not commit. Those who lied and fabricated evidence against me will have to answer for what they have done. I call upon the spirits of my ancestors, the land, the sea, the skies, to clear a path for me, and I swear to them and now, I am coming home."

He finished he statement by saying "Loch sloy," a Scottish battle cry for the McFarland clan in Scotland.

Immediately after he finished his statement, his mother said in a loud voice, "I love you," and his spiritual adviser then said, also in a loud voice, "Loch sloy."

The medical technicians who were to start the lethal injection had been instructed to do so after Frank finished with his phrase, "Loch sloy."

Both rooms fell totally silent. I could see Frank's chest move up and down a few times; his eyes had remained closed since he turned his head away from the viewing room moments before.

Within moments, he appeared to be in a deep sleep, and then, suddenly, he let out a long exhalation, making a coughing/gurgling noise. His chest stopped moving, and he lay perfectly still on the gurney, strapped down tightly with his eyes closed and no expression on his face.

The warden and the chaplain continued to stare down at the floor, never acknowledging Frank's presence.

This scene remained frozen in time, as about four minutes passed. Still, no one in either room said a word.

Finally, Frank's mother, standing immediately next to me, said, still staring through the window at her now-dead son, "He looks so peaceful. He's in a better place." His spiritual adviser then said, "His pain has come to an end."

I stood there in total silence, shock and disbelief as to what had just transpired. I could not believe what I had just seen.

Finally, after four minutes, a medical technician entered the death chamber, and stood next to Frank's lifeless right arm. He took out a little pocket penlight and opened both of Frank's eyes, shining it directly into each of them. Then he put his hand on Frank's carotid artery, feeling for a pulse. Finally, he put his stethoscope on Frank's heart, and bent over his body listening closely for a heartbeat.

The technician then stood up straight, leaned toward the microphone, and said, "Death is at 6:27. Death is at 6:27."

Then he stepped away from the body, toward the head of the gurney, toward the warden, who himself now moved toward the microphone. This was the first time I had seen him look up from the floor.

The warden looked into the viewing room, and repeated the doctor's words, "Death is at 6:27 p.m."

The technician then departed the death chamber.

Frank's mother, his spiritual adviser and I were still looking at his body on the gurney when a prison staff member behind us said, "Will the witnesses please follow me?" The reporters then filed out of the room, followed by Camille, Frank's mother, and myself. I turned one last time to look at Frank on the gurney before I left the viewing room. I could no longer see either the chaplain or the warden, and I did not know if they had left the death chamber.

My final view was to see Frank strapped on a gurney in a middle of a small room, tubing and needles in his arms, a peaceful expression on his face.

We then retraced our steps, through the office where we had waited earlier, back outside across the street, and into the main building of the Walls Unit, walking to the main office where the other family members awaited our return. No one said a word. Frank's mother was completely composed, with no tears.

Upon entering the waiting room with the family members and church members, I could see everyone still sitting at the large table. The room was very quiet. But as soon as we entered, some folks began to cry.

Dawn was off to one side of the room, by herself. It was apparent that she had been crying prior to our arrival, and she immediately broke down in deep sobs when we walked into the room.

Frank's mother went immediately to her, but said to everyone, in a strong voice, that "Frank did not suffer. He went in peace. Give thanks for that."

Everyone huddled together, and some were crying, some said nothing, and all were very hurt by what had just transpired. It was a painful, painful scene. The three aunts finally began to comfort both Theresa and Dawn. It was clear that both of Frank's sisters were terribly upset and distraught over the news of his actual death.

Finally, a prison staff officer appeared and informed the group that reporters wanted to know if the family had a statement. Mrs. McFarland had stated before the execution that she would only be willing to speak with the reporter from The Associated Press.

He entered the room and gave his condolences to Mrs. McFarland. She read him a prepared statement, part of which said that Frank "paid a high price for a debt he did not owe. Frank is at peace, and the family will become stronger."

She spoke with him for about 10 minutes, then rejoined her family in their grieving. I asked the reporter how many executions he had seen, and he responded "over 100." I asked him if, beyond seeing them in his professional capacity as a journalist, they bothered him as a human ... he just smiled and said nothing.

At approximately 7 p.m., the McFarland family decided to retire to their hotel rooms, inviting me to accompany them. But I felt they needed the time for themselves, and I still faced a long drive back to Dallas that night.

We all walked outside, where it was still warm and sunny, and where prison officials said nothing to us.

We all hugged, and got into our respective vehicles to head to our own destinations.

For me, it was a somber drive back to Dallas. I saw the entire process over and over again in my mind, and felt somewhat nauseous at what I had witnessed.

Later that evening, when I returned to my office, the first item I encountered was a news report in which the U.S. Supreme Court berated the 9th Circuit Court of Appeals for delaying executions, reading a quote that Chief Justice William Rehnquist said: "The 9th Circuit Court of Appeals had cheated the victims of crime by delaying executions."

Justice Anthony Kennedy was quoted as saying: "At some point, the state must be allowed to exercise its sovereign power to punish offenders. Only with real finality can the victims of crime move forward knowing the moral judgment will be carried out."

Having just seen the state put a human being to death three hours earlier, I stared at the quotes of the Supreme Court justices, and realized again why I and so many others are in this struggle.

I can state unequivocally that what I witnessed was one of the two or three worst things I have ever seen. It was a process totally devoid of anything civilized. It was not humane, it was not justice.

I knew in my mind and heart that I had been a witness to evil. I was truly amazed at how dehumanizing the entire process is, to the condemned and to the family/friends of the condemned. No state official ever acknowledged Frank's presence in the death chamber, and the guards, in my opinion, fulfilled their tasks like robots. The family members were pretty much left to get through this as best they can, only being urged by the prison staff "to do your best to keep your emotions in check."

The process has little to do with guilt or innocence; it has little to do with justice or fairness. It has everything to do with exterminating an individual whom the state has long-ago declared as "life unworthy of life."

Frank McFarland died with dignity and courage in the face of this terror. At the moment when the poison entered his body, it mattered not whether he was guilty or innocent; the act cast a dark pall over humanity for what was happening.

There is absolutely no way to be mentally prepared for what one sees and experiences. It is incredible to be, literally, only a few feet from a human being who is helpless and premeditatedly exterminated by the state. It is too soft to say that this is capital punishment. It is worse. It is an annihilation, an extermination process which leaves one numb, sickened, helpless, yet morally enraged. The process of human destruction is almost incalculable in its methodical nature of it being "a job."

Abolitionists should come to grasp, whether they ever see this act for themselves or not, with the brutal reality of the absolute terror, power and evil of the act.

I remain amazed and outraged that politicians, judges and others (especially in positions of authority) would have us believe that this is the best we are capable of; it is an extremely sad and pathetic comment on the human spirit, and should serve as both a warning and a catalyst to all abolitionists everywhere to rededicate ourselves with renewed fervor to end this scourge as quickly as possible.

Rick Halperin, Member, Amnesty International and The Texas Coalition to Abolish the Death Penalty
Dallas, Texas

The Execution Team

In the execution chamber, the warden usually stands at the head of the man who is moments away from a state sanctioned killing. If there is a chaplain, that person stands at the feet of the man being executed. Many others are also involved in observing the process. On the other side of the glass are the loved ones of victims and the loved ones of the person being executed. Several members of the media, as well as a member of the TDCJ's public information office and other staff are also present. The person being executed can request to have another witness present in accordance with policy. TDCJ does not disclose who actually delivers the lethal dose to the man. Although every individual has different reactions to being a part of this process, watching a human being die can be a traumatic process. Those who take an active role in an execution and witness a man being strapped to a gurney, stuck with a needle and administrated a lethal dose of a drug can process this emotionally in many different ways. The act of watching a human being die and being the person who gives the final nod to intentionally cause his death can be an impactful experience. Imagine, as well, if the participant believes that the man being executed is innocent. All of these scenarios can leave witnesses with negative emotional consequences that may never subside.

Some wardens and employees who have roles in the process describe executions as simply part of their jobs, to carry out the directives of the state of Texas. To carry out this line of reason, they cling to the notion that if they were not there, someone else would carry out the same job. Therefore, they carry no sense of individual responsibility for the actual death. These explanations often serve to diffuse responsibility to a larger group, making it easier to not internalize or personalize their role in the execution. For some individuals involved in executions, a coping mechanism may be to attribute their participation to external forces, such as the judge, the jurors, the community, the process and legislation. Others justify their roles in an execution as part of taking an active role in protecting society, making that person a hero or one of the "good guys." There are many reasons why a person might choose to participate in these voluntary roles. These individual narratives, and the meaning attributed to their roles, can serve to protect a person's conscious for years. At some point, however, the weight of the executions can become too heavy to bear. This has been the case for many wardens who have presided over executions.

In testimony before the Judiciary Committee of the Minnesota House of Representatives, former warden Donald Cabana, who oversaw executions during his career, relayed his experience.

> The first young man that I executed, a man by the name of Edward Earl Johnson, was convicted of killing a police officer. He insisted to the very end, somewhat oddly, that he did not commit the crime. It is not unusual for death row inmates to deny that they have committed their crime, and yet we find that odd, we let it anger us sometimes. But if you're pursuing appeals, you're hardly in a position to go out and confess your worst kinds of actions. But in the end, my experience with condemned prisoners was always that once strapped to the chair, they came around somehow with something—something as simple as tell the victim's family I'm sorry; tell my mother I'm sorry—something that indicated something bad happened, and I was there and I was a part of it. But not so with this young man. When I performed my ... ritualistic function of asking if he had a final public statement, this young man looked me in the eye, with tears streaming down his cheeks, and he said, "Warden, you're about to become a murderer. I did not kill that policeman, and dear God, I can't make anyone believe me." Well, you know we read about that sort of thing and of course the average person who reads that, the average legislator probably who reads that, says, "Well, what do you expect him to say?" I must tell you that just four days ago I had a rather gut-wrenching meeting with a former high official who is now convinced the young man was in fact telling the truth. And I must say to you that however we do it, in the name of justice, in the name of law and order, in the name of retribution, you, and when I say you, I mean generically, Americans, do not have the right to ask me, or any prison official, to bloody my hands with an innocent person's blood. Not in the name of justice, not in the name of fairness.[190]

In another example, Ron McAndrew, the former warden of Starke Florida State Prison, shared his experience and concern with capital punishment in testimony that he presented before the Montana House Judiciary committee. In addition to his work in Florida, he oversaw five lethal injections in Texas. As part of his testimony, he stated, "In both places, I saw staff traumatized by the duties they were asked to perform. Officers who had never ever met the condemned fought tears, cowering in the corners so as not to be seen. Some of my colleagues turned to drugs and alcohol to numb the pain of knowing that a man had died by their hands." Ron also shared, "I myself was haunted by the men I was asked to execute in the name of the state of Florida. I would wake up in the middle of the night to find them lurking at the foot of my bed."[191]

In yet another experience, Dr. Allen Ault, former warden and director of the Georgia Department of Corrections, who oversaw five executions, described the suffering that was experienced by those involved, including himself. "Those of us who have participated in executions often suffer something very much like post-traumatic stress. Many turn to alcohol and drugs. For me, those nights that weren't sleepless were plagued by nightmares." In addition, he reflected, "I can't always remember their names, but in my nightmares I can see their faces. Having witnessed executions firsthand, I have no doubts: capital punishment is a very scripted and rehearsed murder. It's the most premeditated murder possible."[192]

The public information office for TDCJ has a staff representative present during the preparation and execution process. Jason Clark, a public information officer for TDCJ, stated in an interview, "It [watching the execution] is one of the most difficult aspects of our job."

Chaplains

Chaplains can serve various roles on death row. Some can serve as spiritual advisors to those who are incarcerated, and some may be present during an execution. The relationships that chaplains and other types of spiritual advisors form with the individuals who are incarcerated are unique in their own right. Individuals who are incarcerated share their deepest vulnerabilities and fears and often choose their chaplain to be present because they can be with a person with whom they are familiar and who has been friendly with them. Ministers who develop relationships with the incarcerated individuals often experience the men changing before their eyes. Reverend Carol Picket, former TDCJ death row chaplain and author of *Within these Walls: Memoirs of A Death Row Chaplain,* witnessed close to 100 executions in Texas. "Quite often," he wrote, "the man I met in the final hours of his life was in no way the same person who, in some impulsive and mindless moment in his teen years, had committed a murder."[193] In his book, Reverend Picket reveals the emotional toll that witnessing the executions had on him. He described his nightmares, "At night, I had begun to have dreams in which I was locked away in the death house, its unique scent so real that it filled my nostrils, and that I could hear voices, faint and far away at first, then nearer and growing louder. They always asked the same question: where is the chaplain? And, in dreams or awake, I knew the answer, and it troubled me: he is busy helping prepare men to die."[194]

Even years after he stopped ministering to the individuals on death row, he reported that the executions still haunted him. He also attributed his stress and severe health problems to his experiences witnessing executions.[195] Al Obrien, another prison chaplain in Texas and former director of Prison Ministries Diocese of Beaumont, shares his personal experiences with various aspects of the execution process.

I visited some of the men over a two–three year period and developed a relationship. I did not deal with their offenses; I did not ask them what they did. That is not why I was there. The minute that you enter the Walls Unit for the execution, all of the staff is quiet. There is not much talking; everyone is courteous, helpful and quiet. Offenders were prepared for this night. One offender asked me, "I am going to be executed. Can you describe for me what it is like from the time you enter the chamber until it is all over?"

It did not appear to be painful. I look down at the gurney, and see a slight drop in the lips when lungs collapse. One offender passed me a note and asked me if I could call his mother to tell her that he did not suffer.

It is stunning to be conscious and present to the deliberate killing of someone. You are wordless.

I put the note in my pocket and went in. The drugs run; the doctor enters the room and pronounces him. When everyone leaves, no one talks. They all exit the room; walk out of the unit; go to their cars; and no one says anything. It is the same with every execution. Afterward, I went back to Beaumont. After one hour into the drive, I opened the envelope and took out the note, and called his mom.

I think back on these guys now, still years later, it is not a healthy environment for anyone.

Media

Each execution is permitted to have up to five reporters as witnesses. Media witnesses are usually divided with some on the side with the victim's relatives and friends and some with families and friends of the condemned.

The experiences that media witnesses report represent a wide range of emotional reactions. Michael Graczyk, a reporter from The Associated Press, has witnessed hundreds of executions in Texas. He describes one of the ways in which the executions affect him personally, "It has made me develop a greater appreciation for life. When you see the heroic measures taken by people to try to save an inmate's life, then you reflect on when the execution occurs and the circumstances of how we got to this point. It shows you how quickly life can be taken. I am there to do a job: tell the story. I've always believed my feelings are irrelevant." Graczyk also expressed how the memory of an execution that he witnessed years ago continues to trigger a response, "My work with the death penalty affects me at Christmas because of the song 'Silent Night.' It was sung by inmate Jonathan Nobles on the gurney as his last words as the lethal drugs took effect. His execution in early October 1998 was nowhere near Christmas, but when I hear that song at Christmas Mass, while I'm sure everyone else is focusing on the joy and spirit of the season, I'm jolted into a thought about Nobles."

Some reporters describe an emotional distancing that takes place, which may be seemingly adaptive during the execution, allowing them to focus on the level of detail required for their work rather than emotion. What may seem to be a healthy boundary at the time, however, can turn into dissociation, which is a psychological detachment from reality that proves to be an unhealthy defense mechanism. A study published in the *American Journal of Psychiatry* examined the experience of media witnesses to executions. After analyzing the responses of 15 journalists, it was concluded that dissociative symptoms were associated with serving as an eyewitness to an execution. Other signs of short-term trauma we also demonstrated.[196]

THERE ARE MANY OTHER participants that play a role in the capital punishment process who may be affected but were not mentioned in this chapter. There is a great need for research to better understand the needs of this population. These include prosecutors, governors, investigative personnel, individuals who testify during trials and many others. When one analyzes the ripple effect that even one execution has and the number of lives that it has impacted, there are numerous people—entire juries, judges, attorneys, participants, victims and families of the accused—that have suffered in vain, all for the sole purpose of punishing one individual.

PART IV
ADJUSTING TO
THE DARK

CHAPTER ELEVEN

THE BATTLE TO MAINTAIN SELF

By the time I reached my 22nd birthday, J-21 had stripped away everything from me that I ever possessed, except for my dignity and life principles. Although at times I doubted whether those things were worth salvaging at all, they remained.

—*Nanon M. Williams, Still Surviving*

FEAR AND TREPIDATION SETS in as a man begins his journey to what will be his new habitation. Life has ill-prepared him for the moment that the steel door closes and traps him in. At first, his mind begins to reassure him that he can handle the situation. Soon after, the realization sets in that home will be an inescapable steel tomb that would have to be managed so as to not overcome him.

In the prequel to this book *The Darkest Hour: Stories and Interviews from Death Row*, Christopher Coleman, who was executed Sept. 22, 2009, characterized his reaction upon his arrival to his cell on death row: "I got off the bus at the back gate, handcuffed and shackled from head to toe, like a beast. When I was later placed in a dirty-ass cell, my neighbor kept screaming over and over again. I just stood there looking around and thinking to myself, 'I have to do what I have to do,' and I meant that in regards to many things. Mainly knowing I had to preserve my sanity and to survive at all costs."[197]

The environment is quickly but carefully scanned and survival instincts kick in. A person is then forced to conduct an appraisal of his own internal coping resources that will be needed to survive the new harsh realities. "Survival" is a word that is often associated with the pain and trauma of living in isolation. In addition to the adjustment required to living in captivity, living in a prison *within* the prison, or on death row, adds additional burdens. In an interview with Michael Richard, whose controversial execution by the state of Texas took place on Sept. 25, 2007, the matter of survival was explored.

Nanon: "Do most people survive when they come to prison?"

Michael: "Depends on what you consider survival to be."

Nanon: "What is 'survival' to you?"

Michael: "Being able to remain who you are, keeping your own principles, maintaining dignity and not letting the racial poison destroy you."

Nanon: "Have you survived all of that?"

Michael: "In all honesty, maybe not. I've never given in to allowing others to pressure me into anything. I've been on the losing battle of physical violence, but I have always fought back. What response you want is a wonder to me, but I'm still around. I'm not crazy, stable by drugs or rubbing shit all over my face; so mentally I am strong."[198]

Although everyone has a different meaning of what survival looks like, the body interprets it all the same—life is at risk. Continued attempts at survival can feel like a large wave crashing in and knocking that individual down, leaving him breathless and disoriented, trying to fight with every internal resource to reach the surface for that rescue breath. But instead of a reprieve, a larger wave comes and fills the airways on that first gasp. The waves keep coming, and no one is there to help.

When an individual is exposed to a prolonged, ongoing and inescapable traumatic stressor, the body's physiological stress response is constantly deployed, and the brain does not get an opportunity to rest or recover before being faced with another stressor. As a consequence, for many individuals, the frontal cortex, which is responsible for higher order functions such as decision-making, impulse control, planning and regulation of behavior and emotion, becomes fatigued. Other structures, such as the hippocampus, which is implicated in memory, and the amygdala, which is involved in the fear response, can be damaged, rendering their ability to function as designed, challenged. To live in confinement means to exist in a perpetual state of heightened physiological reactivity. Self-preservation and threat reduction remains the brain's primary function at this high level of stress exposure. As a result, many individuals in isolation are often functioning in survival or "fight or flight" mode, and their behavior is aimed at reducing the perceived threat.

Coping, a term used to describe how people manage stressors, therefore, can mirror the state of desperation that is often experienced in solitary confinement. Ongoing and inescapable traumatic stressors, real or perceived, can overwhelm a person's ability to cope. There are tremendous variations in coping behaviors employed by individuals in confinement. One individual may be seemingly adapting well using one type of coping behavior, where another may do the same thing and falter at every turn. A person's ability to adapt and cope with the ongoing traumatic stress can depend on both internal and external factors. Internal factors can include genetics, age, biology, perception, history, mental and physical health, and personality factors among others. External factors that can be influential can include time spent in isolation, the harshness of the environment, opportunities for social connectivity and availability of needed resources.

According to The National Institute for Mental Health, "personality and cognitive factors, such as optimism and the tendency to view challenges in a positive or negative way, as well as social factors, such as the availability and use of social support, appear to influence how people adjust to trauma. More research may show what combinations of these or perhaps other factors could be used someday to predict who will develop PTSD following a traumatic event."[199] Countless research studies have focused on how people cope with stressful situations and why some people decompensate and others thrive under adverse conditions. Namely, what factors lend themselves to successful coping outcomes, as well as what specific strategies humans engage in when faced with stress. Some of the literature on coping has focused on adaptive versus maladaptive responses to stress. People who are living in survival mode in horrific environments are trying to continuously adapt to maladaptive situations. Behavioral responses should, therefore, be taken contextually in order to be understood. When behaviors are taken out of context, the needs are not addressed, and the consequences can negatively impact many people in the environment.

According to the National Institute of Mental Health, "Thus, while responses to chronic stress can clearly have negative consequences, one has to consider the possibility that they may solve pressing problems of the organism at the expense of future success. Chronic stress responses represent attempts at adaptation, but, as noted above, can constitute physiologic challenges in and of themselves."[200] There are many examples of individuals who are incarcerated chronically using drugs, such as heroin, LSD, amphetamines and downers, as a coping mechanism. There is no question that the behavior is destructive to the body; however, it represents an attempt to escape from the severe and monotonous environment of everyday life on death row or in solitary confinement. Wanting to escape is a rational desire.

Rather than thinking of coping mechanisms as adaptive or maladaptive, it can be more useful to conceptualize behavior as constructive versus destructive. A behavior can be adaptive and destructive at the same time. For example, several men have reported that they are only allowed to clean their cells with the same small square of soap that is provided for bathing. The same bar of soap that is used to clean the person's face and the rest of his body would also clean a toilet and the rest of the cell. When a person lives 23 hours per day in cell, it is normal to want control over as much of the environment as he can by keeping it sanitary and free from bacteria. In order to cope, the man may choose to commit a rule violation. Men will go through great lengths to obtain bleach for cleaning purposes. This is an adaptive response that can end up being destructive if a consequence is imposed for the rule violation. Many of the men will risk having privileges revoked, as well as other disciplinary action, in order to have a clean cell.

Opportunities to engage in constructive coping strategies that are known to mitigate the impact of the stress and assist in more long-term adaptation are highly limited in solitary confinement and death row. As a result, the individual's ability to buffer the impact of the trauma is significantly reduced, and the likelihood that their difficulties coping will create challenges to the others who are incarcerated, the staff, as well as cause self-harm is significantly increased. Desperately needed are strategies that can be taught and made available that will allow these individuals to cope, as much as the harsh situation allows, with the severe reality of their living environment without losing the core of who they are, their physical health and, most importantly, their sanity.

Religiosity and Spiritual Connectedness

Religious practices and spiritual connectedness have been proven by research to reduce recidivism and promote rehabilitation among incarcerated and previously incarcerated people. Spiritual connectedness can also foster a sense of newfound meaning that can be essential to survival.[201] Many incarcerated individuals find that a belief in a higher power can help sustain them. Others may rekindle past beliefs. Some seek redemption, forgiveness and spiritual consultation. For those who have received the death penalty, the prospect of death can be highly unsettling and questions about an afterlife are common. The ability for confined individuals to pursue their religious practices or seek spiritual guidance from a chaplain or spiritual guide, however, is very limited. According to the Texas Department of Criminal Justice public information officer, for example, "There are two chaplains assigned to units with 2,900 or more offenders; one assigned to the less populated units (under 2,900); and several smaller units share a unit chaplain. Chaplains minister to offenders at all custody levels including those on death row and administrative segregation."[202] Since this population of individuals is not permitted to leave their cells to attend services, their only option for spiritual counsel is through a chaplain that visits their cell. This option, however, is highly limited due to the nature of the cells' physical structure and barrier for proper and private communication caused by the small slot on the door, which serves as the only open passage for dialogue.

Connectivity

Connectivity and human interaction is known to be one of the most potent coping mechanisms and primal needs of all humans. Connectivity can be vital to coping and can have a tremendous impact on an individual's ability to regulate distress. Many incarcerated individuals have reported that having the ability to connect with the outside world, on any level, is what kept them sane. Connectivity allows them to maintain some orientation with time and society. Connection can come in the form of a social contact with friends, pen pals, loved ones or being able to follow current events through newspaper or radio.

Oswaldo Soriano related the importance of social connection to his survival on death row and in isolation: "The way I survived was through people that cared out in society, because even though you might be on death row, there are still some people who have compassion. When people tend to extend a hand, you are going to feel compelled to reach out. That is one of the ways I learned to survive, opened up to someone that cared in the world. It makes me realize where I went wrong. Another thing is that people learn to survive through visits. When their family, friends, loved ones or they get letters … it's the only way to survive."

In an excerpt from *Still Surviving*, Nanon reveals the importance that maternal relationships played in coping.

> "Have you ever thought about killing yourself, Khallid?" I asked.
> "No, not really. I have to stay strong for my mother, but if my Queen Mother ever died, well, I would probably give up my remaining appeals. My Queen Mother is all I have."
>
> How well I understood where he was coming from. "Me too, Bro. If my Mama wasn't suffering as I am, trying to gain my freedom so we could live together as a family again, I can't say I would have the desire to live either. My Mama is the voice that whispers "all is well," and I believe her. All is well as long as I know her love exists for me."[203]

Some incarcerated individuals do not have social support outside of prison. This can have devastating consequences on them. At any part of the incarceration process, it is possible that family, friends and loved ones can reject them for various reasons, perhaps as their own way of coping with the incarceration and the events leading up to their loved one's incarceration. Receiving a death sentence brings on an additional layer of fear that they will be abandoned by their family and the outside world.

Oftentimes, incarcerated individuals wait to see if their loved ones will still embrace them after they have been sentenced. Some families stand by their loved one, which can help motivate the men, and they may seek redemption, if only for their family. As a way to cope, many find meaning in taking care of their families, and reassure them that everything will be OK. When families reject the individuals and sever all ties, the process can take an entirely different trajectory.

Moving forward without support can be devastating. Nanon noted his observations: "Some men become more wayward, more suicidal, lash out and almost attempt to terrorize other people, or they go crazy. They feel like there is no one out there to carry the hope for them." Finding connection with other people on the inside serves as an important coping tool. Solidarity can serve as a lifeline between some of the men on death row. This form of connectivity can be a critical instrument in the coping process.

Coping, as opposed to survival, can mean different things to different people. It can mean staying mentally, physically and cognitively stable, continuing to find some meaning and hope in life, the ability to manage emotions and mood, and the ability to relate with others. Living on death row has been related to living in a hospice facility where it is common knowledge that everyone living there is going to die, and they are actively dying together. This commonality forms a unique type of bond that does not occur in any other part of the prison system environment. The men communicate through the vent shafts in their cells or scream down the hall in attempt to reach out and provide support for one another. In one description of solidarity Nanon recalls, "I needed them to survive and perhaps they needed me. We needed each other's personalities, emotions, laughter and the need to relate to each other when no one outside of those walls could understand. We mended each other, and we tore each other apart. We survived because of the natural human need to not be alone—to not feel alone despite the concrete walls and steel that separated us. This is how we coped. People bonded together. We had nothing to celebrate, but we suffered together. We needed to survive together. Few of us, however, survived."

On the day prior to his execution, a fellow death row inmate, Patrick Rogers-El was able to pass a letter to Nanon. Little did he know how impactful this letter would be.

My Dear Brother Nanon, (Yeah, I used your first name. Smile.)

I received your letter today, along with the love and concern for me. I truly don't know where this letter will take us, but for sure it's all out of love for you. Though I do not know what tomorrow will bring, I fear it not! I know what getting to know you has brought me in my life and death can never take that away.

My little big brother, you have taught me so much that these written words can never capture it all. You see, I have little brothers myself, and I see them in you every single day. Even when you think I don't see you, I see you through the window pacing in that single-man recreation yard, frustrated and angry. I often see a young man with deep thoughts, and more consciousness than a man your age should have. I see a young African warrior (even though you look like a Cuban, *smile*). Seriously, I see a young brother that tries to strive for something more than what death row has to offer, and it inspired me long ago when we used to sit up in solitary talking for hours at a time. Even when I would hear you sing in your cell at night, I knew you had a passion for life many do not have. (I bet you didn't know that I heard you, huh? I heard you very well, and it didn't sound bad.)

I never thought about how others looked at me; I only wished to live up to what I proclaimed to be and that is a Moor. I know we do not have the same religious beliefs but that didn't stop us from becoming friends. Early this morning, before I wrote my family final letters that said my goodbyes, I wrote a poem for every brother I knew over the years, and I had you in mind when I wrote it. The poem was called *Love in the Form of a Poem*, and hopefully you will see it in print one day. Whenever I write poetry, I always tried to write about the truth, as I see it. When I read your writings, they inspired me to push myself, because you were pushing yourself every day. I had always attempted to lead by example, but often I found myself following young warriors like yourself. No, I didn't mind, for I knew we were headed in the right direction, even when pain seared through my body causing me to suffer. It didn't matter though; we suffered together and never gave up!

Ego, I didn't possess. I humbled myself, for rare is it that any young man with a consciousness and a will to stand up for others appeared. I consider myself to be blessed to have been around you and a few more brothers like you. I truly miss you already as I sit in this deathwatch cell writing. My thoughts stay focused on my family, on you, and the rest of the brothers and their families. I know that your case got affirmed, but I somehow believe that you will be free one day. Don't ask me why. I know your family will still go through pain until that time comes. I think of my family going through that turmoil, and it hurts like anything anyone could imagine, but I know my little big brother understands. (smile).

L.A., (Nanon) you made my life here meaningful, for we have been able to grow as people, as men and as fellow human beings. When one was hurting, we felt the pain. We have all been able to inspire each other to achieve things we normally would not have attempted! So you must understand this, my young brother, I respect you and by my respecting you, it turned into love. But you made it easy for me to love you, my brother, because you respected yourself!

Me and the other brothers often speak of you, and they all respect you, so don't push yourself away from them when you are deep in your studies. They need your strength too, just like we all need each other's. If these people kill me tomorrow, I will tell the other brothers in heaven that you said hello, and I'll be watching over you. You have to stay strong for me and not do anything stupid when they execute me. I have done many wrongs in my life, but you helped me make them right by giving something back. You made me want to give something back.

I'm not ashamed to admit it, but I'm crying like a baby now as tears fall on this very same paper. I've always planned not to grow this close to anyone, but as time went on, nature took its course, and I grew close to many of you. L.A., don't be afraid to allow others in your life because you have so much to give, but knowing the way you are, you will continue to seclude yourself from the world. You can write some wonderful stories, so if you ever write about me and you, please share this letter with others as I wrote it. Promise me?

Yesterday, I gave an interview with *Dateline*, and I cried two times when I spoke of all of you. When the tears hit the floor, I wasn't even embarrassed, and I was on national television! But they were tears of reflection because I knew I would be leaving you all behind to battle the system without me. My tears were also tears of laughter that we shared, tears of pride in knowing some individuals true to themselves, and tears of joy for God blessing me to know you all. So yeah, I cried, cried, cried and will cry some more tonight, but I'm not ashamed because it doesn't make me any less of a man.

You know I also smashed America and their justice system, but most of them act like a bunch of Klansmen anyway. They also want to put a foot in the door in everyone else's business but can't get their own shit straight. I talked so bad about them all that I know they will edit the interview because they're scared of the truth!

I had a visit with my Queen Mother last week, and I call her Queen because that's what she is to me. Remember that woman that came to say hello to you while you were visiting your mother? Well, whether you knew it or not, that was my mother. I told her that you be trying to beat me up! And she asked me why? And I said because I beat you in basketball all the time! So then my mother said, so when he finally beats you in a game of basketball will you beat him up? And I said, "Mama, you know I'm non-violent," and she just looked at me and shook her head laughing.

You know my mother and auntie loved my bad ass no matter what, and when I see them tomorrow for the last time, I know it will be very hard.

I wish you could be out there with me, but who knows, maybe you will be. Man, I love you forever and always know that, OK? I want you to stay strong and keep up all the writing because we need a voice to tell people how it is, not how the system tells them it is. I'll be watching over you, little big brother, and send my love to all the rest of the brothers. I'll miss y'all.

Peace & Love,
Patrick Rogers-El

June 2, 1997, Rogers-el was executed and an indescribable grief filled death row once again. The letter is illustrative of the role that relationships can have in a person's ability to cope. Individuals can play an instrumental role in taking caring of and looking after each other. In a sense, they help each other regulate their own behavior and try to lift each other up when they are down, or calm them down when they are angry. Despite the serious obstacles to communication, they find a way to render aid to each other from behind a wall, trying to understand what they cannot see. Many of them monitor each other, and if they see something out of the ordinary or have not heard from someone for a while, they will notice and attempt to communicate. Not all men, of course, share this sense of camaraderie. There can be intense conflict and violence that occurs inside those walls, which is also a way to connect.

Opportunities for appropriate social connectivity are highly limited for those in solitary confinement, particularly those on death row who cannot have phone calls or contact visits. If the basic need for connectivity and interaction cannot be met, individuals, by nature, will try to find it. The ability to cope through connection, for some, means banging on the cell door in order to draw the attention of guards and the other men. The need to seek and receive connection in any form can outweigh rationality. Even explosions of violent outbursts hold the promise of a conflict with guards and can be more stimulating than sitting in solitary, feeling as though one's life is rotting away in inescapable monotony. Negative or painful physical contact often becomes more desirable than no physical contact.

Activity

The perpetual state of boredom and monotony can feel paralyzing. One form of coping comes through engaging in various types of activities, which can come in several forms. In his book, *Living in Prison: The Ecology of Survival,* Hans Toch describes the function of activity as a coping mechanism, "It can be a release for feelings, can distract attention from pain, or can keep the mind from being concerned with unpleasant thoughts or memories. Transcending survival needs, activity can provide goals, fulfillment, or scope for creativity."[204] Activity provides a mechanism. Exercise allows for a discharge of stress, energy and tension, which in turn, can promote self-regulation of the body and mind.[205] Many men locked in solitary confinement run in place, pace back and forth and conduct whatever exercise routines they are able to manage in their highly restrictive space. Some individuals engage in artwork to pass the time, and those who are literate often lose themselves in books. Others begin to study something that may better serve them in future, positive endeavors. Coping can also come in the form of writing such as poetry, articles, books and letters. These can all provide an outlet to escape the hardships and engage in self-care, even if it is only temporary.

When Oswaldo Soriano was on death row, he detailed how he spent his time prior to learning to read and write in English, "I can't write well now or even understand a lot of words, but I can draw stuff! It is my way of telling of my fears, my hopes and even my dreams. Art is even a way for me to be who I really am without having to realize that I am here to die."[206]

Incarcerated individuals often find that if they can structure their activities and time or engage in routines it is very helpful to them and can bring a sense of control over their environment. Dennis, whose name has been changed to remain anonymous, tells the story of how he coped in solitary.

SLAM!

Eyes fly open, ears hustling and filtering for human audio, inside the six by nine cell that's been home for decades. My mind tried to calculate the distance of the metal door slammed from the vibration just reaching my metal cot mounted to the steel bars. Best guess four doors down, which meant Rico must have returned after a two-week stint at the county hospital for his fifth attempted suicide. Since his arrival a year ago, the life without the possibility of parole broke Rico into attempting suicide.

Bright flashlight inspected the cell and then me, lying on my side supposedly sleeping.

Brass keys clattered.

Footsteps distancing.

At first, the isolation was traumatic. No one to talk to. Twenty-three hours a day trapped inside a concrete wall cell. Hours felt like years. Radio and books take the edge off. Sleep helps when I could manage to get some. Within the first week, I had measured my pace around the cell. Used a pencil to mark the day. Spent the waking hours trying to figure out when I turned into a speed demon. Was it running past the other kids every day to get to the ice-cream truck first? Or was it pedaling a bicycle to beat a car down the street? Or countless other acts just to be the first? Patience was not my virtue before prison, and the repetitious cycle of prison life angered me at first, but I learned over time that the anger didn't change a single thing. The guard opened the tray slot about four o'clock for breakfast every morning. Pancakes Monday and Wednesday, French toast Thursday and Sunday. Boiled eggs Tuesday. Scrambled eggs Thursday. And fried eggs Saturday. When the tray was picked up and the metal slot closed, I brushed my teeth and grabbed my pencil and marked another day on the wall.

Time taught me a lot. First, it never goes back. Always moving forward like a train down a long tunnel. One way to stop it was suicide, but I was too much a coward to carry that out. I wanted to make a difference someday. I just had to bide my time. Since I had smashed my watch in a fit of rage in county jail, I developed a mental clock. All I had to do was ask the guard the time when they delivered food, mail and made their rounds. I charted this for two weeks, then started pacing my in-cell activities. Then, I developed a routine of writing, reading, exercising, meditating, sleeping and listening to others ramble about their crime, prison lifestyle, family, girlfriends, wives, school, friends and whatever else they boastfully revealed.

Within months, my mental clock was within minutes of the actual time. Occasionally, I would track when someone like Rico attempted suicide or one of the prisoners on their way to medical or rec attacked a guard. Then I was back on my routine.

Footsteps.

Brass keys.

Clang.

Four o-clock.

Breakfast.

Tuesday. Boiled eggs.

Living in confinement can bear overwhelming feelings of powerlessness over the environment. The inability to make choices or have control in such seemingly minor things such as when the lights go on and off, when it is time to eat, when one can shower, when toilet paper is provided, whether or not one can invite conversation, can all take a devastating toll. Prolonged experiences of powerlessness are physically and emotionally damaging. Dennis established a method to feel like he had control over his environment by becoming highly attuned to his senses in a manner that oriented him to the activity in his periphery. He created a structure and an orientation to space and time that helped ground him and provide him with a sense of equilibrium and mastery.

Some men are unable to gain the same type of respite from the typical forms of activity, or those methods may not seem effective in reducing or ameliorating distress. Various types of activity are engaged in to break the monotony. Repeatedly flushing the toilet to watch the water drain, for example, can seem better than existing in their minds or holding an unpleasant thought. It provides stimulation of the mind and brings a new sensory experience. Orchestrating a fight or a conflict with the other men or guards can serve as another form of distraction, and at times, even entertainment for all of those who can hear, feel or witness it.

Detachment

While some individuals engage and fight the pain of confinement, others detach as a method of coping. From a physiological perspective, detachment can represent the "flight" escape part of the "fight or flight" response that is deployed upon exposure to trauma and chronic stress. Detachment can take many forms and can range in severity. Some examples might include avoidance, excessive sleep and withdrawal. Apathy can be another type of detachment that allows for a suppression of emotions and can be triggered by a sense of learned helplessness.

Drugs can be a powerful way to escape reality. Martin Draughon describes his experience with drugs on death row more than a decade ago.

> Myself, as with most prisoners, I was a drug and alcohol user and abuser when I got locked up. This attitude, desire, habit is still there when you get locked up. The only reason you're not still using is because you've been removed from the dope. But then there comes a time when you discover it's there in prison too, and you seek it out.

> I am not sure if drugs and alcohol usage of "the row" was an act of escapism or simply a coping mechanism (or if there is even a difference). I've smoked pot, popped pills, acid, smoked crack and learned to make wine. Ironically enough, I never smoked or even saw crack before death row. I'm recalling an experience when I laid on my mattress on the floor for at least 12 straight hours because the physical weight of my predicament was so heavy it was preventing me from getting up or even moving after I'd eaten three hits of acid. That was very intense. There was merely an "existing" on the row; no classes or self-betterment programs of any kind. Not even church service. Why not get high? It breaks the torturously slow monotony of ... being locked in a concrete room ... indefinitely. There came a time for me when I was getting stoned regularly. One day, I realized I was too stoned to write

a letter, so I kicked back with a book. Later I realized I had just read 20 or more pages and didn't remember a darn thing I had just read. I thought to myself, "this is boring!" That was a revelatory moment and turning point in my life. As soon as I had that thought another thought popped up that went: "Well, why are you still doing it stupid?" So I gave away my weed I had left. Could've easily sold it, but I didn't. Just got rid of it.

Not the end of the story however, because now that I wasn't getting high I quickly slipped into bad depression. I sought out the unit psych person and eventually I got antidepressants. After trying several, I found one that didn't make me sleep and didn't amp me up, just alleviated my anger and frustration, which produced the depression—because there's no outlet for anything on the row. Essentially, I just traded the illegitimate dope and getting high for a legitimate dope and coping mechanism.

When I left the row, I wanted a clean break and fresh start, and so I willingly went cold turkey and shunned all pills and dope of any kind. I've not gotten high or had any pharmaceuticals now in many years. There's smoke and pills and wine available all around me still, but thank God, it no longer entices me or has any pull on me whatsoever. For this, I am very thankful.

Martin was able, at some point, to recognize that he needed help, and reached out for it. A decision that led to his recovery. Martin realized that he needed to address his underlying issues of depression. Not everyone, however, has this level of emotional intelligence, fortitude and self-awareness to be able to seek help. Given that 12-step programs such as Alcoholics Anonymous are not available to death row inmates, people with the disease of addiction often go untreated.

In its extreme form, detachment can progress to severe symptoms that cause a pathological break in reality known as dissociation. Dissociation can occur in the context of an overwhelming traumatic event, such as a rape, where a person might report feeling as though they were watching it occur from above while it was happening. Others describe it as though they went to a different place in their mind, not experiencing the rape in actuality. Others have described it as a type of numbing that occurs. Dissociation can also occur after the event, in the form of flashbacks, for example, that the body can experience as real, even though the stressor might have passed. Dissociation is defined by Eric Vermetten and David Spiegal as "A complex phenomenon that comprises a host of symptoms and factors, including depersonalization, derealization, time distortion, dissociative flashbacks, and alterations in the perception of the self."[207]

A person who is dissociating can appear to be ignoring the other person, which can be interpreted as rebellion. This behavior can also appear to others that the person is glazing over without focus. Some individuals may fly into a rage, appearing completely out of control. The manners by which dissociation manifests differ per individual. The ultimate form of detachment comes when a person develops a disregard for his own life and the life of others. There is nothing to risk and nothing to lose. Death seems, in these instances, the only way to cope, they no longer run from it, they run to it in order to ease the pain. Death is their only chance at freedom.

Overriding the Pain

In the book, *The Darkest Hour: Stories and Interviews from Death Row*, Christopher Coleman, who was eventually executed, explained to Nanon, "Sometimes my anger overrides any fear I have of things so I don't really know what I truly fear. A way to cope with emotion is to cover it up with something less painful and more powerful, like anger." Anger is an emotion that can feel more powerful than sadness or fear. Anger can make a person feel alive and can serve as an escape from emotional pain. In one example, Nanon describes the function of his anger on death row:

> "I must stay strong!" I told myself aloud. The anger seemed at times to be my only ally. It gave me a surging strength when nothing else did. But even the anger took on an existence of its own, at times abandoning me and being constantly re-born into a destructive state until I waged a battle within myself to tame it. I sometimes failed.[208]

Physical pain, for some individuals, can feel more palatable than emotional pain. Physical pain enables these men to escape the emotions and focus on something more salient. Therefore, self-inflicted injuries or intentionally stirring up conflicts that will lead to violent outcomes can be a way to cope. But only for a while.

Fighting for Dignity

> When I hobbled to the concrete in my gorilla-like stance, two guards rushed to my sides and grabbed my arms. One of them was a large black woman three or more inches taller than me. Other guards stood ahead holding batons, shields and pepper spray, as if itching for a problem to arise so they could use their cowardly weapons, but no problems arose. I hobbled inside a building that was all white and clean, and there stood many more guards.

"On your knees," the large, black woman said.

I shook my head and reluctantly obeyed her command. She removed the shackles first, then the handcuffs, and finally the other chains.
"Strip," she said.

I took off the prison jumpsuit, boxer shorts, socks and shoes. I then dropped what remained in the bag, and I stood there, butt-ass naked as the day my Mama gave birth to me.

The large, black woman grinned, "Run your fingers through your hair. OK, now lift your nuts. Now turn around and spread 'em."

I ran my fingers through my hair. I lifted my nuts as she stared openly and unmercifully at me. But then, we came to a roadblock.

"I ain't spreading nothing," I said, standing up straight, no longer conscious of my nakedness.

Her face softened, and she smiled. "It's my job, Inmate," she said.
"Well, it's my dignity," I replied.

"What's your name?" she asked as other guards moved closer, wondering what the holdup was.

I was surprised that she didn't ask for my number too, so of course I did not offer it. "My name is Nanon Williams," I said.

"What's your number?" she asked. "Oh never mind, I found it."

I was just standing there as more prisoners came in behind me and were also told to strip.

"Is there a problem?" another guard asked.

"There's no problem," she said. "Go ahead and get dressed, Williams."[209]

There were many other occasions in which tear gas, tasers, loss of privileges, cell extraction teams and other means were used when Nanon refused an anal cavity search. All of the ongoing, excruciatingly painful punishments, however, took a back seat to his dignity. Many perceived his behavior as stubbornness and could not understand why he did not just give in like everyone else. Dignity is a human quality that is vital to survival and self-efficacy. Yet it is difficult to hold on to in these environments where there is a chance to lose it at every turn. In order to cope with this reality, some men will go to any lengths to keep it, and others will eventually lose their grip.

Individuals who are incarcerated lack ownership of anything material. They, themselves, are property of the state. All of their personal possessions are property of the state and are subject to inspection and can be taken away or defaced at any time. When an individual has nothing in his world that is tangibly his, he may do everything within his power to maintain what is invisible and impossible for anyone to take away without surrender. Once dignity and self-efficacy is lost, helplessness prevails and there is nothing left to hold on to. Having dignity is a basic human need and many will go through any means necessary to hold on to it. Many men will resort to violence before they will allow anyone to rob them of the only thing that is left for them to protect and control.

Nanon described his desire to maintain his dignity when he arrived on death row, "I want to go home, I thought to myself. I was no badass. I was scared of what death row would be like, and deep down I didn't want to go to the wing called J-21. However, I wouldn't let anyone run over me, whether they were wearing a gray uniform like the prison guards or white prison garb like the other prisoners wore. I would keep my dignity and stand by my principles, no matter what the consequences, because I didn't have much else."[210]

Some men carried their dignity and principles through to the very end. In one account, Ponchai Wilkerson refused to walk to his own execution.

Holding true to his word, Ponchai would not participate in his execution. He wanted it to be known that if he walked to his death, it would very well be an execution. But, if he resisted any attempt to take him to the execution chamber, it would not be an execution; it would be murder.

At noon, the 14th of March 2000, Ponchai resisted all attempts to willingly walk to his death. In fact, he was sprayed with gas repeatedly as a five-member "cell extraction team" of guards wearing helmets, shields and protective gear and wielding steel batons, rushed into his cell. After beating him and continuously spraying him with neutralizing gas, Ponchai held onto the steel plate door, but was finally dragged away unconscious.[211]

Meaning, Growth and Hope

Formerly on death row and now serving a life sentence, Gabriel Gonzales has endured much suffering in his many years in Texas prisons. In the letter below, he describes his personal search for meaning in life.

If one can manage to find the internal fortitude to withstand the attack that death row is on one's humanity, in facing death in such a manner, you eventually reach a point where you begin to ask yourself: Who am I? What is the purpose of my life and life in general? What is the purpose of my suffering? What is the purpose of death? And as a father you ask yourself, if I died today, what can I say I left behind for my children that enriches them on every level long after I'm dead and gone? These questions turned my death row experience into a journey of self-discovery ... I turned this man-made hell into my personal sanctuary of growth and development. As you read this, I ask you to bear in mind that I am a man who could not read or write when I first arrived to death row; I taught myself. I am also a man who was never taught the subjects of life in prison, for death row and prison are not places truly made to rehabilitate, but to slaughter. What you read is my own personal growth and development through my own journey. In my answers, I discovered a higher calling and being in life. On death row and in prison, men are "alive" and subsist; so does a man in a coma. In the face of oppression and death, here and beyond. I have made that choice not just to be alive and subsist, but to feel, learn, grow, live and love. Hence why I feel I have changed for the better, and my death row experience was the catalyst to that change.

It is an undisputed fact that prolonged and ongoing exposure to traumatic stressors can cause severe distress, psychological and physical impairments. Although everyone who encounters adversity experiences distress, some are able to demonstrate well-being and even signs of resiliency and growth. How people cope, in the face of adversity has been a subject of intense study. The question has often been posed, "What makes two people living in the same traumatic situation cope completely differently?" One person, for example, may show high levels of mental and physical deterioration, where another may exhibit characteristics of adaptation, resiliency or growth.

HAVING LIVED MORE OF his life in prison than out of prison for a murder that all evidence shows Nanon did not commit, his own search for meaning has been challenging, yet persistent. "I know the work ahead will impact the lives of others and to me, yeah, that means something. My mom always tells me God uses me. Sometimes I need to believe that. I need to believe it when I don't feel like getting out of bed. No matter how tired I am I can be strong enough to be encouraging enough to impact the lives of others. I will give my best despite the hell so many live in. These things are within my reach."

Traumatic events often leave people feeling powerless, having no sense of control over what is happening to them. It is human nature to derive meaning from traumatic events and to question why these things happen. Finding answers and creating meaning can give people a sense of control and security. Oftentimes, a person will assign meaning based on their own personal value system, beliefs, culture and other past experiences. The way an individual seeks explanations can be associated with how a person processes and copes with the personal trauma.

While searching for meaning, some find a greater purpose to their adversity. Some, for example, may find comfort feeling as though God has a bigger plan for them, or that they are experiencing this suffering so that they can help others. This type of coping behavior is reflected in acts such as teaching, mentoring and learning. The capacity for human suffering can always be tested, but the lessons we learn about survival from individual experiences are invaluable. There are countless stories of those who have maintained hope and bettered themselves. There are also individuals who report that they have grown and inspired others, even though they knew that they would die in prison, alone. Nanon shares how he finds meaning and purpose by being of service to others.

It didn't become about my personal interests, it became about making promises to guys who are no longer here to write about them and share what was meaningful to them. I felt like I owed them something because I was their voice. I want to show that you can take the worst of us, and we could become the best of us. It didn't matter what people thought of me, my actions would speak louder than words. I was a reject. I have a capital sentence, and people say I will rot in prison. Why do I work toward an education, why do I pay for this even though I will rot here? If I can do this, I hope I will restore hope for other guys. I take all the guys here and look for the strength. You hear grown men say they would be proud to get their GED diploma. They want to be acknowledged, not *only* be punished. As long as you have breath, you can overcome all obstacles.

Gabriel Gonzales shares how he seeks to find meaning and purpose:

My spirituality, the love and support of my family, and a few great friends help me move forward. Writing poetry has also been very therapeutic. My beliefs are also a sustaining factor.

The greatest tragedy in life is not death, but a life without purpose. Therefore, seek knowledge of self.

If at the end of the day someone realizes that the human experience is the same all around the world, that we all suffer and struggle, seek to love and be loved, seek to bring happiness and be happy, to understand who we are and why we are here and feel closer to the whole of humanity, then I've been of service to humanity and I'm happy.

Being of service to others can foster a sense of dignity, identity and self-worth. Richard Tedeschi, a leading expert in the area of post-traumatic growth explains, "Those who can figure out how to have a rich internal life can do well. They have to set some type of task for themselves without having something to do. They find meaning from these things. Living with dignity is meaningful. They have the power to create good things in others; it gives them life. It goes beyond themselves."

In *Man's Search For Meaning,* Victor Frankl, as a prisoner in a Nazi concentration camp, answered some important questions about survival through adversity, through his own observations. He theorized that it was those individuals who had the capacity to attribute any sense of meaning to their experiences in the death camps who were more likely to survive their horrifying conditions. It was this search for meaning, that enabled those individuals to maintain hope in the in the midst of adversity."[212] Some incarcerated individuals find meaning and a sense of power in activism. Writing books on the death penalty or prison issues, newsletters, creating or becoming members of activist organizations and being advocates for a cause are all ways that individuals can be involved in making the situation better for themselves or others.

Proving oneself can also be a purpose that enables an individual to cope. There is no harsher judgment than being told that your life is worth nothing and needs to be exterminated. Judges and prosecutors have used the words, "evil," "monster" and "animals" in capital trials to describe the individuals. For some of the individuals, the rest of their lives will be spent proving they are not evil, nor are they monsters or animals. In deed and action, activities that are aimed at correcting the labels are fervently engaged in. Masterful artworks and writings are created to demonstrate talent, obtaining an education to demonstrate intelligence and being of service to others, to demonstrate humanity can become the underworking of a purposeful life, spent to prove others wrong, and perhaps, to prove it to themselves and their families.

IN FINDING MEANING TO their traumas, incarcerated individuals construct personal narratives to describe their histories and reasons for moving forward through their adversities. Their life stories, or narratives, are subjectively written by the person who has experienced them, through their own eyes. Stories contain protagonists and antagonists and can be analyzed through the lens of a universal story structure. How individuals convey their histories through their narratives can play a part in leading them to have positive and altruistic behaviors. [213]

A research study focusing on narratives examined two different forms by which people build their life stories. "Redemption and contamination sequences are identifiable narrative forms that appear in life-story accounts. When telling their life stories, people will sometimes juxtapose clearly negative events with positive outcomes (redemption sequences) and highly positive events with negative outcomes (contamination sequences). In two samples, evidence was obtained to suggest that redemption and contamination sequences in life stories are meaningfully associated with independent self-reports of psychosocial adaptation."[214] Other studies also confirm the relationship between redemption meanings in adverse situations and well-being. [215]

Gabriel's story is an example of a redemption sequence, whereby his negative experiences allowed for some level of positive outcome that he described at the time of his writings. Oswaldo Soriano also viewed his work as a type of redemption. When asked how he felt about his pending execution, he responded, "Denial, I think. No, really, I just take it a day at a time, and I try to keep busy writing to leave as much of myself behind as I can. I know my words have touched many hearts since I have been locked up. That's my legacy. That's redemption of sorts." Through the lens of redemption and purpose, he was able to keep going and engaging in productive and healthy coping behaviors.

An example of a narrative that contains a contamination sequence may occur when an incarcerated person experiences having a new family member such as the birth of a child or relative. Positive feelings are experienced, however, the story changes when the true reality sets in that he may never be able to hold that child or be a parent, grandparent, sibling or uncle to the child. A negative outcome, therefore, may result.

Being of service to others and having a purpose is instrumental to healthy coping. When the greater purpose feels important, persevering can come naturally. In *Still Surviving*, Nanon writes about coping:

> Over the years when people have asked me, "How do you do it?" referring to the will to survive under such mind-boggling circumstances. I never tell them the truth. I have often lied to myself, "Oh, it's nothing. Just another day." But there have been times that I have wondered if dying would be much easier. Each time my mother, my grandma and papa have visited, I smiled so they could see that I'm well, but I know my eyes deceive me. Perhaps true courage is the ability to just openly cry and let the pain flow away in a river of tears and hope that time will heal the pain like my body hides the scars. But no, I have to be strong. My loved ones have carried us all on their backs for too long.[216]

STORIES OF GROWTH AND hope through adversity in the context of confinement and in the wake of death are remarkable. Malcolm, whose name has been changed to protect his privacy, shared his story.

I knew that I was going back to solitary confinement. I was released from solitary confinement the last time and since nothing had changed, as far as my gang affiliation, a life of solitude was my destiny. As I laid in my bunk, resigned as the reality finally made its appearance. It was a crippling thing, this sensation that a huge hole had been punched through my chest, excising my most vital organs and leaving ragged, unhealed gashes around the edges that continued to throb and bleed despite the passage of time. Rationally, I knew my lungs must still be intact, yet I gasped for air and my head spun like my efforts yielded me nothing. My heart must have been beating too, but I couldn't hear the sound of pulse in my ears. My hands felt blue with cold. I curled inward, hugging my ribs to hold myself together. I scrambled for my numbness, my denial, but it evaded me. And yet, I found I could survive. I was alert. I felt the pain—the aching loss of my freedom that radiated from my chest, sending wracking waves of hurt through my limbs and head—but it was manageable. I could live through it. It didn't feel like the pain had weakened over time, rather I'd grown strong enough to bear it.

Whatever it was that had happened that night—and whether it was the past memories, the present situation I found myself in or the fact that I understood what I wanted for my future that was responsible—it had wakened me up.

For the first time in a long time, I didn't know what to expect in the morning. Some people would look at the life of solitary confinement as hell on Earth. Some would not be able to live that life if forced into it. But others take it and use it as a chance to better understand one's self and create or find the person they know they can be. The nature of solitary confinement removes the everyday responsibilities and distractions from a person's life. Thereby, forcing the person to become more introspective as the days of solitude roll.

All the time that one spends alone has an effect that is either positive or negative. There are a lot of things to deal with that most people will never know about, due to hectic schedules and the demands of life. For me, the days were long. Every day I was faced with challenges and thoughts. I strived for anything to teach me and to learn from. I did not want life to pass me up. So I engaged my life in ways that would help me to continue living and to do right.

On Aug. 29, 2006, I completed and received a Legal Assistance/Paralegal Diploma. Hardship is the key to make some of us wake up.

I had to go through a program to get back to population after serving eight years in solitary confinement this time. The program is called GRAD, an acronym for Gang Renunciation and Disassociation. The program is nine months long. I successfully completed the program in October 2008. The program and classes have taught me both the positive and negatives about life. I have made poor decisions in the past, of which I am not proud. I have since learned to make positive decisions in negative situations. I have chosen to be an acceptable member within the institution, and I look forward daily to sharing my positive outlook with others. The programs and the undying support from my family, in addition to understanding the entire experience that brought me here, have helped me to realize that living in this situation is not the environment I choose to be a part of. Until I am released from prison, I will do my best to stay focused on my goals and be of help to those whom I can help.

Although people find individual ways to deal with their traumatic environments, coping strategies alone cannot fully prevent damage from occurring. In her book *Solitary Confinement*, author Lisa Guenther, posits, "All of these strategies are partial solutions or coping mechanisms, and they are vitally important as such, but they do not in themselves diminish the violence of intensive confinements." She also explains, "Even those who, like Robert King [case example used in the book], manage to survive solitary confinement and even to emerge with great strength and dignity are haunted by their experience. To be 'still there' in one's prison cell, years after release, is to have one's Being in the world altered by the spatial and temporal dimensions of confinement."[217]

IN HIS BOOK *STILL SURVIVING,* Nanon describes the often elusive sense of hope and the will to always cling to it. "Even when we could see no light at all and hope seemed to elude our grasp, we still stumbled in the darkness searching and searching for some inkling of hope to grasp onto. Sometimes we could still hear the cries of the damned calling out to us, along with the cries of the forsaken who once roamed these very same halls trying to find a reason to keep going, to keep searching, to keep living."

Finding even a minuscule of hope in such a dark place can be an extraordinarily difficult task. Hope is a motivator to keep moving forward. Yet without hope, darkness takes over and gives way to helplessness, which inevitably brings about despair, depression and loss of the will to live.[218] In the days and weeks before the execution of Kevin Varga, he chronicled his emerging thoughts and feelings. It seems that one of the things that got him through, were the rays of hope that a stay of execution would be granted. As the grim reality set in that his death would not be stopped, fear took over.

> One more day closer to insanity. I have tried to stay positive and keep hope alive. Then the day passes with no word on a stay of execution and the hope dies within and the insanity grows once more. How soon before I am talking to the walls and they actually answer back? I have heard it stated that if you question your own sanity then you are not insane. I am beginning to doubt that statement. I am spiraling down into darkness. I know this and cannot do anything to stop that downward spiral. Knowing helps not at all. I do not think I will ever be the insane person who makes a hand puppet with my sock and listens to its every utterance as if it were the word of God. There are so many degrees of insanity. I know only a single cure for the insanity I feel growing within me, and that is to be granted either a stay of execution or to have my sentence commuted to life. Then I feel that I will no longer have these insane thoughts. It is a subtle thing, my insanity. I guess it may just be the thoughts of what comes next after the poison stops my heart beating. Is there truly a kingdom of gold as it stated in the Bible? Is there a hell awaiting me because I am a mean and nasty person? Is there only oblivion, a rotting piece of meat in the ground and nothing else? The only ones who really know the answers to these questions are the dead, and I cannot seem to get any straight answers out of them. I have heard so many people tell me, "everyone dies …" well, until it is them who has to lie on a table and just wait until that poison drips into my heart, I cannot listen to them. I do not fear the actual killing (murder) the state will perform upon me; it is what comes after that has me lying in my bed in a cold sweat at night. I feel that if God truly has a kingdom of gold that I will be welcomed, albeit to the slums as, let's face it, I am not a high class kind of guy here. But the Bible states that the poorest in heaven are richer than the richest man on Earth. That is something I could definitely live with. 15 days to live.[219]

For those who are imprisoned, their hope is freedom—either from the internal or external chains that bind them. For many on death row, hope can come in the form of the appeals processes, believing that perhaps, execution is not going to happen to them. One person can be enough to bring the light of hope and carry it. Many attorneys, advocates, loved ones or family members serve this function and bring tremendous value. Hope grounds an individual to the earth. Without hope, death can become something to look forward to. How then, does one find hope when they know that they are condemned to die, or spend years, or a lifetime in solitary confinement? How can someone find hope when everyone around him, one by one, is being executed?

The answer is not a concrete one. Some find peace in places where others cannot. Some hoist themselves up on the branches of hope and find everything that life has to offer and soak up every bit of it. Opening the door of hope creates an opportunity for change and growth. Without it, there is nothing to lose.

PART V
CALL TO ACTION

CHAPTER TWELVE
WAYS FORWARD

A CALL TO ACTION

Throughout history, it has been the inaction of those who could have acted; the indifference of those who should have known better; the silence of the voice of justice when it mattered most; that has made it possible for evil to triumph.

—Haile Selassie

ABSORBING THE VOLUME OF information detailed in this book can prove to be overwhelming on many levels. When a person examines human rights issues, the injustices can feel so large and so insurmountable that they may feel impossible to hold and consequently lead to feelings of helplessness and paralysis. One can acknowledge and feel deeply for the inhumanities that are occurring globally, but also feel incapable of doing anything that would make any difference. For these, among other reasons, people walk away from injustices. They turn a blind eye, or worse, they refuse to even bear witness to the suffering of others.

Every person holds the power to have a profound effect on the lives of others. One powerful and simple way that we can do that is by shifting our own consciousness as it relates to those in society who have caused harm to others. All too often, we reduce our thinking to the lowest common denominator by categorizing people as a result of their own behavior or as a result of what has been done to them. Society is quick to label someone who has committed a violent crime—and those sentenced to prison for non-violent crimes—as monsters, evil, worthless, etc. Most people refer to individuals who are incarcerated as "perpetrators," "prisoners," "convicts," "inmates" or "offenders." In prison, they are spoken directly to by using their numbers to name them, or the word "inmate," not their names. Not only is this dehumanizing, but it also creates a dangerous form of depersonalization and distancing.

Within this book, those words are only used within a quote. These labels reduce individuals to the sum of their worst behavior, which has been heavily influenced by many variables such as abuse, neglect, poverty, oppression, addiction, mental health and developmental problems, lack of access to resources, education, and many other physical and psychological factors. We erase our responsibility as members of society to play a role of support to those who need it most with a simple label.

The language we use to describe a person shapes our attitudes and actions toward that person. Language also impacts the way that individuals view themselves, and each other, which then impacts their behavior. It is difficult to respect someone who does not call you by your name. By labeling individuals who are incarcerated as "prisoners" and "offenders" we imprison them and ourselves to all the attitudes, expectations, emotions and social belief systems assigned to the word. Labeling individuals provides a subtle sense of permission to treat the person in a way that some believe to be appropriate to the label.

For many individuals in society, nothing separates them from the individuals in prison other that the fact that they were not caught in their crimes, or not prosecuted, yet some people on the outside often feel better than and more deserving of those on the inside. In addition, the connotations behind these labels do not permit others to view these individuals as being capable of change, or having the ability to contribute to society, despite many examples to the contrary. As a consequence, we can lose faith in them as people, believe they are not capable of doing good and treat them accordingly. Holding the mindset that individuals are incapable of growth and redemption significantly impairs rehabilitative efforts. Creating an expectation, however, of recovery, change and productivity fosters an environment in which this rehabilitation can flourish. Each of us carries the responsibility of asking ourselves whether our attitudes, language and actions are contributing to injustices, or are they acting in opposition to the gross inhumanities that occur behind those walls and impact our communities.

A SIMPLE ACT OF kindness in the lives of these individuals and their loved ones can have a tremendous ripple effect. What is a grand gesture to one person may be a small gesture to another, yet the effect that action has is equally powerful. The individuals involved in creating this work have experienced this firsthand. Each person gave what he or she had to give, and in doing so, together, have touched the lives of many. Explore within yourself what causes you to turn a blind eye to injustice. Is it fear, vulnerability, paralysis, not knowing where to dive in, feeling like you are the only one, feeling inadequate or too busy, feeling like the problem is to big? We are all called to be change-makers. What are you called to change? Find out what you are passionate about and ask yourself if you are making a difference in those areas, whether it is this cause or others. What is holding you back, and why?

The authors of this book are asking you to not walk away from such gross inhumanities and human rights abuses that are occurring not only in the state of Texas, but also across this nation and around the world. To help individuals who want to be a part of a positive solution, this chapter outlines ways forward— actionable steps individuals, groups and systems can take. Every reader, if so called, should be able to close this book identifying something that he or she can do to make a difference. Whether you are called to address this issue systemically or to work on an individual level by touching the life of one death row inmate, one person in solitary confinement or one family. Every action has a ripple effect. Every action makes a difference in the lives of others. This chapter is organized by demographics of people and systems. For example, individuals who are the loved ones and family of people who are incarcerated may find helpful ideas in the "Families and Loved Ones" section. Concerned citizens will find guidance in the "Concerned Citizens" section, and so on.

Families and Loved Ones

Five Mualimm-ak was in solitary confinement for five of the 12 years of his incarceration. He was confined in a windowless, gray concrete cell for simple rule violations such as having more than seven pencils, which he used to illustrate portraits. Mualimm-ak was released from solitary directly onto the streets when his prison sentence ended. He is now the program director of Incarcerated Nation Campaign, a grassroots movement comprised of formerly incarcerated persons, family members of those currently incarcerated, activists, students and advocacy organizations who work to educate the community on issues of mass incarceration, improve conditions for the incarcerated and their families and create a support base of re-entry for individuals returning to the community. Mahatma Gandhi taught that we should all be the change we want to see in the world; Mualimm-ak is doing just that as he works tirelessly to bring support to those affected by prison systems while also educating the public, nonprofits and politicians on the injustices of solitary confinement and offering guidance for how to create change.

"Family members and loved ones of those incarcerated need to unite to support each other in this battle, because we are stronger together. Family members should be involved with groups not as members but as leaders. Their voice is of personal experience and is invaluable in this fight. This will require that the family sacrifice their time and resources to be that voice for their loved ones," explained Mualimm-ak.

Family and loved ones represent a very important, sometimes life-saving connection to the outside world, yet they often feel helpless. They can have a positive effect on the lives of their incarcerated loved ones by doing the following:

- Maintain regular, consistent and predictable correspondence. Individuals who are incarcerated need routine, and something to look forward to.
- Maintain regular, consistent and predictable visitation and hold steady on your commitments to do so. If you are unable to visit them due to distance, contact a local church or support organization that can maintain regular contact.
- Help your loved one maintain connections in the outside world, including providing updates on current events.
- Create social media opportunities for them to share their writings, artwork etc.
- Connect your loved ones to outside advocacy organizations or pen-pal programs (see resources).
- Provide your loved ones with money to purchase basic necessities such as hygiene items, paper for drawing, food and stamps.

Perhaps the most important action that loved ones can take is to simply remain connected. Nurture the relationship with your loved one and help him know that he has not been forgotten. People often want to protect those who are incarcerated from hearing about news in the free world, when in fact news of the free world builds a bridge to all that was lost.

Concerned Citizens
Demand Transparency

Citizens and lawmakers must insist upon greater transparency from Texas Department of Criminal Justice and private prisons that systematically push the public out. According to Lisa Guenther, associate professor of philosophy at Vanderbilt University and author of *Solitary Confinement: Social Death and its Afterlives*, the public must demand transparency from prisons.

> Prisons must become more transparent. Not only with their data, but also in allowing the actual conditions of confinement cells and treatment of inmates to be seen and made public. Texas Department of Criminal Justice does not allow media to enter death row or enter an isolation cell. The domestic back sites of our prison systems must be open to the media and to public scrutiny. Currently, "security concerns" trump the public's right to know what is being done in our own name, and for the sake of our apparent safety. But in order to evaluate whether public interests are truly being served by current policies, and whether the civil rights of people in prison are being respected, we need more information and more open dialogue about what is happening in our prisons, jails and detention centers.

One of the many areas that require complete transparency is the execution process. There are ongoing questions about current protocols in Texas, and although questions are not being answered, Texas denies secrecy. The agency refuses to release information about where they are obtaining the execution drug or which alternative drugs they have in their supply in the event that they run out of phenobarbital. Texas Department of Criminal Justice reports that revealing the sources of the drug would put the employees of that company at risk because of previous threats to employees who provided the drug to the agency. A report by the Associated Press revealed that there is "no evidence of an investigation by police agencies into threats to the pharmacies."[220] Concerned citizens should continue asking questions from TDCJ as well as conveying your concerns, by calling and emailing the TDCJ public information office (contact information can be found on the web at http://tdcj.state.tx.us/divisions/pio/index.html), and by reaching out to Texas state legislators. Find your state representatives and their contact information here http://www.fyi.legis.state.tx.us/Home.aspx.

Support Prison Reform Legislation
Citizens must encourage their state and federal lawmakers to support legislation that provides alternatives to solitary confinement and promotes rehabilitative practices. Legislative reform across the country is taking a step in the right direction toward recognizing the need to curb the use of solitary confinement, particularly as it applies to vulnerable populations. Several states have passed laws to reduce the use of harmful isolation practices. Approximately 80,000 people, however, are living in solitary confinement cells in the United States.[221] Most of the people living in solitary confinement will be released into their respective communities with little to no assistance in successfully reintegrating.

In Texas, a few bills have been introduced and lawmakers are expressing concerns about the impact that the practices may have on the community.

- In 2011, HB3764 passed through committee, but the bill did not make it to the House floor for vote. Had this bill become law, it would have required TDCJ to submit an annual report to the legislature on the use of solitary confinement in order to create a plan to improve confinement conditions.[222]
- Authored by Senator John Carona, Senate Bill 1003 requires that the Criminal Justice Legislative Oversight Committee, "subject to the availability of funds from gifts, grants and donations," appoint an independent party to review the use of administrative segregation (i.e., solitary confinement) in state juvenile and adult prison. Per the bill, the independent reviewer was to report

to lawmakers in December 2014 with recommendations to reduce the use of solitary; however, the oversight committee was not funded, and therefore, the independent study was never deployed.[223]

Contact Your Legislators and Texas Department of Criminal Justice

Many people feel intimidated or powerless to contact their state or federal representatives, yet it is important to remember that these individuals work for the people they represent. Although it can be challenging to make a connection with your representatives, persistence is the key. Call them, write them, follow them on social media and engage with them. Most likely, each attempt at connecting with your representative will trigger a form letter response from his or her office. Do not allow that automatic response to serve as a legitimate response by allowing it to thwart your efforts. Be persistent and send the message to your representative that these are matters that must be urgently addressed. A sample letter, written by Five Mualimm-ak, is provided in the resource section of this book. Use this as a guide, but personalize it as you see fit.

TDCJ must be continuously informed of concerns from citizens. In response to the letter from the union president regarding concerns over death row practices, a *Texas Observer* article cites, "TDCJ spokesman Jason Clark said the agency has an ongoing practice of periodically reviewing its policies and that it is 'currently reviewing and updating the Death Row Plan.' In an email, Clark said, 'As with any input from the public, the agency will review the information.'" It is imperative, therefore, that input from the public be persistent and ongoing.

Know the Facts and Create Awareness

Historically, fear has been used to maintain social order and survive. Popular media perpetuates fear and defines public perception regarding what and who needs to be feared. Likewise, public perception of fear feeds the media.[224] Politicians and their constituencies are influenced by the fear of crime in their communities. Individuals and laws that are considered to be "soft on crime" have not gleaned votes, and being "tough on crime" has often gained bipartisan support. Be mindful of whether or not you are allowing fear or personal experience to dictate your views on crime and punishment for all. Learn the facts on the issues you are interested in and understand all of the ramifications of a policy, law or rule before you decide what you will support. Take into account the consequences on the entire community, not just select groups. Public policy must be informed by evidence, facts and research, input from various constituencies and a thorough examination of past failures and successes. The implications for forming legislation around public fear are widespread.

There are many resources available (see resource section) including videos, books and social media that create opportunities to become more educated about the issues discussed in this book. These resources can be used to create awareness amongst your group affiliations.

Incarcerated Individuals

Five Mualimm-ak encourages individuals who are incarcerated to join together as a unified community of people working to end mass incarceration and harsh conditions. Rather than allowing the prison systems to dictate social control through housing assignments and pitting one racial group against another, those who are incarcerated should seek to find commonality and work together toward a common goal and take a stand regarding these issues. By creating organizations within the prison system designed to support one another rather than harm each other, people can use their time in prison productively to create positive change. Mualimm-ak encourages those who are in prison to create peaceful situations that offer support and help one another in order to create a shift in the incarceration experience for all people.

Texas State Prison

State prisons desperately need to increase support and training for prison staff and equip them with tools to be able to do their jobs more effectively and apply preventative measures to address conflict related issues before they progress. Prison staff desperately need conflict management and dispute resolution skills, as well as communication skills, stress management and empathy training. Training should create a mindset and an expectation of actions in the prison environment that fosters a belief in rehabilitation rather than reliance on punishment and control. Much conflict in prison could be constructively addressed if those individuals who are employed by prison systems treated those who are incarcerated as humans— people who are capable of change—and fostered an environment of mutual respect. Highly skilled and trained prison staff with a rehabilitative mindset would go a long way in addressing the existing issues.

The Justice Fellowship addresses this need in the following statement:

Teaching people to become good citizens, rather than just good prisoners, is the charge entrusted to correctional officials by taxpayers. Skilled wardens understand that developing pro-social communities within prison walls is paramount to public safety—both inside and outside of prison fences. Part of creating safe communities inside prisons includes removing individuals who violate societal norms by placing themselves or others' safety at risk. Skilled wardens also understand, however, that this removal process must be temporary, and that a clear path back into the community must be not only clearly available, but achievable. Skilled wardens and corrections officers should welcome oversight, performance measurements, and independent review to ensure their use of segregation increases safety in the prison and the safety of the community upon prisoners' reintegration.[225]

Prison staff do not have enough support to do their jobs effectively or minimize the impact of stress. In order to support prison staff, it is vital that adequate staffing numbers be maintained in order to increase safety for staff and those who are incarcerated. It is important to address the reasons for the difficulties maintaining an appropriate level of staffing. Although monetary sign-on incentives are offered to new correctional officers, the high levels of stress, hostile work environment and low pay rate must be addressed.

Correctional employees at TDCJ are also calling for reform. The prisoner's guard union president wrote a letter to TDCJ citing its strong concerns with the use of solitary confinement and the current practices used on death row. The letter reads:

AFSCME Texas
Correctional Employees
Local 3807

"We Patrol Texas' Toughest Beat"

Jan. 20, 2014

Greetings,
As the president of the largest correctional professional organization in Texas I am calling on the Texas Department of Criminal Justice to change the death row plan to positively impact both the correctional staff and offenders on Texas death row. After the November 1998 escape of Offender Martin Gurule, the Texas Department of Criminal Justice engaged in a knee jerk reaction regarding the administration of Texas death row inmates.

Staff incompetency and lack of proper security equipment were the biggest factors resulting in Gurule's escape from the O.B. Ellis death row. As a result of the escape the agency ignored the root of the problem and addressed the lack of security equipment by increasing the physical perimeter security, in addition to the number of firearm rounds issued to perimeter pickets. Lack of staff competency was never addressed in a positive manner and has resulted in a less experienced force securing Texas death row.

The changes in the death row plan following the Gurule escape have resulted in the solitary housing of "D1" offenders who were capable and had additional privileges which could be used as management tools for negative behavior. As a result of the changes to the Texas death row plan, inmates have very few privileges to lose and staff become an easy targets. The Texas death row plan needs to address tools that can manage positive behavior. D1 offenders who are work capable should be utilized. Housing death row D1 offenders in a solitary cell is a waste of valuable security personnel and money. D1 offenders should be housed 2 offenders to a cell and treated similar to G3 offenders in terms of privileges such as work assignment and allowed TV privileges by streaming over the air television to a computer tablet using a closed Wi-Fi network. Use of technologies such as computer tablets and streaming TV should be offered to offenders who exhibit positive behavior. Lack of visual or audio stimulation result in increased psychological incidents and results in costly crisis management. Staff incompetency should be addressed by offering death row officers a salary differential and substantially increase their training for staff committed to working death row. A greater pay differential will insure [sic] we have the best officers watching Texas' most dangerous population. Other correctional agencies have successfully used differentials to address staffing issues. Let's make Texas a model for successful death row criminal justice reforms.

Respectfully,
Lance l Lowry
President Local 3807
1314 Tenth, Street, Suite 110, Huntsville, Texas 77320
(936) 295-5265 ' 1-800-374-9772[226]

Implement Existing Strategies that Curb the Use of Confinement

Prisons need to implement existing strategies used by other states to drastically reduce the use of solitary confinement and eliminate it completely for vulnerable populations. Michael Mushlin, professor of law at Pace Law School, explains how some prison systems are creating positive change.

These harsh practices continue to exist as if there are no other options. This is not the case, there are other options. What these inmates are subjected to in the name of safety doesn't have to be this way, yet the state of Texas is refusing to implement methods that are known to be effective in other states. Thoughtful corrections officials are finding other ways to run safe prisons by not resorting to these tortuous and unnecessary conditions. In Maine, Colorado and Mississippi, for example, the use of solitary confinement has been drastically reduced by prison officials instituting reforms. Texas should be using practices that have addressed some of these issues, other states.

During the summer of 2011, the Maine Department of Corrections greatly reduced the use of solitary confinement by decreasing the capacity of solitary use from 90 to 40 percent. Breton, the Department of Corrections associate commissioner, reported the decrease after inmates were observed to "do better not isolated ... [and] in normal living conditions."[227] Although Maine plans to continue the use of solitary confinement for safety and security risks to the incarcerated person's self or others, the use will be restricted to hours as opposed to the previously used days or months. These changes, prompted by a mental health professionals' and the Department of Corrections staff's report, now implement a reduction in privileges due to misbehavior in replace of solitary confinement. In addition, the Maine prison system moved lower-security people to more rehabilitative facilities with "minimum security ... [to help] prisoners make the transition back into civilian life."[228] Both the reduction of the use of solitary confinement and moving those who are incarcerated to less restrictive facilities results in state money savings.[229]

Based on research from the American Civil Liberties Union of Colorado's National Prison Project's Director David Fathi, "The vast majority of prisoners who are forced into solitary confinement eventually are released back into the community, making it imperative that we invest in proven alternatives that lead to greater rehabilitation and pave the way for successful re-entry."[230] [231] Colorado legislature proposed and passed a bill to reduce the use of solitary confinement in prisons, specifically within mentally ill populations. The bill also supports mental and behavioral health alternatives and cost-saving mechanisms. Colorado's solitary confinement cells house individuals spending more than 23 hours a day in isolation, for 16 months on average, at an increased additional cost of up to $21,485 per year, per person.[232] From 2011 to 2012, Colorado transferred 400 people out of solitary confinement and into the general prison population.[233]

Severely Limit the Use of Solitary Confinement and Set Strict Guidelines for Its Use

Craig Haney, professor of psychology at University of California Santa Cruz, and Mona Lynch, professor of criminology and law at University of California Irvine, propose standards based on psychological research that create a framework for the use of confinement. Some of these standards include:

- Segregated prisoners must retain all of the fundamental constitutional rights and privileges afforded mainline prisoners.

- Adequate due process should be afforded all prisoners before transfer to disciplinary segregation, solitary or supermax units, irrespective of the particular purpose that correctional officials ascribe to the transfer itself.
- No prisoner should be kept in administrative segregation for longer than 10 days absent or pending a due process hearing to determine disciplinary segregation status.
- No prisoner should be confined to segregated housing for indeterminate or indefinite terms.
- Conditions of total social isolation and extreme sensory deprivation (e.g., darkness) should be prohibited entirely.
- Complete social isolation and restricted movement that precludes social interaction should not exceed 30 days in duration for any prisoners.
- Prisoners should not be placed in disciplinary segregation when the infraction for which they are being punished was the result of pre-existing psychiatric disorders, mental illness or developmental disability.
- Segregated prisoners should be screened in advance of supermax or solitary confinement, and those whose psychological and medical conditions would render them significantly more susceptible to the potentially harmful consequences of the experience should be precluded from it.
- Prison mental health staff should be required to articulate explicit diagnostic procedures for screening prisoners who are to be placed in solitary, and to specify the diagnostic criteria that would disqualify prisoners for such confinement.
- Those prisoners who are unfit for segregated housing should not be confined in it at all. Alternative facilities to house and care for such prisoners should be created by prison administrations.
- Prisoners in segregated housing for longer than three months should be offered the same kinds of activities as those in mainline prison units, albeit on a modified or reduced basis consistent with security concerns, including access to therapy, work, educational, and recreational programs. Whenever possible, activities of this sort should not be precluded for those housed in short-term solitary confinement terms of three months or less.
- Visitation should be offered to segregated prisoners on a basis that resembles mainline visiting as closely as security considerations will allow.
- No prisoner should be subjected to punitive segregation solely on the basis of alleged or documented gang membership in the absence of behavioral infractions.
- Staff members who work in punitive segregation units should be given specialized training that addresses the unique psychological stresses that

such environments have for prisoners and guards alike, including in-depth instruction in recognizing and responding to signs of psychological trauma and the psychopathological effects of such isolation.

- Staff members who work in punitive segregation units should be monitored for the use of excessive force, removed from such assignments whenever their behavior begins to deteriorate in the face of the pressures of these working conditions and periodically rotated out of these units to ensure that they maintain a broader perspective on prisoner behavior and the range of potential relationships between staff and inmates.[234]

Redefine Separation to Include Rehabilitation and Humane Treatment

Five Mualimm-ak advocates that prison systems take a comprehensive approach to both end the torture of long-term solitary confinement beyond 15 days and to create more humane and effective alternatives. This would require that any person separated from the general prison population for more than 15 consecutive days (which U.N. Special Rapporteur on Torture concluded to amount to torture or cruel and unusual punishment, inhumane or degrading treatment) be placed in a separate secure rehabilitative and therapeutic unit aimed at providing residents with additional programs, therapy and support to address the underlying causes of their behavior. Separation does not have to mean isolation and torture, but should instead aim to effectively address the reasons why someone needs to be separated. This will also restrict the criteria that can result in isolation, bars vulnerable populations from being placed in isolation, enhances staff training and provides for procedural protections and outside oversight. It is time for us to replace isolation and torture with rehabilitation and treatment that will be both more humane and more effective, and will help make prisons, jails and our communities safer.

Provide Opportunities for Connectivity

In addition to the above recommendations, incarcerated individuals should be allowed regular opportunities for connectivity with the outside world, human contact and sensory stimulation. The following are examples of how prison systems can support connectivity:

- Allow contact visits for individuals living on death row.
- Allow phone calls for individuals living on death row.
- Facilitation of opportunities for children and families to interact with their parents on death row.
- Provide incentive opportunities that would allow for a greater level of connection with other individuals inside and out.
- Provide monitored group recreation opportunities for individuals living on

death row and in solitary confinement.

- Provide access to current events through newspapers, television or radio for all individuals in prison, not just the ones who have money in their accounts to purchase it.
- Allow two-way electronic correspondence.

Create Opportunities to Build Self-Efficacy

Death row and solitary confinement conditions do not allow for opportunities to engage in many activities that build a sense of self and accomplishment. Re-instating the once successful work program, providing opportunities to engage in various hobbies, mentorship activities and allowing all individuals living on death row and in solitary confinement to engage in educational instruction are just a few examples of how prisons can create opportunities for individuals in prison to build self-efficacy. Teaching skills to incarcerated individuals in conflict resolution, stress management and coping would allow them to gain some skills that will help them in their environment.

Acknowledge and Address the Needs of Vulnerable Populations

Alternative measures must be formed to keep vulnerable populations safe and to increase support services without victimizing them by placing them in confinement. According to the Justice Fellowship, "Creating 'missioned housing' that allows for services targeted to the needs of prisoners with mental illness, developmental delays, or those at risk of sexual victimization. These units provide a smaller community setting for these vulnerable populations without placing them in solitary confinement."[235]

Increase Availability of Support Services

Individuals in solitary confinement, including those people living on death row, do not have access to support groups such as Alcoholics Anonymous nor the opportunity to participate in faith-based activities. Mental health care should be provided in a way that honors confidentiality and privacy. And for those individuals who are not a threat to others, treatment should be conducted face-to-face away from the cell.

Academic Institutions

Academic institutions are uniquely positioned to create opportunities for change in social systems. Some of the ways that academic institutions can get involved are detailed below.

- Create awareness of issues in educational settings through the use of textbooks, book clubs and encouraging professors to bring in speakers and panels that engage students in dialogues about these issues:

- Engage students in creating opportunities for involvement, such as:
- Writing letters to incarcerated individuals and their family members.
- Educating students on how to become advocates for legislative reform.
- Inviting politicians to speak in class on matters of legislative reform process.
- Encouraging student groups and organizations to advocate for change.
- Providing opportunities that encourage research that generates awareness and need for change.

Faith-Based Communities

According to Five Mualimm-ak, "It is important that the religious community fight against torture. The sad fact is that many religious communities are not taking a stand and making a commitment to do more." Mualimm-ak offers the following ways that faith-based communities can get involved:

- Religious organizations can "adopt" a prison family and support the family by providing financial assistance (put money on the incarcerated person's trust account, purchase phone minutes, etc.) and transportation assistance to visit loved ones.
- For death row families, faith-based communities can work with the children of the individual on death row to help meet their emotional, psychological, educational, social and spiritual needs.
- Faith-based communities can launch letter-writing campaigns to support incarcerated individuals and their families.
- Faith-based organizations can become a part in the National Religious Campaign Against Torture and be a part of the interfaith dialogue.

Faith-based communities can also organize spiritual mentorship to those who are on death row and in solitary confinement. They can educate members of their own faith-based community about the inhumane treatment of some of the most vulnerable populations. And, they can sign the Statement Against Prolonged Solitary Confinement (nrcat.org/torture-in-us-prisons/statement) and obtain signatures in their community.

Reconstructing the Narrative

Past and present narratives of crime and punishment in Texas history need to be rewritten to include the experiences of all of the people involved, not just certain groups or individuals. By ignoring the stories of the collective who are impacted by violence, rather than acknowledge them, we are selecting which pieces of history are important and inaccurately rewriting and revising stories and passing them on to generations, keeping the legacy and traditions that were based on only pieces of the whole.

The current criminal justice paradigm uses violent measures to address violence in society. Violence does not cure violence; it perpetuates it. The current paradigm is counterproductive and has proven to be counterproductive throughout history. It is pertinent, then, to question why it continues to be a strategy that is repeated, despite its known consequences. The current criminal justice practices are creating more victims, and it is the responsibility of every member of society to be a part of the solution. We must create a shift in ideology.

The problem of solitary confinement and abusive and tortuous treatment of individuals in prison must be framed as a collective problem in which all people bear responsibility for creating positive change. Individuals returning from prison to the community often return to society with more emotional, psychological and social challenges than when they went in to prison. And, as a result of the laws that disenfranchise formerly incarcerated people (e.g., housing discrimination, lack of nutritional support, job discrimination), these individuals now have even fewer resources available to them. As this book has posited, these problems affect everyone, yet interventions are designed to address only certain segments of the population. The question must be asked, *Is one of the ramifications of these harsh practices an even a higher number of citizens with mental illness?* The ripple effect of that can be devastating. The time is ripe to start new conversations that frame the issues around the impact that the current ideologies are having in our communities, on all of our citizens. Lisa Guenther offers her perspective on the need for dialogue.

We also need to facilitate informed public discussions of violence, crime and public safety. "Tough on crime" rhetoric has fostered the impression that most people in prison are violent offenders and that the main function of incarceration is to punish offenders while protecting the public. But in reality, only a small percentage of people in prison have committed violent crimes. Mass incarceration, and even the overuse of solitary confinement, is driven—at least in part—by the punishment of non-violent unlawful activity (such as the possession of illegal drugs) and non-compliance with rules or expectations in prison (such as possession of a cellphone or having more stamps than are allowed), as if they were extremely serious offenses. This approach is inspired by the "broken window" theory of public safety, which punishes non-serious misdemeanors very harshly in an attempt to create an atmosphere in which everyone feels compelled to follow the laws and the rules. Contrary to popular belief, many of the inmates who are in solitary confinement have not been sentenced for violent acts, yet they are harshly punished, isolated and treated as if they were violent offenders.

The flavor of Texas southern culture, traditional Christian fundamentalism and vigilante justice have been part of the crime and punishment system for centuries and continue to be embedded in capital punishment processes and the prison system to date. *The Rope, The Chair and The Needle,* a book that examines the history of capital punishment in Texas, describes the history that influences modern day punishment: "Slavery, criminal justice, lynchings, and capital punishment are historically intertwined in the United States, Texas is no exception."[236]

In order to move forward, we must acknowledge how the past atrocities continue to play a role in the present day. After African-Americans were freed from slavery, they continued to be mistreated and dehumanized in other forms such as legalized lynching and hangings (which eventually were outlawed), and more insidious forms of racism, such as the War on Drugs, which incarcerates more than a million African-Americans, as well as other disadvantaged groups, for minor crimes. Individuals of color are executed at a rate that it is significantly disproportionate to any other race. The history of oppression and racism in Texas continues to play a role in many aspects of the capital punishment process today. Many scholars have described the practice of state executions as "legal lynching."

We also need to examine the reason why Texas has been so resistant to change despite the known consequences to these inhumane and degrading extreme forms of punishment. In his book *Conflict Revolution: Mediating Evil, War, Injustice and Terrorism* Kenneth Cloke identifies ways by which systems resist change. "Systems may benefit, for example, by encouraging adversarial communications and chronically conflicted relationships, isolating critics and dissenters, and punishing transformational change efforts. These forms of systemic resistance may fuel hostility and magnify conflicts over change, yet they also divert attention from transformational change."[237] It is pertinent then to ask the question, *Who is benefiting from allowing these injustices to continue? What is our attention being diverted from?*

We must also ask the question, *What can we do to facilitate systemic change?* Cloke offers hope to the systemic challenges that often leave people feeling hopeless. "In response to each of these forms of resistance it is possible to invent, adapt and apply democratic, collaborative, interest-based alternatives that encourage systemic change without generating superficial polarizations and adversarial relationships. These alternatives are designed to draw people into constructive dialogue regarding issues that are important to them, invite them to participate actively in the change effort, and simultaneously improve the way they change."[238] These issues are so polarizing, so entrenched in values that the conflict in and of itself takes on its own identity and in some cases, the manifestations, or behaviors associated with the conflict, can thwart efforts to work together.

Change brings fear and uncertainty. It means changing old traditions and even accepting accountability that some of our actions were ineffective and even inhumane. It can mean admitting to ourselves and others that we were wrong. In order for there to be transformational change, there must be a massive shift in the ideology, attitudes and culture that are currently allowing these injustices to continue. Solutions must take into account the perspective of those who are directly impacted. Not only certain groups. Research indicates that large institutional change efforts have failed because the individuals who are impacted by the problems are excluded from the process. Change has also failed when the larger, more pervasive and insidious problems, such as the culture and existing processes, are not addressed; rather, each issue is tackled separately.[239]

Texas has been a leader in executions and has refused to implement what other states and countries have found to be successful and humane measures to address the issue of extreme punishments. Although a shift appears to be happening in a positive direction in the reduction of solitary confinement, the inhumane practices continue on a mass scale, despite the recommendations. The impact of solitary confinement and capital punishment continues to be widespread, affecting all members of Texas communities. Not only do these practices degrade Texas as a state, but it speaks volumes about some of the deepest values that remain entrenched in many of our institutions. Rather than equate Texas pride with being "tough on crime" and retributive justice, which has proven to have negative consequences, Texas has the opportunity to be leaders in rehabilitative, social and restorative justice as well as preventative measures such as education, and create safer communities. It is the responsibility of all Texans to hold Texas Department of Criminal Corrections accountable for allowing practices that contradict its mission statement: "… to provide public safety, promote positive change in offender behavior, reintegrate offenders into society, and assist victims of crime." Finally, we must look in the mirror, and hold ourselves accountable. Change happens from within.

PART VI
RESOURCES

TEXAS RESOURCES

Texas Resources

American Civil Liberties Union of Texas
www.aclutx.org

State Headquarters
P.O. Box 8306
Houston, TX 77288-8306
(713) 942-8146
(888) 653-6498 toll free

State Capitol Office
P.O. Box 12905
Austin, TX 78711-2905
Main: (512) 478-7300

Rio Grande Valley Office
P.O. Box 6087
Brownsville, TX 78523-6087
(956) 465-1905
acluinfo@aclutx.org.

Prisoner's Family Conference
www.prisonersfamilyconference.org
(915) 861-7733
2200 N Yarbrough, B245
El Paso, TX 79925

Texas After Violence Project
www.texasafterviolence.org
(521) 916-1600
P.O. Box 41476
Austin, TX 78704

Texas Civil Rights Project
www.texascivilrightsproject.org
(512) 474-5073
4920 N. IH-35 c/o TRLA
Austin, TX 78751

Texas Coalition to Abolish the Death Penalty
www.tcadp.org
(512) 441-1808
2709 S Lamar Austin
TX 78704

Texas Criminal Justice Coalition
www.texascjc.org
(512) 441-8121
1714 Fortview Road, Suite 104
Austin, TX 78704

Texas Impact
www.texasimpact.org
(512) 472-3903
200 East 30th Street
Austin, TX 78705

Texas Jail Project
www.texasjailproject.org
(512) 597-8746
1712 E. Riverside Drive, Box 190
Austin, TX 78741

NATIONAL RESOURCES

American Civil Liberties Union
www.aclu.org
(212) 549-2500
125 Broad Street, 18th Floor
New York, NY 10004
www.aclu.org/contact-us

Amnesty International, USA
www.amnestyusa.org
(212) 807-8400
5 Penn Plaza, 16th Floor
New York, NY 10001

Campaign for Alternatives to Isolated Confinement (CAIC)
www.nycaic.org
caicny@gmail.com

Human Rights Watch
www.hrw.org
(212) 290-4700
350 Fifth Avenue, 34th floor
New York, NY 10118-3299 USA

Journey of Hope...From Violence to Healing™
www.journeyofhope.org
(877) 924-4483
P.O. BOX 210390
Anchorage, AK 99521-0390

Justice Fellowship
www.justicefellowship.org
703.554.8607
44180 Riverside Parkway
Lansdowne, VA 20176

Murder Victims' Families for Human Rights

www.mvfhr.org
(617) 443-1102
89 South St., Suite 601
Boston MA 02111

Murder Victims' Families for Reconciliation

www.mvfr.org
(877) 896-4702
405 Morson Street
Raleigh, NC 27601

National Religious Campaign Against Torture

www.nrcat.org
(202) 547-1920
110 Maryland Ave. NE, Suite 502
Washington, DC 20002

National Resource Center on Children and Families of the Incarcerated at Rutgers University

http://nrccfi.camden.rutgers.edu
(856) 225-2718
NRCCFI at Rutgers–Camden 405-7 Cooper Street
Room 103
Camden, New Jersey 08102
nrccfi@camden.rutgers.edu

Quaker United Nations Office

www.quno.org
(212) 682-2745
777 U.N. Plaza
New York, NY 10017

INTERNATIONAL RESOURCES

Amnesty International
www.amnesty.org
+44-20-74135500
1 Easton Street
London
WC1X 0DW, UK

Penal Reform International
www.penalreform.org
+44 20 7247 6515
60-62 Commercial Street
London
E1 6LT
United Kingdom
info@penalreform.org

Reprieve
www.reprieve.org.uk
+020 7553 8140
PO Box 72054
London EC3P 3BZ
info@reprieve.org.uk

Sample Letter for Legislators

Dear _____,

I am writing to express my deep concern about the inhumane and counterproductive use of solitary confinement and other forms of isolation in Texas State prisons and jails, and to urge you and your colleagues to sponsor and pass legislation that will end the practice of extreme isolation.

In prisons and jails, on any given day there are thousands of people held in isolated confinement in a cell the size of an elevator for 22 to 24 hours a day, without any meaningful human contact, programs, or therapy, or even the ability to make phone calls. The United Nations Special Rapporteur on Torture has concluded that more than *15 days* in isolated confinement amounts to torture or cruel, inhuman, or degrading treatment. Yet in States people are routinely held in isolation for months and years, and sometimes even decades. Such isolation has been proven to often cause deep and permanent psychological, physical, and social harm. Moreover, isolation exacerbates rather than addresses the underlying causes of difficult behavior and therefore makes our prisons, jails, and communities less safe, including when thousands of people each year are released directly from solitary to the streets. Of additional concern, most of the prison and jail rule violations that result in isolated confinement are for non-violent, often frivolous, conduct, and disproportionately people of color are sent to isolated confinement. Even people particularly vulnerable to the devastating effects of isolation, including young people and people with pre-existing mental health needs, are held in isolation.

Please take a comprehensive approach to both end the torture of long term solitary confinement beyond 15 days and to create more humane and effective alternatives. This would require that any person separated from the general prison population for more than 15 consecutive days be placed in a separate secure rehabilitative and therapeutic unit aimed at providing residents with additional programs, therapy, and support to address the underlying causes of their behavior. Separation does not have to mean isolation and torture, but should instead aim to effectively address the reasons why someone needs to be separated. This will also restrict the criteria that can result in isolation, bars vulnerable populations from being placed in isolation, enhances staff training, and provides for procedural protections and outside oversight.

It is time for us to replace isolation and torture with rehabilitation and treatment that will be both more humane and more effective, and will help make prisons, jails, and our communities safer. I urge you to join as a co-sponsor or create a change in the way we treat humans that are incarcerated, and the impact that this treatment is having on the whole of the community.

Sincerely,

Your Name

PART VII
LAST STATEMENTS

THE LAST WORDS

THE LAST WORDS OF Napoleon Beazley are outlined in the statement below. He was 17 years old at the time of the crime. Napoleon was executed by the state of Texas May 28, 2002. He was 25 years old at the time of his death.

The act I committed to put me here was not just heinous, it was senseless. But the person that committed that act is no longer here ... I am. I'm not going to struggle physically against any restraints. I'm not going to shout, use profanity or make idle threats.

Understand though that I'm not only upset, but I'm saddened by what is happening here tonight. I'm not only saddened, but disappointed that a system that is supposed to protect and uphold what is just and right can be so much like me when I made the same shameful mistake. If someone tried to dispose of everyone here for participating in this killing, I'd scream a resounding, "No." I'd tell them to give them all the gift that they would not give me, and that's to give them all a second chance.

I'm sorry that I am here. I'm sorry that you're all here. I'm sorry that John Luttig died. And I'm sorry that it was something in me that caused all of this to happen to begin with.

Tonight we tell the world that there are no second chances in the eyes of justice. Tonight, we tell our children that in some instances, in some cases, killing is right. This conflict hurts us all. There are no sides. The people who support this proceeding think this is justice. The people that think that I should live think that is justice. As difficult as it may seem, this is a clash of ideals, with both parties committed to what they feel is right. But who's wrong if in the end we're all victims?

In my heart, I have to believe that there is a peaceful compromise to our ideals. I don't mind if there are none for me, as long as there are for those who are yet to come. There are a lot of men like me on death row — good men — who fell to the same misguided emotions, but may not have recovered as I have. Give those men a chance to do what's right. Give them a chance to undo their wrongs. A lot of them want to fix the mess they started, but don't know how.

The problem is not in that people aren't willing to help them find out, but in the system telling them it won't matter anyway.

No one wins tonight. No one gets closure. No one walks away victorious.

The following last statements represent the last words of all the people executed by the state of Texas from December 1982 to April 2014. Until Texas legislators abolish the death penalty, this list will continue to grow. To read the last statements of the individuals executed since April 2014, visit http://www.tdcj. state.tx.us/death_row/dr_executed_offenders.html.

Please note that the last statements are copied directly from the Texas Department of Criminal Justice website and are unedited. The last statements of the people executed by the state of Texas are recorded by a TDCJ stenographer. The employees' notes are indicated in parentheses.

Michael Graczyk, a reporter from *The Associated Press*, who has witnessed hundreds of executions in Texas, speaks to the accuracy of the statements that appear on the website:

The prison system has a stenographer writing an inmate's last statement that is posted on the TDCJ website. Reporters inside the death chamber also take their own notes of what the prisoner says. Occasionally, the accounts may differ slightly. In addition, reporters' accounts may also include comments the inmate uttered before his formal last statement, and what he said following his completed formal statement in the seconds before the lethal drugs took effect. The TDCJ accounts generally include only what the prisoner said in response to the warden asking him if he had a final statement, and ends once the inmate indicated he was finished talking.

Charlie Brooks, Jr.
Execution Date: 12/07/1982
Race: Black
County of Conviction: Tarrant
Last Statement: Statement to the Media: I, at this very moment, have absolutely no fear of what may happen to this body. My fear is for Allah, God only, who has at this moment the only power to determine if I should live or die... As a devout Muslim, I am taught and believe that this material life is only for the express purpose of preparing oneself for the real life that is to come... Since becoming Muslim, I have tried to live as Allah wanted me to live.

James Autry
Execution Date: 03/14/1984
Race: White
County of Conviction: Jefferson
Last Statement: This person declined to make a last statement.

Ronald O'Bryan
Execution Date: 03/31/1984
Race: White
County of Conviction: Harris
Last Statement: What is about to transpire in a few moments is wrong! However, we as human beings do make mistakes and errors. This execution is one of those wrongs yet doesn't mean our whole system of justice is wrong. Therefore, I would forgive all who have taken part in any way in my death. Also, to anyone I have offended in any way during my 39 years, I pray and ask your forgiveness, just as I forgive anyone who offended me in any way. And I pray and ask God's forgiveness for all of us respectively as human beings. To my loved ones, I extend my undying love. To those close to me, know in your hearts I love you one and all. God bless you all and may God's best blessings be always yours. Ronald C. O'Bryan P.S. During my time here, I have been treated well by all T.D.C. personnel.

Thomas Barefoot
Execution Date: 10/30/1984
Race: White
County of Conviction: Bell
Last Statement: When asked if he had a last statement, he replied, "Yes, I do."I hope that one day we can look back on the evil that we're doing right now like the witches we burned at the stake. I want everybody to know that I hold nothing

against them. I forgive them all. I hope everybody I've done anything to will forgive me. I've been praying all day for Carl Levin's wife to drive the bitterness from her heart because that bitterness that's in her heart will send her to Hell just as surely as any other sin. I'm sorry for everything I've ever done to anybody. I hope they'll forgive me. "Sharon, tell all my friends goodbye. You know who they are: Charles Bass, David Powell…" Then he coughed and nothing else was said.

Doyle Skillern
Execution Date: 01/16/1985
Race: White
County of Conviction: Lubbock
Last Statement: I pray that my family will rejoice and will forgive, thank you.

Stephen Morin
Execution Date: 03/13/1985
Race: White
County of Conviction: Jefferson
Last Statement: Heavenly Father, I give thanks for this time, for the time that we have been together, the fellowship in your world, the Christian family presented to me (He called the names of the personal witnesses.). Allow your holy spirit to flow as I know your love as been showered upon me. Forgive them for they know not what they do, as I know that you have forgiven me, as I have forgiven them. Lord Jesus, I commit my soul to you, I praise you, and I thank you.

Jesse De La Rosa
Execution Date: 05/15/1985
Race: Hispanic
County of Conviction: Bexar
Last Statement: This person declined to make a last statement.

Charles Milton
Execution Date: 06/25/1985
Race: Black
County of Conviction: Tarrant
Last Statement: There's no God but Allah, and unto thy I belong and unto thy I return. I want to continue to tell my brothers and sisters to be strong.

Henry Porter
Execution Date: 07/09/1985

Race: Hispanic
County of Conviction: Tarrant
Last Statement: I want to thank Father Walsh for his spiritual help. I want to thank Bob Ray (Sanders) and Steve Blow for their friendship. What I want people to know is that they call me a cold-blooded killer when I shot a man that shot me first. The only thing that convicted me was that I am a Mexican and that he was a police officer. People hollered for my life, and they are to have my life tonight. The people never hollered for the life of the policeman that killed a thirteen-year-old boy who was handcuffed in the back seat of a police car. The people never hollered for the life of a Houston police officer who beat up and drowned Jose Campo Torres and threw his body in the river. You call that equal justice. This is your equal justice. This is America's equal justice. A Mexican's life is worth nothing. When a policeman kills someone he gets a suspended sentence or probation. When a Mexican kills a police officer this is what you get. From there you call me a cold-blooded murderer. I didn't tie anyone to a stretcher. I didn't pump any poison into anybody's veins from behind a locked door. You call this justice. I call this and your society a bunch of cold-blooded murderers. I don't say this with any bitterness or anger. I just say this with truthfulness. I hope God forgives me for all my sins. I hope that God will be as merciful to society as he has been to me. I'm ready, Warden.

Charles Rumbaugh
Execution Date: 09/11/1985
Race: White
County of Conviction: Potter
Last Statement: D.J., Laurie, Dr. Wheat, about all I can say is goodbye, and for all the rest of you, although you don't forgive me for my transgressions, I forgive yours against me. I am ready to begin my journey and that's all I have to say.

Charles Bass
Execution Date: 03/12/1986
Race: White
County of Conviction: Harris
Last Statement: I deserve this. Tell everyone I said goodbye.

Jeffery Barney
Execution Date: 04/16/1986
Race: White
County of Conviction: Harris
Last Statement: This person declined to make a last statement.

Jay Pinkerton
Execution Date: 05/15/1986
Race: White
County of Conviction: Nueces
Last Statement: "Be strong for me," Pinkerton told his father, Gene Pinkerton, as witnesses entered the execution chamber. "I want you to know I'm at peace with myself and with my God," Pinkerton said. He recited a prayer to Allah, the supreme being of Islam. "I bear witness that there is no God but Allah. With your praise I ask for forgiveness and I return unto you," Pinkerton said. "I love you, Dad."

Rudy Esquivel
Execution Date: 06/09/1986
Race: Hispanic
County of Conviction: Harris
Last Statement: Goodbye to all my friends; be cool. Thank you for being my friends. Give my love to everybody.

Kenneth Brock
Execution Date: 06/19/1986
Race: White
County of Conviction: Harris
Last Statement: I have no last words. I am ready.

Randy Woolls
Execution Date: 08/20/1986
Race: White
County of Conviction: Tom Green
Last Statement: Goodbye to my family; I love all of you, I'm sorry for the victim's family. I wish I could make it up to them. I want those out there to keep fighting the death penalty.

Larry Smith
Execution Date: 08/22/1986
Race: Black
County of Conviction: Dallas
Last Statement: Tell my mother I love her and continue on without me. God bless her. Tell the guys on death row to continue their struggle to get off death row. That's about it.

Chester Wicker
Execution Date: 08/26/1986
Race: White
County of Conviction: Galveston
Last Statement: This person declined to make a last statement.

Michael Evans
Execution Date: 12/04/1986
Race: Black
County of Conviction: Dallas
Last Statement: I want to say I'm sorry for the things I've done and I hope I'm forgiven. I don't hold nothing against no one – Everyone has treated me well and I know it's not easy for them – That's all, I'm sorry.

Richard Andrade
Execution Date: 12/18/1986
Race: Hispanic
County of Conviction: Nueces
Last Statement: This person declined to make a last statement.

Ramon Hernandez
Execution Date: 01/30/1987
Race: Hispanic
County of Conviction: El Paso
Last Statement: This person declined to make a last statement.

Eliseo Moreno
Execution Date: 03/04/1987
Race: Hispanic
County of Conviction: Fort Bend
Last Statement: This person declined to make a last statement.

Anthony Williams
Execution Date: 05/28/1987
Race: Black
County of Conviction: Harris
Last Statement: Mother, I am sorry for all the pain I've caused you. Please forgive me. Take good care of yourself. Ernest and Otis, watch out for the family. Thank all of you who have helped me.

Elliot Johnson

Execution Date: 06/24/1987
Race: Black
County of Conviction: Jefferson
Last Statement: This person declined to make a last statement.

John Thompson

Execution Date: 07/08/1987
Race: White
County of Conviction: Bexar
Last Statement: This person declined to make a last statement.

Joseph Starvaggi

Execution Date: 09/10/1987
Race: White
County of Conviction: Montgomery
Last Statement: This person declined to make a last statement.

Robert Streetman

Execution Date: 01/07/1988
Race: White
County of Conviction: Hardin
Last Statement: This person declined to make a last statement.

Donald Franklin

Execution Date: 11/03/1988
Race: Black
County of Conviction: Nueces
Last Statement: This person declined to make a last statement.

Raymond Landry, Sr.

Execution Date: 12/13/1988
Race: Black
County of Conviction: Harris
Last Statement: This person declined to make a last statement.

Leon King

Execution Date: 03/22/1989
Race: Black

County of Conviction: Harris
Last Statement: I would like to tell Mr. Richard that I appreciate all he has done for me. I love you all. God bless. Goodbye, David.

Stephen McCoy
Execution Date: 05/24/1989
Race: White
County of Conviction: Harris
Last Statement: This person declined to make a last statement.

James Paster
Execution Date: 09/20/1989
Race: White
County of Conviction: Harris
Last Statement: I hope Mrs. Howard can find peace in this.

Carlos De Luna
Execution Date: 12/07/1989
Race: Hispanic
County of Conviction: Nueces
Last Statement: I want to say I hold no grudges. I hate no one. I love my family. Tell everyone on death row to keep the faith and don't give up.

Jerome Butler
Execution Date: 04/21/1990
Race: Black
County of Conviction: Harris
Last Statement: I wish everybody a good life. Everything is O.K.

Johnny Anderson
Execution Date: 05/17/1990
Race: White
County of Conviction: Jefferson
Last Statement: I would like to point out that I have written a statement and the Warden will give you a copy. I still proclaim I am innocent, and that's all I have to say.

James Smith
Execution Date: 06/26/1990

Race: Black
County of Conviction Harris
Last Statement: This person declined to make a last statement.

Mikel Derrick
Execution Date: 07/18/1990
Race: White
County of Conviction: Harris
Last Statement: I just ask everybody I ever hurt or done anything wrong to, to just forgive me for whatever wrongs I done to them.

Lawrence Buxton
Execution Date: 02/26/1991
Race: Black
County of Conviction: Harris
Last Statement: I'm ready, Warden.

Ignacio Cuevas
Execution Date: 05/23/1991
Race: Hispanic
County of Conviction: Harris
Last Statement: I'm going to a beautiful place. O.K., Warden, roll 'em.

Jerry Bird
Execution Date: 06/17/1991
Race: White
County of Conviction: Cameron
Last Statement: I don't think so. That's all. Go ahead. Start things rolling. *(Mouthed "Hi, Mom" to his mother.)*

James Russell
Execution Date: 09/19/1991
Race: Black
County of Conviction: Fort Bend
Last Statement: His final statement lasted 3 minutes. He thanked everybody that fought against his sentence. He spoke to his family and said he would carry their love with him.

G. W. Green
Execution Date: 11/12/1991
Race: White
County of Conviction: Montgomery
Last Statement: Let's do it, man. Lock and load. Ain't life a *[expletive deleted]*?

Joe Cordova
Execution Date: 01/22/1992
Race: Hispanic
County of Conviction: Harris
Last Statement: This person declined to make a last statement.

Johnny Garrett
Execution Date: 02/11/1992
Race: White
County of Conviction: Potter
Last Statement: This person declined to make a last statement.

David Clark
Execution Date: 02/28/1992
Race: White
County of Conviction: Brazos
Last Statement: None. But as he lay there he did praise the Lord and seemed to be praying.

Edward Ellis
Execution Date: 03/03/1992
Race: White
County of Conviction: Harris
Last Statement: I just want everyone to know that the prosecutor and Bill Scott are sorry sons of bitches. *To his family he added that he loved them all.*

Billy White
Execution Date: 04/23/1992
Race: Black
County of Conviction: Harris
Last Statement: This person declined to make a last statement.

Justin May
Execution Date: 05/07/1992
Race: White
County of Conviction: Brazoria
Last Statement: Thanked his family.

Jesus Romero, Jr.
Execution Date: 05/20/1992
Race: Hispanic
County of Conviction: Cameron
Last Statement: When his attorney came into the witness room, he said, "Tell Mom I love her." The attorney said back to him, "I love you, too."

Robert Black, Jr.
Execution Date: 05/22/1992
Race: White
County of Conviction: Brazos
Last Statement: High Flight (aviation poem).

Curtis Johnson
Execution Date: 08/11/1992
Race: Black
County of Conviction: Harris
Last Statement: This person declined to make a last statement.

James Demouchette
Execution Date: 09/22/1992
Race: Black
County of Conviction: Harris
Last Statement: This person declined to make a last statement.

Jeffery Griffin
Execution Date: 11/19/1992
Race: Black
County of Conviction: Harris
Last Statement: This person declined to make a last statement.

Kevin Lincecum
Execution Date: 12/10/1992

Race: Black
County of Conviction: Brazoria
Last Statement: This person declined to make a last statement.

Carlos Santana
Execution Date: 03/23/1993
Race: Hispanic
County of Conviction: Harris
Last Statement: This person declined to make a last statement.

Ramon Montoya
Execution Date: 03/25/1993
Race: Hispanic
County of Conviction: Dallas
Last Statement: This person declined to make a last statement.

Darryl Stewart
Execution Date: 05/04/1993
Race: Black
County of Conviction: Harris
Last Statement: This person declined to make a last statement.

Leonel Herrera
Execution Date: 05/12/1993
Race: Hispanic
County of Conviction: Cameron
Last Statement: I am innocent, innocent, innocent. Make no mistake about this; I owe society nothing. Continue the struggle for human rights, helping those who are innocent, especially Mr. Graham. I am an innocent man, and something very wrong is taking place tonight. May God bless you all. I am ready.

John Sawyers
Execution Date: 05/18/1993
Race: White
County of Conviction: Harris
Last Statement: This person declined to make a last statement.

Markum Duff-Smith
Execution Date: 0629/1993

Race: White
County of Conviction: Harris
Last Statement: I am the sinner of all sinners. I was responsible for the '75 and '79 cases. My trial was not just; it was not fair; they lied against me. I love all of those on Death Row, and I will always hold them in my hands. Those who stood by me, I will always love you. Jim and Judy Peterson and Chaplain Lopez, I thank you for staying by my side.

Curtis Harris

Execution Date: 07/01/1993
Race: Black
County of Conviction: Brazos
Last Statement: This person declined to make a last statement.

Danny Harris

Execution Date: 07/30/1993
Race: Black
County of Conviction: Brazos
Last Statement: I would like to tell my family I love them very dearly, and I know they love me. I love all of the people who supported me all of these years. I would like to tell the Merka family I love them, too. I plead with all the teenagers to stop the violence and to accept Jesus Christ and find victory. Today I have victory in Christ and I thank Jesus for taking my spirit into His precious hands. Thank you, Jesus.

Joseph Jernigan

Execution Date: 08/05/1993
Race: White
County of Conviction: Navarro
Last Statement: This person declined to make a last statement.

David Holland

Execution Date: 08/12/1993
Race: White
County of Conviction: Jefferson
Last Statement: This person declined to make a last statement.

Carl Kelly

Execution Date: 08/20/1993

Race: Black
County of Conviction: McLennan
Last Statement: I'm an African warrior, born to breathe, and born to die.

Ruben Cantu
Execution Date: 08/24/1993
Race: Hispanic
County of Conviction: Bexar
Last Statement: This person declined to make a last statement.

Richard Wilkerson
Execution Date: 08/31/1993
Race: Black
County of Conviction: Harris

Last Statement: This execution is not justice. This execution is an act of revenge! If this is justice, then justice is blind. Take a borderline retarded young male who for the 1st time ever in his life committed a felony then contaminate his TRUE tell all confession add a judge who discriminates plus an ALL-WHITE JURY pile on an ineffective assistance of counsel and execute the option of rehabilitation persecute the witnesses and you have created a death sentence for a family lasting over 10 years. I will say once again.....This execution isn't justice – but an act of revenge. Killing R.J. will not bring Anil back, it only justifies "an eye for an eye and a tooth for a tooth." It's too late to help R.J., but maybe this poem will help someone else out there. "Seeing Through the Eyes of a Death Row Inmate" Sometime I wonder why, why he? Why did he go out into the world to see? To be out there and see what really did exist, now his name is written down on the Death Row list. I can only imagine how lonesome he was all by himself. We both knew he had no future left! His hopes and dreams became a fantasy. He often said, "There's nothing left of me." I have asked myself, why did he get involved with drugs? He could never explain why he hung around with thugs? Did it really make him feel like a king – Did he actually think he was capable of getting away with anything? He knew the thought of life wasn't ticking in his head. There's nothing left but the memory of those who lay dead. What was did, cannot be undone. He was confessed, he was one of the guilty ones. What would he say to the victim's family? – I'm sorry and my head wasn't on straight. I hope you will accept my apology, even though it's too late. I never knew I would take a life and commit a crime. I regret it because now I have to face the lethal injection while doing death row time. I knew I would pay with struggle and strife, but I never thought the cost would be me losing my life. Richard J. Wilkerson. Written through his sister Michelle Winn.

Johnny James
Execution Date: 09/03/1993
Race: White
County of Conviction: Chambers
Last Statement: This person declined to make a last statement.

Antonio Bonham
Execution Date: 09/28/1993
Race: Black
County of Conviction: Harris
Last Statement: This person declined to make a last statement.

Anthony Cook
Execution Date: 11/10/1993
Race: White
County of Conviction: Milam
Last Statement: I just want to tell my family I love them, and I thank the Lord Jesus for giving me another chance and for saving me.

Clifford Phillips
Execution Date: 12/15/1993
Race: Black
County of Conviction: Harris
Last Statement: I want to express my feelings regarding the mishap of the deceased Mrs. Iris Siff. That was a very unfortunate incident and only God knows why it was an unintentional situation that took place. I want to express my remorse to the family and the discomfort and pain I caused in their lives. Only God will determine if I am truly guilty or innocent of being the type of person I have been drawn up to be by the press and media. I have given my wife the power and energy to be a disciple of Islam. I rescued her from a wretched life in Ireland. I thank Allah for sending her to me. Certainly murder cannot be an instrument of Allah. My wife is very devoted.

Harold Barnard
Execution Date: 02/02/1994
Race: White
County of Conviction: Galveston
Last Statement: God, please forgive me of my sins. Look after my people. Bless and

protect all people. I am sorry for my sins. Lord, take me home with you. Amen. *(A couple of sentences garbled.)*

Freddie Webb
Execution Date: 03/31/1994
Race: Black
County of Conviction: Nueces
Last Statement: Peace.

Richard Beavers
Execution Date: 04/04/1994
Race: White
County of Conviction: Harris
Last Statement: This person declined to make a last statement.

Larry Anderson
Execution Date: 04/26/1994
Race: White
County of Conviction: Harris
Last Statement: This person declined to make a last statement.

Paul Rougeau
Execution Date: 05/03/1994
Race: Black
County of Conviction: Harris
Last Statement: This person declined to make a last statement.

Stephen Nethery
Execution Date: 05/27/1994
Race: White
County of Conviction: Dallas
Last Statement: Well, I just wanted to ask people to pray for two families: my family and the family of Officer McCarthy. I appreciate the prayers. Lord Jesus, receive my spirit.

Denton Crank
Execution Date: 06/14/1994
Race: White
County of Conviction: Harris
Last Statement: To my family who has kept me strong, I give my love.

Robert Drew
Execution Date: 08/02/1994
Race: White
County of Conviction: Harris
Last Statement: *(First two or three words not understood.)* I don't know why Marta Glass wasn't allowed in here. I love you all. Keep the faith. Remember the death penalty is murder. They are taking the life of an innocent man. My attorney, Ron Kuley [unintelligible], will read my letter at a press conference after this is over. That is all I have to say. I love you all.

Jessie Gutierrez
Execution Date: 09/16/1994
Race: Hispanic
County of Conviction: Brazos
Last Statement: I just love everybody, and that's it.

George Lott
Execution Date: 09/20/1994
Race: White
County of Conviction: Potter
Last Statement: This person declined to make a last statement.

Walter Williams
Execution Date: 10/05/1994
Race: Black
County of Conviction: Bexar
Last Statement: *(Mumbled something about he wished his whole life would have been spent as Islamic.)*

Warren Bridge
Execution Date: 11/22/1994
Race: White
County of Conviction: Galveston
Last Statement: I'll see you.

Herman Clark, Jr.
Execution Date: 12/06/1994
Race: Black
County of Conviction: Harris

Last Statement: I told the daughter not to come. Discontinue; be quiet, please. Specifically, I want to say that the bad evil man I was when I came to death row 13 years ago is no more – by the power of God; Jesus Christ; God Almighty; Holy Spirit, he has transformed me as a new creature of Christ. I know that I am a Christ child and that my Lord will welcome me into His arms. Jesus Christ is the Lord of Lords and the King of Kings. I love all of you, those I can and can't see. With the love of Christ, my love for you is secure and I love you purely and wholeheartedly in the name of the Almighty God.

Raymond Kinnamon

Execution Date: 12/11/1994
Race: White
County of Conviction: Harris
Last Statement: ...guys like them got tied up in something like this. Thank Chaplain Taylor and Jane. I just got your letter. Thanks to Carolyn and Gloria, who have been my friends for over four years. I want to remember Patsy Buntion, Gladys and a lot more friends. I want to thank the prosecutor in my case; it took courage for him to do what he did but he did what he did because he believed in the judicial system. I'm not ready to go, but I have no choice; I sent several letters to my family; they'll be very moving when you get them. I want to say goodbye again to my boys. I know I'm missing somebody, but if there's anything I have left to say, it would be that I wish I had a Shakespearean vocabulary, but since I was raised in TDC, I missed out on some of my vocabulary. If my words can persuade you to discontinue this practice of executing people, please do so. If the citizens don't do away with the death penalty, Texas won't be a safe place to be. I have no revenge because hate won't solve anything.(I gave Warden Hodges the phone at this time and he listened for 5-10 minutes. When he returned the phone to me, I could hear Kinnamon talking but evidently the phone was not close to the mike, because I could not understand him.)

Jesse Jacobs

Execution Date: 01/04/1995
Race: White
County of Conviction: Walker
Last Statement: I have committed lots of sin in my life, but I am not guilty of this crime. I would like to tell my son, daughter and wife that I love them –Eden, if they want proof of them, give it to them. Thanks for being my friend.

Mario Marquez
Execution Date: 01/17/1995
Race: Hispanic
County of Conviction: Bexar
Last Statement: Thank you for being my Lord Jesus and Savior and I am ready to come home. Amen.

Clifton Russell, Jr.
Execution Date: 01/31/1995
Race: White
County of Conviction: Taylor
Last Statement: I would like to thank my friends and family for sticking with me through all of this. I would like to encourage my brothers to continue to run the race. I thank my Father, God in Heaven, for the grace he has granted me – I am ready.

Willie Williams
Execution Date: 01/31/1995
Race: Black
County of Conviction: Harris
Last Statement: There's love and peace in Islam.

Jeffery Motley
Execution Date: 02/07/1995
Race: White
County of Conviction: Harris
Last Statement: I love you, Mom. Goodbye.

Billy Gardner
Execution Date: 02/16/1995
Race: White
County of Conviction: Dallas
Last Statement: I forgive all of you – hope God forgives all of you too.

Samuel Hawkins
Execution Date: 02/21/1995
Race: Black
County of Conviction: Lubbock
Last Statement: This person declined to make a last statement.

Noble Mays
Execution Date: 04/06/1995
Race: White
County of Conviction: Wilbarger
Last Statement: This person declined to make a last statement.

Fletcher Mann
Execution Date: 06/01/1995
Race: White
County of Conviction: Dallas
Last Statement: I would like to tell my family I love them. My attorneys did their best. All of my brothers on death row, those who died and those who are still there, to hang in there. And that's all I have to say.

Ronald Allridge
Execution Date: 06/08/1995
Race: Black
County of Conviction: Tarrant
Last Statement: This person declined to make a last statement.

John Fearance
Execution Date: 06/20/1995
Race: Black
County of Conviction: Dallas
Last Statement: I would like to say that I have no animosity toward anyone. I made a mistake 18 years ago – I lost control of my mind but I didn't mean to hurt anyone. I have no hate toward humanity. I hope He will forgive me for what I done. I didn't mean to.

Karl Hammond
Execution Date: 06/21/1995
Race: Black
County of Conviction: Bexar
Last Statement: This person declined to make a last statement.

Vernon Sattiewhite
Execution Date: 08/15/1995
Race: Black
County of Conviction: Bexar

Last Statement: I would like to say – I just hope Ms. Fielder is happy now. I would like to thank my lawyer, Nancy, for her help on my case and for being with me now.

Carl Johnson
Execution Date: 09/19/1995
Race: Black
County of Conviction: Harris
Last Statement: I want the world to know that I'm innocent and that I've found peace. Let's ride.

Harold Lane
Execution Date: 10/04/1995
Race: White
County of Conviction: Dallas
Last Statement: This person declined to make a last statement.

Bernard Amos
Execution Date: 12/06/1995
Race: Black
County of Conviction: Dallas
Last Statement: This person declined to make a last statement.

Hal Vuong
Execution Date: 12/07/1995
Race: Other
County of Conviction: Jefferson
Last Statement: I thank God that He died for my sins on the cross, and I thank Him for saving my soul, so I will know when my body lays back in the grave, my soul goes to be with the Lord. Praise God. I hope whoever hears my voice tonight will turn to the Lord. I give my spirit back to Him. Praise the Lord. Praise Jesus. Hallelujah.

Esequel Banda
Execution Date: 12/11/1005
Race: Hispanic
County of Conviction: Hamilton
Last Statement: This person declined to make a last statement.

James Briddle
Execution Date: 12/12/1995
Race: White
County of Conviction: Harris
Last Statement: This person declined to make a last statement.

Leo Jenkins
Execution Date: 02/09/1996
Race: White
County of Conviction: Harris
Last Statement: This person declined to make a last statement.

Kenneth Granviel
Execution Date: 02/27/1996
Race: Black
County of Conviction: Tarrant
Last Statement: This person declined to make a last statement.

Joe Gonzales, Jr.
Execution Date: 09/18/1996
Race: Hispanic
County of Conviction: Potter
Last Statement: There are people all over the world who face things worse than death on a daily basis, and in that sense I consider myself lucky. I cannot find the words to express the sadness I feel for bringing this hurt and pain on my loved ones.I will not ask forgiveness for the decisions I have made in this judicial process, only acceptance. God bless you all.

Richard Brimage, Jr.
Execution Date: 02/10/1997
Race: White
County of Conviction: Kieberg
Last Statement: Not from me but I have a message to you from God. Save the children. Find one who needs help and make a small sacrifice of your own wealth and save the innocent ones. They are the key for making the world a better place.

John Barefield
Execution Date: 03/12/1997
Race: Black

County of Conviction: Harris
Last Statement: *(Mumbled.)* Tell Mama I love her.

David Herman

Execution Date: 04/02/1997
Race: White
County of Conviction: Tarrant
Last Statement: It was horrible and inexcusable for me to take the life of your loved one and to hurt so many mentally and physically. I am here because I took a life and killing is wrong by an individual and by the state, and I am sorry we are here but if my death gives you peace and closure then this is all worthwhile. To all of my friends and family, I love you and I am going home.

David Spence

Execution Date: 04/03/1997
Race: White
County of Conviction: McLennan
Last Statement: Yes, I do. First of all, I want you to understand I speak the truth when I say I didn't kill your kids. Honestly I have not killed anyone. I wish you could get the rage from your hearts and you could see the truth and get rid of the hatred. I love you all – *(names of children)* – Corey, Steve *(garbled)* – This is very important. I love ya'll and I miss ya'll. O.K., now I'm finished.

Billy Woods

Execution Date: 04/14/1997
Race: White
County of Conviction: Harris
Last Statement: This person declined to make a last statement.

Kenneth Gentry

Execution Date: 04/16/1997
Race: White
County of Conviction: Denton
Last Statement: Thank the Lord for the past 14 years that have allowed me to grow as a man – To J.D.'s family, I am sorry for the suffering you have gone through the past 14 years. I hope you can get some peace tonight. To my family, I am happy to be going home to Jesus. Sweet Jesus, here I come. Take me home. I am going your way.

Benjamin Boyle
Execution Date: 04/21/1997
Race: White
County of Conviction: Potter
Last Statement: This person declined to make a last statement.

Ernest Baldree
Execution Date: 04/29/1997
Race: White
County of Conviction: Navarro
Last Statement: This person declined to make a last statement.

Terry Washington
Execution Date: 05/06/1997
Race: Black
County of Conviction: Walker
Last Statement: This person declined to make a last statement.

Anthony Westley
Execution Date: 05/13/1997
Race: Black
County of Conviction: Harris
Last Statement: I want you to know that I did not kill anyone. I love you all. *(Offender's words were not clear)*

Clifton Belyeu
Execution Date: 05/16/1997
Race: White
County of Conviction: McLennan
Last Statement: First of all I want to thank the LORD, my family and my wife Nora for all the support and encouragement they've shown me through all this. I love you!! Now I want to thank all of you that came here today to be with me. I know most of you are here to see me suffer and die but you're in for a big disappointment because today is a day of joy. Today is the day I'll be set free from all this pain and suffering. Today I'm going home to HEAVEN to live for all eternity with my HEAVENLY FATHER JESUS CHRIST, and as I lay here taking my last breath, I'll be praying for all of you because you're here today with anger and hatred in your hearts letting Satan deceive you into believing that what you're doing is right and just. GOD help you, because what you're doing here today and what's in your hearts here today makes you no better than any man or woman on death-rows

across this country. Today you're committing murder too!!! I pray on my own behalf for forgiveness for any and all of the pain I've caused you, I pray that some day you'll realize your own mistakes and ask GOD to forgive you as I have, because there is no peace without GOD's forgiveness. Amen.

Richard Drinkard
Execution Date: 05/19/1997
Race: White
County of Conviction: Harris
Last Statement: This person declined to make a last statement.

Clarence Lackey
Execution Date: 05/20/1997
Race: White
County of Conviction: Tom Green
Last Statement: I would like to thank my Lord Jesus Christ for keeping me strong all these years. I would also like to thank my mother for standing by me all these years. I would also like to thank my pen pals, Joe and Camille Tilling and JoAnn for helping me stay strong all these years. I also thank my two lawyers, Rita and Brent, for fighting to keep me alive. I love you, Mom –

Bruce Callins
Execution Date: 05/21/1997
Race: Black
County of Conviction: Tarrant
Last Statement: I want to let all of my people know and everybody who is here and supported me that I love them and wish them all the best.

Larry White
Execution Date: 05/22/1997
Race: White
County of Conviction: Harris
Last Statement: I would like to apologize for all of the hurt, pain and disappointment I caused to my family and all my friends. I hope all the veterans and teenagers out there who have a drug problem will get help. I hope the lord will forgive me of all of my sins. I thank Jack and Kathy for being with me. I hope that those who support the Death Row inmates will continue to work and maybe we can get this resolved and do away with the Death Penalty. I hope this is a lot better place where I am going.

Robert Madden

Execution Date: 05/28/1997
Race: White
County of Conviction: Leon
Last Statement: Yes sir, I do. Well, here we are. I apologize for your loss and your pain, but I didn't kill those people. Hopefully we will all learn something about ourselves and about each other and we will learn enough to stop the cycle of hate and vengeance and come to value what is really going on in this world. We can't look back. I forgive everyone for this process, which seems to be wrong. We all end up doing experiences which we create. That is all I have to say about that. *(There were some unintelligible sentences.)*

Patrick Rogers

Execution Date: 06/02/1997
Race: Black
County of Conviction: Collin
Last Statement: Yes, I would like to praise Allah and I am praying to Allah. Allah is most gracious. I will ask Allah for forgiveness because he created me and he will forgive me. All of the brothers on the row stay strong. *(Some words about Allah that I couldn't understand.)* I love my family, my mother. I will see her sooner or later. Life goes on. Don't let these people break *(couldn't understand)* you. Keep true to nature. You do not have to act like them. Rise above it. *(couldn't understand)* Praise Allah – *(some more Allah mumbling)*

Kenneth Harris

Executive Date: 06/03/1997
Race: Black
County of Conviction: Harris
Last Statement: I would like to thank all of you for coming. I am sorry for all of the pain I have caused both families – my family and yours. I would like for you to know that I am sorry for all the pain I caused for all these years. I have had time to understand the pain I have caused you. I am ready, Warden.

Dorsie Johnson, Jr.

Execution Date: 06/04/1997
Race: Black
County of Conviction: Scurry
Last Statement: I would like to tell my family that I love them and always be strong and keep their heads up and keep faith in Jesus. That's it.

Davis Losada

Execution Date: 06/04/1997

Race: Hispanic

County of Conviction: Cameron

Last Statement: Yes, I do. If it matters to anyone, I did not kill Olga. Brian, thank you for caring. Dee Dee, you have been a good sister to all of us. Ana and Chico *(not sure of name he said)*, trust in God. I will always love you, Lynn. I will always love you. O.K., Warden.

Earl Behringer

Execution Date: 06/11/1997

Race: White

County of Conviction: Tarrant

Last Statement: It's a good day to die. I walked in here like a man and I am leaving here like a man. I had a good life. I have known the love of a good woman, my wife. I have a good family. My grandmother is the pillar of the community. I love and cherish my friends and family. Thank you for your love. To the Hancock family, I am sorry for the pain I caused you. If my death gives you any peace, so be it. I want my friends to know it is not the way to die, but I belong to Jesus Christ. I confess my sins. I have...

David Stoker

Execution Date: 06/16/1997

Race: White

County of Conviction: Hale

Last Statement: I have a statement prepared that I have given to the Chaplain that I want released to the media. I am ready, Warden.

Eddie Johnson

Execution Date: 06/16/1997

Race: Black

County of Conviction: Aransas

Last Statement: I would like to say to the Magee family and the Cadena family that I was friends with David and Virginia and I did not commit this offense. I have tried to do something to compensate the families by writing a book. I would like for the proceeds to go to the Magee family and the Cadena family. There is someone who will be contacting them or they can get in touch with my attorney. I would like to thank you for standing by me and loving me and carry my best to my "sun," my butterfly. Goodbye, sun, I love you.

Irineo Montoya
Execution Date: 06/18/1997
Race: Hispanic
County of Conviction: Cameron
Last Statement: Goodbye. I will wait for you in Heaven. I will be waiting for you. I love my parents. I am at peace with God. Fight for the good.

Robert West, Jr.
Execution Date: 07/29/1997
Race: White
County of Conviction: Harris
Last Statement: I would like to apologize for all of the pain and suffering I put you all through. I hope this will give you closure now and later on down the line. Bob, I appreciate you coming – Stacey and Jess. I will wait for you –

James Davis
Execution Date: 09/09/1997
Race: Black
County of Conviction: Travis
Last Statement: Well, my friends in my heart, I'm ready –

Jessel Turner
Execution Date: 09/22/1997
Race: Black
County of Conviction: Harris
Last Statement: First, I would like to give praise to God for the love and grace that he has allowed for all of this to come together. I would like to thank and ask blessings for all of the men who are imprisoned and have shared in my struggle and have allowed me to help them. I would like to thank my family for their blessings and for sharing my struggle and having been there for me and endured this with me. I would like to thank the Chaplain and all the rest who have offered their prayers.

Benjamin Stone
Execution Date: 09/25/1997
Race: White
County of Conviction: Nueces
Last Statement: This person declined to make a last statement.

John Cockrum
Execution Date: 09/30/1997
Race: White
County of Conviction: Bowie
Last Statement: I would like to apologize to the victim's family for all of the pain I have caused them. I would like to tell my family I love them and I hope to see them again soon. Lord Jesus, thank you for giving me the strength and the time in my life to find Jesus Christ and to be forgiven for all of my sins. Thank you for the changes in my life you have given me, the love and closeness of my family, and my beautiful daughter. Thank you for using me –

Dwight Adanandus
Execution Date: 10/01/1997
Race: Black
County of Conviction: Bexar
Last Statement: Ms. Craft and Ms. Bethrie, I don't know what to say to you but I apologize for the pain I have caused you and your family over the years. I hope you will accept my apology and that you will know that it is sincere. I hope this will allow you and your family to move on and I hope you will forgive me and I hope Mr. Hanon [illegible] will forgive me for taking his life. Please accept my apology. I love you all. I am finished.

Ricky Green
Execution Date: 10/08/1997
Race: White
County of Conviction: Tarrant
Last Statement: I want to thank the Lord for giving me this opportunity to get to know Him. He has shown me a lot and He has changed me in the past two months. I have been in prison 8½ years and on Death Row for 7, and I have not gotten into any trouble. I feel like I am not a threat to society anymore. I feel like my punishment is over, but my friends are now being punished. I thank the Lord for all He has done for me. I do want to tell the family that I am sorry but killing me is not going to solve nothing. I really do not believe that if Jesus were here tonight that he would execute me. Jesus is all about love. I want to thank all of my friends for supporting me and for being here for me. Thank all of my friends on the row. Thank you Lord. I am finished.

Kenneth Ransom
Execution Date: 10/28/1997

Race: Black
County of Conviction: Harris
Last Statement: First and foremost I would like to tell the victims' families that I am sorry because I don't feel like I am guilty. I am sorry for the pain all of them have gone through during holidays and birthdays. They are without their loved ones. I have said from the beginning and I will say it again that I am innocent. I did not kill no one. I feel like this is the Lord's will that will be done. I love you all. You know it. Don't cry. Tell my brothers I love them. You all be strong.

Aus Lauti

Execution Date: 11/04/1997
Race: Other
County of Conviction: Harris
Last Statement: I am so glad I found God and I am so happy for it. I love my family and I want them to know that. That is about all I have to say.

Aaron Fuller

Execution Date: 11/06/1997
Race: White
County of Conviction: Dawson
Last Statement: Jesus, the Lord, is everything to me. I am nothing without him. Praise Jesus. Praise God

Michael Sharp

Execution Date: 11/19/1997
Race: White
County of Conviction: Crockett
Last Statement: Yes, I do. I would like to tell the surviving victims here, society, my family and friends, that I ask that they forgive me for anything I have done. I beg for your forgiveness. I would like to ask the Lord Jesus Christ for forgiveness and say that in spite of my circumstances, I have been blessed by Him. My first thought is that Jesus Christ came down and separated the humans from God. I would like to see that wall that separates these groups here tonight brought down and that we would all have love and compassion for one another and that you all build a future for all of us. There are a lot of men on the Row who need to be remembered. I love all...

Charlie Livingston

Execution Date: 11/21/1997

Race: Black
County of Conviction: Harris
Last Statement: You all brought me here to be executed, not to make a speech. That's it.

Michael Lockhart

Execution Date: 12/09/1997
Race: White
County of Conviction: Bexar
Last Statement: A lot of people view what is happening here as evil, but I want you to know that I found love and compassion here. The people who work here, I thank them for the kindness they have shown me and I deeply appreciate all that has been done for me by the people who work here. That's all, Warden, I'm ready.

Karla Tucker

Execution Date: 02/03/1998
Race: White
County of Conviction: Harris
Last Statement: Yes sir, I would like to say to all of you – the Thornton family and Jerry Dean's family that I am so sorry. I hope God will give you peace with this. Baby, I love you. Ron, give Peggy a hug for me. Everybody has been so good to me. I love all of you very much. I am going to be face to face with Jesus now. Warden Baggett, thank all of you so much. You have been so good to me. I love all of you very much. I will see you all when you get there. I will wait for you.

Steven Renfro

Execution Date: 02/09/1998
Race: White
County of Conviction: Harrison

Last Statement: I would like to tell the victims' families that I am sorry, very sorry. I am so sorry. Forgive me if you can. I know it's impossible, but try. Take my hand, Lord Jesus, I'm coming home.

Jerry Hogue

Execution Date: 03/11/1998
Race: White
County of Conviction: Tarrant
Last Statement: Mindy, I'm with you, honey. I do not know why, Mindy, you are

doing this, but I will still forgive you. You know he is a murderer. Why don't you support me? He will do it again. Mindy, you are lucky you are still alive. Give my love to my family. I love them. Mindy, you can stop this. O.K., I'm ready.

Joseph Cannon
Execution Date: 04/22/1998
Race: White
County of Conviction: Bexar
Last Statement: I am sorry for what I did to your mom. It isn't because I'm going to die. All my life I have been locked up. I could never forgive what I done. I am sorry for all of you. I love you all. Thank you for supporting me. I thank you for being kind to me when I was small. Thank you, God. All right.

Lesley Gosch
Execution Date: 04/24/1998
Race: White
County of Conviction: Victoria
Last Statement: This person declined to make a last statement.

Frank McFarland
Execution Date: 04/29/1998
Race: White
County of Conviction: Tarrant
Last Statement: I owe no apologies for a crime I did not commit. Those who lied and fabricated evidence against me will have to answer for what they have done. I know in my heart what I did and I call upon the spirit of my ancestors and all of my people and I swear to them and now I am coming home.

Robert Carter
Execution Date: 05/18/1998
Race: Black
County of Conviction: Harris
Last Statement: I love all of you all. Thank you for caring so much about me. Keep the faith. I am going to a better place. I hope the victim's family will forgive me because I didn't mean to hurt no one or kill no one. I love you all.

Pedro Muniz
Execution Date: 05/19/1998
Race: Hispanic

County of Conviction: Williamson

Last Statement: I know you can't hear me now but I know that it won't matter what I have to say. I want you to know that I did not kill your sister. If you want to know the truth, and you deserve to know the truth, hire your own investigators. That's all I have to say.

Clifford Boggess

Execution Date: 06/11/1998
Race: White
County of Conviction; Clay

Last Statement: I'd like to say that for the murders of Ray Hazelwood and Frank Collier, I'm sorry for that pain it has caused you. To my friends, I'd like to say that I love you and I'm glad you've been a part of my life. Thank you. I'll miss you. Remember that today I'll be with Jesus in paradise. I'll see you again. Lord Jesus Christ, son of Almighty God, [have] mercy on me as a sinner, forgive me of my sins. I would like to offer up my death for the conversion of sinners on Death Row. Lord Jesus, into your hands I command my spirit.

Johnny Pyles

Execution Date: 06/15/1998
Race: White
County of Conviction: Dallas

Last Statement: I want to tell you folks there, of a... I have a love in my heart for you. I hope you don't look for satisfaction or comfort or peace in my execution. Jesus Christ is my Lord and Savior and I want him to be yours. I'm sorry for the pain and heartache I've caused your family. Too many years I've caused all my family problems and heartache. I'm sorry. I wanted to let you know that the Lord Jesus is my life and I just want to go. I'm gonna fall asleep and I'll be in his presence shortly. I got reason to rejoice and I pray to see all of you there someday.

Leopoldo Narvaiz

Execution Date: 06/26/1998
Race: Hispanic
County of Conviction: Bexar

Last Statement: This person declined to make a last statement.

David Castillo

Execution Date: 08/23/1998
Race: Hispanic

County of Conviction: Hidalgo

Last Statement: Keep it brief here. Just want to say, uh, family, take care of yourselves. Uh, look at this as a learning experience. Everything happens for a reason. We all know what really happened, but there are some things you just can't fight. Little people always seem to get squashed. It happens. Even so, just got to take the good with the bad. There is no man that is free from all evil, nor any man that is so evil to be worth nothing. But it's all part of life, and my family, take care of yourselves. Tell my wife I love her. I'll keep an eye on everybody, especially my nieces and nephews. I'm pretty good. I love ya'll. Take care. I'm ready.

Genaro Camacho, Jr.

Execution Date: 08/26/1998
Race: Hispanic
County of Conviction: Dallas
Last Statement: I love you all. We had a good service and I'll be with you. I'll be waiting for you in Heaven. Ok. Adios. That's all I have to say.

Delbert Teague, Jr.

Execution Date: 09/09/1998
Race: White
County of Conviction: Tarrant
Last Statement: I have come here today to die, not make speeches. Today is a good day for dying. Est Sularus Oth Mithas (My Honor Is My Life).

Javier Cruz

Execution Date: 10/01/1998
Race: Hispanic
County of Conviction: Bexar
Last Statement: Thank you for setting me free. God bless you all. I love you, Miguel. Take care of my angel, Leslie. Love, Javier Cruz

Jonathan Nobles

Execution Date: 10/07/1998
Race: White
County of Conviction: Travis
Last Statement: 1 Corinthians 12:31B – 13:13 (NIV) And now I will show you the most excellent way. If I speak in the tongues of men and of angels, but have not love, I am only a resounding gong or a clanging cymbal. If I have the gift of prophecy and can fathom all mysteries and all knowledge, and if I have a faith

that can move mountains, but have not love, I am nothing. If I give all I possess to the poor and surrender my body to the flames, but have not love, I gain nothing. Love is patient, love is kind. It does not envy, it does not boast, it is not proud. It is not rude, it is not self-seeking, it is not easily angered, it keeps no record of wrongs. Love does not delight in evil but rejoices with the truth. It always protects, always trusts, always hopes, always perseveres. Love never fails. But where there are prophecies, they will cease; where there are tongues, they will be stilled; where there is knowledge, it will pass away. For we know in part and we prophesy in part, but when perfection comes, the imperfect disappears. When I was a child, I talked like a child, I thought like a child, I reasoned like a child. When I became a man, I put childish ways behind me. Now we see but a poor reflection as in a mirror; then we shall see face to face. Now I know in part; then I shall know fully, even as I am fully known. And now these three remain: faith, hope and love. But the greatest of these is love.

Kenneth McDuff
Execution Date: 11/17/1998
Race: White
County of Conviction: Harris
Last Statement: I'm ready to be released. Release me.

Daniel Corwin
Execution Date: 12/07/1998
Race: White
County of Conviction: Montgomery
Last Statement: I guess the first thing I want to do is thank some very special people, Sara and Sabrina. And for affording me the opportunity that ya'll did. It made a real big difference in my life. I thank you. Thank you again from the deepest part of my heart. I'm sorry. The biggest thing I wanted to say was to you and family and I know I haven't had a chance to talk with ya'll in any form or fashion or way or manner. And I regret what happened and I want you to know that I'm sorry. I just ask and hope that sometime down the line that you can forgive me. I think in a lot of ways that without that it becomes very empty and hollow and the only thing we have is hatred and anger. I guess the only thing I have to say about the Death Penalty is that a lot of times people think of it as one sided, but it's not. It's two sided. There pain on both sides and it's not an issue that people just sit there and voice off and say, well, this is a good thing, or this is a bad thing. But it's something that's, you know, needs to be looked at and desired in each heart. I just hope that all of you can understand that and someday forgive me. I want to thank ya'll for

affording me the opportunity to talk and meet with ya'll. It meant so much. Thank you so much for being with me and my family. Thank you. I love you.

Jeff Emery
Execution Date: 12/08/1998
Race: White
County of Conviction: Brazos
Last Statement: I just want to tell Catharina I love you. Take care of yourself. That's all I have to say.

James Meanes
Execution Date: 12/15/1998
Race: Black
County of Conviction: Harris
Last Statement: As the ocean always returns to itself, love always returns to itself. So does consciousness, always returns to itself. And I do so with love on my lips. May God bless all mankind.

John Moody
Execution Date: 01/05/1999
Race: White
County of Conviction; Taylor
Last Statement: I'd like to apologize and ask forgiveness for any pain and suffering I have inflicted upon all of you, including my family. All of you, I am very sorry. There is a point where a man wants to die in judgment. Though my judgment is merciful, I hope and pray that all those involved as well as the judgment upon ya'll, will one day be more merciful than mine. God bless you all. God speed. I love you. Remain strong. Ask God to have mercy. I love you all, too. I'm very sorry. I've got to go now. I love you.

Troy Farris
Execution Date: 01/13/1999
Race: White
County of Conviction: Tarrant
Last Statement: First off, to the Rosenbaum family, to Cindy, to Scott, to everyone, I just want to say I have nothing but love for you. And I mean that from the deepest part. I can only tell you that Clark did not die in vain. I don't mean to offend you by saying that, but what I mean by that is, through his death, he led this man to God. I have nothing but love for you. To my family, my soul beloved, you're so beautiful,

for all your love and support is just miraculous, everything that ya'll have done. Be sure and tell T.D. he's in my heart. I send my love to Jay, to everyone. To Roger Burdge. I have nothing but love for all of you. Like they say in the song, I guess, I just want to go out like Elijah, on fire with the spirit of God. I love you. I'm done.

Martin Vega
Execution Date: 01/26/1999
Race: Hispanic
County of Conviction: Caldwell
Last Statement: I really don't have much to say. All I want to say is that when the state introduced my sister and my niece as state witnesses, it's not that they testified against me. The thing is, my lawyers would not subpoena anyone, so they allowed the state to subpoena them to paint a picture to the jury that my own sister and niece was testifying against me. Linda is innocent of this. I am innocent of this. Now all you all are seeing in the process a perfect example of ol' freaky deaky Bill Clinton when he signed that anti-terrorism law to shorten the appeals. This is a conspiracy. They used false testimony of a woman that said I had raped her, when the test showed that the foreign pubic hair that was found on her body belonged to no one in that room. They found a drop of sposmosa in the crotch of her pants that was tied to blood type B. My blood type is A. Now the same woman there they brought to testify against this murder case. That woman was under indictment for possession of methamphetamine, delivery of methamphetamine. She could have gotten out of both of those cases. Yet, she swore under oath that she had never been in trouble with the law and none of that mattered. So what does that make this great state? A very high-priced prostitute that sells itself, called justice, to the highest bidder. I am being charged under article 19.83 of the Texas Penal Code of murder with the promise of remuneration. That means they got to have three people, the one that paid, the one that killed, and the deceased. And the alleged remunerator is out on the streets, so how come I'm being executed today, without a remunerator? This is a great American justice. So if you don't think they won't, believe me they will. Ain't no telling who gonna be next. That's all I have to say. Especially for the people of the deceased, Sims is innocent and so am I. So the murder is still not there. Today you are a witness, the state (cough). Bye.

George Cordova
Execution Date: 02/10/1999
Race: Hispanic
County of Conviction: Bexar
Last Statement: For the pain I have caused you. I am ashamed to even look at

your faces. You are great people. To my brothers on Death Row. Mexico, Mexico...
(Spanish).

Danny Barber
Execution Date: 02/11/1999
Race: White
County of Conviction: Dallas
Last Statement: Hello, Ms. Ingram, it is good to see you. I said I could talk but I don't think I am gonna be able to. I heard one of your nieces had some angry words. I didn't have anything to do with the stay. I spent the last twenty years waiting to figure out what's going on. I pray that you get over it and that's the only thing I can think to say. I'm regretful for what I done, but I'm a different person from that time. If you could get to know me over the years, you could have seen it. I've got some people over here that believes that. I want to talk to my friends over here for a second. Well, it's good to see you guys. Look after Mary Lynn for me. Like I said, I've called my mother already, so she knows. Goodbye.

Andrew Cantu
Execution Date: 02/16/1999
Race: Hispanic
County of Conviction: Taylor
Last Statement: This person declined to make a last statement.

Norman Green
Execution Date: 02/24/1999
Race: Black
County of Conviction: Bexar
Last Statement: This person declined to make a last statement.

Charles Rector
Execution Date: 03/26/1999
Race: Black
County of Conviction: Travis
Last Statement: The first statement I would like to make it's my sister. I want her to know that every thing that is said, every move that is made, every motion, I hold it true to my heart. I hold it in my soul. I want you to know that I am not guilty and I will say this to the family. I did not kill your daughter. Take it the way you want. Sorry for the pain. Sister, I love you and will be there with you, to help you. I want to talk to you about being there by her. You know what I am saying. I want to thank

you, thank you for the words. The dying words, you know. They mean a lot. Make sure he knows what I want him to know. I want to quote a song that I wrote called "God Living with Us 24 Hours." It goes: Tell the kids I love them and I'll be there. That's all I have to say.

Excell White
Execution Date: 03/30/1999
Race: White
County of Conviction: Collin
Last Statement: This person declined to make a last statement.

Aaron Foust
Execution Date: 04/28/1999
Race: White
County of Conviction: Tarrant
Last Statement: Adios, amigos, I'll see ya'll on the other side. I'm ready when ya'll are.

Jose De La Cruz
Execution Date: 05/04/1999
Race: Hispanic
County of Conviction: Nueces
Last Statement: This person declined to make a last statement.

Clydell Coleman
Execution Date: 05/05/1999
Race: Black
County of Conviction: McLennan
Last Statement: This person declined to make a last statement.

William Little
Execution Date: 06/01/1999
Race: White
County of Conviction: Liberty
Last Statement: This person declined to make a last statement.

Joseph Faulder
Execution Date: 06/17/1999
Race: White

County of Conviction: Gregg
Last Statement: This person declined to make a last statement.

Charles Tuttle
Execution Date: 07/01/1999
Race: White
County of Conviction: Smith
Last Statement: To Kathy's family and friends that were unable to attend today, I am truly sorry. I hope my dropping my appeal has in some way began your healing process. This is all I am going to do to help you out in any way for the nightmare and pain that I have caused you, but I am truly sorry and I wish I could take back what I did, but I can't. I hope this heals you. To my family: I love you. When the tears flow, let the smiles grow. Everything is all right. To my family: I love you. Warden, ATW.

Tyrone Fuller
Execution Date: 07/07/1999
Race: Black
County of Conviction: Grayson
Last Statement: Yes, to my family, I love you. Please do not mourn my death or my life. Continue to live as I want you to live. I hold no bitterness toward no one. Just remember the light. I'm gonna let this light shine. Let it shine. Let the light shine.

Ricky Blackmon
Execution Date: 08/04/1999
Race: White
County of Conviction: Shelby
Last Statement: This person declined to make a last statement.

Charles Boyd
Execution Date: 08/05/1999
Race: Black
County of Conviction: Dallas
Last Statement: I want you all to know I did not do this crime. I wanted to wait for a thirty day stay for a DNA test so you know who did the crime.

Kenneth Dunn
Execution Date: 08/10/1999
Race: Black

County of Conviction: Harris
Last Statement: This person declined to make a last statement.

James Earhart

Execution Date: 08/11/1999
Race: White
County of Conviction: Lee
Last Statement: This person declined to make a last statement.

Joe Trevino, Jr.

Execution Date: 08/18/1999
Race: Hispanic
County of Conviction: Tarrant
Last Statement: This person declined to make a last statement.

Raymond Jones

Execution Date: 09/01/1999
Race: Black
County of Conviction: Jefferson
Last Statement: This person declined to make a last statement.

Willis Barnes

Execution Date: 09/10/1999
Race: Black
County of Conviction: Harris
Last Statement: Yes, I would like to give love to my mother, sisters and brothers and let them know that I am thinking of them right now and I want to thank God for giving me such a loving family. To the victim's family: I hope you will find it in your heart to forgive me as I have forgiven you. I'm ready, Warden.

William Davis

Execution Date: 09/14/1999
Race: Black
County of Conviction: Harris
Last Statement: I would like to give thanks to God Almighty, by whose grace I am saved through His son, Jesus Christ, without whom I would be nothing today. Because of this mercy and grace, I have come a long way, and I would like to thank God and others who have been instrumental. I would like to say to the Lang family how truly sorry I am in my soul and in my heart of hearts for the pain and misery

that I have caused from my actions. I am truly sorry. And to my family I would also like to extend to them the same apology for the pain and misery that I have put them through, and I love them dearly from the bottom of my heart, and one day I would like to see them on the other side. Some I will; some I won't. I would like to thank all of the men on Death Row who have showed me love throughout the years, but especially the last two or three weeks, and I hold nothing against no man. I am so thankful that I have lived as long as I have. I hope that I have helped someone. I hope that [by] donating my body to science that some parts of it can be used to help someone, and I just thank the Lord for all that he has done for me. That is all I have to say, Warden. Oh, I would like to say in closing, "What about those cowboys?"

Richard Smith
Execution Date: 09/21/1999
Race: White
County of Conviction: Harris
Last Statement: This person declined to make a last statement.

Alvin Crane
Execution Date: 10/12/1999
Race: White
County of Conviction: Denton
Last Statement: I would like to say a little something. I just want to say I'm sorry to the family. I know I caused you a lot of pain and suffering and I hope that you will find some peace and comfort in this. That if there is any anger you can let it go. Not let it come between you and God. Sorry for causing everybody such trouble tonight, Bruce, Joe, ya'll all treat me with respect I appreciate it. I really do. I just want to tell my family, everybody I love and I want you to know that I love you, and that God loves you too. Everything is going to be just fine, just fine. I love ya'll. That's it.

Jerry McFadden
Execution Date: 10/14/1999
Race: White
County of Conviction: Upshur
Last Statement: This person declined to make a last statement.

Domingo Cantu, Jr.
Execution Date: 10/28/1999
Race: Hispanic
County of Conviction: Dallas

Last Statement: *English:* I love you. I will be waiting for you on the other side. Son be strong no matter what happens, know that God is looking over you. Jesus mercy, Jesus mercy, Jesus mercy! *Spanish:* Brother-in-law, take care of the family and let it be united. Yoli. German: Menic schone prizessin. Du list all mine herz and seele, rind ich liele dich so sehm! (Translation: My beautiful princess. You are all my heart and soul and I love you so much.)

Desmond Jennings
Execution Date: 11/16/1999
Race: Black
County of Conviction: Tarrant
Last Statement: This person declined to make a last statement.

John Lamb
Execution Date: 11/17/1999
Race: White
County of Conviction: Hunt
Last Statement: I'm sorry, I wish I could bring them back. I'm done, let's do it.

Jose Gutierrez
Execution Date: 11/18/1999
Race: Hispanic
County of Conviction: Brazos
Last Statement: Mama Isabel told me to tell you hello. Holy, holy, holy! Lord God Almighty! Early in the morning our song shall rise to Thee; Holy, holy, holy, merciful and mighty! God in three Persons, blessed Trinity. Holy, holy, holy! Merciful and mighty. All Thy works shall praise Thy name, in earth, and sky, and sea; Holy, holy, holy, merciful and mighty! God in three Persons, blessed Trinity. Oh, our Father who art in heaven, holy, holy, holy be Thy name. Thy kingdom come, Thy will be done, on earth as it is in heaven. Give us this day our daily bread and forgive us our sin as we forgive our debtors. Lead us not into temptation, but deliver us from evil, for Thine is the kingdom and the power and the glory forever and ever. Now, Father, into Thy hands I commit my spirit. Amen.

David Long
Execution Date: 12/08/1999
Race: White
County of Conviction: Dallas
Last Statement: Ah, just ah sorry ya'll. I think of tried everything I could to get in

touch with ya'll to express how sorry I am. I, I never was right after that incident happened. I sent a letter to somebody, you know a letter outlining what I feel about everything. But anyway I just wanted, right after that apologize to you. I'm real sorry for it. I was raised by the California Youth Authority, I can't really pin point where it started, what happened but really believe that's just the bottom line, what happened to me was in California. I was in their reformatory schools and penitentiary, but ah they create monsters in there. That's it, I have nothing else to say. Thanks for coming Jack.

James Beathard

Execution Date: 12/09/1999
Race: White
County of Conviction: Trinity
Last Statement: I want to start out by acknowledging the love that I've had in my family. No man in this world has had a better family than me. I had the best parents in the world. I had the best brothers and sisters in the world. I've had the most wonderful life any man could have ever had. I've never been more proud of anybody than I have of my daughter and my son. I've got no complaints and no regrets about that. I love everyone of them and have always been loved all of my life. I've never had any doubts about that. Couple of matters that I want to talk about since this is one of the few times people will listen to what I have to say. The Unites States has gotten to a now where they zero respect for human life. My death is just a symptom of a bigger illness. At some point the government has got to wake up and stop doing things to destroy other countries and killing innocent children. The ongoing embargo and sanctions against places like Iran and Iraq, Cuba and other places. They are not doing anything to change the world, but they are harming innocent children. That's got to stop at some point. Perhaps more important in a lot of ways is what we are doing to the environment is even more devastating because as long as we keep going the direction we're going the end result is it won't matter how we treat other people because everybody on the planet will be on their way out. We have got to wake up and stop doing that. Ah, one of the few ways in the world the truth is ever going to get out, or people are ever going to know what's happening as long as we support a free press out there. I see the press struggling to stay existent as a free institution One of the few truly free institutions is the press in Texas. People like the Texas Observer and I want to thank them for the job they've done in keeping me and everybody else informed. I hope people out there will support them, listen to them and be there for them. Without it, things like this are going to happen and nobody will even know. I love all of you. I always have I always will. I would like to address the State of Texas and specially Joe Price,

the District Attorney who put me here. I want to remind Mr. Price of the mistake he made at Gene Hawthorn's trial when he said that Gene Hawthorn was telling the truth at my trial. Mr. Price is a one-eyed hunting dog. He in fact is not a one-eyed hunting dog, and in fact Gene Hawthorn lied at my trial. Everybody knew it. I'm dying tonight based on testimony, that all parties, me, the man who gave the testimony, the prosecutor he used knew it was a lie. I am hoping somebody will call him to the floor for recent comments he's made in the newspaper. It's bad enough that a prosecutor can take truth and spin on it and try to re-doctor it. But when they actually make facts up and present to the public as trial's evidence. That goes beyond fail, that's completely unforgivable and I hope somebody makes Mr. Price account for or explain the tennis shoes he is talking about that put me here. I'm still completely lost on that and I'm hoping that somebody will go back and verify the trial record and make him accountable for lying to the public and the press that way. That's really all I have to say except that I love my family. and nobody, nobody has got a better family than me. I love you booger bear. I love doodle bug, too. Don't let them ever forget me. I'll never forget them. I'll see you on the other side, okay. Bye bye Debbie. Bye bro, bye booger bear. Father Mike, Father Walsh, love you all. That's all, sir.

Robert Atworth

Execution Date: 12/14/1999
Race: White
County of Conviction: Dallas
Last Statement: Well, first, My people, you guys have heard everything I needed to say today. I hope I said the right things. I hope you heard me. And I hope you go beyond here and do what you need to do, do the right thing. Strength in numbers. Look out for each other. You still got a chance with Shawn. Edwin you know what you gotta do. You have my love. It's the right thing. And for everybody else, those people who have malice in their heart, allow ambitions to over ride what they know. Be right. Even though they just gotta do their job. For all of you with hatred in their veins, and think this is ashamed. You've done nothing. I did this, I chose this, you've done nothing. Remember this, if all you know is hatred, if all you know is blood love, you'll never be satisfied. For everybody out there that is like that and knows nothing but negative, kiss my proud white Irish ass. I'm ready Warden, send me home.

Sammie Felder, Jr.

Execution Date: 12/15/1999
Race: Black

County of Conviction: Harris
Last Statement: Like to tell my friends that I love them. Appreciate them being here to support me. Alison, I love you.

Earl Heiselbetz, Jr.
Execution Date: 01/12/2000
Race: White
County of Conviction: Sabine
Last Statement: Love ya'll, see you on the other side.

Spencer Goodman
Execution Date: 01/18/2000
Race: White
County of Conviction: Fort Bend
Last Statement: To my family, I love them. To Kami, I love you and will always be with you. That's it Warden.

David Hicks
Execution Date: 01/20/2000
Race: Black
County of Conviction: Freestone
Last Statement: Hey, how y'all doing out there? I done lost my voice. Y'all be strong now, alright? Don, thanks man. I love you, Gloria, always baby. That's all I got to say. Hey, don't y'all worry about me, okay?

Larry Robison
Execution Date: 01/21/2000
Race: White
County of Conviction: Tarrant
Last Statement: This person declined to make a last statement.

Billy Hughes, Jr.
Execution Date: 01/24/2000
Race: White
County of Conviction: Matagorda
Last Statement: Yes, I do. I want to tell you all how much I love you all, how much I appreciate everything. I love you all and my family. I treasure every moment that I have had. I want the guys to know out there not to give up, not to give in, that I hope someday the madness in the system, something will come about, something

will be resolved. I would gladly trade the last 24 years if it would bring back Mark Fredericks. Give him back his life, give back my father his life, and my mother her health. All I ask is that I have one day and all the memories of you and my family and all the things that have happened. They are executing an innocent man because things did not happen as they say they happen and there's. The truth will come out someday. I am not the same person as I was 24 years ago. Who would have thought it would have taken 24 years to get to this moment? Don't give up, don't give in. If I am paying my debt to society, I am due a rebate and a refund, but I love you all and you all watch out for Mom and you all keep up, keep going. Thank you, Warden.

Glen McGinnis

Execution Date: 01/25/2000
Race: Black
County of Conviction: Montgomery
Last Statement: This person declined to make a last statement.

James Moreland

Execution Date: 01/27/2000
Race: White
County of Conviction: Henderson
Last Statement: Dad, love you both. You've been the best. All of you, all of you have truly been the best. And ah, I believe I'm going home. I'm sorry, and I really mean that, it's not just words. My life is all I can give. I stole 2 lives and I know it was precious to ya'll. That's the story of my whole life, that's what alcohol will do for you. Oh Jesus, Lord God, take me home. Precious Lord. Take me home Lord. Take me home. Yes, sir. Take me home oh Lord.

Cornelius Goss

Execution Date: 02/23/2000
Race: Black
County of Conviction: Dallas
Last Statement: I'd like to apologize to the victim's family. Ah, no ah, I really can't say, I don't think I can say anything that will help, but I hope through your God, you can forgive me. I'm definitely not the person now that I was then. I was sick, afraid, and looking for love in all the wrong ways. I've caused you pain and grief beyond ever dreaming to cause someone of. I hope you will be able to forgive me. To my mother, I love you very much. Thanks, Jones.

Betty Beets
Execution Date: 02/24/2000
Race: White
County of Conviction: Henderson
Last Statement: This person declined to make a last statement.

Odell Barnes, Jr.
Execution Date: 03/01/2000
Race: Black
County of Conviction: Lubbock
Last Statement: I'd like to send great love to all my family members, my supporters, my attorneys. They have all supported me throughout this. I thank you for proving my innocence, although it has not been acknowledged by the courts. May you continue in the struggle and may you change all that's being done here today and in the past. Life has not been that good to me, but I believe that now, after meeting so many people who support me in this, that all things will come to an end, and may this be fruit of better judgments for the future. That's all I have to say.

Ponchai Wilkerson
Execution Date: 03/14/2000
Race: Black
County of Conviction: Harris
Last Statement: This person declined to make a last statement.

Timothy Gribble
Execution Date: 03/15/2000
Race: White
County of Conviction: Galveston
Last Statement: Verbal Statement: Okay, thank you. To the Weis family, and ah I just want you to know from the bottom of my heart that I am truly sorry. I mean it, I'm not just saying it. Through the years of being in prison I come to hear and respect our life. It was wrong what I did. I know you had to go through a lot of pain and I'm sorry. To the Jones family, the same is true, I am truly truly sorry. I wanted to prepare a longer statement but time ran out. I had the chaplain write down a few words for my friends and for you, my family. I would like him to read them for me, and ah, just please find peace. Chaplain Brazzil recites written statement: To the Jones Family: Please accept my sincerest apology and regrets for what happened to your loved one. It was truly a horrible thing that I did and I regret it deeply. I do not know if this will ease your pain but I truly pray that this will

help you find peace. I am sincerely truly sorry. For the Weis Family: The same is true. I regret what happened. I have lived with the guilt and the pain in my heart for taking Donna away from you. There is no way that I can know your pain and sorrow for losing someone so close to you. I truly hope that you will find peace. Please know that I am sorry. I feel that I have to speak out against the practice of the death penalty, although I have no regrets in my case. The death penalty is an unnecessary punishment for society who has other means to protect itself. You cannot rectify death with another death. Whenever the state chooses to take a life and take the power of God into their own hands, whenever our leader's kill in the name of justice, we are all diminished. To my family and friends, father, sister and brother, those that have traveled so far to be here today, please just know that I am at peace. You have all been so good to me through this whole ordeal. I can never find the words to express my love for all of you. Just know that I go with God. Oum - Nama Shiveya I go with God. Last Verbal Statement: No sir, I just want to pray a chant, do what you have to do.

Tommy Jackson
Execution Date: 05/04/2000
Race: Black
County of Conviction: Williamson
Last Statement: Yes sir, I would like to address the Robinson family. There is nothing I can say here or anything I could probably do. Now you are all probably mad at me and I would probably be in the same situation you all in if anybody I thought killed anybody in my family ahh. If I knew who killed Rosalyn I would let you know, but, I am going to say this: I am going to heaven with God as my witness. Ros was a personal friend of mine. She was a beautiful person, very educated, her. I'm very tight with the Robinson family. She was proud that she had a father that was a doctor. My family is not here present and that is by my wish and my wish only. Now the tables is turned. You are all here, the Robinson family is her to see me executed. That is something that I would not want for my family. In no form or fashion would I have ever want to see Rosalyn dead. I left the scene of where the incident happened. I guarantee you if I would have been there you would not be standing where you are if I would have been there. You all have some very serious look on your face and something very serious fixin' to happen now. I will say this on my own behalf but then again I know it is not going to make any difference but what you fixing to witness is not a nice thing. It's not nice. It's not nice. The media. I would just like to address to the media with everybody's permission. I would like to say before I go that it has been said that I have shown no remorse, but if you look at my record and my background, ask anybody that know me that in order for me

to show any kind of remorse for killing that ever been done, this one time I can't show no remorse for something that I did not do and if I did I would be faking. I would totally be faking and believe me there is nothing fake about me. Nothing fake. I've done wrong, sure, I've paid the time. This is one time that I know I cannot show no remorse for something that I did not do. I am at peace, please believe me. Wherefore, I figure that what I am dying for now is what I have done in my past. This is what I am dying for. Not for killing Rosalyn. I don't know what ya'll call her but I call her Ros, I call her Ros. That's it.

William Kitchens
Execution Date: 05/09/2000
Race: White
County of Conviction: Taylor
Last Statement: Yes, sir. James Webb, I don't know which one you are out there. I can't remember from the trial. I personally just want to let you know if there has ever been any doubt in your mind at all of what happened, I want you to know that Patty was always faithful to you, that I forced her for everything that she did and I am sorry. I just don't know how to tell ya'll I am sorry for what I did. There is no way for expressing I am sorry. I just hope that in some kind of way that ya'll can move on and find peace in your life. The Lord has given me peace and that is all that I pray for is that ya'll can find that peace. I just want you to know that I am sorry for what I done. I can't change that, all I can do is say I am sorry, that's nothing for what I have done. I can't replace your loss. I am sorry. I just want you to know that I love all of ya'll. It's been a pleasure, ya'll just keep on with life, it's gonna be good. The Lord's gonna be with us. If it's alright, I just want to say a prayer first. Father, God, I just thank you for the time that you have given me on this earth, for having mercy on somebody like me for all the despicable thing's I've done in my life, Father, but you still with your love and your mercy reach down into my heart and changed it before it's too late. I ask that you bestow peace upon the family of Patricia Webb, that you let them know, Father, that you are in a place where they can obtain that peace, and you will help them move on in their life, Father. Help them, Father, to find it in their hearts, not for my sake , but for yours, and their sake to, Father, find it in their heart to forgive me for what I have done. Father, I just ask that you be with my family and comfort them to move on Father. Father, we are all here today for the mistake that I have made and I thank you for your mercy for sending your Son into this life, that we might come to know you, Father. Father, I pray for these Wardens and the officers and the people that deal with all of this, Father, I ask that you touch their hearts, Father, and if there is any wrong to it, that you will forgive them, Father. Just let them know that you love

them, Father, and that You are the way. I just thank you and in Jesus' name, I pray, Amen. I love ya'll, ya'll take care. I am so sorry.

Michael McBride
Execution Date: 05/11/2000
Race: White
County of Conviction: Lubbock
Last Statement: Written: The following is the personal final statement of and by Michael L. McBride. The Beatitudes: Jesus lifted up his eyes on His disciples, and said, "Blessed be the poor: for yours is the kingdom of God. Blessed are ye that hunger now: for ye shall be filled. Blessed are ye that weep now: for ye shall laugh. Blessed are ye, when men shall hate you, and they shall separate you from their company, and shall reproach you, and cast out your name as evil for the Son of Man's sake. Rejoice ye in that day, and leap for joy: for behold, your reward is great in Heaven: for in the like manner did their fathers unto the prophets. But woe unto you that are rich! for ye have received your consolation. Woe unto you that are full! for ye shall hunger. Woe unto you that laugh now! for ye shall moan and weep. Woe unto you, when all men shall speak well of you! for so did their fathers to the false prophets. The supremacy of love over gifts: I Corinthians, Chapter 13: 4-8: Love is patient, love is kind, and is not jealous, love does not brag and is no arrogant, does not act unbecoming; it does not seek its own, is not provoked, does not take into account a wrong suffered, does not rejoice in unrighteousness, but rejoices with the truth; bears all things, believes all things, hopes all things, endures all things. Love never fails; but if there are gifts of prophecy, they will be done away; if there tongues, they will cease. Now abide faith, hope, love, these three: but the greatest of these is love. Poem: Do not stand at my grave and weep, I am not there I do not sleep. I am the diamond glints in the snow, I am the sunlight on the ripened grain. I am the gentle autumn rain. When you awaken in the morning's hush, I am the swift uplifting rush of quiet birds in circled flight, I am the soft stars that shine at night. Do not stand at my grave and cry, I am not there. I did not die. Signed Michael L. McBride #903 May 11, 2000 Huntsville, Texas Spoken: Thank you, um, I anticipated that I would try to memorize and recite beatitudes New Testament, more or less, Luke's beatitudes, I should say, and a , a chapter on love in 1st Corinthians chapter 13, ah, I pretty much knew that I would not be able to memorize so much. There was also a poem that went along with it and in anticipation of not being able to, um, fulfill that desire, I provided a written statement that will be made available to anybody that wants it, I believe. Isn't that correct? So, uh, I wanted you to hear me say that and I apologize and for any other grief I have caused you know, including the, ah, what you're about to witness now.

It won't be very long. As soon as you realize that appear I am falling asleep. I would leave because I won't be here after that point. I will be dead at that point. It's irreversible. God bless all of you. Thank you.

James Richardson

Execution Date: 05/23/2000
Race: Black
County of Conviction: Navarro
Last Statement: Can they talk back? Say I pray for it, I accept it. Pray with me. This is still a statement. Ready? Dear Heavenly Father, forgive us, Lord. I ask that you watch over my Mama and over my sister. I ask this in the name of Christ. I also repent for all my sins, Lord. I pray that you will bring me home tonight. Please, I ask that I rest in your arms in the name of Christ Jesus I pray this. I truly believe that Jesus died for my sins that I may be resurrected, Lord, that you would do that much. Please, I ask that you not let me down and that I will be with you today in Heaven. Christ Jesus name I pray this. Donna and everybody else, Mr. Johnson, I ask that y'all will pray for me and that God will bring me home tonight, that he will keep me in Heaven, that I will still be in heaven. Please Lord, I don't want to be in Heaven, I mean I don't want to be in Hell. And, please Lord, I confess my sins. This is your son, Lord Jesus, this is your servant, please, this is your slave. I love you, too. Donna and Mama and Mr. Johnson, I wrote a message. Don't give up, love you all, even the ones that are my enemies. I truly forgive all of y'all in Christ Jesus, we pray. I ask God that he take all the hate out of my heart and away from my soul. Please, please, Lord, don't fail me. I don't know is Margie here now? But if she is, I ask her forgiveness. I ask that you not hold nothing against me or my family from this day forward, and hold no hate toward them. I don't know. I can't hear you, you may forgive me, and you may not. Forgive Mike Allison, forgive McHenry, forgive us all. Whatever the cost may be I love you. Take care of my Mama. Donna, I ask you to take care of my Mama, too. Whenever you get mad at her, you remember me. Remember I may be back. Mama, I am going to try to make that promise to you. I gonna ask God to allow his child to come back to see you. Cause I am in Heaven. At time I can come (unintelligible). Okay, Mr. Johnson, you take care, let my Mama's will be done. One more prayer, then we may proceed. Heavenly Father, I confess my sins, really I do. Let me know that I will be in Heaven tonight. Please let me know. I don't want to be in Hell with Satan or anyone else. Please, that is something I need to know. I ask that Jesus give me help. In Jesus precious name, I pray this. I ask that you give me those promises, that you assure me that those promises are real. That I am praying right. In Jesus precious name, I pray this. Goodbye, Mama. Goodbye, Donna.

Richard Foster

Execution Date: 05/24/2000
Race: White
County of Conviction: Parker
Last Statement: I have been crucified with Christ. It is no longer I who lives, but Christ who lives in me. So for the life for which I live now in the flesh, I live by faith in the Son of God who loved me and gave himself for me. I love you, Annie. You have been the best friend I have ever had in the world. I'll see you when you get there, okay? I am ready, Warden.

James Clayton

Execution Date: 05/25/2000
Race: Black
County of Conviction: Taylor
Last Statement: I would like to take this time to, ah, to use this moment an example for Christ. I would like to follow his example and leave with peace in my heart and forgiveness. There is no anger in my heart about this entire situation. I just want to testify to all of y'all that I have loved you. I appreciate your concern and genuine love for me. God bless you. I love all of all. Jesus is Lord.

Robert Carter

Execution Date: 05/31/2000
Race: Black
County of Conviction: Bastrop
Last Statement: To the Davis family, I am sorry for all of the pain that I caused your family. It was me and me alone. Anthony Graves had nothing to do with it. I lied on him in court. My wife had nothing to do with it. Anthony Graves don't even know anything about it. My wife don't know anything about it. But, I hope that you can find your peace and comfort in strength in Christ Jesus alone. Like I said, I am sorry for hurting your family. And it is a shame that it had to come to this. So I hope that you don't find peace, not in my death, but in Christ. Cause He is the only one that can give you the strength that you need. And to my family, I love you. Ah, you have been a blessing to me and I love you all and one day I will see y'all, so I hope y'all find y'all peace, comfort, and strength in Christ Jesus alone, because that's where it's at. Abul, behold your son, and Anitra, behold your mother. I love you. I am ready to go home and be with my Lord.

Thomas Mason

Execution Date: 06/12/2000

Race: White

County of Conviction: Smith

Last Statement: I understand that Michael Skains is supposed to be here somewhere. They did everything but make sure I got a fair trial to prove I was innocent. I wasn't the one who had the gun to give to police and all these altered records from the District Attorney's office and the Attorney General's office, that's why Michael Sputnick got fired and ran off when I filed these appeals. Not one of my sell out lawyers would use this evidence, because they all work as a conspiracy with the court. No doubt about it. Jack King did everything he could to keep me from making arms and showing this evidence. They wait till the hearing was over and then make the arguments in the court or on paper where nobody can rebut it or contradict the testimony or arguments. There's more than 30 altered and falsified records saying I told so and so this or that, but you go look in their record, it does not say Thomas Mason called them at all and told them anything. But that's okay. All this evidence is being saved, so Jack King can laugh all he wants like he's the big hero, after this is over with, that's fine. But the person that had the gun, they know was not Thomas Mason, so who's getting the last laugh after all? The guy that got away. But Jack King knows he illegally convicted me of all these falsified altered records. My sister's got the document that my lawyer filed, but he didn't file with the court. It's got the signature on it. He put this all in one record. So it's going to be saved. It ain't going to be destroyed just because I'm dead. Everybody's got to go sooner or later and sooner or later everyone of ya'll will be along behind me. That's all I got to say.

John Burks

Execution Date: 06/14/2000

Race: Black

County of Conviction: McLennan

Last Statement: Hey, how are ya'll doing? Alright, it's gong to be alright. There's some guys I didn't get a chance to visit with, ah I met when I first drove up here… Lester Byers, Chris Black, Alba, John Alba, and Rosales Rock. You know who you are. The Raiders are going all the way, ya'll (mumbles…Mo-B). Ya'll pray for me. And it's going to be alright. That's it and it's time to roll up out of her. It's going down, let's get it over with. That's it.

Paul Nuncio

Execution Date: 06/15/2000

Race: Hispanic

County of Conviction: Hale

Last Statement: Verbal: I have a written statement for the press. It will be released as soon as they can. And I also responded to a comment to me from Sandy, daughter of Ms. Farris. I have felt deeply sorry for the deceased. But I'm sorry that I wasn't the one that did it or anything. She will tell you that when she gets a chance to. When the time comes. I just wish just to be patient when the time for each and everyone of ya'll individually have ya'll time. But I'm not putting pressure on either one of ya'll being having any guilt. I just want to say two thing, executing someone that is innocent, cause even though I am. The burden will be wiped away and you will be at ease to know that I know how it is and they will pay for it when their time comes. And all I have to say is that right now I'm sorry that it happened and I was part, not part in it but, part responsible for not properly getting the word out in time to get the right victim or the right convict or the right person that did it. I just wish to say a little prayer for the family for their appearance and forgiveness in this matter. Our Father, who art in heaven, hallowed by thy name. Thy kingdom come, thy will be done, on earth as it is in Heaven. Give this day your daily bread and forgive us our trespasses as we forgive those who trespass against us. Lead us not into temptation, but deliver us from evil. Our Lord, Amen. And ah, don't be surprised if your Mom be the helper of God that would grab my hand and say "You are now into eternal life with God." This is her being one of the chosen ones to give as proof of innocence. That's what I meant by telling you I don't mean to injure you anymore. When your time comes that she would let you know, if I was innocent or guilty. That about all I have to say. Love you all. Written: I wish the public to see my point of inside view that the officers of Death Row of the State of Texas. All the years of 5 or 6 years of my first time being locked up for not doing a crime of this sort. Now, officers of Texas TDCJ are of Terrell Unit, Walls Unit and some of Ellis I are just doing their job for their family. Now there are also respectful inmates death row and population that I've meet, now I say to all of you just realizing what crime is about, don't do it. One way I've thought of was having your friends "inmate" to witness your execution talking about those of population and first timers. I just want to give those officers that respected me while in prison of TDCJ Death Row. May God bless you all of TDCJ and inmates especially the free-world population. With Gods and my words of faith, Paul Selso Nuncio.

Gary Graham
Execution Date: 06/22/2000
Race: Black
County of Conviction: Harris
Last Statement: I would like to say that I did not kill Bobby Lambert. That I'm an innocent black man that is being murdered. This is a lynching that is happening

in America tonight. There's overwhelming and compelling evidence of my defense that has never been heard in any court of America. What is happening here is an outrage for any civilized country to anybody anywhere to look at what's happening here is wrong. I thank all of the people that have rallied to my cause. They've been standing in support of me. Who have finished with me. I say to Mr. Lambert's family, I did not kill Bobby Lambert. You are pursuing the execution of an innocent man. I want to express my sincere thanks to all of ya'll. We must continue to move forward and do everything we can to outlaw legal lynching in America. We must continue to stay strong all around the world, and people must come together to stop the systematic killing of poor and innocent black people. We must continue to stand together in unity and to demand a moratorium on all executions. We must not let this murder/lynching be forgotten tonight, my brothers. We must take it to the nation. We must keep our faith. We must go forward. We recognize that many leaders have died. Malcom X, Martin Luther King, and others who stood up for what was right. They stood up for what was just. We must, you must brothers, that's why I have called you today. You must carry on that condition. What is here is just a lynching that is taking place. But they're going to keep on lynching us for the next 100 years, if you do not carry on that tradition, and that period of resistance. We will prevail. We may loose this battle, but we will win the war. This death, this lynching will be avenged. It will be avenged, it must be avenged. The people must avenge this murder. So my brothers, all of ya'll stay strong, continue to move forward. Know that I love all of you. I love the people, I love all of you for your blessing, strength, for your courage, for your dignity, the way you have come here tonight, and the way you have protested and kept this nation together. Keep moving forward, my brothers. Slavery couldn't stop us. The lynching couldn't stop us in the south. This lynching will not stop us tonight. We will go forward. Our destiny in this country is freedom and liberation. We will gain our freedom and liberation by any means necessary. By any means necessary, we keep marching forward. I love you, Mr. Jackson. Bianca, make sure that the state does not get my body. Make sure that we get my name as Shaka Sankofa. My name is not Gary Graham. Make sure that it is properly presented on my grave. Shaka Sankofa. I died fighting for what I believe in. I died fighting for what was just and what was right. I did not kill Bobby Lambert, and the truth is going to come out. It will be brought out. I want you to take this thing off into international court, Mr. Robert Mohammed and all ya'll. I want you, I want to get my family and take this down to international court and file a law suit. Get all the video tapes of all the beatings. They have beat me up in the back. They have beat me up at the unit over there. Get all the video tapes supporting that law suit. And make the public exposed to the genocide and this brutality world, and let the world see what is really happening here behind closed doors. Let the world see the barbarity and injustice of what is really happening here. You must get those video tapes. You must make it exposed, this injustice, to the world. You must continue to demand a moratorium on all executions. We must move forward Minister Robert Mohammed. Ashanti Chimurenga, I love you for standing with me, my sister. You are a strong warrior queen. You will continue to be string in everything that you do. Believe in yourself, you must hold your head up, in the spirit of Winnie Mandela, in the spirit of Nelson Mandela. Ya'll must move forward. We will stop this lynching. Reverend Al Sharpton, I love you, my brother. Bianca Jagger, I love all of you. Ya'll make sure that we continue to stand together. Reverend Jesse Jackson and know that this murder, this lynching will not be forgotten. I love you, too, my brother. This is genocide in America. This is what happens to black men when they stand up and protest for what is right and just. We refuse to compromise, we refuse to surrender the dignity for what we know is right. But we will move on, we have been strong in the past. We will continue to be strong as a people. You can kill a revolutionary, but you cannot stop the revolution. The revolution will go on. The people will carry the revolution on. You are the people that must carry that revolutionary on, in order to liberate our children from this genocide and for what is happening here in America tonight. What has happened for the last 100 or so years in America. This is the part of the genocide, this is part of the African (unintelligible), that we as black people have endured in America. But we shall overcome, we will continue with this. We will continue, we will gain our freedom and liberation, by any means necessary. Stay strong. They cannot kill us. We will move forward. To my sons, to my daughters, all of you. I love all of you. You have been wonderful. Keep your heads up. Keep moving forward. Keep united. Maintain the love and unity in the community. And know that victory is assured. Victory for the people will be assured. We will gain our freedom and liberation in this country. We will gain it and we will do it by any means necessary. We will keep marching. March on black people. Keep your heads high. March on. All ya'll leaders. March on. Take your message to the people. Preach the moratorium for all executions. We're gonna stop, we are going to end the death penalty in this country. We are going to end it all across this world. Push forward people. And know that what ya'll are doing is right. What ya'll are doing is just. This is nothing more that pure and simple murder. This is what is happening tonight in America. Nothing more than state sanctioned murders, state sanctioned lynching, right here in America, and right here tonight. This is what is happening my brothers. Nothing less. They know I'm innocent. They've got the facts to prove it. They know I'm innocent. But they cannot acknowledge my innocence, because to do so would be to publicly admit their guilt. This is something these racist people will never do. We must remember brothers, this is what we're faced with.

You must take this endeavor forward. You must stay strong. You must continue to hold your heads up, and to be there. And I love you, too, my brother. All of you who are standing with me in solidarity. We will prevail. We will keep marching. Keep marching black people, black power. Keep marching black people, black power. Keep marching black people. Keep marching black people. They are killing me tonight. They are murdering me tonight.

Jessy San Miguel
Execution Date: 06/29/2000
Race: Hispanic
County of Conviction: Dallas
Last Statement: Be strong, brother. Be strong, my brother. Be strong, Mom. It's going to be alright. I love all of you. Don't forget that. Ironic, isn't it? I'm a cross. Ya'll take care of each other. I'll be watching over you. Thank you, Dana......Yes.

Orien Joiner
Execution Date: 07/12/2000
Race: White
County of Conviction: Lubbock
Last Statement: Kathy, y'all take and I bless all of you and I am glad I have had y'all in my life. As I have said from the very first thing, I am innocent of this crime and God knows I am innocent and the four people that was murdered know I am innocent and when I get to heaven I'll be hunting you and we'll talk. I feel sorry for the families that's had to suffer and my family and I have 'em all in my prayers. I love you all. Y'all take and y'all look after Sheila and Shannon and them, call 'em and get the pictures to 'em and everything and, ah, again, like I said, I feel sorry for the families, but if it takes my death to make them happy, then I will bless them. I have no hard feelings toward anyone cause the Lord feels that it is my time to come home to Him, my work on earth is done and that, ah, like I said, I am just sorry for, but they will have to go through this one time again, cause sooner or later, whoever did this crime is going to be caught and they'll have to come down here and do this again and they will realize they witnessed an innocent man going to be with Jesus Christ.

Juan Soria
Execution Date: 07/26/2000
Race: Hispanic
County of Conviction: Tarrant
Last Statement: I wish we could pray to Allah, the father of the universe. I ask for

your protection and my salvation, my night and my day. I want you to lead me and I will follow. We give praise to Allah the divine and holy prophet. We know that you are Allah, that you are the prophet in these days that is in charge of the human race in this new era of time. These two (unintelligible) to the masters of the temple of the son we have been honored to dwell in our father's house at least for the time in which this finite time has come to it's assigned time for one. There is nothing strange, love governs all events, what is (unintelligible), who is who was his mother and father, we extend my love to all my brothers and sister extend to life and my religion, it is Allah. It is going in salvation of the nation I come from South, Central, and North America. (Unintelligible) that would save us. So, I call on to all of my brothers and sisters and to members of the human race that still have some knowledge for what love divine love is. That comes learned from your ancient forefathers. Love is brought by this prophet Allah. We extend our love to everyone who believes the faith of Islamic and chooses to love along with all their being. We come to understand what is finite and what is infinite. Again, I say it is an honor to live in my father's house. To see this divine great paradise that which I have come to see with the eye of the spirit, the spirit which was revealed by my prophet which was (unintelligible). We extend our love to everybody. Extend my love to my divine sister. Sister Dorothy, and my brother Tomas and we know that our father Allah will bless them in the following days to come. We know that Allah is with us now and forever. The say I am going to have surgery, so I guess I will see everyone after this surgery is performed. It is finished.

Brian Roberson
Execution Date: 08/09/2000
Race: Black
County of Conviction: Dallas
Last Statement: Since I have already said all I need to say to all my loved ones, I'm not going to say anything to y'all at this time. Y'all know I love you and y'all know where we're at. I will see y'all when you get there. So this is my statement. To all of the racist white folks in America that hate black folks and to all of the black folks in America that hate themselves: the infamous words of my famous legendary brother, Matt Turner, "Y'all kiss my black ass." Let's do it.

Oliver Cruz
Execution Date: 08/09/2000
Race: Hispanic
County of Conviction: Bexar
Last Statement: First of all, I want to apologize to the family of Kelly Elizabeth

Donovan. I am sorry for what I did to her twelve years ago. I wish they could forgive me for what I did. I am sorry. I am sorry for hurting my family, for hurting my friends. Jesus forgive me. Take me home with you. I am ready. I love you all.

John Satterwhite

Execution Date: 08/16/2000
Race: Black
County of Conviction: Bexar
Last Statement: This person declined to make a last statement.

Richard Jones

Execution Date: 08/22/2000
Race: White
County of Conviction: Tarrant
Last Statement: I want the victim's family to know that I didn't commit this crime. I didn't kill your loved one. Sharon Wilson, y'all convicted an innocent man and you know it. There are some lawyers hired that is gonna prove that, and I hope you can live with it. To my family and loved ones, I love you. Thank you for supporting me. Y'all stay strong. Warden, take me home.

David Gibbs

Execution Date: 08/23/2000
Race: White
County of Conviction: Montgomery
Last Statement: Mr. Bryant, I have wronged you and your family and for that I am truly sorry. I forgive and I have been forgiven. Death is but a brief moments slumber and a short journey home. I'll see you when you get there. I am done, Warden.

Jeffery Caldwell

Execution Date: 08/30/2000
Race: Black
County of Conviction: Dallas
Last Statement: I would like to extend my love to my family members and my relatives for all of the love and support you have showed me. I extend my special love to my daughter who I love greatly. I hope that you forever remember me. I hope that you will always cherish the love and the strength that I have provided you. My love for you will remain with you winthin your heart and in part of your soul. As to all my brothers I love you all with all of my heart. But during your time

of departure from this earth plane you will have to face the judgement of God for the lack of love you have shown my aunt and my cousins. We were never brought up to be that way. As you know our parents brought us up to love one another no matter what. There was no love showed to my aunt or none of my cousins. I can forgive you all but you must ask forgiveness from God for how you have hurt our aunt and our family. I leave now at this moment to join my parents and my only sister whose lives were not taken by me. To all the fellows on death row, I thank you for the love that you have shown me and for the strength that you provided me. You all keep your heads up. As for my attorney's I thank you all for being there for me. As defense attorneys you have shown me a lot strength. May my love touch each one of you all's souls as I leave this body.

Ricky McGinn
Execution Date: 09/27/2000
Race: White
County of Conviction: Brown
Last Statement: Robin you know this ain't right. Mama, Adam, Mike, Sonny, Michelle, y'all know I love you. Tell everybody I said hi and that I love them and I will see them on the other side. Okay? And now I just pray that if there is anything against me that God takes it home. I don't want nobody to be mad at nobody. I don't want nobody to be bitter. Keep clean hearts and I will see y'all on the other side. Okay? I love y'all, stay sweet. I love ya.

Jeffery Dillingham
Execution Date: 11/01/2000
Race: White
County of Conviction: Wichita
Last Statement: I would just like to apologize to the victim's family for what I did. I take full responsibility for that poor woman's death, for the pain and suffering inflicted on Mr. Koslow. Father, I want to thank you for all of the beautiful people you put in my life. I could not have asked for two greater parents than you gave me. I could just ask for two greater people in their life now. It is a blessing that there are people that they love so much but even more so, people that I love so much. I thank you for all the things you have done in my life, for the ways that you have opened my eyes, softened my heart. The ways that you have taught me. For teaching me how to love, for all of the bad things you have taken out of my life. For all the good things you have added to it. I thank you for all of the beautiful promises that you make us in your word, and I graciously received every one of them. Thank you Heavenly Father for getting me off of death row and for bringing me home out of

prison. I love you Heavenly Father, I love you Jesus. Thank you both for loving me. Amen.

Miguel Flores
Execution Date: 11/09/2000
Race: Hispanic
County of Conviction: Collin
Last Statement: I want to thank my attorneys, Father Walsh...Sylvia, te quiero mucho y a Consulado, te quiero decir muchas gracias por todo. I want to say I am sorry and I say a prayer today for you so you can have peace and I hope that you can forgive me. God is waiting and God is waiting now.

Stacey Lawton
Execution Date: 11/14/2000
Race: Black
County of Conviction: Smith
Last Statement: I am saying, I want y'all to keep your heads up, hold on and stay strong for everybody. I mean ah, I don't want y'all to look at me like I am a killer or something man, cause I ain't no killer. I mean, I didn't, I didn't kill your father. I mean, I know how it look, but I didn't do it. You know what I am saying? You were out there with me, Tommy. I mean, you know man. (mumbled) You know I always did want to say something to y'all. Right? I can't say that I done it because I didn't do it. I've got love for everybody. I am a Christian now. I'm saying I want everybody to keep thier heads up and stay strong. I'm going to stay strong. I'll be seeing you, this is my last breath. Ricky, keep your head up baby. All y'all, Doreen, Melodee. I mean, I know y'all don't come down here. I just really don't know what y'all want me to say. I mean, I know, ah, I mean, I'm sorry anybody, ah, anybody got killed that night. It wasn't supposed to happen, but I didn't do it. I really didn't do it. I don't want y'all to go through life thinking that I did. You know what I am saying? I love everybody and I want y'all to stay strong. Right? It would take me an hour or a long time, man, but, ah, man, I don't want to hold y'all up, man, like that, ah. Y'all just keep your head up and stay strong, man. Give my love to everybody. I love y'all.

Tony Chambers
Execution Date: 11/14/2000
Race: Black
County of Conviction: Smith
Last Statement: Mom, I just want y'all to know that I love you. No matter what in

life, I want you to stay strong. Doreen, you have been a very special part of my life, too. I want you to keep doing what you are doing. Stay strong. Dad, I want you to stay strong.

Garry Miller
Execution Date: 12/05/2000
Race: White
County of Conviction: Jones
Last Statement: Maggie, I am sorry. I always wanted to tell you but I just didn't know how. I have been praying for y'all. I hope that y'all find the peace that y'all have been wanting. Lord, thank you for all my family, all my friends, and all my brothers on the row. Thank you for my spiritual family. Lord, be merciful with those who are actively involved with the taking of my life, forgive them as I am forgiving them. Be merciful to me a sinner. Protect us Lord as we stay awake and watch over us as we sleep as we wake may we may keep watch with Christ and sleep rest in His peace. All right, Warden. I am ready to go home.

Daniel Hittle
Execution Date: 12/06/2000
Race: White
County of Conviction: Dallas
Last Statement: Santajaib Singh Ji.

Claude Jones
Execution Date: 12/07/2000
Race: White
County of Conviction: San Jacinto
Last Statement: To your family, ah, I hope that this can bring some closure to y'all. I am sorry for your loss and hey, I love all y'all. Let's go.

Jack Clark
Execution Date: 01/09/2001
Race: White
County of Conviction: Lubbock
Last Statement: First, I would like to say to the family that I am sorry, and I do ask for forgiveness. There will be also a funeral mass at St. Thomas and I would like to invite all of those from the State and the family to be there if they would like to come. My last words will be: And He was the light that shineth in the hearts of all

man from the foundations of the world. If we confess our sins He is just and true to forgive us of our sins and cleanse us from all unrighteousness. Peace and goodness.

Alvin Goodwin
Execution Date: 01/18/2001
Race: White
County of Conviction: Montgomery
Last Statement: He spoke in Irish, translating to "Goodbye."

Caruthers Alexander
Execution Date: 01/29/2001
Race: Black
County of Conviction: Bexar
Last Statement: This person declined to make a last statement.

Adolph Hernandez
Execution Date: 02/08/2001
Race: Hispanic
County of Conviction: Lubbock
Last Statement: I want to thank my family for their help and moral support and for their struggle. It would have been a lot harder without their love. So, I am just going home. I will see ya'll one of these days. Just don't rush it. I will be there always. I 'll always be watching over you. I love you. Okay? Y'all be strong. God bless you. That is where I am going. I love y'all huh. I'll see y'all in Slayton, Texas. Dios te mandas contigo mi espiritu. (Spanish - God, I command my spirit to go with you.) Alabamos a Dios todos. (Spanish - We all praise God.) Amen Cuida mi familia. (Take care of my family.) I love you. That's it Warden.

Dennis Dowthitt
Execution Date: 03/07/2001
Race: White
County of Conviction: Montgomery
Last Statement: I am so sorry for what y'all had to go through. I am so sorry for what all of you had to go through. I can't imagine losing two children. If I was y'all, I would have killed me. You know? I am really so sorry about it, I really am. I got to go sister, I love you. Y'all take care and God bless you. Gracie was beautiful and Tiffany was beautiful. You had some lovely girls and I am sorry. I don't know what to say. All right, Warden, let's do it.

Jason Massey
Execution Date: 04/03/2001
Race: White
County of Conviction: Ellis
Last Statement: Yes, first I would like to speak to the victims' family. First of all, I would like to say that I do not know any of y'all and that is unfortunate, because I would like to apologize to each and every one of you individually. I can't imagine what I have taken from y'all, but I do want to apologize and I want to let you know that I did do it. You guys know that I am guilty and I am sorry for what I have done. I apologize and I know that you may not be able to forgive me and I know that may not be able to forgive me in this life and in this world, but I hope sometime in the future you will be able to find it in you to forgive me. And I want you to know that Christina, she did not suffer as much as you think she did. I promise you that. I give you my word. I know you guys want to know where the rest of her remains are. I put her remains in the Trinity River. I have said that since I have come to death row. I want to apologize to you again. I hope sometime in the future you can forgive me. Okay, now I want to speak to my mom and my family. Brother Anderson, Kathy, I want you to know that I appreciate all these years that you have been coming to see me on death row and Daddy, I love you. I appreciate y'all being here and being strong for me, and Mama, you know I love you, and I appreciate all of these visits, the letters and everything y'all have done for me. Y'all have been wonderful. You too, Granny. I love y'all and you know, I want to apologize to y'all too for what I have done. For all of the pain that I have caused, but all of this pain has brought us closer together and all of this suffering that we have been through has brought us all closer to the Lord and in the end that is what counts. Isn't it? That's what counts in the end; where you stand with Almighty God. I know that God has used this to change my life. And it's all been worth it because of that. If I lie here today where I lie, I can say in the face of death, Jesus is Lord. He has changed my life and I know that when I leave this body, I am going home to be with the Lord forever. That is all I want to say. I love y'all and I won't say goodbye, I will say I will see you again. I love you, Daddy. Tonight I dance on the streets of gold. Let those without sin cast the first stone.

David Goff
Execution Date: 04/25/2001
Race: Black
County of Conviction: Tarrant
Last Statement: I want to give all the praise to God and glory and thank him for all that he done for me. With this let all debts be paid that I owed - real or imagined.

The slate is wiped clean, all marked erased other than that there is no justice. That's not justice. Praise the Lord. Glory to Jesus Christ. Praise the Lord God.

John Wheat
Execution Date: 06/13/2001
Race: White
County of Conviction: Tarrant
Last Statement: I deeply regret what happened. I did not intentionally or knowingly harm anyone. That's it and didmau. (Vietnamese for let's get out of here.)

Miguel Richardson
Execution Date: 06/26/2001
Race: Black
County of Conviction: Bexar
Last Statement: I love you, I love everyone, I go out with great love and respect. This is a great day to pass on. This so called dying. This is a great day to approach this glorious event. Approach the present. (mumbling) Thy will be done. (more mumbling) I love you all. Don't waste your time arguing and bickering. God loves you all. All that really matters is love. Love is the only thing for us. There is no closure without love. Forgive one another. You got to learn how to forgive and embrace one another. Be one. Our love is just like...it is the nectar of God. We have so much to give when we give out of our hearts. The hear is the wishing well that waters the tree. I wish and desire one thing. I wish only the best for all of you. (unknown tongues) I love the love in every man and child. Mankind is my family and tribe. I am ready grumah. A poet once said, "...is my country. There is no separation between you and me There is no enemies, only family. I am a minister of love. I go out loving everyone and everything. God bless my...country. I shed tears of love may they nourish everyone. Stop killing start loving. Stop the violence. Let my death change society. You don't need any more killing. You don't need any minimum, maximum security, death row. You don't need the death penalty. We need more loving fathers and mothers. It is a good day to die. Take me God, Hold me in yours and carry me home.

James Wilkens
Execution Date: 07/11/2001
Race: White
County of Conviction: Smith
Last Statement: Sandy, all of you, I am sorry. Please hear me. Please in the name of God forgive me. Please understand. Please find that peace. I am really sorry. Please

for your sake forgive me. All of you please. I love my sister, my friends, father. Thank you for loving me and being with me. You are magnificent people. God has blessed me more than I deserve. I would like to end with a prayer. Heavenly Father, as I come to you to praise and thank you that even now I can endure the pain that you endured when you died for me on the cross. You have forgiven me of my sins and travesties. Thank you, Lord, for giving me strength. Give them strength to forgive me. Ask them to have them forgive me in their hearts. I ask you to touch each and every one of them. I am truly repentant. In the name of Jesus Christ I love you. Warden I am ready to go home please. Remember God is peace, God is love.

Mack Hill

Execution Date: 08/08/2001
Race: White
County of Conviction: Lubbock
Last Statement: First, I would like to tell my family that I love them. I will be waiting on them. I am fine. I hope that everyone gets some closure from this. I am innocent. Lubbock County officials believe I am guilty. I am not. Travis Ware has the burden on him to prove that he did not commit felonies. He needs to be stopped or he is going to do it time and time again. The power is invested in you as a public official to do your job. That's all Warden. I love y'all. June 25, 2008.

Jeffery Daughtie

Execution Date: 06/16/2001
Race: White
County of Conviction: Nueces
Last Statement: For almost nine years I have thought about the death penalty, whether it is right or wrong and I don't have any answers. But I don't think the world will be a better or safer place without me. If you had wanted to punish me you would have killed me the day after, instead of killing me now. You are not hurting me now. I have had time to get ready, to tell my family goodbye, to get my life where it needed to be. It started with a needle and it is ending with a needle. Carl, you have been a good friend, man. I am going to look for you. You go back and tell your daughter I love her. Tell her I came in here like a man and I will leave like a man. It's been good, dude. Thank you, Shorty. I appreciate you. I came in like a man and I will leave like a man. I will be with you. I will be with you every time you take a shower. If you leave crying you don't do me justice. If you don't see peace in my eyes you don't see me. I will be the first one you see when you cross over. They got these numbers that I called today. Calling my family. That is it. Ready, Warden.

James Knox
Execution Date: 09/18/2001
Race: White
County of Conviction: Galveston
Last Statement: This person declined to make a last statement.

Gerald Mitchell
Execution Date: 10/22/2001
Race: Black
County of Conviction: Harris
Last Statement: Yes, sir. Where's Mr. Marino's mother? Did you get my letter? Just wanted to let you know, I sincerely meant everything I wrote. I am sorry for the pain. I am sorry for the life I took from you. I ask God for forgiveness and I ask you for the same. I know it maybe hard, but I'm sorry for what I did. To my family I love each and every one of you. Be strong. Know my love is always with you…always. I know I am going home to be with the Lord. Shed tears of happiness for me. I love each and everyone of you. Keep on living. Betty, you have been wonderful. You guided me to the Lord. You have been like a mother to me. Sean, Rusty, Jenny, Marsha, God Bless each and every one of y'all. Jesus, I confess you as my Lord and Savior. I know when I die, I'll have life in heaven and life eternal everlasting. I am ready for that mansion that you promised me. Take care. It's alright Sean, it's alright. I'm going to a better place.

Jeffery Tucker
Execution Date: 11/14/2001
Race: White
County of Conviction: Parker
Last Statement: I'd like to tell the Humphrey family, I am sorry for the pain and suffering that I have caused you. I never intended for your husband and father to be killed, it was just an accident. I sincerely regret any pain and sorrow. I realize that my actions have caused this death and a lot of pain and grief. I pray that Jesus will give you peace. I just ask that my death bring you peace and solace. If my death brings you that, then I will gladly give it. I know that I leave this world for the crime that I committed. To my friends, Jack and Irene Wilcox. Bless you both, you've been my rock. Irene, you have been like a mother and Jack, you have been like a father. To my lawyers, Danalyn and Robert Owen, you are not just my lawyers but you are my friends. I know you weren't happy when I stopped my appeals, but you know the reason why. Thank you for understanding. Have a happy heart knowing I leave this world in peace. Father Walsh, you have helped me so much to come to

a knowledge of the Lord. I would never have understood that without you. You give me patience and diligence. Someday I will see you there. I'll be there waiting for you but don't be in a hurry. You have a lot of work left to do. Just know that I'll be watching over you. I love you all and thank you for being a part of my life. (recites the Lord's Prayer)

Emerson Rudd
Execution Date: 11/15/2001
Race: Black
County of Conviction: Dallas
Last Statement: Ok. I guess I'll address the Morgan family. Mrs. Morgan, the sister from the trial. Thirteen or fourteen years ago, I had a non-caring attitude at the time. I'm sorry for shooting your son down at that particular robbery. Politicians say that this brings closure. But my death doesn't bring your son back—it doesn't bring closure. I wish that I could do more, but I can't. I hope this brings you peace. Ursula, Manon, and Irene, I love y'all—take it easy. They've gotta do this thing. I'm still warm from the pepper gas. I love you. I'm ready to go. Call my mom and tell her that this particular process is over. Tell all the brothers to keep their heads up, eyes toward the sky.

Vincent Cooks
Execution Date: 12/12/2001
Race: Black
County of Conviction: Dallas
Last Statement: Tell my family I love y'all. Watch out for Momma. Don't want to talk too much, I will cry. I'll just cry everywhere. I'm sorry, Teach, for not being a better son and not doing better things. It wasn't your fault. You raised me the way you should, at least I won't be there no more. I miss you, too. I see you there, you doing alright? I sent you a letter. Neckbone, there's a sheet, I got your name on it. Keep on writing, now. Write to the, hun. Charles, keep the right, now. You people over there. You know what these people are doing. By them executing me ain't doing nothing right. I don't weigh 180 pounds and 5'7". Take care, love y'all. Did Roger come up here yet? Tell Pat and them I love them. I'm gonna go ahead and let them do what their gonna do. Help your sister, see ya later Pat, love ya Becca. Do what you do, Warden.

Michael Moore
Execution Date: 01/09/2002
Race: White

County of Conviction: Coryell

Last Statement: I'll start by saying I love all of you. I will be waiting for your arrival, don't disappoint me by not showing up. I will be there with the give of Christ. We'll all be there. I promise I'll go up smiling. I am sorry. If I could think of a word in the vocabulary stronger, you need to hear something stronger, you deserve it. I'm sorry, I can't take back what I have done. I have asked Christ for forgiveness, and I ask that you forgive me. And I understand your feelings. God bless all of you. I will be waiting for your arrival. Do not disappoint me by not showing up. God bless everybody.

Jermarr Arnold

Execution Date: 01/16/2002
Race: Black
County of Conviction: Nueces

Last Statement: Yes sir, members of Mrs. Sanchez's family, I don't know who you are and other people present. As I said, I'm taking responsibility fro the death of your daughter in 1983. I'm deeply sorry for the loss of your loved one. I am a human being also. I know how it feels, I've been there. I cannot explain and can't give you answers. I can give you one thing, and I'm going to give that today. I'm give a life for a life. I pray you will have no ill will or animosity. You have the right to see this, I am glad you are here. All I can do is ask the Lord for forgiveness. I am not saying this to be facetious. I am giving my life. I hope you find comfort in my execution. As for me, I am happy, that is why you see me smiling. I am glad I am leaving this world. I am going to a better place. I have made peace with God, I am born again. Thank you for being here, I'm sorry. I hope you get over any malice or hatred you feel. Because it yields sorrow and suffering. I take responsibility for the loss of your daughter. I can't give answers. I hope you can find peace in the days to come. God bless all of you. Thank you all for being here. Begins singing: Amazing Grace.

Windell Broussard

Execution Date: 01/30/2002
Race: Black
County of Conviction: Jefferson

Last Statement: Yes, Warden. I just want to let everyone know that this here is a tragedy. What happened to Diana, Corey, and what is happening to me...it is a tragedy. That is all Warden.

Randell Hafdahl, Sr.

Execution Date: 01/31/2001

Race: White
County of Conviction: Randall
Last Statement: Spoken: Yes, I do. My last full statement is being released in a way other than me right here. All I want to say, I love you all. Approximately 28 years ago, I remember looking down at a bassinet, I saw an angel. I am looking at her right now. I love you, Colleen. Let's get going. The road goes on forever, and the party never ends. Let's rock and roll. Let's go Warden. Me and you, all of us. Remember wet Willie - keep on smiling, keep on smiling. I love you. It's on the way, I can feel it. It's OK, baby. We have a party to go to. I can feel it now. Written: Over the last few days we've had a chance to say it all. If I lived to be a 100, the love we all share couldn't be more beautiful. Than you for loving me. II Timothy 1.7 tells us that God DID NOT instill in us the spirit of fear: but of power, love, and of sound mind...For those of you who seek to find fear in my eyes? Look into yourself, thats where you'll find the fear you so desperately search for. I leave this life with a clear conscience and heart; I can say that only because I have spoke the truth over the last 16+ years. I am the only one that can say that truthfully. Chief Neal: as to what you said to me when you had me in the back seat of your car on the night of Nov 11? Thank you for being so determined to only seek a specific conclusion, truth be damned! I say that because the thought of having to die of old age in prison is the worst death any person could endure. To Modina Holmes: I thank you for planting that bullet in the ground, and the cigarette butt, also the knives Danny Helgren had packed in his suit case in the trunk of the car; which you placed in the cab for your photo shoot. I also want to thank you and Chief Neal, because of your actions, it shows me that you are human and can love, the same as I love my Club Brothers. We're a lot more alike than you think. To Wes Clayton: You were nothing but a paid chump. You were brought in to do all the dirty work on this case so as to shield Randy Sherrod, "AKA Daffy Duck" from possibly soiling his reputation if the bottom fell out of this conviction through the appeals. For 16 years now you have been the one I have dreamed of having the chance to meet again: UNrestrained! I really would have loved to have had the chance to take your lying ass to school, boy! James Farren: You ain't as slick as you think you are. I read that article the Globe printed on the 27th, where you expressed how Eardmann wasn't important because there was at least one witness at trial who testified the first shot diarmed Mitchell and rendered him defenseless. Your sure right about that. Just wonder how many people out there other than me and you know that one witness you used to justify Eardmann was actually Eardmann himself! You know as well as I do the only witness to testify about sequence of shots was Eardmann himself. I have to admit, when it comes to walking the line between a lie and a deception, your good! You sure your not related to Clayton? And to the Mitchell family: I truely am sorry

for the tragedy that took place on Nov 11, 85. Thats all I can give you. Thats all I will give you. Because today your making my family and loved ones a victim just as you have cried to the world you were in this tragedy. I did not deliberately shoot James Mitchell. I had no premeditation in my thoughts when I spun around and fired, no matter how many fantasy motives Clayton and Sherrod fabricated. So today my family becomes a victim. You know, the truth sets you free, and the truth is, if your loved one had acted with any professionalism at all, he would be alive today! And thats all I got to say about it. Scooter, get the beer and get in the truck, take me home baby, we got a party to get ready for. I love ya'll. Remember Wet Willy Boocub.

Monty Delk
Execution Date: 02/28/2002
Race: White
County of Conviction: Anderson
Last Statement: "I've got one thing to say, get your Warden off this gurney and shut up. I am from the island of Barbados. I am the Warden of this unit. People are seeing you do this."

Gerald Tigner
Execution Date: 03/07/2002
Race: Black
County of Conviction: McLennan
Last Statement: Yes. My last statement. I was wrongfully convicted of this crime against Michael Watkins and James Williams on 10th Street on August 31, 1993. I got convicted on a false confession because I never admitted to it, but my lawyer did not put this out to the jury. I did not kill those drug dealers. I send love to my family and friends; my east side family and friends. I am being real with the real. That's all that counts in my heart. I will see you later. That's it.

Jose Santellan, Sr.
Execution Date: 04/10/2002
Race: Hispanic
County of Conviction: Kerr
Last Statement: First of all, I would like to apologize to the Guajardo family even though they are not present. I loved Yolanda a lot. I hope and pray they can forgive me for all the pain. To my family, stay strong. Tom, Orlando, Celia, stay strong. Michael, thank you for your friendship. Thank you for the support you have given me. I thank all of you and I love all of you. To the guys on death row, stay strong

and I hope to see you someday. Bye bye, I love you guys, don't worry about me. It's going to be alright.

William Burns
Execution Date: 04/11/2002
Race: Black
County of Conviction: Bowie
Last Statement: I just want to tell my Mom that I am sorry that I caused her so much pain and my family and stuff. I love them and I hurt for the the fact that they are going to be hurting. I really hate that; and that I'm hoping they are going to be O.K.

Gerald Casey
Execution Date: 04/18/2002
Race: White
County of Conviction: Montgomery
Last Statement: This person declined to make a last statement.

Rodolfo Hernandez
Execution Date: 04/30/2002
Race: Hispanic
County of Conviction: Comal
Last Statement: Yes, sir. I want to give thanks to Father Walsh, my spiritual advisor and Mr. Whiteside and Irene Wilcox and her husband, Jack, and Richard Lopez for being there for me through all of this. I don't see O'Brien. Oh, there he is. Thanks to everybody. Everybody will be all right, because y'all are going where I am going. Remember what I said, I want to see you all where I'm going. I want to give thanks. God, come and do Your will. I'm ready Warden.

Reginald Reeves
Execution Date: 05/09/2002
Race: Black
County of Conviction: Red River
Last Statement: I pray that we all may learn to love and forgive so that we can have peace in the world. It is with loving and forgiveness and living to learn to love and loving to live that we can learn the power of forgiveness and learn to live as brothers and sisters on this earth. Until then, this will continue to happen -- capital punishment; and if we don't forgive, sooner or later we will all self-destruct. You need to open up your heart and let God in. I apologize for taking the life of your

daughter and I know how much pain you must be in because I saw my family today. And although my pain is not as deep as yours, I am very sorry. Today, this does not bring you peace because this is not really the way. We should forgive and love and I do apologize with all my heart and soul and I love you and I know your spirit and God dwells within us and we are all one big family of humanity; we must all learn to love and live together. I will see you on the other side. Thank you for your hospitality.

Ronford Styron
Execution Date: 05/16/2002
Race: White
County of Conviction: Liberty
Last Statement: Yes sir, Thank you. I love y'all and I want y'all to know that. Y'all always told me not to worry about myself. I worry more about you all because I know where I am going. I want to see you there, so get your heart right. You know I love you and care for you. I am going to go with my little boy and play with him. Y'all take care and I love y'all. I love y'all. Chaplain Wilcox, Roger, Robin, Sarah, Grandma. I love you. Y'all be careful. Lord Jesus, I see your Spirit, it's o.k. I love you.

Johnny Martinez
Execution Date: 05/22/2002
Race: Hispanic
County of Conviction: Nueces
Last Statement: First of all, I want to say that I want to apologize to Clay Peterson's father. I am sorry. And I want to thank you for everything you tried to do; it meant a lot to me. I want to thank David Dow; you have been great to me and I know that I am fixing to die - but not for my mistakes. My trial lawyers - they are the ones that are killing me. I love my family and I know where I am going. You all take care - Celina, David and tell Mama I love her, too. I didn't call her 'cause I just couldn't. I am going to heaven and I'll see you there. Tom Crouch, and everybody, I love you. Chiara, thank you for everything. Fred, Rachel, Daniel, Oralia - thank you for being there for me. I will be there with you all in spirit. David Dow, you have been great. Mary Moreno, from the Corpus Christi Caller Times, thank you for what you wrote. You have been sincere and I wanted to talk to you, but they wouldn't let me. David Dow, let them know what happened. I am fine; I am happy; I will see you on the other side.

Napoleon Beazley
Execution Date: 05/28/2002
Race: Black
County of Conviction: Smith
Last Statement: The act I committed to put me here was not just heinous, it was senseless. But the person that committed that act is no longer here - I am. I'm not going to struggle physically against any restraints. I'm not going to shout, use profanity or make idle threats. Understand though that I'm not only upset, but I'm saddened by what is happening here tonight. I'm not only saddened, but disappointed that a system that is supposed to protect and uphold what is just and right can be so much like me when I made the same shameful mistake. If someone tried to dispose of everyone here for participating in this killing, I'd scream a resounding, "No." I'd tell them to give them all the gift that they would not give me...and that's to give them all a second chance. I'm sorry that I am here. I'm sorry that you're all here. I'm sorry that John Luttig died. And I'm sorry that it was something in me that caused all of this to happen to begin with. Tonight we tell the world that there are no second chances in the eyes of justice...Tonight, we tell our children that in some instances, in some cases, killing is right. This conflict hurts us all, there are no SIDES. The people who support this proceeding think this is justice. The people that think that I should live think that is justice. As difficult as it may seem, this is a clash of ideals, with both parties committed to what they feel is right. But who's wrong if in the end we're all victims? In my heart, I have to believe that there is a peaceful compromise to our ideals. I don't mind if there are none for me, as long as there are for those who are yet to come. There are a lot of men like me on death row - good men - who fell to the same misguided emotions, but may not have recovered as I have. Give those men a chance to do what's right. Give them a chance to undo their wrongs. A lot of them want to fix the mess they started, but don't know how. The problem is not in that people aren't willing to help them find out, but in the system telling them it won't matter anyway. No one wins tonight. No one gets closure. No one walks away victorious.

Stanley Baker, Jr.
Execution Date: 05/30/2002
Race: White
County of Conviction: Brazos
Last Statement: Well, I don't have anything to say. I am just sorry about what I did to Mr. Peters. That's all.

Daniel Reneau
Execution Date: 06/13/2002
Race: White
County of Conviction: Gillespie
Last Statement: This person declined to make a last statement.

Robert Coulson
Execution Date: 06/25/2002
Race: White
County of Conviction: Harris
Last Statement: I'm innocent. I had nothing to do with my family's murders. I want to thank everyone who has supported me. I hope they continue to fight. You know who you are. That's all. Thank you, Warden

Jeffrey Williams
Execution Date: 06/26/2002
Race: Black
County of Conviction: Harris
Last Statement: The Lord is my Shepherd, I shall not want. He maketh me lie down in green pastures; He leadeth me beside the still waters, He restoreth my soul. He leadeth me in the paths of righteousness for His name's sake. Yea, though I walk through the valley of the shadow of death, I will fear no evil; for Thou art with me. Thy rod and Thy staff, they comfort me. Thou preparest a table before me, in the presence of mine enemies. he anointeth my head with oil; my cup runneth over. Surely goodness and mercy shall follow me all the days of my life, and I will dwell in the House of the Lord forever. Amen. Amen.

Richard Kutzner
Execution Date: 08/07/2002
Race: White
County of Conviction: Montgomery
Last Statement: Well, yes, sir. Rebecca, I understand that you wanted this day to come, you got what you wanted. I didn't kill your mother. The two guys that worked for me killed your mother and they are still out there. If Mr. McDougal had allowed the DNA evidence, I would be exonerated. Mr. Tolson, I understand you are out there. If there is any justice in this world, please use this to keep other people from being where I'm at. Warden, this is murder just as surely as the people that killed Rebecca's mother. Send me home.

T. J. Jones
Execution Date: 08/08/2002
Race: Black
County of Conviction: Gregg
Last Statement: I would like to say to the family, I regret the pain I've put you through and I hope you can get over it someday. Mom and Dad, I love you. Take care. I'm ready.

Javier Medina
Execution Date: 08/14/2002
Race: Hispanic
County of Conviction: Dallas
Last Statement: First of all, I would like to apologize to the family members of the Cadena family for whatever hurt and suffering I have caused you. This opportunity has never come up before. It's not that I haven't been remorseful, things just never worked out before. Please forgive me and I hope you find it in your heart to forgive me. The peace you will find will be a temporary peace, true peace will come through find Christ. I pray through this execution, that you will find the peace you seek. Give yourself to Christ and find peace through him. I thought about your loved one very much. He will be waiting in heaven for me. I will be able to talk to him and ask him for forgiveness personally. To my family, I thank you and love you for being there for me and supporting me. This is just a stepping stone to home. The hardest part of all the years I was on death row. To all people that supported me, you will always be in my heart, as I have always been in yours. God bless you. Keep your heads up, see you again soon. Forgive me for the pain I caused you. (Spanish) To all the people of Mexico, I would like to thank them for the help. I also want to carry each and every one of you in my heart. If you are going to demonstrate, I don't want you to do anything crazy to these people. They have suffered enough. Long lives Mexico. Raise the flag of Mexico with honor. Thanks for everything. I love you. (English) To everyone on death row, keep your heads up and I will see you again. I am truly sorry, may you find peace in this. Forgive me for the pain. God bless you, I love you all, and I'm ready to go home.

Gary Etheridge
Execution Date: 08/20/2002
Race: White
County of Conviction: Brazoria
Last Statement: Yes, sir. To the victim's family, I'm sorry for what was taken from you. I hope you find peace. To my sweet Claudia, I love you. Stay strong, keep building, and be careful. Be careful. I love you. I'm through.

Toronto Patterson
Execution Date: 08/28/2002
Race: Black
County of Conviction: Dallas
Last Statement: I am sorry for the pain: sorry for what I caused my friends, family and loved ones. I feel a great deal of responsibility and guilt for all this crime. I should be punished for the crime, but I do not think I should die for a crime I did not commit. I am sorry, but nothing can bring Kim, Ollie, and Gigi back. But I pray my death brings peace for my family that may unite the family. I ask for your forgiveness and that you will all forgive me. I have no animosity; I am at peace and invite you all to my funeral. We are still family. I love you all, Momma, Aunt Deidra, family and everybody. I love you. I am ready, Warden.

Tony Walker
Execution Date: 09/10/2002
Race: Black
County of Conviction: Morris
Last Statement: Spoken: I would like to say goodbye to a good friend of mine in Switzerland - Diego. I appreciate all the help and support he gave me through the years. A friend of mine in England. Wildflower: I love you and will never forget you. And to my family. That's all. Written: I wish to tell the family how sorry I am about what I done. I know that nothing I say will bring Mr. and Mr. Bo Simmons back. I ask that if Linda and Gary and their family can find it in their hearts to forgive me, but if not, I will understand. I am truly sorry.

Jessie Patrick
Execution Date: 09/17/2002
Race: White
County of Conviction: Dallas
Last Statement: This person declined to make a last statement.

Ron Shamburger
Execution Date: 09/18/2002
Race: White
County of Conviction: Brazos
Last Statement: A lot of people have always asked if there is a Heaven, and I say there is. There is a Heaven and a Hell. They ask, "Who goes to Heaven?" I believe that it is those who have placed their faith in Jesus Christ. Romans 3:25: For all have sinned and come short of the glory of God. Romans 6:23: The wages of sin is

death, but the gift of God is eternal life. Romans 5:8: While we were yet sinners, Christ died for us. Romans 10:9: If you confess with your mouth the Lord Jesus Christ, and that He was raised from the dead, thou shalt be saved. John 3:16: For God so loved the world, that He gave his only begotten Son, that whosoever believeth in Him shall have everlasting life. A lot of people forget about: John3:36: If you have the Son, you have life and if you have not the Son, the wrath of God lies on you. In this life, we sin and we make mistakes: 1 John 1:19: If we confess our sins, He is faithful and just to forgive our sins. I had a verse that jumped out at me a few days ago. Psalm 99:8 speaks of the holiness of God and He was to the people a God who forgave, but He took vengeance on his deeds. I am not here because of my faith in the Lord Jesus, but I am here for not other reason than my own actions. To the Bakers, I am really sorry for the pain and sorrow I caused you. I really do not know what to say, but I am sorry - forgive me. And to my parents, I am sorry for the pain I have caused you. Forgive me; thank you for your love.

Rex Mays
Execution Date: 09/24/2002
Race: White
County of Conviction: Harris
Last Statement: I would like to say a final prayer: Dear Heavenly Father, I come to you today, Lord, and thank You for this opportunity to be with You in paradise. I ask You for forgiveness for the ones that need to be forgiven. Dear Lord, deliver us from evil and give us the comfort and peace and joy that we need. Dear Lord, I ask You right now to be with each of the witnesses and lift them up and be on solid ground. Let them know what has gone on and may we all see each other again. Amen. I would like to thank each witness: Ms. Cox, Whiteside, Reed, Scott, and Chad. I am going to go and see Jesus tonight and reserve a special place for each one of you. You all have been there when no one else was. Thank you for all of your love and support. Just know that I am ready to go. You all know what I've gone through. I am going to a better place with the Lord. I'm mad for one reason, that I'm leaving you behind, when I am going to a better place. Y'all still have to go through this hell on earth. Just remember the good things and not the bad. You are all loved and respected. Warden, just give me parole and let me go home to be with the Lord.

Calvin King
Execution Date: 09/25/2002
Race: Black
County of Conviction: Jefferson
Last Statement: I want to say God forgives as I forgive. God is the greatest. Thank you.

James Powell
Execution Date: 10/01/2002
Race: White
County of Conviction: Newton
Last Statement: I am ready for the final blessing.

Craig Ogan
Execution Date: 11/19/2002
Race: White
County of Conviction: Harris
Last Statement: I would like to say first of all the real violent crimes in this case are acts committed by James Boswell and Clay Morgan Gaines. We have the physical evidence to prove fabrication and cover-up. The people responsible for killing me will have blood on their hands for an unprovoked murder. I am not guilty; I acted in self-defense and reflex in the face of a police officer who was out of control. James Boswell had his head beat in; possibly due to this he had problems. My jurors had not heard about that. They did not know he had suffered a head injury from the beating by a crack dealer five months earlier; that he was filled with anger and wrote an angry letter to the Houston Chronicle. He expressed his frustration at the mayor, police chief and fire chief. He was mad at the world. Three and a half months before I worked on a deal with the DEA, the informant was let off. At the moment he left the courtroom, he became angry with me; Officer Boswell was upset about this. Officer Boswell and an angry woman were in the police car and they were talking in raised voices. In other words, Officer Boswell was angry at the time I walked up. Officer Boswell may have reacted to the...(Offender stopped speaking in mid-sentence.)

William Chappell
Execution Date: 11/20/2002
Race: White
County of Conviction: Tarrant
Last Statement: Jane, Grace and all of you all, I know you think I did this, and I'm sure you think this is wonderful in you eyes. But, let me tell you something, there were two DNA tests run and none matched me. I wanted a third, but that never happened. Three people at different times confessed to killing these people - your parents. They did not know me. My request is that you get yourselves in church and pray for forgiveness because you are murdering me. I did not kill anyone in my life. If you will look at your house and the police report, there are several bullet patterns shot into the West wall over the bed and the East wall and North wall and

your sister was in the front bedroom while 30 shots were fired. There's no way in hell she would have laid in that bed. If you think I did this, you need to think again. There were three people in the house and have confessed to it. Larry Ashworth in Fort Worth killed seven people. All I was asking for was a DNA and I could not get it. But get in church and get right with God. Jane, you know damn well I did not molest that kid of yours. You are murdering me and I feel sorry for you. Get in church and get saved. I really don't know what else to tell you.

Leonard Rojas
Execution Date: 12/04/2002
Race: Hispanic
County of Conviction: Johnson
Last Statement: This person declined to make a last statement.

James Collier
Execution Date: 12/11/2002
Race: White
County of Conviction: Wichita
Last Statement: The only thing I want to say is that I appreciate the hospitality that you guys have shown me and the respect; and the last meal was really good. That is about it. Thank you guys for being there and giving me a little bit of spiritual guidance and support.

Samuel Gallamore
Execution Date: 01/14/2003
Race: White
County of Conviction: Comal
Last Statement: Written: There are many things I would like to say, but none more important that how I feel toward Mr. & Mrs. Kenney, and Ms. Arnott. I would like to apologize and say I'm sorry but words seem so hollow and cheap. Their death should not have happened, but it did. I'm so sorry that all of this took place. Now I have devastated my family as well, but my heart has grown in the last few minutes because I was forgiven by the family of Mr. & Mrs. Kenney, and Ms. Arnott. Thank You. You have given me more hope then I have had in a long time. If I could change things I would, not for my sake but for all those who have loved me over the years, and for those who have forgiven me. Thank you for all that you have given me.

John Baltazar
Execution Date: 01/15/2003

Race: Hispanic
County of Conviction: Nueces
Last Statement: This person declined to make a last statement.

Robert Lookingbill

Execution Date: 01/22/2003
Race: White
County of Conviction: Hidalgo
Last Statement: I would like to thank all my loved ones that are standing over there for all the kindness and support you have shown me over the years. Be strong. Do not hate, but learn from this experience. Just because it happens, do not think that God doesn't care. He will be with you. I will be there with all of you. I love you all and appreciate all of you. You won't be forgotten and there are a lot of people out there that love you. It has been a blessing to know all of you. This is not easy for any of us. Don't be upset about my situation, because I am not. I am still faithful and I am still strong. Just give my love to everyone out there. Don't forget me and burn a candle for me when you can. I love you all.

Alva Curry

Execution Date: 01/28/2003
Race: Black
County of Conviction: Travis
Last Statement: I pray with the help of God that you will forgive me for the pain I caused your family. I am truly sorry. I wish I could take it back, but I just pray and ask that you forgive me.

Richard Dinkins

Execution Date: 01/29/2003
Race: White
County of Conviction: Jefferson
Last Statement: Written To the families of Ms. Thompson and Ms. Cutler. I am sorry for what happened and that it was because of me that they are gone. If there were any way I could change things and bring them back I would. But I can't. Because of what I caused to happen many people were affected and I am very sorry that I did. I have made my peace with God and I pray that soon everyone will be able to have closure in their hearts and lives. To my family and friends, I love you and some day we will all be together again.

Granville Riddle

Execution Date: 01/30/2003
Race: White
County of Conviction: Potter
Last Statement: I would just...(speaking in French). I love all of you. I love you Lundy, Levi, my dad. I have no grudges against anyone, or any of the things that have gone wrong. I would like to say to the world, I have always been a nice person. I have never been mean-hearted or cruel. I wish everybody well.

John Elliott

Execution Date: 02/04/2003
Race: Hispanic
County of Conviction: Travis
Last Statement: This person declined to make a last statement.

Henry Dunn, Jr.

Execution Date: 02/06/2003
Race: Black
County of Conviction: Smith
Last Statement: Spoken: To all my family and friends, I want you to know that I love you very much. I appreciate all the good and bad times together. I'll always remember you, and love you forever. And to the West family, I hope you can find it in your heart to find forgiveness and strength, to move on and find peace. Written: The Death Penalty in Texas is broke. When an attorney can be forced to represent you, who is not qualified to represent you under Texas laws, the system does not work. When an attorney can dismiss your appeal process, by missing a filing deadline or for failing to file documents on behalf of a client, thats not Due Process of Law as guaranteed under the Unites States Constitution, the system does not work. When officials of any state, such as the State of Texas, has so much confidence in their justice system, mistakes will be made, and innocent people will be executed. Texas has executed innocent people, and tonight, Texas has shown just how broke and unfair its system is. There is no clemency in Texas, a process that needs to be reviewed, and fixed. Most importantly, the Texas Justice System need to be fixed. I hope the politicians such as Elliot Nashtat, Harold Dutton, Rodney Ellis, and others, continue to do their part in trying to fix the Texas Justice System, and until so is done, continue to work for a moratorium on the death penalty in Texas. The victim of this case is NOT forgotten. To the West family, I hope you find in your hearts forgiveness and peace, and find the strength to move forward and the closure they are looking for. Nicholas West is not forgotten, and never will be

forgotten. To my family and friends, Anne Dolatschko, Debbie Bilodeau, and the many supporters around the world, as well as my attorneys, Michael Charlton, who has always been there for me and done everything in their will and power to help me and stand by my side, I love you dearly, and you will always be in my heart forever. Please continue to struggle and fight against the death penalty, as its only use has been for revenge, and it does not deter crime. Its time for a moratorium in the State of Texas.

Richard Williams
Execution Date: 02/25/2003
Race: Black
County of Conviction: Harris
Last Statement: Spoken: The statement I would like to make is to all my loved ones - and to the Abrahams and Williams families. We came a long way through the tragedy - from hate to love and I would like to apologize for the pain I have caused all my families on both sides. I am looking at you Mr. Frank: I am sorry brother for what happened to your sister and I hope that you would forgive me one day. Ask God to forgive me and ask God to forgive you and allow me to pass through. My brother Farooq, I love you my brother and send my love to all my family members. And I was not a monster like they said I was. I made a mistake and this mistake cost - but they won't cost no more. I leave you with all my love and blessings. may Allah bless each and every one of you. Written: Hello to all: Tonight I take my last walk as well breath in this world called Earth. I state that to show I'm not saddened or enjoied to see this moment. Because I leave behind alot of people that loved me, that believe I could had been that someone. If I been given a real chance in life instead of denial or incarceration everytime I was arrested for something the community believed I did. To be here on Texas death Row show all people that we people of American don't care about helping. This is about destroying lives to show they can kill, but they hide behind laws of American. I'm not disappointed of the system or nobody because this is how it's supposed to be. Texans was breed that way to live, think, act. But someone is mad that a system that's supposed to protect and uphold what is just and right, has shown it's just as crooked as I am said to be. Now I lay here dead. But we have gave all Texans the sign that in some instances, and in some cases "KILLING IS ALRIGHT TO DO AS LONG IT'S FOR JUSTICE OF THE AMERICAN PEOPLE". So who win? No one do! Ain't no such thing as a closure! Because we all still will remember who ain't here on them special detes, occasion's ect... So no victorious, heros and happiness. but in ALLAH's (GOD) eye justice is his, and we should cry out for his forgiveness. I leave with ALLAH's blessing as well mercy for my soul. I'm free now! Let me rest in peace. Nam-myoho-renge-

kyo! Salaamu! Amen! Bro. D'Reehcer Ali Smaillii Muhammd. (formely known as) Richard Earl Head-Williams III

Bobby Cook
Execution Date: 03/11/2003
Race: White
County of Conviction: Anderson
Last Statement: I would like to say to the victim's family, if this goes on record, that I know they have gotten grief and I know with this execution, it will not be any relief to them. That with my death, it will just remind them of their loved one, Mr. Holder. I would like to say to them, "please forgive me for what happened; it was self defense...and I was never able to get up on the stand to tell them." I know this is wrong. I am going home to the Lord.

Keith Clay
Execution Date: 03/20/2003
Race: Black
County of Conviction: Harris
Last Statement: I would like to say first and foremost to the Lord God Almighty that I am sorry and forgive me of every single solitary sin I have committed these 35 years I have lived upon this Earth. To the Varghese family, I would ask that you forgive me because I know you have suffered a great loss and I am truly, truly sorry. I know what you have suffered, but please grant me your forgiveness. I am truly sorry, and there is not a day that I have not prayed for you. And to my Mom, I love you. I am going to see the Lord. The Lord is my Shepherd. Let everyone know that I love them; this is not goodbye. I will see you later.

James Colburn
Execution Date: 03/26/2003
Race: White
County of Conviction: Montgomery
Last Statement: The statement that I would like to make is, none of this should have happened and now that I'm dying, there is nothing left to worry about. I know it was a mistake. I have no one to blame but myself. It's no big deal about choosing right from wrong. I pray that everyone involved overlooks the stupidity. Everybody has problems and I won't be a part of the problem anymore. I can quit worrying now, it was all a mistake. That's all I want to say.

John Chavez
Execution Date: 04/22/2003
Race: Hispanic
County of Conviction: Dallas
Last Statement: To the media, I would like for you to tell all the victims and their loved ones that I am truly, truly sorry for taking their loved ones' lives. And I hope they will find it in their heart to forgive me for what I did to them. I am a different person now, but that does not change the fact of the bad things I have committed. God can give you the same peace He gave me and you can be in His hands. And to my beautiful family, be strong. Remember what I said, "God is the Way, the Truth, and the Life." OK, Warden.

Roger Vaughn
Execution Date: 05/06/2003
Race: White
County of Conviction: Wilbarger
Last Statement: This person declined to make a last statement.

Bruce Jacobs
Execution Date: 05/15/2003
Race: White
County of Conviction: Dallas
Last Statement: Can you hear me, Chris? The Lord is my Shepherd; I shall not want. He makes me to lie down in green pastures; He leads me beside the still waters. He restores my soul; He leads me in the paths of righteousness for His name's sake. Yea, though I walk through the valley of the shadow of death, I will fear no evil; for Thou art with me; Thy rod and Thy staff comfort me. Thou preparest a table before me in the presence of my enemies; Thou anointest my head with oil; My cup runneth over. Surely goodness and mercy shall follow me all the days of my life; And I will dwell in the house of the Lord forever. I want to thank you for being there with me all these years and supporting me and keeping me in the Word. Michael, you take care of her and thank you Father Don and Chris. And I want to thank the media for being nice to me all this time. Bye, Chris. I will see you. Take care of yourselves and you all stay strong. You keep doing your ministry.

Kia Johnson
Execution Date: 06/11/2003
Race: Black
County of Conviction: Bexar

Last Statement: Tell Mama I love her and tell the kids I love them, too. I'll see you all.

Hilton Crawford
Execution Date: 07/02/2003
Race: White
County of Conviction: Montgomery
Last Statement: First of all, I would like to ask Sister Teresa to send Connie a yellow rose. I want to thank the Lord, Jesus Christ, for the years I have spent on death row. They have been a blessing in my life. I have had the opportunity to serve Jesus Christ and I am thankful for the opportunity. I would like to thank Father Walsh for having become a Franciscan, and all the people all over the world who have become my friends. It has been a wonderful experience in my life. I would like to thank Chaplain Lopez, and my witnesses for giving me their support and love. I would like to thank the Nuns in England for their support. I want to tell my sons I love them; I have always loved them - they were my greatest gift from God. I want to tell my witnesses, Tannie, Rebecca, Al, Leo, and Dr. Blackwell that I love all of you and I am thankful for your support. I want to ask Paulette for forgiveness from your heart. One day, I hope you will. It is a tragedy for my family and your family. I am sorry. My special angel, I love you. And I love you, Connie. May God pass me over to the Kindom's shore softly and gently. I am ready.

Christopher Black, Sr.
Execution Date: 07/09/2003
Race: Black
County of Conviction: Bell
Last Statement: This person declined to make a last statement.

Cedric Ransom
Execution Date: 07/23/2003
Race: Black
County of Conviction: Tarrant
Last Statement: I just want to address Katrina and Rebecca. You have been beautiful to me. Without you in my life, I would not have been able to make it like this. Probably, I would have put up a good fight; you have calmed me. I love you. I respect you. Big brother, you put up the best fight you could and I love you. That is it.

Allen Janecka
Execution Date: 07/24/2003
Race: White
County of Conviction: Harris
Last Statement: First of all, I want to say God bless everyone here today. For many years I have done things my way, which caused a lot of pain to me, my family and many others. Today I have come to realize that for peace and happiness, one has to do things God's way. I want to thank my family for their support. I love you. I am taking you with me. You all stay strong. I love you. I also want to say thanks to the Chaplains who I have met through the years and who have brought me a long way. And I cherish you as my family and at this time...oh, Ken, my little son, I am coming to see you. Oh Lord, into your hands I commit my spirit. Thy will be done.

Larry Hayes
Execution Date: 09/10/2003
Race: White
County of Conviction: Montgomery
Last Statement: I would like for Rosalyn's family and loved ones and my wife, Mary's, family to know that I am genuinely sorry for what I did. I would like you to reach down in your hearts and forgive me. There is no excuse for what I did. Rosalyn's mother asked me at the trial, "Why?" and I do not have a good reason for it. Please forgive me. As for my friends and family here - thanks for sticking with me and know that I love you and will take part of you with me. I would like to thank one of the arresting officers that I would have killed if I could have. He gave me CPR, saved my life, and gave me a chance to get my life right. I know I will see Mary and Rosalyn tonight. I love you all.

Robert Henry
Execution Date: 11/20/2003
Race: White
County of Conviction: San Patricio
Last Statement: This person declined to make a last statement.

Richard Duncan
Execution Date: 12/03/2003
Race: White
County of Conviction: Harris
Last Statement: I did have, but now I see my family here and everything - all I want to say is I love you all so much. I am innocent. I love you all so much. You are beautiful. Okay Warden, I am through.

Ivan Murphy
Execution Date: 12/04/2003
Race: White
County of Conviction: Grayson
Last Statement: Yes sir, I do. I would like to thank everybody for coming out tonight and celebrating life. This is a celebration of life, not death. Through Jesus Christ, we have victory over death. I would like to thank the Holy Father and Pope John Paul for their angelic blessings and all the prayers and support. And thanks to Father (name unknown) and Guido Todeschini for your love and support. I want to thank everybody around the world and Father, let your will be done. I am going to keep this statement short. I love you all. I am ready, Warden.

Ynobe Matthews
Execution Date: 01/06/2004
Race: Black
County of Conviction: Brazos
Last Statement: This person declined to make a last statement.

Kenneth Bruce
Execution Date: 01/14/2004
Race: Black
County of Conviction: Collin
Last Statement: Yes sir. I would like to thank God for all the blessings He has given me. And I pray that through His mercy, He will allow me into His grace. And to the family of Ms. Ayers, I would like to apologize for all the pain and suffering and that God gives you closure. And I pray that He blesses you. And to my family, know that I love every single one of you and pray that God gives you peace and strength. I may not be with you in the physical, but by grace, my heart will be with you all and I know God loves every one of you all.

Kevin Zimmerman
Execution Date: 01/21/2004
Race: White
County of Conviction: Jefferson
Last Statement: Yes. Connie, Nanny, Bea, Kathy and Richard - I love you all and I thank you all very much for supporting me with your love. In the name of Jesus, I am sorry for the pain I caused you all. I am sorry. Gilbert didn't deserve to die and I want you all to know I am sorry. I pray that the good Lord will give you all peace. Okay.

Billy Vickers
Execution Date: 01/28/2004
Race: White
County of Conviction: Lamar
Last Statement: Yes. I would just like to say to my family that I am sorry for all the grief I have caused. I love you all. Tell Mama and the kids I love you; I love all of you. And I would like to clear some things up if I could. Tommy Perkins, the man that got a capital life sentence for murdering Kinslow -- he did not do it. I did it. He would not even have had anything to do with it if he had known I was going to shoot the man. He would not have gone with me if he had known. I was paid to shoot the man. And Martin, the younger boy, did not know what it was about. He thought it was just a robbery. I am sorry for that. It was nothing personal. I was trying to make a living. A boy on Eastham doing a life sentence for killing Jamie Kent - I did not do it, but I was with his daddy when it was done. I was there with him and down through the years there were several more that I had done or had a part of. And I am sorry and I am not sure how many - there must be a dozen or 14 I believe all total. One I would like to clear up is Cullen Davis - where he was charged with shooting his wife. And all of these it was never nothing personal. It was just something I did to make a living. I am sorry for all the grief I have caused. I love you all. That is all I have to say.

Edward Lagrone
Execution Date: 02/22/2004
Race: Black
County of Conviction: Tarrant
Last Statement: Yes. I just want to say I am not sad today or bitter with anybody. Like I've said from day one, I did not go in there and kill them - but I am no better than those that did. Jesus is Lord.

Bobby Hopkins
Execution Date: 02/12/2004
Race: Black
County of Conviction: Johnson
Last Statement: This person declined to make a last statement.

Cameron Willingham
Execution Date: 02/17/2004
Race: White
County of Conviction: Navarro

Last Statement: Yeah. The only statement I want to make is that I am an innocent man - convicted of a crime I did not commit. I have been persecuted for 12 years for something I did not do. From God's dust I came and to dust I will return - so the earth shall become my throne. I gotta go, road dog. I love you Gabby. [Remaining portion of statement omitted due to profanity.]

Marcus Cotton
Execution Date: 03/03/2004
Race: Black
County of Conviction: Harris
Last Statement: Yes Warden, I do. Well Mom, sometimes it works out like this. Love life; live long. When you are dealing with reality, real is not always what you want it to be. Take care of yourselves. I love you. Tell my kids I love them. God is real. He is fixing to find out some deep things that are real. Bounce back, baby. You know what I'm saying. You all take care of yourselves. That is it.

Kelsey Patterson
Execution Date: 05/18/2004
Race: Black
County of Conviction: Anderson
Last Statement: Statement to what. State What. I am not guilty of the charge of capital murder. Steal me and my family's money. My truth will always be my truth. There is no kin and no friend; no fear what you do to me. No kin to you undertaker. Murderer. [Portion of statement omitted due to profanity] Get my money. Give me my rights. Give me my rights. Give me my rights. Give me my life back.

David Harris
Execution Date: 06/30/2004
Race: White
County of Conviction: Jefferson
Last Statement: Yes I do. Sir, in honor of a true American hero. "let's roll". Lord Jesus receive my spirit.

Jasen Busby
Execution Date: 08/25/2004
Race: White
County of Conviction: Cherokee
Last Statement: Yes I do. I want to tell everyone, my family, thanks for standing by me. I want to tell Mr. and Ms. Gray and everyone that I didn't do what I did to

hurt you all. I am sorry that I did what I did. I don't think you know the true reason for doing what I did, but Brandy and I had a suicide pact and I just didn't follow through with it. That did not come out in the trial. I am not trying to hurt you by telling you this. I am trying to tell you the truth. I want Cindy to know that I know she is out there -- and Vicente Hernandez that I love them. Thank you for all you have done and I want to make sure you are alright. That is all I want to say. I am ready. See you later. I am ready.

James Allridge III
Execution Date: 08/26/2004
Race: Black
County of Conviction: Tarrant
Last Statement: Yeah. I want to thank my family and friends; my family for all loving me and giving me so much love. I am sorry; I really am. You, Brian's sister, thanks for your love -- it meant a lot. Shane -- I hope he finds peace. I am sorry I destroyed you all's life. Thank you for forgiving me. To the moon and back -- I love you all.

Andrew Flores
Execution Date: 09/21/2004
Race: Hispanic
County of Conviction: Bexar
Last Statement: Yes sir. Today I go home to the Lord. But first, I have to say something. I am real sorry. I took family member's life and I shouldn't have. I hope that you can move on. I am just sorry. I don't know what else to say. I can't bring anyone back. I would if I could. I hope you will be fine. I won't ask for your forgiveness. God will be my judge. To my family and friends, I love you all. You all take care and somebody find Void. Be strong and I will see you all; hopefully not soon. Keep your head up. That is all I have to say.

Edward Green
Execution Date: 10/05/2004
Race: Black
County of Conviction: Harris
Last Statement: Yes I do. To my family, to my friends, and people who have accepted me for being the person that I am. To the Sullivan and Hayden families, I do not come here with the intention to make myself out to be a person that I am not. I never claimed to be the best person. I am not the best father, the best son, or the best friend in the world. I did the best I could with what I had. I come with no

hate in my heart or bitterness. To my family and to you people, I can only apologize for all the pain I caused you. May God forgive us on this day. I am ready when you are.

Peter Miniel
Execution Date: 10/06/2004
Race: Hispanic
County of Conviction: Harris
Last Statement: Into your hands Oh Lord, I commence my spirit. Amen.

Donald Aldrich
Execution Date: 10/12/2004
Race: White
County of Conviction: Kerr
Last Statement: Yes sir, I would. To the West Family, I would just like to apologize for your loss. I hope that you can forgive me. To my family and loved ones and friends, I thank all of you all for your support and I am sorry for the pain and hurt I have caused you. I love you all and I will see you on the other side. O.K. Warden.

Ricky Morrow
Execution Date: 10/20/2004
Race: White
County of Conviction: Dallas
Last Statement: Yes, I do. I want to say first that I love you Pam. I love you, Ann, Jenny, Carla, Fran, Mom and Dad. What a blessing, what a blessing you have been in my life. And I am so sorry you are going through what you are now. But we are both headed to a better place. Thank you, baby girl - love you people. Sister, Blackie, Dixie, Rusty, Andy, Buster, Milo - we got so many - Grace and Sonny man. I love you all. You have a treat coming to you. Thank you for having been there for me -- and our Father and Mother. Give them a hug and give them my love. I am ready Warden.

Dominique Green
Execution Date: 10/26/2004
Race: Black
County of Conviction: Harris
Last Statement: Yes. Man, there is a lot of people there. There was a lot of people that got me to this point, and I can't thank them all. But thank you for your love and support; they have allowed me to do a lot more than I could have on my own.

Sheila, I wish I would have met you seven years ago; it would have been a lot easier. But I have overcame a lot. I am not angry, but I am disappointed that I was denied justice. But I am happy that I was afforded you all as family and friends. You all have been there for me; it's a miracle. I love you. And I have to tell Jessica I am sorry. I never knew it would come to this. Lorna, you know you have to keep my struggle going. I know you just lost your baby; but you have to keep running. Andy, I love you man. Tell Andre and them that I didn't get a chance to reach my full potential, but you can help them reach theirs. You needed me, but I just did not know how to be there for them. There is so much I have to say, but I just can't say it all. I love you all. Please just keep the struggle going. If you turn your back on me, you turn your back on them. I love you all and I'll miss you all. Thanks for allowing me to touch so many hearts. I never knew I could do it, but you made it possible. I am just sorry. And I am not as strong as I thought I was going to be. But I guess it only hurts for a little while. You all are my family. Please keep my memory alive.

Lorenzo Morris

Execution Date: 11/02/2004
Race: Black
County of Conviction: Harris
Last Statement: This person declined to make a last statement.

Robert Morrow

Execution Date: 11/04/2004
Race: White
County of Conviction: Liberty
Last Statement: Yes I do. Mike and Ms. Allison, I would like to tell you that I am responsible and I am sorry for what I did and the pain I caused you all. I love you Earline and all of my friends that stood by me. I feel blessed to have had you all. Stay strong and take care of them kids. Set me free Warden. Father, accept me.

Demarco McCullum

Execution Date: 11/09/2004
Race: Black
County of Conviction: Harris
Last Statement: I do. I just wanted to say to all of those that have supported me over the years that I appreciate it and I love you. And I just want to tell my mom that I love her and I will see her in Heaven.

Frederick McWilliams

Execution Date: 11/10/2004
Race: Black
County of Conviction: Harris
Last Statement: Yes. Well here we are again folks, in the catacombs of justice. You know there is a lot I wanted to say - a lot I thought I'd say - but there is not a whole lot to say. There are people that will be mad thinking I try to seek freedom from this, but as long as I see - freedom belongs to me and I'll keep on keeping on. The shackles and chains that just might hold my body can't hold my mind, but will kill me otherwise. I love you momma, and Misty and Annette, Brenda and Anthony - and all my friends and everybody that supported me. I leave my love here; I am never going to stop loving you. My love is going to stay here.

Anthony Fuentes

Execution Date: 11/17/2004
Race: Hispanic
County of Conviction: Harris
Last Statement: Yes sir. Sorry that I have to put my family through this. All of you know I got my peace. And I hope you find peace. And to the family, the truth will come out and I hope you find peace. I got my peace. I hope everybody has their peace. I am tired. I am going to be in your heart. I love you all. To everybody else, the truth will be known. It didn't come out in time to save my life. It is wrong to put the families through this. But when it comes out, I hope it stops this. It is wrong for the prosecutors to lie and make witnesses say what they need them to say. The truth has always been there. I just hope everybody has their peace. Today I get mine. I love you all.

James Porter

Execution Date: 01/04/2005
Race: White
County of Conviction: Bowie
Last Statement: Yes sir, I do. I would like to apologize to the family of the victim. I am sorry for the pain I have caused you. I know it is a great loss and I want to apologize. I am sorry. And to my family, I love you and I will see you all in Heaven. O.K.

Troy Kunkle

Execution Date: 01/25/2005
Race: White

County of Conviction: Nueces
Last Statement: Yes sir. I would like to ask you to forgive me. I made a mistake and I am sorry for what I did. All I can do is ask you to forgive me. I love you and I will see all of you in Heaven. I love you very much. Praise Jesus. I love you. Our Father, who art in Heaven, hallowed be thy name. Thy kingdom come, Thy will be done, on earth as it is in Heaven. Give us this day our daily bread, and forgive us our trespasses as we forgive those who have trespassed against us. And lead us not into temptation, but deliver us from evil. Amen.

Dennis Bagwell
Execution Date: 02/17/2005
Race: White
County of Conviction: Atascosa
Last Statement: Yes sir, can you hear me? To you Irene, Thank You. I love you all. All right Warden, I'm ready.

George Hopper
Execution Date: 03/08/2005
Race: White
County of Conviction: Dallas
Last Statement: I want to apologize to you, and I am sorry. I have made a lot of mistakes in my life. The things I did changed so many lives. I can't take it back, it was an atrocity. I am sorry. I beg your forgiveness, I know I am not worthy of it. I love you Mom and Dad, and all my family. Thank you for everything. Jesus, thank you for your love and saving grace. Thank you for shedding your blood on Calvary for me. Thank you Jesus for the love you have shown me.

Douglas Roberts
Execution Date: 04/20/2005
Race: White
County of Conviction: Kendall
Last Statement: Yes sir, Warden Okay I've been hanging around this popsicle stand way too long. Before I leave, I want to tell you all. When I die, bury me deep, lay two speakers at my feet, put some headphones on my head and rock and roll me when I'm dead. I'll see you in Heaven someday. That's all Warden.

Lonnie Pursley
Execution Date: 05/03/2005
Race: White

County of Conviction: Polk
Last Statement: Yes. I would like to address the victim's family. I received your poem and I am very grateful for your forgiveness. I still want to ask for it anyway. I have Jesus in my heart and I am sorry for any pain I caused you all. Thank you for your forgiveness. I am sorry. Ashlee, Pam -- I am going to miss you all. I love you all. Give everybody my love. Give everybody my love, O.K.? Mother, James, Justin, Corey, Brent, grand-babies and Daddy - I love you Pam. I love you Ashlee, Pammy and Irene. I will see you all on the other side. Couple friends on death row who have helped me; Shy Town and Crazy Jay...I love you all and for all your support. Uncle Ray too. I am saved and I am going home, O.K.? You all stay strong. You all stay strong. That is all.

Bryan Wolfe
Execution Date: 05/18/2005
Race: Black
County of Conviction: Jefferson
Last Statement: Yes sir. To Edie, Tom, and and Carma - I love all you all. I appreciate all your support. I love you Margherita, Father Guido, and Father Angelo. I appreciate your spiritual support and all those that were in prayer for me. I will be O.K. I am at peace with all of this and I won't have to wake up in prison any more. I love you all. I totally surrender to the Lord. I am ready, Warden.

Richard Cartwright
Execution Date: 05/19/2005
Race: White
County of Conviction: Nueces
Last Statement: Yes, I do. I just want to thank all my friends and family who gave me support these past eight years. I want to apologize to the victim's family for the pain I caused them. And to everyone at the Polunsky Unit, just keep your heads up and stay strong.

Alexander Martinez
Execution Date: 06/07/2005
Race: Hispanic
County of Conviction: Harris
Last Statement: Yes. The victim's family is not here so I won't address them. I want to thank my family and friends for everything. My wife, Ailsa, my sister-in-law, Laura - thank you for being here for me. I love you. And thanks for the friends at the Polunsky Unit that helped me get through this that didn't agree with my decision - and still gave me their friendship. I thank them. Warden...

David Martinez
Execution Date: 07/28/2005
Race: Hispanic
County of Conviction: Travis
Last Statement: Only the sky and the green grass goes on forever and today is a good day to die.

Gary Sterling
Execution Date: 08/10/2005
Race: Black
County of Conviction: Navarro
Last Statement: I would like the Chaplain to say a prayer, not only for me but for the victim's family. For them being misled, I am sorry. That is all I have to say.

Robert Shields
Execution Date: 08/23/2005
Race: White
County of Conviction: Galveston
Last Statement: This person declined to make a last statement.

Francis Newton
Execution Date: 09/14/2005
Race: Black
County of Conviction: Harris
Last Statement: This person declined to make a last statement.

Ronald Howard
Execution Date: 10/06/2005
Race: Black
County of Conviction: Travis
Last Statement: Yes sir, I do. To the victim's family. I hope it helps a little. I do not know how, but I hope it helps. I love you all, all of you. You know I love you. Thank you for bringing my children back to my life. Thank you. I love you all. I love you all very much. Thank you very much. (Statement amended 01/09/06)

Luis Ramirez
Execution Date: 10/20/2005
Race: Hispanic
County of Conviction: Tom Green

Last Statement: Yes I do. I would like to address you first. I did not kill your loved one, but I hope that one day you find out who did. I wish I could tell you the reason why, or give some kind of solace; you lost someone you love very much. The same as my family and friends are going to lose in a few minutes. I am sure he died unjustly, just like I am. I did not murder him; I did not have anything to do with his death. And to you my family and friends, I love you dearly. Even though I die, that love for you will never die. Into Your hands, Lord, I commit my spirit. Thank you. Thank you all.

Melvin White
Execution Date: 11/03/2005
Race: White
County of Conviction: Pecos
Last Statement: Tell Beth and them I am sorry, truly sorry for the pain that I caused your family. I truly mean that too. She was a friend of mine and I betrayed her trust. I love you all. Tell momma I love her. The Lord is my shepherd; I shall not want, He maketh me to lie down in green pastures; he leadeth me beside the still waters. He restoreth my soul; he leadeth me in the paths of righeousness for his name's sake. Yea, though I walk through the valley of the shadow of death, I will fear no evil; for thou art with me. Thou preparest a table before me in the presence of mine enemies; thou anointest my head with oil; my cup runneth over. Surely goodness and mercy shall follow me all the days of my life; and I will dwell in the house of the Lord for ever. Our Father, who are in heaven, Hallowed be thy Name. Thy kingdom come. Thy will be done, On earth as it is in heaven. Give us this day our daily bread. And forgive us our trespasses, As we forgive those who trespass against us. And lead us not into temptation, But deliver us from evil. For thine is the kingdom, and the power, and the glory, for ever and ever. Amen All right Warden, let's give them what they want.

Charles Thacker
Execution Date: 11/09/2005
Race: White
County of Conviction: Harris
Last Statement: Jack and Irene, I love you guys. Tell my family I love them. I am sorry for the things I have done. I know God will forgive me. Keep track of Danielle for me. I will miss you guys. I love you. I guess that's all.

Robert Rowell
Execution Date: 11/15/2005

Race: White
County of Conviction: Harris
Last Statement: Yes sir. I would like to apologize to the victim's family and all the grief I have caused them. I would like to say I love the girls next to them. Praise the Lord. Let's go, Warden. That's it.

Shannon Thomas
Execution Date: 11/16/2005
Race: Black
County of Conviction: Harris
Last Statement: Yes. Man, I just want you to know how much I love them. I want you to be strong and get through this time. Do not fall back. Keep going forward. Don't let this hinder you. Let everybody know I love them (several names listed), Kevin - as well as everyone else in the family. Tell them that I love them and stay strong. This is kind of hard to put words together; I am nervous and it is hard to put my thoughts together. Sometimes you don't know what to say; I hope these words give you comfort. I don't know what to say. I want you to know I love you; just stay strong and don't give up. Let everybody know I love them...and love is unconditional, as Mama has always told us. I may be gone in the flesh, but I am always with you in spirit. I love you.

Marion Dudley
Execution Date: 01/25/2006
Race: Black
County of Conviction: Harris
Last Statement: This person declined to make a last statement.

Jaime Elizaide, Jr.
Execution Date: 01/31/2006
Race: Hispanic
County of Conviction: Harris
Last Statement: Yes sir. Darling Kerstin, these last few years have been blessed having you in my life. And to all my friends that have been out there, thank you for your friendship and support and all you have done for me. The guys back there waiting, keep the faith and stay strong and put your faith in the Lord. Many times in life we take the wrong road and there are consequences for everything. Mistakes are made, but with God all things are possible. So put your faith and trust in Him. We talk about a reprieve or stay from the Supreme Court, but the real Supreme Court you must face up there and not down here. Keep your heads up and stay strong. I love you all. That is it. Stay strong. Thank you.

Robert Neville, Jr.

Execution Date: 2/08/2006
Race: White
County of Conviction: Tarrant
Last Statement: Yes. Ms. Carolyn Barker, and Tina, I would like to apologize to you all. To Amy's sister, and everybody else here. I love you all. I hope you can find it in yourselves to forgive me and I hope all this here will kinda settle your pain and I hope the Lord will give you comfort and peace. And I just want you to know I am very sorry for what I have done. And if I see Amy on the other side, I will tell her how much you love and miss her and we will have a lot to talk about. Mom, Dad, and Charlotte - I am sorry for putting you through all this pain and stuff. I did talk to Brandon and I think I got a little stuff stopped. I love you all and I will see you on the other side. O.K.

Clyde Smith, Jr.

Execution Date: 02/15/2006
Race: Black
County of Conviction: Harris
Last Statement: Yes. I want to thank you all for being here and for your love and support. And thanks for the efforts, Peter and Lorrell. I love you all. Celina, I love you. I'm done.

Tommie Hughes

Execution Date: 03/15/2006
Race: Black
County of Conviction: Dallas
Last Statement: I love my family. You all stay strong. Watch over each other. Stay strong. I love you. I love you. It's my hour. It's my hour. I love you. Stay strong.

Robert Salazar, Jr.

Execution Date: 03/22/2006
Race: Hispanic
County of Conviction: Lubbock
Last Statement: Yes. Yes, I do. Do I just talk to the front? O.K. To everybody on both sides of that wall--I want you to know I love you. I am sorry that the child had to lose her life, but I should not have to be here. Tell my family I love them all and I will see them in Heaven. Come home when you can. I am done. Love you all.

Kevin Kincy
Execution Date: 03/29/2006
Race: Black
County of Conviction: Harris
Last Statement: Yes. I would like to thank all my friends and supporters, Anne West, who I love and respect. Gabrielle Uhl from Germany, and so many countless other friends. And of course my family, my mother and father, brothers and sisters, nieces and nephews, my wife Barbara and my children - Nadia, Amenia, Kira, and Noemi. I love my children. I love my family. That's it.

Jackie Wilson
Execution Date: 05/04/2006
Race: White
County of Conviction: Dallas
Last Statement: May I speak to my family? Honey, I love you. Be strong and take care of yourselves. Thanks for being there. Take care of yourself. Ms. Irene, thank you for everything you have done. Chaplain Hart, thank you for helping me. Gary, thank you. Maria, Maria, I love you baby. Thank you for being there for me and all these people here will find the one who did this damn crime. I am going home to be with God. Thank you. Thank you, Warden.

Jermaine Herron
Execution Date: 05/17/2006
Race: Black
County of Conviction: Refugio
Last Statement: Yes sir. To Mr. Jerry Nutt, I just hope this brings some kind of peace to your family. I wish I could bring them back, but I can't. I hope my death brings peace; don't hang on to the hate. Momma, stay strong. Lord forgive me for my sins because here I come. Let's go, Warden.

Jesus Aguilar
Execution Date: 05/24/2006
Race: Hispanic
County of Conviction: Cameron
Last Statement: Yes sir. I would like to say to my family, I am alright. (Spanish) Where are you Leo; are you there Leo? (Spanish) Don't lie man. Be happy. Are you happy? Are you all happy? (Spanish)

Timothy Titsworth
Execution Date: 06/06/2006
Race: White
County of Conviction: Randall
Last Statement: Yes, your honor. I know you people are here to find closure for the things that you have done or that I have done. There are no words to describe the pain and suffering that you have gone through all these years, that is something that I cannot take back from you all. I hope that Megan, if she is here present today, know that today I hope you get peace and joy. I am sorry that it has taken 14 years to get closure. If it would have brought closure or brought her back, I would have done this years ago, I promise, I promise. My family all knows the sincerity in my heart when I say these words to you. I didn't mean to inflict the pain and suffering on your family. I pray that she is safe in Heaven. I pray that you find closure and strength. My family prays for you and everybody, if these words can ever touch your heart, I am sorry, I am truly sorry. Ya'll take care. I love ya'll. Pastor tell Megan I am sorry.

Lamont Reese
Execution Date: 06/20/2006
Race: Black
County of Conviction: Tarrant
Last Statement: Yeah. Momma, I just want you to know I love you. I want all of you to know I love you all. I am at peace; we know what it is. We know the truth. Stay out of crime; there is no point in it. I am at peace. We know the truth and I know it. I have some peace. I am glad it didn't take that long - no 10 or 20 years. I am at peace. And I want everyone to know I did not walk to this because this is straight up murder. I just want everybody to know I didn't walk to this. The reason is because it's murder. I am not going to play a part in my own murder. No one should have to do that. I love you all. I do not know all of your names. And I don't know how you feel about me. And whether you believe it or not, I did not kill them. I just want you all to have peace; you know what I'm saying. There is no point in that. It is neither here nor there. You have to move past it. It is time to move on. You know what I'm saying. I want each one of my loved ones to move on. I am glad it didn't last long. I am glad it didn't last long. I am at peace. I am at peace to the fullest. The people that did this - they know. I am not here to point fingers. God will let them know. If this is what it takes, just do what you got to do to get past it. What it takes. I am ready, Warden. Love you all. Let my son know I love him.

Angel Resendiz
Execution Date: 06/27/2006
Race: Hispanic
County of Conviction: Harris
Last Statement: Yes sir. I want to ask if it is in your heart to forgive me. You don't have to. I know I allowed the devil to rule my life. I just ask you to forgive me and ask the Lord to forgive me for allowing the devil to deceive me. I thank God for having patience with me. I don't deserve to cause you pain. You did not deserve this. I deserve what I am getting.

Derrick O'Brien
Execution Date: 07/11/2006
Race: Black
County of Conviction: Harris
Last Statement: I do. I am sorry. I have always been sorry. It is the worst mistake that I ever made in my whole life. Not because I am here, but because of what I did and I hurt a lot of people - you, and my family. I am sorry; I have always been sorry. I am sorry. You look after each other. I love you all. Be there for one another. Alright. But I am sorry; very sorry. I love you too. Alright.

Mauriceo Brown
Execution Date: 07/19/2006
Race: Black
County of Conviction: Bexar
Last Statement: Yes, I do. To the victim's family, I am sorry you lost a brother, loved one, and friend. To my family, I love you all. Keep your heads ups and know I will be in a better place. And you all look after Aleda and make sure she is a part of this family. I appreciate you all and love you. I apologize that you lost a loved one this way. God bless you all. O.K. Warden.

Robert Anderson
Execution Date: 07/20/2006
Race: White
County of Conviction: Potter
Last Statement: Yes, I would like to make a short brief one please. To Audrey's grandmother, I am sorry for the pain I have caused you for the last 15 years and your family. I have regretted this for a long time. I am sorry. I only ask that you remember the Lord because He remembers us and He forgives us if we ask Him. I am sorry. And to my family, and my loved ones - I am sorry for the pain for all

those years and for putting you through all the things we had to go through. I ask the Lord to bless you all. Tammy, Irene, Betty, Dan Judy - I love you all. And Jack, thank you. Warden...

William Wyatt, Jr.
Execution Date: 08/03/2006
Race: Black
County of Conviction: Bowie
Last Statement: Yes I do. I would like to say to my two brother-in-laws and the rest of my family that I would like to thank you for supporting me through all of this. I went home to be with my Father and I went home as a trooper. I would like to say to Damien's family I did not murder your son. I did not do it. I just want you to know that -- I did not murder Damien and would ask for all of your forgiveness and I will see all of you soon. I love you guys. I love you guys. That's it.

Richard Hinojosa
Execution Date: 08/17/2006
Race: Hispanic
County of Conviction: Bexar
Last Statement: Yes sir, to my family and children, I love you very much. Dianne, Virginia, Toby and Irene I love all of you. I apologize for not being the man you wanted me to be. I am going to be free, I am going to Heaven. Please be strong and I love you all. To the Wright family, I pray for you, please find peace in your heart. I know you may hate me for whatever reason, the Lord says hate no one. I hope you find peace in your heart. I know my words cannot help you, I truly mean what I say. God Bless you all. I love you Dianne, Mary Virginia. Kick the tires and light the fire, I am going home to see my son and my mom, I love you and God Bless you.

Justin Fuller
Execution Date: 08/24/2006
Race: Black
County of Conviction: Smith
Last Statement: Yes I do, I would like to tell my family thank you for your support, and my friends. And let everyone know that you must stay strong for each other. Take care of yourselves. That's it, Warden.

Derrick Frazier
Execution Date: 08/31/2006
Race: Black

County of Conviction: Refugio
Last Statement: Yes I do. Debbie, my Baby, I love you; do you know I love you. You are my life. You are my wife - always stay strong. Stay strong everybody. I am innocent. I am being punished for a crime I did not commit. I have professed my innocence for nine years, and I continue to say I am innocent. Let my people know I love them. We must continue on. Do not give up the fight; do not give up hope for a better future. Because we can make it happen. I love you, I love my son, and I love my daughter. Bruno, Chuckie, Juanita, Ray - I love you, all of you. Stay strong baby. I love you forever.

Farley Matchett
Execution Date: 09/12/2006
Race: Black
County of Conviction: Harris
Last Statement: To my family and my mother and my three precious daughters, I love you all. And to my brother and sister for standing with me throughout this situation. Stay strong and know that I'm in a better place. I ask for forgiveness. And to the victim's family, find peace and cancellation with my death and move on. Our Lord Jesus Christ, I commend myself to you. I am ready.

Gregory Summers
Execution Date: 10/25/2006
Race: White
County of Conviction: Denton
Last Statement: This person declined to make a last statement.

Donnell Jackson
Execution Date: 11/01/2006
Race: Black
County of Conviction: Harris
Last Statement: To my family, first and foremost - I love you all. The calmness that I was telling you about, I still have it. You are Mario's Uncle, correct? I just wanted you to know that I wronged your family. I received nothing, I was not paid. I took his life for the love of a friend. I love you all. I just want you to know that. I know he does, I feel it. I'm alright. Make sure momma knows, alright. Jermaine, I love you too man. Alright Warden.

Willie Shannon
Execution Date: 11/08/2006

Race: Black
County of Conviction: Harris
Last Statement: All praises be to God. I would like to say to the Garza family, see my smile, it is not from happiness. I took a father, it wasn't my fault, it was an accident... God knows the truth. If my life could bring your father back, then let it be. Don't take my smile for Disrespect. If I see your father I will ask him forgiveness. I told the Judge the truth it was an accident. I'll smile and I am not sad. If my life could make you happy, be free. I'll say when I see him I'm sorry. I have no anger nor fear. Mom have no fear. Mommy I will be home when I get there.

Carlos Granados
Execution Date: 01/10/2007
Race: Hispanic
County of Conviction: Williamson
Last Statement: Yes, Love you mom, love you pop, love you Sara, and Amanda. Um, Cathy you know I never meant to hurt you. I gave you everything and that's what made me so angry. But I didn't mean to hurt you. I am sorry. That's it.

Jonathan Moore
Execution Date: 01/17/2007
Race: White
County of Conviction: Bexar
Last Statement: Jennifer, where are you at? I'm sorry, I did not know the man but for a few seconds before I shot him. It was done out of fear, stupidity, and immaturity. It wasn't until I got locked up and saw the newspaper. I saw his face and his smile and I knew he was a good man. I am sorry for all your family and my disrespect - he deserved better. Sorry Gus. I hope all the best for you and your daughters. I hope you have happiness from here on out. Quit the heroin and methadone. I love you dad, Devin, and Walt. We're done Warden.

Christopher Swift
Execution Date: 01/30/2007
Race: White
County of Conviction: Denton
Last Statement: This person declined to make a last statement.

James Jackson
Execution Date: 02/07/2007
Race: Black

County of Conviction: Harris

Last Statement: You know, once upon a time diamonds were priceless. I never knew until I ran across my own. I just want Eve to know that. One of these days I'm going to return and get that for myself. Thank you to my family, I love you. Each and every one of you. This is not the end, but the beginning of a new chapter for you and I together forever. I love you all. Remember what I told you Brad. Ms. Irene, God bless you, I love you. See you on the other side. Warden, murder me. Saddam and Gomorrah which is Harris County.

Newton Anderson

Execution Date: 02/22/2007
Race: White
County of Conviction: Smith
Last Statement: Yes, for all of those that want this to happen, I hope that you get what you want and it makes you feel better and that it gives you some kind of relief. I don't know what else to say. For those that I have hurt, I hope after a while it gets better. I love you, I love you. I am sorry. That's it, goodbye. I love you Irene, I love you sis.

Donald Miller

Execution Date: 02/27/2007
Race: White
County of Conviction: Harris
Last Statement: This person declined to make a last statement.

Robert Perez

Execution Date: 03/06/2007
Race: Hispanic
County of Conviction: Dallas
Last Statement: Yes sir, Ernest, Christopher, Ochente, Mary and Jennifer tell all the kids I love them and never forget. Tell Bobby, Mr. Bear will be dancing for them. Tell Bear not to feel bad. My love always, I love you all. Stay strong Mary, take care of them. I love you too. I am ready Warden.

Joseph Nichols

Execution Date: 03/07/2007
Race: Black
County of Conviction: Harris
Last Statement: Profanity directed toward staff.

Charles Nealy

Execution Date: 03/20/2007
Race: Black
County of Conviction: Dallas
Last Statement: Ya'll know I love you, you too Ward. You have been a good friend. You are a good investigator. Doug, I thank you for coming from Michigan. Chris and David, I love you. Thank them for their support Doug. Debra, James, I'm not crying so you don't cry. Don't be sad for me. I'm going to be with God, Allah, and Momma. I'm gonna ask dad why didn't give you away at your wedding. Randy Greer, my little brother, I'll be watching you, stay out of trouble. All my nieces and nephews, I love you all. Sammie, Vincent, and Yolanda, I will be watching over you all. The reason it took them so long is because they couldn't find a vein. You know how I hate needles - I used to stay in the Doctor's Office. Tell the guys on Death Row that I'm not wearing a diaper. I can't think of anything else. You all stay strong. Now you can put this all aside. Don't bury me in the prison cemetery. Bury me right beside momma. Don't bury me to the left of dad, bury me on the right side of mom. Kim Schaeffer, you are a evil woman. You broke the law. The judges and courts helped you and you didn't have all the facts. When you look at the video, you know you can't see anyone. You overplayed your hand looking for something against me and to cover it up the State is killing me. I'm not mad or bitter though. I'm sad that you are stuck here and have to go through all of this. I am going somewhere better. My time is up. Let me get ready to make my transition. Doug, don't forget Marcy.

Vincent Gutierrez

Execution Date: 03/28/2007
Race: Hispanic
County of Conviction: Bexar
Last Statement: I do, I would like to tell everybody that I'm sorry about the situation that happened. My bad - everybody is here because of what happened. I'd like to thank everybody that's been here through the years. The little kids overseas - they really changed me. Sister Doris, mom, brothers, sister, dad; I love ya'll. My brother... where's my stunt double when you need one? My Lord is my life and savior, nothing shall I fear.

Roy Pippin

Execution Date: 03/29/2007
Race: White
County of Conviction: Harris
Last Statement: Yes sir, I charge the people of the jury. Trial Judge, the Prosecutor

that cheated to get this conviction. I charge each and every one of you with the murder of an innocent man. All the way to the CCA, Federal Court, 5th Circuit and Supreme Court. You will answer to your Maker when God has found out that you executed an innocent man. May God have mercy on you. My love to my son, my daughter, Nancy, Kathy, Randy, and my future grandchildren. I ask for forgiveness for all of the poison that I brought into the US, the country I love. Please forgive me for my sins. If my murder makes it easier for everyone else let the forgiveness please be a part of the healing. Go ahead Warden, murder me. Jesus take me home.

James Clark
Execution Date: 04/11/2007
Race: White
County of Conviction: Denton
Last Statement: Uh, I don't know, Um, I don't know what to say. I don't know. (pauses) I didn't know anybody was there. Howdy.

Ryan Dickson
Execution Date: 04/26/2007
Race: White
County of Conviction: Potter
Last Statement: Yes, Sir I do. I'd like to say I love my mother, brother, sister, grandmother, cousins, and nieces, and my brothers and sisters I have never met. I do apologize to the Surace family. I am responsible for them losing their mother, their father, and their grandmother. I never meant for them to be taken. I am sorry for what I did and I take responsibility for what I did. That is all Warden.

Charles Smith
Execution Date: 05/16/2007
Race: White
County of Conviction: Pecos
Last Statement: This person declined to make a last statement.

Michael Griffith
Execution Date: 06/06/2007
Race: White
County of Conviction: Harris
Last Statement: This person declined to make a last statement.

Lionell Rodiguez

Execution Date: 06/20/2007
Race: Hispanic
County of Conviction: Harris
Last Statement: First of all, you have every right to hate me and every right to want to see this. To you and to my family, you don't deserve to see this. I wasn't going to apologize by letter, I wanted to apologize face to face. None of this should have happened. It is the right thing to do. I have a good family, just like you are a good family. I hope that any bitterness that you have because of what I did, I hope you can learn to forgive. I asked my family to contact you, because they did no wrong. I am responsible and I am sorry to you all. Thank you all my Jefe (dad), my brothers, Maria and my Grandfather. Thank you, we will see each other again. Thank you, Lord Jesus receive my spirit.

Gilberto Reyes

Execution Date: 06/21/2007
Race: Hispanic
County of Conviction: Bailey
Last Statement: I love ya'll and I'm gonna miss ya'll.

Patrick Knight

Execution Date: 06/26/2007
Race: White
County of Conviction: Randall
Last Statement: Yes, I do. I thank the Lord for giving me my friends, for getting me the ones I love. Lord reach down and help innocent men on death row. Lee Taylor needs help, Bobby Hines, Steve Woods. Not all of us are innocent, but those are. Cleve Foster needs help. Melyssa, I love you girl. I know I wasn't going to say anything, but I've got to. Jack, Irene, Danny, Doreen, I love you guys. I said I was going to tell a joke. Death has set me free. That's the biggest joke, I deserve this. And the other joke is I am not Patrick Bryan Knight, and ya'll can't stop this execution now. Go ahead, I'm finished. Come on, tell me Lord. I love you Melyssa, take care of that little monster for me.

Lonnie Johnson

Execution Date: 07/24/2007
Race: Black
County of Conviction: Harris
Last Statement: Yes I would. Carrie it's been a joy and a blessing. Take care, give

everybody my regards. I love you, and I'll see you in eternity. Father take me home. I am ready to go.

Kenneth Parr
Execution Date: 08/15/2007
Race: Black
County of Conviction: Matagorda
Last Statement: Can ya'll hear me? Tell my family that I love ya'll. Joe, Tim, everybody - keep your head up. I love you.

Johnny Conner
Execution Date: 08/22/2007
Race: Black
County of Conviction: Harris
Last Statement: Could you please tell that lady right there, can I see her, she is not looking at me. I want you to understand something, hold no animosity towards me. I want you to understand please forgive me. When I get to the gates of Heaven I will open my arms for you. Please forgive me, do not worry about what is going to happen. I don't want you to worry. I don't want you to suffer, I am not mad at you. Shed no tears for me. Even though you don't know me, I love you, I love all of ya'll. I ask ya'll in your heart to forgive me. To my family, I love all of you. What's happening now, you are suffering. I didn't mean to hurt you. Stephanie, Felicia, Carlos and my Father. I love my Father. I want you to understand that life goes on. Continue to live your life and don't be angry at what is happening to me. This is destiny, this is life. This is something I have to do and I am going to be with my momma and your momma. I want everyone to continue to live your life. Thank you and I love all of you. What is happening to me now is unjust and the system is broken. At the same time I bear witness there is no God but Allah and the Prophet Mohammad. Unto Allah, I belong unto Allah I return. I love you.

Daroyce Mosley
Execution Date: 08/28/2007
Race: Black
County of Conviction: Gregg
Last Statement: Yes. I just want to let you all know that I appreciate the love and support over the years. I will see you when you get there. Keep your heads up. To all the fellows on the Row, the same thing. Keep your head up and continue to fight. Same thing to all my pen friends and other friends, I love you all. I can taste it.

John Amador
Execution Date: 08/29/2007
Race: Hispanic
County of Conviction: Bexar
Last Statement: God forgive them, God forgive them for they know not what they do. After all these years my people are still lost in hatred and anger. Give them peace God for people seeking revenge towards me. I love you guys, I love you guys. God give them peace. I love you Chiquita. Peace, Freedom, I'm ready.

Tony Roach
Execution Date: 09/05/2007
Race: White
County of Conviction: Potter
Last Statement: Yes sir, I do. Go ahead? First of all I want to thank God for the love; thank God for the love from the family and friends that I have. To God I give the glory though the years. I love and care about the Lord. The Lord knows that I prayed for the victim's family. I know you all probably have bitterness and hate for what I did. There is not a day goes by that I have not prayed for Ronni Dawn Hewitt and Carol Dawson and her daughter who was left behind. I pray to God, the Lord Almighty that like he did for me, he will reach out and help you. I just pray that the Lord takes away your bitterness. There is so much hurt that I have caused you all. On the phone, I talked to my family for two hours. It was hard to see such a big man just break down and cry like a little baby. I hope this will touch your hearts like you have touched mine. I know it is hard for you all. I am to blame for this, I will take that Lord, when I get there. Back in 2003, I want to tell you this. I got down on my knees. The Lord knew my heart. I wanted to kill myself. I spoke to Ms. Ronnie Dawn Hewitt. The next day I received a letter that they had lost a friend to suicide. She said that she forgave me and that was something that I needed to hear. God helped me to forgive myself and move on. I just pray that some day you will find forgiveness in your heart. Know that your loved one is in a good place. I am sorry for what I have done. I cannot agree with this injustice. The Bible says that you shalt not kill, but it also says to obey the government. I am sorry, forgive me. Francis, I love you and thank you for being here. I have no ill will towards anyone carrying out this so called justice. Thank you. I am ready Warden.

Clifford Kimmel
Execution Date: 09/20/2007
Race: White
County of Conviction: Bexar
Last Statement: This person declined to make a last statement.

Michael Richard
Execution Date: 09/25/2007
Race: Black
County of Conviction: Harris
Last Statement: Yes, I would like for my family to take care of each other. I lovel you Angel, Let's ride. I guess this is it.

Karl Chamberlain
Execution Date: 06/11/2008
Race: White
County of Conviction: Dallas
Last Statement: I want you all to know, everyone with all my heart, soul, mind and strength. Thank you for being here today to honor Falicia Prechtl, whom I didn't even know. To celebrate my death. My death began on August 2, 1991 and continued when I began to see the beautiful and innocent life that I had taken. I am so terribly sorry. I wish I could die more than once to tell you how sorry I am. I have said in interviews, if you want to hurt me and choke me, that's how terrible I felt before this crime. I am sorry, it is her innocence and her life which began the remorse every since December 1, 1991. I have embraced life. Thank you for being a part of my life. I love you. May God be with us all. May God have mercy on us all. I am ready. Please do not hate anybody because.......(end of statement)

Carlton Turner
Execution Date: 07/10/2008
Race: Black
County of Conviction: Dallas
Last Statement: First of all I would like to tell my Uncle Kyle that I am sorry. I have been sorry for the last 10 years for what I did. I wish you could accept my apology. I know you can't accept my apology, I know you can't give your forgiveness; it's okay and I understand. I have done what I could to heal the rest of the family. I wish that someday you could come to terms and understand. I know I was wrong; I accept responsibility as a man. I take this penalty as a man. This doesn't solve anything, 'cause it hurts others that love me. I am sorry. I love you Kjersti. I love you too Roland. I love you too Uncle Kyle; I am still your nephew, no matter what you believe.

Derrick Sonnier
Execution Date: 07/23/2008
Race: Black

County of Conviction: Harris
Last Statement: This person declined to make a last statement.

Larry Davis
Execution Date: 07/31/2008
Race: Black
County of Conviction: Potter
Last Statement: Blessed are they that mourn, for they shall be comforted. It is finished.

Jose Medellin
Execution Date: 08/05/2008
Race: Hispanic
County of Conviction: Harris
Last Statement: I am sorry my actions caused pain. I hope this brings closure to what you seek. Don't ever hate them for what they do. Never harbor hate. I love you. Alright Warden.

Heliberto Chi
Execution Date: 08/07/2008
Race: Hispanic
County of Conviction: Tarrant
Last Statement: Jesus receive my spirit. I love you Edgardo; I appreciate your hard work. Thank you. Okay, Receive my spirit. Thanks sir.

Leon Dorsey
Execution Date: 08/12/2008
Race: Black
County of Conviction: Dallas
Last Statement: Yeah, I love all ya'll. I forgive all ya'll. See you when you get there. Do what your are going to do.

Michael Rodriguez
Execution Date: 08/14/2008
Race: Hispanic
County of Conviction: Dallas
Last Statement: Yes I do, I know this no way makes up for all the pain and suffering I gave you. I am so so sorry. My punishment is nothing compared to the pain and sorrow I have caused. I hope that someday you can find peace. I am not strong

enough to ask for forgiveness because I don't if I am worth. I realize what I've done to you and the pain I've given. Please Lord forgive me. I have done some horrible things. I ask the Lord to please forgive me. I have gained nothing, but just brought sorrow and pain to these wonderful people. I am sorry. So so sorry. To the Sanchez family who showed me love. To the Hawkings' family, I am sorry. I know I have affected them for so long. Please forgive me. Irene, I want to thank you and thank your husband Jack. I'll be waiting for you. I am so sorry. To these families I ask forgiveness. Father God I ask you too for forgiveness. I ask you for forgiveness Lord. I am ready to go Lord. Thank you. I am ready to go. My Jesus my Savior there is none like you. All of my days I want to praise, let every breath. Shout to the Lord let us sing.

William Murray

Execution Date: 09/17/2008
Race: White
County of Conviction: Kaufman
Last Statement: First I want to say to the family, I'm sorry I hope you find it in your heart to forgive me. The Lord has forgiven me. All I can say is I'm sorry. God Bless. To my family, I'll be there waiting for ya'll, alright? God Bless.

Alvin Kelly

Execution Date: 10/14/2008
Race: White
County of Conviction: Gregg
Last Statement: Yes, I would like to thank God for my salvation and all he has done in my life. I thank my family, loved ones, and friends. I give Him thanks, honor, and glory. I love you Mary Taylor with all my heart, I always have. You are my girl. I love you, Michelle. You are my little kitten. Kevin, it's all you now. You are my boy. Sylvia, my sister, keep your eyes on Christ, forever. Everything is going to be okay. Angela Christine, keep your eyes on the prize and nothing else. I love all of you. God's been good. I would like to address the family: I offer my sorrow and my heart goes out to ya'll. I know you believe that you're going to have closure tonight and as I stand before God today, the true judge, I had nothing to do with the death of your family. I ask God to hold this. I would like to address the family of John T. Ford: I ask for forgiveness, because I do stand guilty for my involvement for that. Thank you Lord Jesus Christ for coming to my life. (quiet singing) Thank you Lord Jesus for coming into my life, you walked me through prison. Thank you Lord Jesus because you died for me. Thank you Lord Jesus for remembering me...

Kevin Watts

Execution Date: 10/16/2008
Race: Black
County of Conviction: Bexar
Last Statement: Yes. I appreciate everybody for their love and support. You all keep strong, thank you for showing me love and teaching me how to love. Forgive me, Lord. Ya'll forgive me, remember me. For everybody incarcerated, keep your heads up. For my family, keep your heads up. I never stopped loving ya'll. Stay strong and keep fighting, it's not over yet. I love you all. I am out of here. I am gone. Keep me in your hearts.

Joseph Ries

Execution Date: 10/21/2008
Race: White
County of Conviction: Hopkins
Last Statement: Laura, I love you, stay strong. Jesus is coming back soon. Danny, something will pull us through. I will see you, keep your head up. For all of you, I am really sorry for what I've done. I wish you could have seen the videotape at the end of trial, so you could know the truth. I pray you find the peace through salvation. As my Lord, King of my life, find salvation through Christ. I hope He heals your heart. The truth is that you are going to feel empty after tonight. Standing with Christ in your heart, He can only give you peace. I pray you can find it, I really do. I love you Laura. I love you Danny. I love you Irene. (singing) Our god is an awesome God. Lord, I lift your name on high.

Eric Nenno

Execution Date: 10/28/2008
Race: White
County of Conviction: Harris
Last Statement: This person declined to make a last statement.

Gregory Wright

Execution Date: 10/30/2008
Race: White
County of Conviction: Dallas
Last Statement: Yes I do. There has been a lot of confusion on who done this. I know you all want closure. Donna had her Christianity in tact when she died. She never went to a drug house. John Adams lied. He went to the police and told them a story. He made deals and sold stuff to keep from going to prison. I left the

house, and I left him there. My only act or involvement was not telling on him. John Adams is the one that killed Donna Vick. I took a polygraph and passed. John Adams never volunteered to take one. I have done everything in my power. Donna Vick helped me; she took me off the street. I was a truck driver; my CDL was still active. Donna gave me everything I could ask for. I helped her around the yard. I helped her around the house. She asked if there were anyone else to help. I am a Christian myself, so I told her about John Adam. We picked him up at a dope house. I did not know he was a career criminal. When we got to the house he was jonesin for drugs. He has to go to Dallas. I was in the bathroom when he attacked. I am deaf in one ear and I thought the T.V. was up too loud. I ran in to the bedroom. By the time I came in, when I tried to help her, with first aid, it was too late. The veins were cut on her throat. He stabbed her in her heart, and that's what killed her. I told John Adams, "turn yourself in or hit the high road." I owed him a favor because he pulled someone off my back. I was in a fight downtown. Two or three days later he turned on me. I have done everything to prove my innocence. Before you is an innocent man. I love my famly. I'll be waiting on ya'll. I'm finished talking.

Elkie Taylor

Execution Date: 11/6/2008
Race: Black
County of Conviction: Tarrant
Last Statement: Hello, ain't got to worry about nothing. I am going home. I hope to see all of ya'll one day. Lord have mercy on my soul. For the Flake family, stay strong. It's bad to see a man get murdered for something he didn't do, but I am taking it like a man, like a warrior. I am going home to Jesus. I love ya'll, peace. Iam ready sir... Don't forget to tell my daughter,,, I am ready, Warden.

George Whitaker III

Execution Date: 11/12/2008
Race: Black
County of Conviction: Harris
Last Statement: First off I'd like to say to Mr. and Mrs. Carrier, I apologize for your pain and suffering. I pray Lord, please forgive me. To my family, to my brother Gerard, I love you, Harold, I love you. To my step father Paul, I love you. Momma, I will always love you. Take care of my daughters, Kaneisha and Ieisha. Dad loves you. Continue to pray for me, I am fine. I have made peace with God. Please don't ever forget me. I love you mom. I love you all, take care. I love you too pop, keep your head up. Take care. I am going to sleep.

Denard Manns
Execution Date: 11/13/2008
Race: Black
County of Conviction: Bell
Last Statement: Yes. From Allah we came and to Allah we shall return. I would like to give thanks for the unjust way my trial attorneys John Donahue and Frank Hollbrook purposely denied me a fair trial. I would like to thank Walter E. Reeves for bringing up claims that did not exist. Most importantly, I would like to thank John Hurley, who was suppose to be off my case but was granted to be back on. For those who kept agreeing with me, keep it real. Ya'll will always stay real in my heart. Barbara, I love you, Al and Paul, I love you. Jess and Chong, I love you now and forever. I am ready for the transition.

Robert Hudson
Execution Date: 11/20/2008
Race: Black
County of Conviction: Dallas
Last Statement: I love you all. You have been there for me through this whole thing. Take comfort in each other, I love you all. I will take you to Heaven with me. I will always be with you. I love you, Chantal. I love you, Zena. Tell Robin I love her, she is my one and only. She is a beautiful child. I will pray with this man down here and we will go: Our Father, who art in Heaven, hallowed by thy name. Thy kingdom come, thy will be done, on Earth as it is in Heaven. Give us this day our daily bread and forgive us our tresspasses, as we forgive those who trespass against us. And lead us not into temptation, but deliver us from evil. For thine is the kingdom, and the power, and the glory forever. And ever, Amen. I love you Chantal I love you baby. I am yours, and we are one. Let's go, Warden.

Curtis Moore
Execution Date: 01/14/2009
Race: Black
County of Conviction: Tarrant
Last Statement: Yes, Sir. I love you Irene and I want to thank you for all the beautiful years of friendship and ministry. I love you.

Frank Moore
Execution Date: 01/21/2009
Race: Black
County of Conviction: Bexar

Last Statement: I would like to say that Capital self defense is not Capital Murder. I would like to make a statement to my wife and family, thank you for your support. I love you Roxanne, Kaye. Thank you Saint Gabriel's Church. Sylvia I appreciate you and thank you. All right Warden. (After the official last statement ended, he said I love you Mom.)

Reginald Perkins
Execution Date: 01/22/2009
Race: Black
County of Conviction: Tarrant
Last Statement: I already gave my statement. (talked to family) Love you all, take care. Bobby Nell Love ya.

Virgil Martinez
Execution Date: 01/28/2009
Race: Hispanic
County of Conviction: Brazoria
Last Statement: Yes I do. Um Abel, Love ya'll, Evelyn love ya'll, Armando and Delia I love ya'll. Do what I told you and you will see me one day. Do that and promise me. First, Veronica's sister. I know what you've been told and that's all a lie. John Gomez killed your kids and sister. I know ya'll love John Gomez but he was a violent man. I wish I would have shot him in the leg, then he would be here. Those investigators were just trying to convict somebody. My gun had a hair trigger. Veronica told me to come and get my herb book and she went to the back of the closet. Her kids had asthma and I lent her the book. She said she would give it to me next time. She didn't want to break up, we still talked. She told me to come over. John Gomez said Veronica does not have the money for your book so don't come over. Me being a hot shot I went over there and I had my gun. I had children and nephews where I lived so I had to keep my gun in my truck for self defense. Veronica invited me in her house, the kids were still awake fixing to go to bed. I put the gun under my shirt and said Hi to Josh and Cassandra. John Gomez was there he told Veronica that "he doesn't love you" I didn't care.

Ricardo Ortiz
Execution Date: 01/29/2009
Race: Hispanic
County of Conviction: El Paso
Last Statement: I love my family. Thank you for all of your support. Stay strong. I am at peace. I love you and my kids. See you.

David Martinez
Execution Date: 02/04/2009
Race: Hispanic
County of Conviction: Bexar
Last Statement: Yes, nothing I can say can change the past. I am asking for forgiveness. Saying sorry is not going to change anything. I hope one day you can find peace. I am sorry for all of the pain that I have caused you for all those years. There is nothing else I can say, that can help you. Mija, I love you. Sis, Cynthia, and Sandy, keep on going and it will be O.K. I am sorry to put you through this as well. I can't change the past. I hope you find peace and know that I love you. I am sorry. I am sorry and I can't change it.

Dale Scheanette
Execution Date: 02/10/2009
Race: Black
County of Conviction: Tarrant
Last Statement: Is the mic on? My only statement is that no cases have ever tried have been error free. Those are my words. No cases are error free. You may proceed Warden.

Johnny Johnson
Execution Date: 02/12/2009
Race: Black
County of Conviction: Harris
Last Statement: The Polunsky dungeon should be compared with the Death Row Community as existing not living. Why do I say this, the Death Row is full of isolated hearts and suppressed minds. We are filled with love looking for affection and a way to understand. I am a Death Row resident of the Polunsky dungeon. Why does my heart ache. We want pleasure love and satisfaction. It. The walls of darkness crushed in on me. Life without meaning is life without purpose. But the solace within the Polunsky dungeon, the unforgivesness within society, the church Pastors and Christians. It is terrifying. Does anyone care or who I am. Can you feel me people. The Polunsky dungeon is what I call the pit of hopelessness. The terrfying thing is the US is the only place, country that is the only civilized country that is free that says it will stop murder and enable justice. I ask each of you to lift up your voices to demand an end to the Death Penalty. If we live, we live to the Lord. If we die we die to the Lord. Christ rose again, in Jesus name. Bye Aunt Helen, Luise, Joanna and to all the rest of yall. You may proceed Warden. (began singing)

Willie Pondexter

Execution Date: 03/03/2009

Race: Black

County of Conviction: Red River

Last Statement: Well, first I want to say. They may execute me but they can't punish me because they can't execute an innocent man. I am not mad. Jack Herrington, I am not mad. You were given a job to do but that's neither here nor there. I am not mad. I am disappointed by the courts. I feel like I was upset and let down by them. But that's O.K. I just played the hand that life dealt me. Look at my life and learn from it. I am very remorseful about what I did. I apologize. To my kids, Daddy loves you. Irene Wilcox, Thank you. It's been a long journey. Thank you for being there. Tell Jack hello. I know I am wrong but I am asking ya'll to forgive me.

Kenneth Morris

Execution Date: 03/04/2009

Race: Black

County of Conviction: Harris

Last Statement: Yes, I have to say that I am sorry for all the pain that I have caused you and your family. I only have love in my heart. I hope that you can all forgive me. I pray that you can all forgive me. Thank you for standing by me and being there for me. I am ready to go home. My baby I will always be with you. I really am sorry.

James Martinez

Execution Date: 03/10/2009

Race: Hispanic

County of Conviction: Tarrant

Last Statement: Yes sir, I want to tell my mom that I love her and thank her for everything that she has done for me. Tell my sister that I love her too thank her for everything that she has done for me. I hope you can move on after this. I'll be fine. I'll be O.K. I love you too. I love you too. Take care O.K. That's all I have to say Warden. Thank you sir.

Luis Salazar

Execution Date: 03/11/2009

Race: Hispanic

County of Conviction: Bexar

Last Statement: Yes, I do. Thank you for your friendship Reverend Whiteside and thank you for your fellowship. God help me to say this statement correctly. I would like to say goodbye to mom and my brother, brother, sister, Chelsea, Danny, Johnny, Tito and Sylvia. My heart goes is going ba bump ba bump ba bump. I love my children, Roxanne, Roseanne, Melissa, and Louis. I miss them; I will take them with me in my heart. I will keep them in my heart. Thank you Mrs. Dyson for praying for me and everyone that has been praying for me. God loves everybody and myself. I can't say this correctly. Let's see. That's all right. I guess that's it. Our Father, who art in heaven, Hallowed by thy Name. Thy kingdom come. Thy will be done, On earth as it is in heaven. Give us this day our daily bread. And forgive us our trespasses, As we forgive those who trespass against us. And lead us not into temptation, But deliver us from evil. For thine is the kingdom, and the power, and the glory, for ever and ever. Amen. Lord Jesus forgive of my sins, please forgive me for the sins that I can remember.

Michael Rosales
Execution Date: 04/15/2009
Race: Hispanic
County of Conviction: Lubbock
Last Statement: No, I love you. May the Lord be with you. Peace, I'm done.

Derrick Johnson
Execution Date: 04/30/2009
Race: Black
County of Conviction: Dallas
Last Statement: Don't cry, it's my situation. I got it. Hold tight, It's going to shine on the golden child. Hold tight. I love you , I'm through with my statement.

Michael Riley
Execution Date: 05/19/2009
Race: Black
County of Conviction: Wood
Last Statement: Yes I do. To the Harris family. I have been trying to tell you for years that I am sorry. I know that I hurt your family bad. I am sorry. Wynona should not of even have happened. I am sorry. I truly am sorry for the hurt and pain I caused you. I hope you can forgive me. One day I hope you can move on and if not I understand. Tim Jackson, Bobby Dan Spade and Mr. Segal thank you for your lies. Your lies set me free. I couldn't do a life sentence. To my mom, I'm sorry. I love you. I'm not the big son that you wanted me to be. But, I love you. To my friends, Synnova, Kay I thank you for everything. I'm ready. I told you years ago that I was ready. Synnova tell everyone I got full on Chicken and Pork Chops. Rodney, take care of my mom. To the fellas on the row, stay strong. Renee, I love

you baby. Fleetwood is up out of here. I'm ready Warden.

Terry Hankins
Execution Date: 06/02/2009
Race: White
County of Conviction: Tarrant
Last Statement: Yes, I am sorry for what I've done and for all of the pain and suffering that my actions have caused. Jesus is Lord. All glory to God.

Stephen Moody
Execution Date: 09/16/2009
Race: White
County of Conviction: Harris
Last Statement: Yes sir, to Joseph's mom and son. I was unable to respond to you in the courtroom. I can only ask that you have the peace that I do. To my brother, you are a good brother. You're the best. And I love you. Can't beat ya. The beautiful lady standing next to you. Kathy you are next to my heart. Amber I love you. Warden, pull the trigger. I love you brother never forget it. Ronnie, Linda, Amber, Kathy. Chaplain Hart you're the best. Love you Thomas.

Christopher Coleman
Execution Date: 09/22/2009
Race: Black
County of Conviction: Harris
Last Statement: Yes, Ain't no way fo' fo', I Love all yall.

Reginald Blanton
Execution Date: 10/27/2009
Race: Black
County of Conviction: Bexar
Last Statement: Yes I do. I know ya'lls pain, believe me I shed plenty of tears behind Carlos. Carlos was my friend. I didn't murder him. This what is happening right now is an injustice. This doesn't solve anything. This will not bring back Carlos. Ya'll fought real hard here to prove my innocence. This is only the beginning. I love each and everyone dearly. Dre My queen. I love you. Yaws, Junie I love yall. Stay strong, continue to fight. They are fixing to pump my veins with a lethal drug the American Veterinary Association won't even allow to be used on dogs. I say I am worse off than a dog. They want to kill me for this; I am not the man that did this. Fight on. I will see ya'll again. That's all I can say.

Khristian Oliver
Execution Date: 11/05/2009
Race: White
County of Conviction: Nacogdoches
Last Statement: Collins family, I know your not going to get the closure you are looking for tonight. I wish you the best. I prayed for ya'll every day and every night. I have only the warmest wishes. I am sorry for what you are having to go through. Mom, Pa, Kristy, Khristopher, Tony I love all ya'll. Thank you Mr. Whiteside. The Lord is my shepherd; I shall not want. He maketh me to lie down in green pastures; He leadeth me beside the still waters. He restoreth my soul; He guides me down the right paths. Yea, though I walk through the valley of the shadow of death, I will fear no evil; for thou art with me. Thou preparest a table before me in the presence of mine enemies; Thou anointest my head with oil; my cup over runneth.

Yosvanis Valle
Execution Date: 11/10/2009
Race: Hispanic
County of Conviction: Harris
Last Statement: I am sorry, I never wanted to kill your family. I never wanted to kill your family or these people. I am sorry for the way I talk in English. I did it to myself. I was forced to do it. I was a gang member. I never wanted to kill your brother. I was forced to do this. I blame myself. I am not going to blame nobody. I got my mother and my family too. I was forced. I tell you from my heart. I am sorry with all my heart. That's the reality of life, I am sorry. I got to pay for it. To my family, I love you, be strong. They have family too; the way they suffer is the way I am suffering. I am asking you to go and give them hugs. Please accept their hugs. Be strong in the Lord. I love you sister. I love you all, please go and try and talk to the family. I love my family. I understand why I am paying this price. Do not have any excuses for not extending your love. I am ready Warden, I am sorry everybody, I did it. Thank you brother, don't hate nobody, I feel good. I love my family, I love you Jesus. Be strong mama, I love you sister. I love Jesus. Warden I am ready.

Danielle Simpson
Execution Date: 11/18/2009
Race: Black
County of Conviction: Anderson
Last Statement: Yeah, I want to tell my family I love ya'll. Tell Kate I love her too. Tell brother, my kids I live ya'll. I'm gonna miss ya'll. I'm ready, ready.

Robert Thompson
Execution Date: 11/19/2009
Race: Black
County of Conviction: Harris
Last Statement: Yes, I bear witness that there is no God, but Allah. From Allah we came and from Allah we will return. To my mother, friends I would like to thank you for all that you have done for me. For you love. This is another testimony of faith. We all have to walk this path. Smile, be happy don't cry. To the family of any victims, AsSalaam Alaikum, unto Allah I belong, unto Allah we return. I just want you to know that I never meant any of your family to get hurt. I hope you forgive me. I know Allah will forgive me, Allah is the forgiver. Go ahead Warden. I love you, love you too.

Bobby Woods
Execution Date: 12/03/2009
Race: White
County of Conviction: Llano
Last Statement: Bye, I'm Ready.

Kenneth Mosley
Execution Date: 01/07/2010
Race: Black
County of Conviction: Dallas
Last Statement: This person declined to make a last statement.

Gary Johnson
Execution Date: 01/12/2010
Race: White
County of Conviction: Walker
Last Statement: Tell my family goodbye. I can't see them. Jenny, you keep your promise to me, O.K.? Dell, you take care of Gaylene always. Dixie watch over all the kids. Tell them thank you for coming down. Jennie talk to them O.K.? Talk to Jennie, O.K. Dell. Dell you tell the rest of them what they did was wrong for letting me fall for what they did. I never done anything in my life to anybody.

Michael Sigala
Execution Date: 03/02/2010
Race: Hispanic
County of Conviction: Collin

Last Statement: Yes sir, I would like to ask forgiveness of the family. I have no reason for why I did it, I don't understand why I did it. I hope that you can live the rest of your lives without hate. I pray the Lord grant me forgiveness. All powerful and almighty Lord I commit myself to thee, Amen.

Joshua Maxwell

Execution Date: 03/11/2010
Race: White
County of Conviction: Bexar
Last Statement: I do, I want to address you, I am sorry. I don't know who you are. I am sorry I put you through some things that I can't take back. I am sorry. This isn't going to change anything. Sorry for putting you through this. This is creating more victims. I am sorry, I put you through this. I love you man, I love you. This is not gonna change anything. This person shoe did that 10 years ago isn't the same person you see today. I hurt a lot of people with decisions I made. I can't be more sorry than I am right now. I hurt the Lopes family, let this be a lesson. Your decisions affect everybody. Look after your sister for me. I am always gonna be with you. I love you too Shay I love you if your listening I am sorry to be putting everybody through this. This is the end of this, time to move on. I hope this brings you peace, I am sorry. I told your sister my last words. Danielle, you know that I love you. You know that you have my heart, I've enjoyed these times. I love you little hef.

Franklin Alix

Execution Date: 03/30/2010
Race: Black
County of Conviction: Harris
Last Statement: Yes I do, I would like to thank my family for their support, love and understanding. I would like to point out some things, I got your letter. It touched me and changed me. What happened was I been wanting to apologize to yall for your son. They told me not to do it in court. I wrote him a letter but they told me that they tore it up in court. I am not the monster they made me out to be. I made lots of mistakes that took your son. I'll take it to the grave, I will be at peace. You have test and drug results to show it. I am not just taking. I messed up, made poor choices. No rapes, I don't do drugs, I am not an alcoholic. Back to my family, Thank yall for being here. It is what it is. I got peace in my heart. Thank you. Bye bye yall. Bye bye peanut.

William Berkley

Execution Date: 04/22/2010

Race: White
County of Conviction: El Paso
Last Statement: Samantha, I love you with all my heart and soul. Cori, thanks for everything, make sure my princess is all right. Death before dishonor. Cori, I think you should continue with criminal law. It's your decision; they need lawyers out there that will fight. Death before dishonor. Warden let her rip. Thank you for coming Irene.

Samuel Bustamante

Execution Date: 04/27/2010
Race: Hispanic
County of Conviction: Fort Bend
Last Statement: This person declined to make a last statement.

Kevin Varga

Execution Date: 05/12/2010
Race: White
County of Conviction: Hunt
Last Statement: I am going to start with the victim's family. I know I took someone very precious to you. Myself and Mr. Galloway who you will see tomorrow. Please forgive me. God has given me peace. I love each and every one of you. You have to forgive me for you to gain the kingdom of Heaven. I wish what was torn from you was not. I do know how it feels to have lost loved ones. This was the only way God could save me; I would pay it back a thousand times to bring back your loved ones. I would pay it gladly. I love each and every one of you and hope you can find forgiveness for me. I don't require your forgiveness, because God has forgiven me. Sorry, I hope you find peace. God's love is infinite. If you hate me, please give it up. I forgive you and I hope you can forgive me. Mom, you are my strength. Kathy we've had some good memories, you are still the monkey. Mom, this is nothing, I am going to go to sleep and wake up with Jesus. This is the only way God could save me. Stefanie, she is my heart, say goodbye to Stefanie. I do not want anybody to mourn my death, celebrate my life. God loves me and God loves you. Mom, you didn't do anything wrong. Thank you, Warden, Thank you Chaplain, Thank you God, I am ready to go. God please take me home. I am ready Warden. Thank you Jesus. I am going mom.

Billy Galloway

Execution Date: 05/13/2010
Race: White

County of Conviction: Hunt
Last Statement: If I can go back and change the past I would, there's nothing I can do. I'm sorry. I love you Adonya. That's it.

Rogelio Cannady

Execution Date: 05/19/2010
Race: Hispanic
County of Conviction: Bee
Last Statement: Yes, I do, Victor, Gary Hey bros, I know you can hear me, I can't hear you. I was in there right now thinking how we grew up... You know how we grew up in the same house. We need to love each other like we use to. Deena, Bob we were raised in the same house, we need to take care of each other and love each other like we use to. Adela I love you, Mijta, I need you to take care of your mom. We need to love each other like we use to. Juana, all the kindness that you showed me. Taking the time to show me the friendship that you did. I can never repay that. Take of yourself OK; you see I am doing good. I am OK. Thank you for showing me that I can be loved again. You showed me a love that I sometimes didn't deserve. I love you for that. You need to take care of yourself. I am going to be OK; I know where I'll be. I love you, I love you, I love you, I love you , I love you, I love you too bro. Take care of yall. May God have mercy on my soul. I thought it was going to be harder than this. I am ready to go. I am going to sleep now. I can feel it, it's affecting me now.

John Alba

Execution Date: 05/25/2010
Race: Hispanic
County of Conviction: Collin
Last Statement: Yes, first I want to tell the victim's family, Wendy's family, I am sorry for taking something so precious to you and to my kids. I wish I could take it all back and change it, but I know I can't. I hope you can find it in your heart to forgive me. Please tell Robert and Eric, I love them. I hope they forgive me. To my family, thanks for being beside me, Sabrina, you are a wonderful daughter, I am proud of you. Jr., John, you turned out to be a great young man. Hector, you too. Amy, thank you for always being there. Tell your family I love them. To my family, I appreciate you always standing by me and everything ya'll have done. Tell, everyone I love them. I'll be OK. You will too. Remember what asked you. Give my love to the grandchildren. Tell Jake and Mia, Papa Alba loves them. Okay Warden, let's do it, I love yall. I can taste it already. I am starting to go.

George Jones
Execution Date: 06/02/2010
Race: Black
County of Conviction: Dallas
Last Statement: Yes, I do, uh at this time I would like to thank my parents who have been my pillar of strength throughout this. To my brothers and sisters and all my family members who have supported me and who have loved me despite my faults and imperfections. I would like to thank Pastor Williams for counseling me and guiding me. As I look to my right and I see the family of Forest Hall. I hope this brings you closure or some type of peace. I hope it helps his family, son and loved ones. This has been a long journey, one of enlightenment. It's not the end, it's only the beginning.

David Powell
Execution Date: 06/15/2010
Race: White
County of Conviction: Travis
Last Statement: This person declined to make a last statement.

Michael Perry
Execution Date: 07/01/2010
Race: White
County of Conviction: Montgomery
Last Statement: Yes, I want to start off by saying to everyone know that's involved in this atrocity that they are all forgiven by me. Mom, I love you.....(crying) I am ready to go Warden. Coming home dad, coming home dad.

Derrick Jackson
Execution Date: 07/20/2010
Race: Black
County of Conviction: Harris
Last Statement: No last statement.

Peter Cantu
Execution Date: 08/17/2010
Race: Hispanic
County of Conviction: Harris
Last Statement: No

Larry Wooten
Execution Date: 10/21/2010
Race: Black
County of Conviction: Lamar
Last Statement: No sir. Warden, Since I don't have nothing to say, you can go ahead and send me to my Heavenly Father.

Michael Hall
Execution Date: 02/15/2011
Race: White
County of Conviction: Tarrant
Last Statement: First of all I would like to give my sincere apology to Amy's family. We caused a lot of heartache, grief, pain and suffering, and I am sorry. I know it won't bring her back. I would like to sing, I would like to sing for that person's dead. The old is gone. I am not the same person that I used to be, that person is dead. It's up to you if you would find it in your heart to forgive.As for my family, I am sorry I let you down. I caused a lot of heartache, and I ask for your forgiveness. I am not crying for myself, I am crying for the lost and those that are dying for their sins, those that are committing suicide, those that don't know God and have never been set free. I've been locked up 13 years. I am not locked up inside, all of these years I have been free. Christ has changed me. Even though I have to die for my mistake, he paid for mine by wages I could never pay. Here I am a big strong youngster, crying like a baby. I am man enough to show my emotions and I am sorry. I am sorry for everything. I wish I could take it back, but I can't.

Timothy Adams
Execution Date: 02/22/2011
Race: Black
County of Conviction: Harris
Last Statement: This person declined to make a last statement.

Cary Kerr
Execution Date: 05/03/2011
Race: White
County of Conviction: Tarrant
Last Statement: Yes, Tell my sister Tracey, I love you. Nicole, thank you and I love you. Wanda and all of my friends, I love you and thank you for your support. To the State of Texas, I am an innocent man. Never trust a court-appointed attorney. I am ready Warden. Thank you, Brad, I'm sorry. Check that DNA, check Scott. Here we go. Lord Jesus, Jesus.

Gayland Bradford
Execution Date: 06/01/2011
Race: Black
County of Conviction: Dallas
Last Statement: Noel, I love you man. You have been there for me through thick and thin, you and Brigitta. Be there for each other. I am at peace, we have no worries, just as I have no more worries. To the victim's family, may you be at peace also.

Lee Taylor
Execution Date: 06/16/2011
Race: White
County of Conviction: Bowie
Last Statement: Yes, sir. Jennifer, I love you. Mom, I love you. Rick, take care of you. For all of you people, I defended myself when I killed your family member. Prison is a bad place. There was eight against me. I didn't set out to kill him. I am sorry that I killed him, but he would not have been in prison if he was a saint. I hope ya'll understand that. I love you, baby.I hope people understand the grave injustice by the state. There are 300 people on death row, and everyone is not a monster. Texas is carrying out a very inhumane and injustice. It's not right to kill anybody just because I killed your people. Everyone changes, right? Life is about experience and people change. I love you, Jennifer. Mom, I love you and all my friends that I have known over the years that have always been there for me. I am ready to teleport. I love you, baby. I hope you don't find satisfaction in this, watching a human being die.

Milton Mathis
Execution Date: 06/21/2011
Race: Black
County of Conviction: Fort Bend
Last Statement: Yes, sir. I just want to say to all my supporters, family and friends; I love y'all and appreciate y'all. To the ones representing me today, thank you for everything. The system has failed me. This is a miscarriage of justice. There are people on death row that need help. I love my family. I love you too, Mom. I am alright. I asked the Lord to have mercy on me and I hope He has mercy on these people carrying out this mass slaughter. They have no respect for humanity. To Melanie, I never meant to hurt you. You were just in the wrong place at the wrong time. I am not asking for your forgiveness. All I have to worry about is God forgiving me. I hope you get better and for the doctors to continue to take care of

you. Take care of my mother for me. To everybody, know that I love you and I am OK. Lord, have mercy on my soul. Lord, have mercy on my soul. Lord, have mercy on these peoples' soul. Life is not supposed to end this way. No more pain and frustration. When I knock at the gates, they will open up and let me in. To my mom and everybody, I love you. I can feel it right now. My life, my life.

Humberto Leal

Execution Date: 07/07/2011
Race: Hispanic
County of Conviction: Bexar
Last Statement: I am sorry for everything that I have done. I've hurt a lot of people. For years I have never thought that I deserved any type of forgiveness. Lord Jesus Christ in my life, I know He has forgiven me, I have accepted His forgiveness. I have accepted everything. Let this be final and be done. I take the full blame for this. I am sorry and forgive me. I am truly sorry. I ask for forgiveness. Life goes on and it surely does. I am sorry for the victim's family for what I had did. May they forgive me. I don't know if you believe me, life goes on. I am sure it does. To the man to the right of me, I ask for forgiveness for you. Life goes on, it surely does. I ask for forgiveness. I am truly sorry. That is all. Let's get this show on the road. One more thing, Viva Mexico, Viva Mexico.

Mark Stroman

Execution Date: 07/20/2011
Race: White
County of Conviction: Dallas
Last Statement: Even though I lay on this gurney, seconds away from my death, I am at total peace. May the Lord Jesus Christ be with me. I am at peace. Hate is going on in this world and it has to stop. Hate causes a lifetime of pain. Even though I lay here I am still at peace. I am still a proud American, Texas loud, Texas proud. God bless America, God bless everyone. Let's do this damn thing. Director Hazelwood, thank you very much. Thank you everyone. Spark, I love you, all of you. I love you Conna. It's all good, it's been a great honor. I feel it; I am going to sleep now. Goodnight, 1, 2 there it goes.

Martin Robles

Execution Date: 08/10/2011
Race: Hispanic
County of Conviction: Nueces
Last Statement: I love you Israel.

Steven Woods
Execution Date: 09/13/2011
Race: White
County of Conviction: Denton
Last Statement: You're not about to witness an execution, you are about to witness a murder. I am strapped down for something Marcus Rhodes did. I never killed anybody, ever. I love you, Mom. I love you, Tali. This is wrong. This whole thing is wrong. I can't believe you are going to let Marcus Rhodes walk around free. Justice has let me down. Somebody completely screwed this up. I love you too, Mom. Well Warden, if you are going to murder someone, go ahead and do it. Pull the trigger. It's coming. I can feel it coming. Goodbye.

Lawrence Brewer
Execution Date: 09/21/2011
Race: White
County of Conviction: Brazos
Last Statement: No, I have no final statement.

Frank Garcia
Execution Date: 10/27/2011
Race: Hispanic
County of Conviction: Bexar
Last Statement: Thank you, Jesus Christ. Thank you for your blessing. You are above the president. And know it is you, Jesus Christ, that is performing this miracle in my life. Hallelujah, Holy, Holy, Holy. For this reason I was born and raised. Thank you for this, my God is a God of Salvation. Only through you, Jesus Christ, people will see that you're still on the throne. Hallelujah, Holy, Holy, Holy. I invoke Your name. Thank you, Yahweh, thank you Jesus Christ. Hallelujah, Amen. Thank you, Warden.

Guadalupe Esparza
Execution Date: 11/16/2011
Race: Hispanic
County of Conviction: Bexar
Last Statement: To the family of Alyssa Vazquez, I hope you will find peace in your heart. My sympathy goes out to you. I hope you find it in your heart to forgive me. I don't know why all of this happened. I would like to say to my friends, Jung and Arthur, thank you for being there for me through all of these years. Say goodbye to my family. Pray for me, for my soul, rest in peace. I don't know why all of this

happened. I don't know. Jesus, take me home, take me away from this place. Goodbye my friends. Jung and Arthur, tell my family I love them. I love everybody. Tell Emmanuel and Joseph I love them.

Rodrigo Hernandez
Execution Date: 01/26/2012
Race: Hispanic
County of Conviction: Bexar
Last Statement: Yes, I want to tell everybody that I love everybody. Keep your heads up. We are all family, people of God Almighty. We're all good. I'm ready. Are they already doing it? I'm gonna go to sleep. See you later. This stuff stings, man almighty.

George Rivas
Execution Date: 02/29/2012
Race: Hispanic
County of Conviction: Dallas
Last Statement: Yes, I do. First of all for the Aubrey Hawkins family, I do apologize for everything that happened. Not because I am here, but for closure in your hearts. I really believe that you deserve that. To my wife, Cheri, I am so grateful you're in my life. I love you so dearly. Thank you to my sister and dear friend Katherine Cox, my son and family, friends and family. I love you so dearly. To my friends, all the guys on the row, you have my courtesy and respect. Thank you to the people involved and to the courtesy of the officers. I am grateful for everything in my life. To my wife, take care of yourself. I will be waiting for you. I love you. God Bless. I am ready to go.

Keith Thurmond
Execution Date: 03/07/2012
Race: White
County of Conviction: Montgomery
Last Statement: All I want to say is I'm innocent, I didn't kill my wife. Jack Leary shot my wife then her dope dealer Guy Fernandez. Don't hold it against me, Bill. I swear to God I didn't kill her. Go ahead and finish it off. You can taste it.

Jesse Hernandez
Execution Date: 03/28/2012
Race: Hispanic
County of Conviction: Dallas
Last Statement: Tell my son I love him very much. God bless everybody. Continue

to walk with God. Go Cowboys! Love ya'll man. Don't forget the T-ball. Ms. Mary, thank you for everything that you've done. You too, Brad, thank you. I can feel it, taste it, not bad.

Beunka Adams
Execution Date: 04/26/2012
Race: Black
County of Conviction: Cherokee
Last Statement: First, I want to let my mom know not to cry, there is no reason to cry, everybody dies. Everybody has their time, don't worry about me. I'm strong. To my family: my old man, my kids, daddy is sorry. I love each and every one of you. I'll be looking for you. To my wife, I love you. The last two years have been the best. All my kids, mom, nieces, and nephews, I am proud of all of ya'll. I love each and every one of ya'll. I really love ya'll.To the victims, I'm very sorry for everything that happened. I am not the malicious person that you think I am. I was real stupid back then. I made a great many mistakes. What happened was wrong. I was a kid in a grown man's world. I messed up, and I can't take it back. I wasn't old enough to understand. Please don't carry around that hurt in your heart. You have got to find a way to get rid of the hate. Trust me, killing me is not going to give you closure. I hope you find closure. Don't let that hate eat you up, find a way to get past it.Linda, I love you, I appreciate you. I hate the way things turned out. Ms. Sheri, thank you. To the victims again, I hate the way all of this happened to ya'll. I don't think any good will come of this. I am going to see ya'll again. I love ya'll, be strong for me. Keep your heads up. I came into the world strong. I'll leave the world strong. Warden, go ahead. I am sorry for the victim's family. Murder isn't right, killing of any kind isn't right. Got to find another way.

Yokemon Hearn
Execution Date: 07/18/2012
Race: Black
County of Conviction: Dallas
Last Statement: Yes, I would like to tell my family that I love ya'll and I wish ya'll well. I'm ready.

Marvin Wilson
Execution Date: 08/07/2012
Race: Black
County of Conviction: Jefferson
Last Statement: Bohannon, Peg and Kim, I love ya'll. Son, get your life right with

Christ, also your mother. Give mom a hug for me and tell her that I love her. Ya'll do understand that I came here a sinner and leaving a saint. Take me home Jesus, take me home Lord, take me home Lord. I ain't left yet, must be a miracle. I am a miracle. I see you, Rich. Don't cry son, don't cry baby. I love ya'll. I'm ready.

Robert Wayne Harris
Execution Date: 9/20/2012
Race: Black
County of Conviction: Dallas
Last Statement: I want to tell ya'll, know that I love you. Billy, I love you, English, Hart and Eloise. Dwight, take care of Dwight. I'm going home, I'm going home. I'll be alright, don't worry. I love ya'll. God bless and the Texas Rangers, Texas Rangers.

Cleve Foster
Execution Date: 9/15/12
Race: White
County of Conviction: Tarrant
Last Statement: Yes, you know I sat in my cell many days wondering what my last words would be: love for my family, grandson, friends. I love you very much. Tonight when I close my eyes, I'll be with my Father. Some time ago I got a letter, I read it, and stuck it in with a bunch of stuff; and I thought to myself, what a cold-hearted person. I was asked about the letter, I spent half the night looking for the letter. A little part of the letter touched me. Over the years I have learned to love. God is everything. God is my life. Tonight, I will be with Him. I am a parent myself. I have so much for this dear lady. I understand where they're coming from, I thought every person was cruel. I love you so, Susan. You know what it is girl, love ya. Maurie, appreciate it girl. Much love to you all. Mrs. Cox, love you. Momma, you are my hero. I wish this world was just like you. Another mother got hurt, as a parent I understand the pain. That letter she wrote wasn't wrong, she was just hurting. She showed God's love for letting me know that love will be there to welcome me home. I love you all. I don't know what you are going to feel after tonight. I love you. I pray one day we will all meet in heaven. A man told me 11 years ago the hardest thing to say is, "I forgive you." Hope one day we all be together again. I love you all: Susan, Mrs. Cox, momma, Maurie, Michael. Grandbabies make the world go around. I love you all. Warden, I am looking to leave this place on wings of a homesick angel. Ready to go home to meet my maker. What a friend we have in Jesus, oh my God, I lay in awe 'cause I love you God. I love you momma. I love you Susan.

Jonathan Green

Execution Date: 10/10/12

Race: Black

County of Conviction: Montgomery

Last Statement: I'm an innocent man. I did not kill anyone. Ya'll are killing an innocent man. My left arm is killing me. It hurts bad.

Bobby Hines

Execution Date: 10/24/12

Race: White

County of Conviction: Dallas

Last Statement: To the victim's family, I am sure I know that I took somebody special from ya'll. I know it wasn't right, it was wrong. I wish I could give it back, but I know I can't. If giving my life in return makes it right, so be it. I ask that ya'll forgive me. I know God forgave me. I know He has forgiven me for what I did. I don't believe that taking my life will solve anything. I believe that if I was locked up for the rest of my life, that would be more of a punishment. To do this is setting me free. God bless ya'll. I wish there was something I could do.

Bernard, thank you. Bill, thanks for being there for me and showing me to the Lord. I give glory to God, I believe I am going home. I love my family. I love everybody. I have love in my heart for ya'll and for my family, we're all victims behind what I did. I wish there was some other way to show I'm sorry. I have a prayer that me and my wife have come up with that I'd like to say. God, hear our prayer. We want to give thanks for this day. I can't do that prayer, that prayer is not right for ya'lls family or my family. Please forgive me. I love ya'll. OK Warden, I am ready. I'm going home. I love ya'll. I'm feeling it.

Donnie Roberts

Execution Date: 10/31/12

Race: White

County of Conviction: Polk

Last Statement: To all of ya'll over here: Mr. Bivins, Allen, Joey, all of ya'll back there, I am truly sorry. I never meant to cause ya'll so much pain. Not one day has passed that I wish I could take it back. After today, I hope you can go on. I hope this brings you closure. God knows I didn't want to do what I did. I loved your daughter. I hope to God, He lets me see her in Heaven so I can apologize to her. I'm sorry. I'm glad ya'll came. Joey, I am really sorry, Joe.

Marjo, you have been there for me for six and a half years. I appreciate that. Take good care of her. I love both of ya'll. I want to say goodbye to all of ya'll. Goodbye.

Please tell my daughter I love her. I'll see ya'll. I'm sorry, Joey, I'm sorry.

Mario Swain

Execution Date: 11/08/12
Race: Black
County of Conviction: Gregg
Last Statement: This person declined to make a last statement.

Ramon Hernandez

Execution Date: 11/14/2012
Race: Hispanic
County of Conviction: Bexar
Last Statement: Can you hear me? Did I ever tell you, you have dad's eyes? I've noticed that in the last couple of days. I'm sorry for putting you through all this. Tell everyone I love them. It was good seeing the kids. I love them all; tell mom, everybody. I am very sorry for all of the pain. Tell Brenda I love her. To everybody back on the row, I know you're going through a lot over there. Keep fighting, don't give up everybody.

Preston Hughes

Execution Date: 11/15/12
Race: Black
County of Conviction: Harris
Last Statement: Yes, Warden. Mom, Celeste: Please know I'm innocent and I love you both. Please continue to fight for my innocence even though I'm gone. John, Cort, Allen, Barbara, Louis, and Anna: Thank you for helping me and trying to save my life. I love you. Give everybody my love. Jason, thank you for your friendship. Thank Laura, too. I love all of you. Bye. Ok, Warden.

Carl Blue

Execution Date: 02/21/13
Race: Black
County of Conviction: Brazos
Last Statement: Hey mom and pop. I love ya'll, all of you people in there. You know, ya'll have to come together, you too Terrella. Ya'll work on that. We all have to stand before God at the end of the day. Don't ever think you're perfect, none of us are perfect. God is the only one that is perfect. Jesus is perfect. I did wrong, now I am paying the ultimate price, even though it's a crooked way. I don't hate ya'll. Don't judge, I'm not judging. God has to judge those people. I forgive. Always

remember, Romans 12:19 is for real, hell is for real. If ya'll don't have your life right, get it right. We all have to die to get to heaven. Get your life right with Christ; it's coming to an end. I'm talking to each and every soul in this building, in this room. I don't hate nobody, you're doing what you think is your job. God's law is above this law. Hang on. Cowboy up, I'm fixing to ride. Jesus is my ride. Tell my babies daddy will look down on them. Put a "C" in his name for Carl. Tell my boys and tell Tracy to keep on keeping on. Love one another, go to church, change your life for Christ, live your life for Christ. All right, Warden. Terella, I feel it babe, love.

Ricky Lewis

Execution Date: 04/09/13
Race: Black
County of Conviction: Smith
Last Statement: Ms. Connie Hilton, I'm sorry for what happened to you. If I hadn't raped you, then you wouldn't have lived. If you look at the transcripts, I didn't kill Mr. Newman and I didn't rob your house. There are two people still alive. I was just there. When I saw you in the truck driving away, I could have killed you but I didn't. I'm not a killer. My momma was abused. I'm sorry for what you've gone through. It wasn't me that harmed and stole all of your stuff. If you look at the transcripts you will see. I ask the good Lord to forgive me.

I love ya'll; Sheena, my sister, momma, and daddy. Ya'll pray for me, keep up the fight. Get the transcripts, let the truth come out so that I do not die in vain. I thank the Lord for the man I am today. I have done all I can to better myself, to learn to read and write. Take me to my King. I love ya'll and thank you for the love you gave me. I respect all of ya'll. Ms. Hilton. Ok. Let me rest. It's burning.

Ronnie Threadgill

Execution Date: 04/16/13
Race: Black
County of Conviction: Navarro
Last Statement: To my loved ones and dear friends, I love ya'll and appreciate ya'll for being there. I am going to a better place. To all the guys back on the row, keep your heads up, keep up the fight. I am ready. Let's go.

Richard Cobb

Execution Date: 04/26/13
Race: White
County of Conviction: Cherokee
Last Statement: Life is death, death is life. I hope that someday this absurdity that

humanity has come to will come to and an end. Life is too short. I hope that anyone that has negative energy towards me will resolve that. Life is too short to harbor feelings of hatred and anger. That's it.

Carroll Parr
Execution Date: 05/07/13
Race: Black
County of Conviction: McLennan
Last Statement: First of all; Shonna talk to your brother. He'll tell you the truth about what happened to your husband. I told Bubba to tell you what happened. Now, my statement to the world: I am in the midst of truth. I am good, I am straight, don't trip. To all my partners, tell them I said like Arnold Schwarzenegger, "I'll be back." These eyes will close, but they will be opened again, my understanding of God is, Jesus has got me through. To my family, I love ya'll.

Jeffrey Williams
Execution Date: 05/15/13
Race: Black
County of Conviction: Harris
Last Statement: You clown police. You gonna stop with all that killing all these kids. You're gonna stop killing innocent kids, murdering young kids. When I kill one or pop one, ya'll want to kill me. God has a plan for everything. You hear? I love everyone that loves me. I ain't got no love for anyone that don't love me.

Elroy Chester
Execution Date: 6/12/13
Race: Black
County of Conviction: Jefferson
Last Statement: I just want to say I don't want you to have hate in your heart for me, because I took your loved one. I know it doesn't mean anything; I told the truth because I feel like you should know who killed your loved one. God watches everything. Don't hate me, if you do, you'll have to deal with Him later. For me, live your life but don't hate me. I'm sorry for taking your loved one. Ms. Suzy, Susan, thank you for fighting for me in the courts. Thank you for supporting me for all these years. Elroy Chester wasn't a bad man, I knew me. A lot of people say I didn't commit those murders, I really did it. That's my statement. Warden, you can go ahead.

Kimberly McCarthy
Execution Date: 06/26/13
Race: Black
County of Conviction: Dallas
Last Statement: I just wanted to say thanks to all who have supported me over the years: Reverend Campbell, for my spiritual guidance; Aaron, the father of Darrian, my son; and Maurie, my attorney. Thank you everybody. This is not a loss, this is a win. You know where I am going. I am going home to be with Jesus. Keep the faith. I love ya'll. Thank you, Chaplain.

John Quintanilla
Execution Date: 07/16/13
Race: Hispanic
County of Conviction: Victoria
Last Statement: Yes, I would like to tell my wife that I love her and thank her for all the years of happiness. That will be all, Warden.

Vaughn Ross
Execution Date: 07/18/13
Race: Black
County of Conviction: Lubbock
Last Statement: Yes, I want to thank my family for supporting me through this. I love ya'll. I don't fear death. I'm fine, I'm OK. To my friends and my loved ones, Miriam, I love you, thanks for being here for me. This is what it is. I know this is hard for ya'll, but we are going to have to go through it. We know the lies they told in court. We know it's not true. I want you to be strong and keep going.

Douglas Feldman
Execution Date: 07/31/13
Race: White
County of Conviction: Dallas
Last Statement: I hereby declare, Robert Steven Everett and Nicholas Velasquez, guilty of crimes against me, Douglas Alan Feldman. Either by fact or by proxy, I find them both guilty. I hereby sentence both of them to death, which I carried out in August 1998. As of that time, the State of Texas has been holding me illegally in confinement and by force for 15 years. I hereby protest my pending execution and demand immediate relief.

Robert Garza
Execution Date: 0919/13
Race: White
County of Conviction: Dallas
Last Statement: I want to thank all of my family and friends for supporting me. I love you and I'm glad that ya'll are by my side through this whole thing. I know it's hard for ya'll. I love you Jennifer, mom, Jaime, Cory, David. Thank God for you being there for me. It's not easy, this is a release. Ya'll finally get to move on with your lives. Take care of my kids and stay strong, life has to go on. We've all lost grandpas, brothers, and sisters. Support and love each other. Don't fight with each other. I love you.

Arturo Diaz
Execution Date: 9/26/13
Race: Hispanic
County of Conviction: Hispanic
Last Statement: I don't know if you remember back in 2000, you were happy the way it happened. You were looking for me yourself and would have taken care of me yourself. I am glad it happened this way. I wouldn't want to see you in my shoes. You would have probably been here, not me. I wouldn't wish this on you. I hope this can bring some relief to you and your family. I have no hate for you.

(In Spanish): Grandmother, Lilia, and Robert; have hope for me. I am with God. Thanks for being with me and all of your love. Mom, take care of my daughter. Many kisses, Mom.
Robert don't forget what I told you, I hope that this serves as an example for the youngsters. Think about it before you make a bad decision.
Let's go, Warden. I'm ready.

Michael Yowell
Execution Date: 10/9/13
Race: White
County of Conviction: Lubbock
Last Statement: I love you. To Gerald: you're a zero. I love you Mandy, Tiffany. I love you, too.

Jamie McCoskey
Execution Date: 11/12/13
Race: White

County of Conviction: Harris

Last Statement: The best time in my life is during this period. If I had to do again, I would not change a thing. I have been touched by an angel's wings. If I had it to do again, I would change Dwyer's parents suffering, because I know they are. I know that is not going to eliminate the pain, because I have a child. God, I want to say something so bad. I appreciate the people that helped me out. I appreciate the people that helped me out, and uh, know that I love you, Angel and your family and all the people that helped me out. And if this takes the pain away, so be it. I love you. I'm ready to go.

Jerry Martin

Execution Date: 12/3/13

Race: White

County of Conviction: Leon C/V from Walke

Last Statement: I would like to tell the Canfield family I'm sorry; sorry for your loss. I wish I could take it back, but I can't. I hope this gives you closure. I did not murder your loved one, it was an accident. I didn't mean for it to happen. I take full responsibility.

To my family, we've talked earlier and you know I'm at peace. God is the ultimate judge, he knows what happened. We talked earlier. I love all of y'all. I'm ready Warden.

Edgar Tamayo

Execution Date: 1/22/14

Race: Hispanic

County of Conviction: Harris

Last Statement: This person declined to make a statement.

Suzanne Basso

Execution Date: 2/5/14

Race: White

County of Conviction: Harris

Last Statement: This person declined to make a statement.

Ray Jasper

Execution Date: 3/19/14

Race: Black

County of Conviction: Bexar

Last Statement: (Written statement) I just want to make a statement to all my friends, family, and supporters. Thank you all for the love. To the Christian hip-hop community, all the positive brothers I've done time with. To all the people that took the time to write a letter. Thank you. To my family, we are one. To my beautiful daughter, the best thing that ever happened to me. I love you endlessly. I am you and you are me forever.

Lastly to God himself....Thank you being a gracious friend to me. I love you with all my heart, mind, strength, in Jesus name. (Spoken statement) I want to say to my family, please take care of each other, stay strong and faithful to God. I thank everyone for supporting me. Christine, I love you. To my daughter: baby, be strong, be positive, have a great life. You know what you meant to me, and I love you. Stay faithful to the Lord. Daughter, I love you, I love you, I love you. May the Lord God almighty in heaven, Jesus Christ see my spirit. Amen.

Anthony Doyle
Execution Date: 3/27/14
Race: Black
County of Conviction: Dallas
Last Statement: This person declined to make a statement.

Tommy Lynn Sell
Execution Date: 4/3/14
Race: White
County of Conviction: Val Verde
Last Statement: This person declined to make a statement.

Ramiro Hernandez
Execution Date: 4/9/14
Race: Hispanic
County of Conviction: Bandera
Last Statement: Yes, sir. First I would like to thank God for letting me see my family. I say this with love, I'm sorry. I say this for my family with love and with God, I love you. I'm happy, and I would like to say on behalf of my family, I love y'all. I am happy. I look into my family's eyes, and I see sadness. Don't be sad, I'm happy. I am sorry for what I have done. Be mindful that I am happy till the end. To the family of my boss, I love you. Young people, listen to your parents; always do what they tell you to do, go to school, learn from your mistakes. Be careful before you sign anything with your name. Never, despite what other people say. God is with y'all. God is the only witness that knows what happened that night. I, Ramiro

Hernandez, say this with lots of love to young people, listen to your parents please. Live your life to the fullest, you only live your life once. To the prison system, I would like to thank y'all. Thanks to the officers and to the warden that are going to witness this. I say this with a lot of love and happiness. I have no pain and no guilt. All I have is love. Love will win. Thank you God, I am going with you.

Jose Villegas
Execution Date: 4/16/14
Race: Hispanic
County of Conviction: Nueces
Last Statement: (Written statement) I always said that if I even get to this point, I would have already said everything that needed to be said to all of those who I love and have been with me throughout this whole journey. Today, I realized that I can never say everything that needed to be said, because there is still so much that needs to be said. First of all, I love you. My children, my friends, and all my brothers who have shared this experience with me on the row and who continue to experience this without me, keep your heads up. I love all of you. Secondly, I am ok. I have peace in my heart and ready for the next journey. I'm really ok. Last but not least, to my true brother in life, Crazy J, I love you, man. You and Bella have been the best. I'm sorry I couldn't talk with you before all of this, but you know me...You are my bro. I love you. I'm ok. My babies, remember what I said. We'll be together soon. I love all of you. John 14:27. (Spoken statement) Yes, I left a written statement. I do have a verbal statement. I would like to remind my children once again, I love them. Crazy J, I forgot to write a list. Everything is ok. I love you all, and I love my children. I am at peace. John 14:27. I am done, Warden.

ACKNOWLEDGMENTS

Betty Gilmore

WHEN I BEGAN THIS book project, I had absolutely no idea what world I was stepping into. I was ill-prepared for what I would learn, what I would experience, the toll it would take and the way that my life would change. Despite the many challenges that were presented during the course of this work, I am forever grateful for this experience and am deeply humbled by the number of people who helped us make this book possible. So many people have put themselves in highly vulnerable positions, despite the potential consequences, to ensure that voices are heard and to make transparent a system that is often hidden behind a curtain.

I could not have written this book if it were not for my friend, colleague and co-author, Nanon Williams. Nanon is a living example of how resilient the human spirit can be. He has taught me to always persist at doing the right thing, no matter how tired you get, no matter what people try to take away and no matter how others may try to make you feel. Nanon continues to teach me that no one has the power, no matter how hard they try, to strip us of our dignity. Nanon, you have been unbelievably patient during this entire process, and you have put yourself at risk to see this project to fruition. We made it, and I wish you could be here to see this book and hold it in your hands. Texas Department of Criminal Justice will likely censure it, as they have *Still Surviving* and many others.

There are so many people who have been invaluable to the process of writing this book. Thank you to all the individuals I interviewed for your personal experiences and expertise; there are too many to name, but your contributions were essential to this work. To those of you who helped edit and give feedback on the manuscript and support me, Gary Gilmore, Sara Saravo, John Potter, Bernie Mayer and Robyn Short, your feedback has been invaluable. I am honored the manuscript went through your filters.

There were countless individuals who chose to remain anonymous but wanted their stories to be told. I know that it took a lot of courage to share your experiences. Your voices matter. To Martin Draughon, Son Vu Tran, Oswaldo Soriano and Gabriel Gonzales, your experiences put life into this book. Thank you for sharing your lives with us.

To the victim survivors who shared their painful stories and perspectives, thank you for letting me be a part of your world and helping me better understand the needs of survivors, many of which are not being addressed by the system. Your experiences highlight the importance of making restorative practices available to victims' families who choose that as an option on the road to healing.

My research assistants, Kristin Baker Croom, Mary Grace Mewitt, Caroline Horner, Ryan Saravo and Josh Gilmore who assisted me with research collection, hopefully you have learned and grown along the way. You all are incredible people. Thank you.

There are many people who have been very patient with my unending curiosity and desire to understand these issues from many perspectives. They have been incredible resources to me. In particular, I would like to acknowledge the support of David Atwood, Five Mualimm-ak, Lisa Guenther, Walter Long, Craig Haney and Rick Halperin. Your passion and dedication toward human rights have been an inspiration to me. I want to be you when I grow up.

Thank you Frans Douw and Susan Sarandon for your involvement in this book. Your passion and dedication for this work is a true inspiration and has made a difference in the lives of many.

My friend, colleague and publisher Robyn Short has quietly tolerated my unconventional methods of getting work done and has been incredibly patient with the length of time it has taken to see this project to completion. Not only did Robyn oversee this project, she became personally involved on every level, and as a result, she experienced a backlash. But she stood taller and kept going. Her incredible talent, guidance, strength, courage, creativity, support and sense of humor were instrumental to me. We went through this journey together, and I am forever grateful for that.

I appreciate the support of all of my friends who listened to me talk endlessly about this project. I am so grateful for your presence in my life.

I feel a tremendous amount of gratitude to my family, who remained patient for more than a year while I immersed myself in this work physically and emotionally. The writing of this book took its toll on all of us. Each of my family members played an important role in helping me complete this work and supporting me. I believe that through this process, they have grown and learned along the way. We all have.

Nanon M. Williams

T HIS BOOK WAS MET with challenges that not only affected my life, but the lives of others that I care deeply about. If there is such a thing as institutional violence, I can now clearly define it as the punishment that ensued upon myself and my loved ones as a result of this work. Walking away from this project would have been the easiest thing to do, but it was not the right thing to do. I admit, at times I have wondered if I would even live to see this book published before I ended up tucked away in some solitary cell for attempting to write it. The love of so many people encouraged me to keep pressing forward. As my grandmother always said, "Keep on keepin' on!"

In my heart, I know this body of work will not only shed light on those living in solitary confinement and on death row, but it will also teach us all to learn to forgive, to understand and to bestow mercy.

First on the list of people to thank is Robyn Short, my publisher, friend, comrade and partner on this journey. Robyn, you have been punished, persecuted and discouraged from moving forward with this book. Through great suffering, many sacrifices and much heartache, you saw this project through. Thank you for believing in me and being willing to learn with me. I am very proud of you.

To my co-author Dr. Betty Gilmore, you surprise me! You are a mother, a professor and a great friend. You are the first person to refer to me as a "colleague," and I am cool with that (smile). It is an honor to be your friend and few people will know how much you digested in doing this work. It is indeed an emotional roller coaster, but you hung in there. I look forward to the work ahead with you.

Thank you to Elyse Short for the copious amounts of transcribing you did converting my archaic typewritten letters into a Word document. I don't know what Robyn and Betty would have done without your generous contribution of your time and energy.

Thank you to Susan Sarandon and Frans Douw for contributing to this book and to the many people who contributed anonymously. Thank you to Harvey Earvin, Martin Draughon, Gabriel Gonzales, Oswaldo Soriano, Son Vu Tran and the many men who shared their stories with me on death row and who have long since been executed.

Many people shared their ideas for this book and have offered invaluable friendship and support throughout my incarceration. Thank you to Bryonn Bain,

James Gilley, Kamau Mposi, Gloria Rubac, Mary Hennig, David Atwood, Rick Halperin, Walter Giger, Morris Moon, Danalynn Recer, Helen Beardsley, Walter Long and Mark Olive. We all hold similar principles grounded in creating a necessary change for a better future.

I am also grateful to have had some wonderful professors at Ramsey One Unit: Dr. Shreekha Subramanian, Tina Mougouris, Bridget Fernandes, Dr. Travis and the new professors who will surely come. Education is the greatest tool for those living in prison to connect the dots to the world they live in and find a connection with what they do not understand. So many of us appreciate you for treating us as people. Thank you.

Over the decades, I have met many people. To all the students that write, I will always respond. Questions bring us closer to finding answers, and I am honored to respond to everyone who has written and the teachers that make the effort. And to those who live in prison with me ... everything is possible when we dig down deep and not just look at our own suffering, but the suffering experienced by others as well. So many of us desire forgiveness, but we do not know how to ask for it or how to give it. Please believe so many of the men who are imprisoned are trying. I am proud to see some guys do amazing things despite the jungle we live in.

Last but not least, this is for my family. There is much to be said to my Mama, Lee Bolton, who always stresses that I must put God first. I listen, I learn and I do my best to make you proud. And to my stepmom Diane Pitts, you have always loved me as your own child, and if it means I'll have to dig through a mountain with a spoon to find my way home, know that I am digging and I'll keep digging. I love you both so very much. Our numbers are growing through our little ones. I may never be a father of my own, but I take great pride in being Uncle Nanon. I love each and every one of you with every breath I take and every step I take.

ABOUT THE AUTHORS

Betty Gilmore

FROM A VERY YOUNG age, Dr. Betty Gilmore developed a passion for serving under-represented groups and creating opportunities for giving a voice to those who are marginalized in society. Her academic pursuits allowed her many opportunities to work with diverse populations while obtaining her doctorate and master's degrees in clinical psychology.

She has delivered training programs and professional presentations nationally and internationally in peace building, crisis management and conflict resolution. Her other areas of interest and specialized training include trauma, human rights and social justice.

As a licensed clinical psychologist, Dr. Gilmore has worked in clinical, teaching, training, supervisory and consulting roles in a wide variety of settings including academic, workplace, private practice, community, outpatient and inpatient psychiatric facilities.

Dr. Gilmore currently serves as director and faculty for the Center for Dispute Resolution at Southern Methodist University where she teaches in both the counseling and dispute resolution graduate programs. She is also a lecturer at the Werner Institute at Creighton University School of Law.

She earned her bachelor's degree in psychology from Southern Methodist University. In addition, she received her master's and doctoral degrees from the California School of Professional Psychology in Los Angeles, California.

Dr. Gilmore is on the board of the Texas After Violence Project and lives in Dallas, Texas.

Nanon M. Williams

NANON MCKEWN WILLIAMS grew up in Los Angeles amid the violence and poverty that plagued the city. As a teenager, Nanon stood out for his academic and sporting achievements and dreamed of a career as a football player. He was an All-American and the recipient of more than 17 athletic and academic scholarships. In 1992, when Nanon was only 17 years old, he was wrongfully convicted of murder and sentenced to death by the state of Texas.

As a young man on death row, Nanon discovered a passion for writing and committed his life to being a voice for those who have been silenced. He began with poems, which he published in 2000 under the title *The Ties That Bind Us*, and continued on to write numerous essays as well as several books, providing a poignant look at life on death row. In 1997, Nanon began publishing *The Williams Report* as a contribution to the debate against the death sentence and to provide an international voice for incarcerated individuals around the world. Readers interested in subscribing to *The Williams Report* may do so on Nanon's website, www.NanonWilliams.com.

In 2005, as a result of the U.S. Supreme Court's ruling in *Roper v. Simmons*, Nanon's death sentence was commuted to a life sentence. With his transition to general population, Nanon was able to study for and complete his GED in 2007. He then began college courses offered through Trinity Valley Community College. He earned an associates degree in Liberal Arts and Science and also took trade courses in Horticulture and Cognitive Intervention. He is currently working toward his Bachelor of Science in Behavioral Sciences through the University of Houston-Clear Lake. Upon completion of his Bachelor degree, Nanon will begin working toward his Masters in Literature.

Through writing, Nanon has found a way in which to endure daily life in prison, connect with and enrich the world beyond prison walls. Nanon actively works to bring attention to the atrocities that routinely occur behind bars and seeks to be a voice for those who have been silenced while offering a platform of education for those who may learn compassion and kindness for a population of people who are all too easy to shun and turn our backs on.

While Nanon continues to live a life of service to others, it is the hope of his publisher and loving community of family and friends that his work be a force of change that will bring him justice and freedom so that he may continue to be a force for peace in this world.

BIBLIOGRAPHY

1 Executed offenders. (n.d.). Retrieved May 1, 2014, from http://www.tdcj.state.tx.us/death_row/dr_executed_offenders.html
2 Williams, N. (2012). *The Darkest Hour: Stories and Interviews from Death Row*. Dallas: GoodMedia Press.
3 Williams, N. (2012). *The Darkest Hour: Stories and Interviews from Death Row*. Dallas: GoodMedia Press.
4 Roper v. Simmons - Official U.S. Supreme Court opinion (1183 March 01, 2005).
5 Associated Press. (2005, March 1). Justices abolish death penalty for juveniles. Retrieved May 5, 2014, from http://www.nbcnews.com/id/7051296/ns/us_news-crime_and_courts/t/justices-abolish-death-penalty-juveniles/#.U2ffrPldVMh
6 Williams, N. (2012). *The Darkest Hour: Stories and Interviews from Death Row*. Dallas: GoodMedia Press.
7 Email communication with public information office. (2012)
8 Testimony on "Reassessing Solitary Confinement: The Human Rights, Fiscal, and Public Safety Consequences" (2012, June 19). Retrieved April 27, 2014, from https://www.aclu.org/prisoners-rights/testimony-reassessing-solitary-confinement-human-rights-fiscal-and-public-safety
9 Information obtained through email from Public Information Office. (2014).
10 Offenders on death row. (n.d.). Retrieved May 1, 2014, from http://www.tdcj.state.tx.us/death_row/dr_offenders_on_dr.html
11 Information obtained through email from Public Information Office.
12 McGiverin, B. (2014, April 5). McGiverin: Prison rape as a political football. Retrieved April 27, 2014, from http://www.news-journal.com/opinion/forum/mcgiverin-prison-rape-as-a-political-football/article_313bac1c-3fce-57ee-947c-616a5fb44e18.html
13 TDCJ Human Resource Division. (2014, March 20). *TDCJ Benefits Publication*, 8.
14 USA, Texas Department of Criminal Justice, Correctional Institutions Division. (2012). *Administrative segregation plan*. TX.
15 USA, Texas Department of Criminal Justice, STG. (2007). *Security threat groups: On the inside*. TX: Texas Department of Criminal Justice. Retrieved April 27, 2014, from http://tdcj.state.tx.us/documents/Security_Threat_Groups_GRAD.pdf
16 Texas Department of Criminal Justice. (2012). *Disciplinary rules and procedures for offenders* (USA, Texas Department of Criminal Justice, Correctional Institutions Division). TX.
17 TDCJ. (n.d.). Definitions & Acronyms. Retrieved April 27, 2014, from http://tdcj.state.tx.us/definitions/index.html
18 Information obtained through email from Public Information Office. (2014).
19 USA, Texas Department of Criminal Justice, Correctional Institutions Division. (2012). *Administrative segregation plan*. TX.
20 Hurt, J. (2012, November 7). Protective Custody [E-mail].
21 TDCJ. (n.d.). Definitions & Acronyms. Retrieved April 27, 2014, from http://tdcj.state.tx.us/definitions/index.html
22 Texas Department of Criminal Justice. (2004). *Offender orientation handbook*(USA, Texas Department of Criminal Justice, Correctional Institutions Division). TX. Retrieved April 27, 2014, from http://www.tdcj.state.tx.us/documents/Offender_Orientation_Handbook_English.pdf
23 Steve Martin, attorney, consultant and former General Counsel of TDCJ [Telephone interview]. (2012, October 23).
24 The Backgate Website. (n.d.). Retrieved from http://tdcjbackgate.blogspot.com/. Accessed 5/10/2014

25 Screenshot, Backgate Websiste, available upon request.

26 The Backgate Website. (n.d.). Retrieved from http://tdcjbackgate.blogspot.com/

27 Testimony on "Reassessing Solitary Confinement: The Human Rights, Fiscal, and Public Safety Consequences" (2012, June 19). Retrieved April 27, 2014, from https://www.aclu.org/prisoners-rights/testimony-reassessing-solitary-confinement-human-rights-fiscal-and-public-safety

28 Williams, N. (2012). *The Darkest Hour: Stories and Interviews from Death Row*. Dallas: GoodMedia Press.

29 Williams, N. (2012). *The Darkest Hour: Stories and Interviews from Death Row*. Dallas: GoodMedia Press.

30 *Execution procedure* [PDF]. (2012, July). Texas Department of Criminal Justice Correctional Institutions Division.

31 *Execution procedure* [PDF]. (2012, July). Texas Department of Criminal Justice Correctional Institutions Division.

32 Email communication with Public Information Office. (2014).

33 Death Row Facts. (n.d.). Retrieved April 19, 2014, from http://www.tdcj.state.tx.us/death_row/dr_facts.html

34 Texas Department of Criminal Justice. (2004). *Offender orientation handbook*(USA, Texas Department of Criminal Justice, Correctional Institutions Division). TX. Retrieved April 27, 2014, from http://www.tdcj.state.tx.us/documents/Offender_Orientation_Handbook_English.pdf

35 Gender and racial statistics of death row offenders. (2014, February 16). Retrieved from https://www.tdcj.state.tx.us/death_row/dr_gender_racial_stats.html

36 Race of death row inmates executed since 1976. (n.d.). Retrieved June 8, 2014, from http://www.deathpenaltyinfo.org/race-death-row-inmates-executed-1976#deathrowpop

37 Testimony on "Reassessing Solitary Confinement: The Human Rights, Fiscal, and Public Safety Consequences" (2012, June 19). Retrieved April 27, 2014, from https://www.aclu.org/prisoners-rights/testimony-reassessing-solitary-confinement-human-rights-fiscal-and-public-safety

38 Testimony of Secretary of Defense Donald H. Rumsfeld. (n.d.). Retrieved April 27, 2014, from http://www.defense.gov/speeches/speech.aspx?speechid=118

39 Fiske, S. T., Harris, L. T., & Cuddy, A. J. C. (2004). Policy Forum: Why ordinary people torture enemy prisoners. *Science, 306,* 1482-1483.

40 Milgram, S. (1963). Behavioral study of obedience. *Journal of Abnormal and Social Psychology,* 67, 371-378

41 Milgram, S. (1974). *Obedience to authority: An experimental view*. Harpercollins

42 McLeod, S. A. (2007). Milgram Experiment. *Simple Psychology*. Retrieved April 19, 2014, from http://www.simplypsychology.org/milgram.html

43 The perils of obedience. (1973, December). *Harper's, 247*(1483), 62.

44 Milgram, S. (1963). Behavioral study of obedience. *The Journal of Abnormal and Social Psychology, 67*(4), 371-378. doi: 10.1037/h0040525

45 Zimbardo, P.G. (2007). Revisiting the Stanford prison experiment: A lesson in the power of situation. *Chronicle of Higher Education, 53*(30), B6–B7

46 Dittman, M. (2004, October). What makes bad people do good things. *Monitor on Psychology, 35*(9), 68. doi: http://www.apa.org/monitor/oct04/goodbad.aspx

47 Breckler, S. (2004, June 10). How can the science of human behavior help us understand Abu Ghraib? Retrieved April 19, 2014, from http://www.apa.org/about/gr/science/advocacy/2004/abu-ghraib.aspx

48   Mayer, B. (2012). *The dynamics of conflict: A guide to engagement and intervention* (pp. 3-32). San Francisco: Jossey-Bass.

49   Stroch, K. (2012, July 12). Texas prisons water problems attract national attention. *Texas Monthly*. Retrieved May 10, 2014, from http://www.texasmonthly.com/story/texas-prisons-water-problems-attract-national-attention

50 Mayer, B. (2012). *The dynamics of conflict: A guide to engagement and intervention* (pp. 3-32). San Francisco: Jossey-Bass.

51 Smith, J. (20017, March 16). TDCJ Negligence Alleged. *The Austin Chronicle*. Retrieved from http://www.austinchronicle.com/news/2007-03-16/456313/

52 Doe v Carter, No. 7:10-CV-147-O slip op. at 787 (United States District Court for the Northern district of Texas, Wichita Falls division October 19, 2011).

53 Data gleaned from Texas Department of Criminal Justice (TDCJ) Response to Open Records.

54 USA, Texas Department of Criminal Justice. (2009). *General rules of conduct and disciplinary action guidelines for employees.* TX.

55 Data gleaned from Texas Department of Criminal Justice (TDCJ) Response to Open Records.

56 Moore, C. W. (2003). *The mediation process: Practical strategies for resolving conflict* (3rd ed.). San Francisco: Jossey-Bass

57 Moore, C. W. (2003). *The mediation process: Practical strategies for resolving conflict* (3rd ed.). San Francisco: Jossey-Bass

58 Guenther, L. (2013). *Solitary confinement: Social death and its afterlives* (p. 229). Minneapolis, MN: University of Minnesota Press.

59 Johnson, R., & Toch, H. (2000). *Crime and punishment: Inside views*. Los Angeles, CA: Roxbury Pub.

60 Haney, C. (2008). A culture of harm: Taming the dynamics of cruelty in super-max prisons. *Criminal Justice and Behavior, 35*(8), 956-984. doi: 10.1177/0093854808318585

61 Animal Legal Defense Fund (ALDF) v. Glickman, 204 F.3d 229 (United States Court of Appeals, District of Columbia Circuit 2000).

62 Haney, C. (2003). Mental health issues in long-term solitary and "super-max" confinement. *Crime & Delinquency, 49*(1), 124-156. doi: 10.1177/0011128702239239

63 Eighth Amendment (United States Constitution). (n.d.). Retrieved April 30, 2014, from http://www.britannica.com/EBchecked/topic/181251/Eighth-Amendment

64 Foxhill, A. (2012, June 26). Family sues TDCJ over heat related death. *The Texas Tribune*. Retrieved April 19, 2014, from http://www.highbeam.com/doc/1G1-294512084.html?refid=easy_hf

65 Smith, J. (20017, March 16). TDCJ Negligence Alleged. *The Austin Chronicle*. Retrieved from http://www.austinchronicle.com/news/2007-03-16/456313/

66 Testimony on "Reassessing Solitary Confinement: The Human Rights, Fiscal, and Public Safety Consequences" (2012, June 19). Retrieved April 27, 2014, from https://www.aclu.org/prisoners-rights/testimony-reassessing-solitary-confinement-human-rights-fiscal-and-public-safety

67 Testimony on "Reassessing Solitary Confinement: The Human Rights, Fiscal, and Public Safety Consequences" (2012, June 19). Retrieved April 27, 2014, from https://www.aclu.org/prisoners-rights/testimony-reassessing-solitary-confinement-human-rights-fiscal-and-public-safety

68 Metzner, J., MD, & Fellner, J., Esq. (2010). Solitary confinement and mental illness in U.S. prisons: A challenge for medical ethics. *Journal of the American Academy of Psychiatry and the Law, 38*(1), 104-108. doi: http://www.jaapl.org/content/38/1/104.full

69 The Universal Declaration of Human Rights, UDHR, Declaration of Human Rights, Human Rights Declaration, Human Rights Charter, The Un and Human Rights. (n.d.). Retrieved April 29, 2014, from http://www.un.org/en/documents/udhr/index.shtml#atop

70 Metzner, J., MD, & Fellner, J., Esq. (2010). Solitary confinement and mental illness in U.S. prisons: A challenge for medical ethics. *Journal of the American Academy of Psychiatry and the Law, 38*(1), 104-108. doi: http://www.jaapl.org/content/38/1/104.full

71 United Nations Human Rights. (n.d.). UN Special Rapporteur on torture calls for the prohibition of solitary confinement. Retrieved May 3, 2014, from http://www.ohchr.org/en/NewsEvents/Pages/DisplayNews.aspx?NewsID=11506&LangID=E

72 Mushlin, Michael B., "Dying Twice: Conditions on New York's Death Row" (2002). *Pace Law*

Faculty Publications. Paper 462.

73 Kubler-Ross, E. (2005). *On death and dying.* Guangzhou, PRC: Guangdong jingji.

74 Doka, K. J. (1999). Disenfranchised grief. *Bereavement Care, 18*(3), 37-39. doi: 10.1080/02682629908657467

75 Kamerman, J., & Doka, K. J. (1991). Disenfranchised grief: Recognizing hidden sorrow. *Contemporary Sociology, 20*(1), 136. doi: 10.2307/2072146

76 Doka, K. J. (2002). Spirituality, loss and grief. *Bereavement Care, 21*(1), 3-5. doi: 10.1080/02682620208657535

77 Shear, M. K., Simon, N., Wall, M., Zisook, S., Neimeyer, R., Duan, N., ... Keshaviah, A. (2011). Complicated grief and related bereavement issues for DSM-5. *Depression and Anxiety, 28*(2), 103-117. doi: 10.1002/da.20780

78 Horowitz, M., Milbrath, C., Bonanno, G. A., Field, N., Stinson, C., & Holen, A. (1998). Predictors of complicated grief. *Journal of Personal and Interpersonal Loss, 3*(3), 257-269. doi: 10.1080/10811449808409703

79 Information obtained through email from Public Information Office. (2014).

80 Adapted from: Williams, N. M. (2002). *The Darkest hour: Stories and interviews from death row* (pp. 85-105). Dallas, TX: GoodMedia Press.

81 Collins, K., Connors, K., Donohue, A., Gardner, S., Goldblatt, E., Hayward, A., Kiser, L., Strieder, F. Thompson, E. (2010). Understanding the impact of trauma and urban poverty on family systems: Risks, resilience, and interventions. Baltimore, MD: Family Informed Trauma Treatment Center. http://nctsn.org/nccts/nav.do?pid=ctr_rsch_prod_ar

82 Cunningham, M. D., & Vigen, M. P. (2002). Death row inmate characteristics, adjustment, and confinement: A critical review of the literature. *Behavioral Sciences & the Law, 20*(1-2), 191-210. doi: 10.1002/bsl.473

83 Kupers, T. A. (1996). Trauma and its sequelae in male prisoners: Effects of confinement, overcrowding, and diminished services. *American Journal of Orthopsychiatry, 66*(2), 189-196. doi: 10.1037/h0080170

84 Hammer, David and Cody, Art C. and Gerson, Risa and Greene, Norman L. and Mushlin, Michael B. and Wolf, Richard T., Dying Twice: Conditions on New York's Death Row (2002). Pace Law Review, Vol. 22, 2002. Available at SSRN: http://ssrn.com/abstract=1147050

85 Adapted from: Williams, N. M. (2002). *The Darkest hour: Stories and interviews from death row* (pp. 9-24). Dallas, TX: GoodMedia Press.

86 Williams, N. M. (2013). *Still Surviving.* Dallas, TX: GoodMedia Press.

87 Toch, H. (1977). *Living in prison: The ecology of survival.* New York: Free Press.

88 Hammer, David and Cody, Art C. and Gerson, Risa and Greene, Norman L. and Mushlin, Michael B. and Wolf, Richard T., Dying Twice: Conditions on New York's Death Row (2002). Pace Law Review, Vol. 22, 2002. Available at SSRN: http://ssrn.com/abstract=1147050

89 Solitary men: Does prolonged isolation drive death row prisoners insane? (2010, November 10). *Texas Observer.* Retrieved April 19, 2014, from http://www.texasobserver.org/solitary-men/

90 Williams, N. M. (2013). *Still Surviving.* Dallas, TX: GoodMedia Press.

91 Haney, C. (2003). Mental health issues in long-term solitary and "super-max" confinement. *Crime & Delinquency, 49*(1), 124-156. doi: 10.1177/0011128702239239

92 Otto, C., Leveton, L., & Ridgway O'Brien Bachman, K. (2012).*Countermeasures to mitigate the negative impact of sensory deprivation and social isolation in long-duration space flight* (Rep. No. NASA/TM-2012-217365, S-1127, JSC-CN-26147, JSC-CN-25581). Houston, TX: NASA Johnson Space Center. doi: http://ntrs.nasa.gov/archive/nasa/casi.ntrs.nasa.gov/20120002722.pdf

93 Mild cognitive impairment (MCI). (n.d.). Retrieved April 19, 2014, from http://www.mayoclinic.org/diseases-conditions/mild-cognitive-impairment/basics/definition/con-20026392

94 Williams, N. M. (2013). *Still Surviving.* Dallas, TX: GoodMedia Press.

95 Grassian, S. (2006). Psychiatric effects of solitary confinement. *Journal of Law &*

Policy, 22(325), 325-383. doi: http://law.wustl.edu/journal/22/p325grassian.pdf

96   Haney, C. (2003). Mental health issues in long-term solitary and "super-max" confinement. *Crime & Delinquency, 49*(1), 124-156. doi: 10.1177/0011128702239239

97   Hypothalamus. (n.d.). Retrieved April 19, 2014, from http://www.healthline.com/human-body-maps/hypothalamus

98   Retrieved April 19, 2014, from http://www.ncbi.nlm.nih.gov/pubmed/16594265

99   Amygdala. (n.d.). Retrieved April 19, 2014, from http://www.sciencedaily.com/articles/a/amygdala.htm

100 Haney, C. (2003). Mental health issues in long-term solitary and "super-max" confinement. *Crime & Delinquency, 49*(1), 124-156. doi: 10.1177/0011128702239239

101 Grassian, S. (2006). Psychiatric effects of solitary confinement. *Journal of Law & Policy, 22*(325), 325-383. doi: http://law.wustl.edu/journal/22/p325grassian.pdf

102 Testimony on "Reassessing Solitary Confinement: The Human Rights, Fiscal, and Public Safety Consequences" (2012, June 19). Retrieved April 27, 2014, from https://www.aclu.org/prisoners-rights/testimony-reassessing-solitary-confinement-human-rights-fiscal-and-public-safety

103 Haney, C., & Lynch, M. (1997). Regulating prisons of the future: A psychological analysis of super-max and solitary confinement. *New York University Review of Law and Social Change*. doi: http://www.probono.net/prisoners/stopsol-reports/416694.Regulating_Prisons_of_the_Future

104 Shalev, S. (2008). *A sourcebook on solitary confinement* (p. 17). London: Mannheim Centre for Criminology, London School of Economics and Political Science.

105 Abbott, J. H. (1991). *In the belly of the beast: Letters from prison* (p. 29). New York: Vintage Books.

106 Stuart, H. (2003). Suicide behind bars. *Current Opinion in Psychiatry, 16*(5), 559-564. doi: 10.1097/00001504-200309000-00012

107 Dye, M. H. (2010). Deprivation, importation, and prison suicide: Combined effects of institutional conditions and inmate composition. *Journal of Criminal Justice, 38*(4), 796-806. doi: 10.1016/j.jcrimjus.2010.05.007

108 Lobos, A. M. (2011). Influencing factors on suicide in correctional settings. In M. S. Plakhotnik, S. M. Nielsen, & D. M. Pane (Eds.), Proceedings of the Tenth Annual College of Education & GSN Research Conference (pp. 123-129). Miami: Florida International University. http://coeweb.fiu.edu/research_conference/

109 Dye, M. H. (2010). Deprivation, importation, and prison suicide: Combined effects of institutional conditions and inmate composition. *Journal of Criminal Justice, 38*(4), 796-806. doi: 10.1016/j.jcrimjus.2010.05.007

110 *A death before dying: Solitary confinement on death row* (Rep.). (2013). New York, NY: American Civil Liberties Union. doi: https://www.aclu.org/files/assets/deathbeforedying-report.pdf

111 Data gleaned from Texas Department of Criminal Justice (TDCJ) Response to Open Records. (2012).

112 Segerstrom, S. C., & O'Connor, D. B. (2012). Stress, health and illness: Four challenges for the future. *Psychology & Health, 27*(2), 128-140. doi: 10.1080/08870446.2012.659516

113 Stress. (n.d.). Retrieved April 19, 2014, from http://umm.edu/health/medical/reports/articles/stress

114 New Amnesty International report exposes severe, inhumane solitary confinement conditions for 3,000 California prisoners. (n.d.). Retrieved April 19, 2014, from http://www.amnestyusa.org/news/press-releases/new-amnesty-international-report-exposes-severe-inhumane-solitary-confinement-conditions-for-3000-ca

115 Testimony on "Reassessing Solitary Confinement: The Human Rights, Fiscal, and Public Safety Consequences" (2012, June 19). Retrieved April 27, 2014, from https://www.aclu.org/prisoners-rights/testimony-reassessing-solitary-confinement-human-rights-fiscal-and-public-safety

116 Holt-Lunstad, J., Layton, J. B., & Brayne, C. (2010). Social relationships and mortality risk: A meta-analytic review (T. B. Smith, Ed.). *PLoS Medicine,7*(7), E1000316. doi: 10.1371/journal.

pmed.1000316

117 Cacioppo, J. T., Hughes, M. E., Waite, L. J., Hawkley, L. C., & Thisted, R. A. (2006). Loneliness as a specific risk factor for depressive symptoms: Cross-sectional and longitudinal analyses. *Psychology and Aging, 21*(1), 140-151. doi: 10.1037/0882-7974.21.1.140

118 Testimony on "Reassessing Solitary Confinement: The Human Rights, Fiscal, and Public Safety Consequences" (2012, June 19). Retrieved April 27, 2014, from https://www.aclu.org/prisoners-rights/testimony-reassessing-solitary-confinement-human-rights-fiscal-and-public-safety

119 Basner, M., Rao, H., Goel, N., & Dinges, D. F. (2013). Sleep deprivation and neurobehavioral dynamics. *Current Opinion in Neurobiology, 23*(5), 854-863. doi: 10.1016/j.conb.2013.02.008

120 Rich, J. D., Wakeman, S. E., & Dickman, S. L. (2011). Medicine and the epidemic of incarceration in the United States. *New England Journal of Medicine, 364*(22), 2081-2083. doi: 10.1056/NEJMp1102385

121 USA, Texas Department of Criminal Justice, Correctional Institutions Division. (2012). *Administrative segregation plan.* TX.

122 Doe v Carter, No. 7:10-CV-147-O slip op. at 787 (United States District Court for the Northern district of Texas, Wichita Falls division October 19, 2011).

123 Johnston, E. Lea, vulnerability and just desert: A theory of sentencing and mental illness (March 25, 2013). Journal of Criminal Law and Criminology, Vol. 103, No. 1, 2013. Available at SSRN:http://ssrn.com/abstract=2239082, accessed April 19, 2014.

124 Williams, N. M. (2013). *Still Surviving.* Dallas, TX: GoodMedia Press.

125 Madrid v. Gomez, 889 F. Supp. 1146, 1265 (N.D. Cal. 1995) (U.S. District court for the northern district of California).

126 Administrative segregation. (n.d.). Retrieved April 30, 2014, from http://www.texasinterfaithcenter.org/content/administrative-segregation

127 Haney, C. (1993). "The infamous punishment": The psychological consequences of Isolation. *The National Prison Project Journal, 8*(2), 3-7.

128 American Psychiatric Association. (1997). Practice guideline for the treatment of patients with schizophrenia. *American Journal of Psychiatry, 154,* 1-63.

129 Weir, K. (2012). Psychologists probe the mental health effects of solitary confinement. *Monitor on Psychology, 43*(5). doi: http://www.apa.org/monitor/2012/05/solitary.aspx

130 Data gleaned from Texas Department of Criminal Justice (TDCJ) Response to Open Records.

131 Data gleaned from Texas Department of Criminal Justice (TDCJ) Response to Open Records.

132 Data gleaned from Texas Department of Criminal Justice (TDCJ) Response to Open Records.

133 Johnston, L. E. (2013). Vulnerability and just desert: A theory of sentencing and mental illness. *Journal of Criminal Law and Criminology, 103*(1).

134 Williams, N. M. (2013). *Still Surviving* (pp. 46-48). Dallas, TX: GoodMedia Press.

135 Lanes, E. C. (2011). Are the "worst of the worst" self-injurious prisoners more likely to end up in long-term maximum-security administrative segregation? *International Journal of Offender Therapy and Comparative Criminology, 55*(7), 1034-1050. doi: 10.1177/0306624X10378494

136 Johnston, L. E. (2013). Vulnerability and just desert: A theory of sentencing and mental illness. *Journal of Criminal Law and Criminology, 103*(1).

137 Jones 'El v. Berge civil case 00-C-0421-C, Testimony from 39 (United States District Court, W.D. Wisconsin September 20, 2001).

138 Johnston, L. E. (2013). Vulnerability and just desert: A theory of sentencing and mental illness. *Journal of Criminal Law and Criminology, 103*(1).

139 Data gleaned from Texas Department of Criminal Justice (TDCJ) Response to Open Records.

140 Knaack, F. (2011, October 19). Torturing children in Texas [Web log post]. Retrieved April 19, 2014, from http://www.aclutx.org/blog/?p=876

141 Email communication, February 24(2014).

142 Data gleaned from Texas Department of Criminal Justice (TDCJ) Response to Open Records.

143 Email communication with public information office. (2012).

144 Kondrad, K., Firk, C., & Uhlhaas, P. J. (2013). Brain development during adolescence neuroscientific insights Into this developmental period. *Journal of Dtsch Arztebl Int, 110*(25), 425-431. doi: 10.3238/arztebl.2013.0425

145 ACLU. (2013). *Alone and afraid: Children held in solitary confinement and isolation in juvenile detention and correctional facilities* (Rep.). New York, NY: American Civil Liberties Union. doi: https://www.aclu.org/files/assets/Alone%20and%20Afraid%20COMPLETE%20FINAL.pdf

146 Texas Family Code §§261.001 (1) (A) & (B)

147 Vasiliades, Elizabeth. "Solitary confinement and international human rights: why the U.S. prison system fails global standards." American University International Law Review 21, no.1 (2005): 71-99.

148 American Academy of Child and Adolescent Psychiatry: Juvenile Justice Reform Committee. (2012, April). Policy statement: Solitary confinement of juvenile offenders. Retrieved April 19, 2014, from http://www.aacap.org/AACAP/Policy_Statements/2012/Solitary_Confinement_of_ Juvenile_Offenders.aspx

149 Survivor profiles - TCADP. (n.d.). Retrieved May 1, 2014, from http://tcadp.org/what-we-do/ victims-outreach/survivor-profiles/

150 Burton, C., & Tewksbury, R. (2013). How families of murder victims feel following the execution of their loved one's murderer: A content analysis of newspaper Reports of executions from 2006-2011. *Journal of Qualitative Criminal Justice and Criminology, 1*(1), 53-77. doi: http://www. jqcjc.org/documents/v1i1.pdf#nameddest=page53

151 Equal Justice USA. (n.d.). The Closure Myth. Retrieved April 19, 2014, from http://ejusa.org/ learn/victims-voices

152 TDCJ. (n.d.). TDCJ website: Executed Offenders. Retrieved April 19, 2014, from http://www. tdcj.state.tx.us/death_row/dr_executed_offenders.html

153 TDCJ. (n.d.). TDCJ website: Executed Offenders. Retrieved April 19, 2014, from http://www. tdcj.state.tx.us/death_row/dr_executed_offenders.html

154 TDCJ. (n.d.). TDCJ website: Executed Offenders. Retrieved April 19, 2014, from http://www. tdcj.state.tx.us/death_row/dr_executed_offenders.html

155 TDCJ. (n.d.). TDCJ website: Executed Offenders. Retrieved April 19, 2014, from http://www. tdcj.state.tx.us/death_row/dr_executed_offenders.html

156 TDCJ. (n.d.). TDCJ website: Executed Offenders. Retrieved April 19, 2014, from http://www. tdcj.state.tx.us/death_row/dr_executed_offenders.html

157 Fernandez, M. (2013, June 29). From America's busiest death chamber, a catalog of last rants, please and apologies. *The New York Times.* Retrieved April 19, 2014, from http://www.nytimes. com/2013/06/30/us/from-americas-busiest-death-chamber-a-catalog-of-last-rants-pleas-and-apologies.html?_r=1&

158 Victims Services Division portion of the TDCJ website. (n.d.). Retrieved April 19, 2014, from http://tdcj.state.tx.us/divisions/vs/victim_viewing_executions.html

159 http://www.worldwithouthate.org

160 Clark County Prosecutor. (n.d.). Karla Faye Tucker #437. Retrieved April 19, 2014, from http:// www.clarkprosecutor.org/html/death/US/tucker437.htm

161 Sharp, S. F. (2005). *Hidden victims: The effects of the death penalty on families of the accused.* New Brunswick, NJ: Rutgers University Press.

162 Gender and racial statistics of death row offenders. (n.d.). Retrieved May 1, 2014, from http:// www.tdcj.state.tx.us/death_row/dr_gender_racial_stats.html

163 Sharp, S. F. (2005). *Hidden victims: The effects of the death penalty on families of the accused.* (p. 7) New Brunswick, NJ: Rutgers University Press.

164 Kovaleski, S. F. (2012, February 04). Killers' families left to confront fear and shame. *New York Times.*

165 Long, W. (2010, November 15). *Research proposal for interactive internet trauma and*

complicated grief therapy for death row family members.

166 TDCJ. (n.d.). Victim Services Division section of website. Retrieved April 19, 2014, from https://www.tdcj.state.tx.us/divisions/vs/victim_viewing_executions.html

167 Texas After Violence Project (TAVP), & Human Rights Documentation Initiative (HRDI). (n.d.). Texas After Violence Project, archived interviews. Retrieved May 3, 2014, from http://av.lib.utexas.edu/index.php?title=Category:Texas_After_Violence_Project

168 Texas After Violence Project (TAVP), & Human Rights Documentation Initiative (HRDI). (n.d.). Texas After Violence Project, archived interviews. Retrieved May 3, 2014, from http://av.lib.utexas.edu/index.php?title=Category:Texas_After_Violence_Project

169 Texas After Violence Project (TAVP), & Human Rights Documentation Initiative (HRDI). (n.d.). Texas After Violence Project, archived interviews. Retrieved May 3, 2014, from http://av.lib.utexas.edu/index.php?title=Category:Texas_After_Violence_Project

170 Texas After Violence Project (TAVP), & Human Rights Documentation Initiative (HRDI). (n.d.). Texas After Violence Project, archived interviews. Retrieved May 3, 2014, from http://av.lib.utexas.edu/index.php?title=Category:Texas_After_Violence_Project

171 Texas After Violence Project (TAVP), & Human Rights Documentation Initiative (HRDI). (n.d.). Texas After Violence Project, archived interviews. Retrieved May 3, 2014, from http://av.lib.utexas.edu/index.php?title=Category:Texas_After_Violence_Project

172 *Children of parents sentenced to death* (Rep.). (2002). Quaker United Nations Office. doi: http://www.quno.org/sites/default/files/resources/ENGLISH_Children%20of%20parents%20sentenced%20to%20death.pdf

173 Feurbacher, S. (2013). *Tough Guys*. Lecture presented in Southern Methodist University Department of Counseling, Family Violence course, Plano.

174 TDCJ Website. (n.d.). TDCJ Mission and Philosophy. Retrieved April 19, 2014, from https://www.tdcj.state.tx.us/gokids/index.html

175 Information obtained through email from Texas Department of Criminal Justice. (TDCJ) Rehabilitation Programs Division.(2014).

176 Data gleaned from Texas Department of Criminal Justice (TDCJ) Response to Open Records. (2013).

177 Brett, R., & Robinson, O. (2013). *Lightening the Load of the Parental Death Penalty on Children* (Rep.). Quaker United Nations Office. doi: http://www.quno.org/sites/default/files/resources/Lightening%20the%20Load.Web_.EN_.pdf

178 Texas After Violence Project (TAVP), & Human Rights Documentation Initiative (HRDI). (n.d.). Texas After Violence Project, archived interviews. Retrieved May 3, 2014, from http://av.lib.utexas.edu/index.php?title=Category:Texas_After_Violence_Project

179 Brett, R., & Robinson, O. (2013). *Lightening the Load of the Parental Death Penalty on Children* (Rep.). Quaker United Nations Office. doi: http://www.quno.org/sites/default/files/resources/Lightening%20the%20Load.Web_.EN_.pdf

180 TDCJ. (n.d.). TDCJ website: Executed Offenders. Retrieved April 19, 2014, from http://www.tdcj.state.tx.us/death_row/dr_executed_offenders.html

181 Corrections officials sign-on for Troy Davis. (2011, September 21). Retrieved April 26, 2014, from https://www.schr.org/action/resources/corrections_officials_sign_on_for_troy_davis

182 Antonio, M. E., (2008). Stress and the capital jury: How male and female jurors react to serving on a murder trial. *The Justice System Journal, 29*(3), 396-407.

183 Cusak, R.M (1999). "Stress and Stress Symptoms in Capital Murder Jurors: Is Jury Duty Hazardous to Juror's Mental Health?" Unpublished doctoral dissertation, St. Mary's University, San Antonio, Texas

184 Antonio, M. E., (2008). Stress and the capital jury: How male and female jurors react to serving on a murder trial. *The Justice System Journal, 29*(3), 396-407)

185 Slick, J. (2011, October 14). The weight of 'playing God': In capital punishment cases, jurors are punished. Retrieved April 26, 2014, from http://www.oregonlive.com/opinion/index.

ssf/2011/10/the_weight_of_playing_god_in_c.html

186   Browning, J. G., (2012). When the trial isn't over: Counseling services for jurors. *Texas Bar Journal, 75*(4), 289-291

187   Sheffer, S. (2013). *Fighting for their lives: Inside the experience of capital defense attorneys.* Nashville, TN: Vanderbilt University Press.

188   Sheffer, S. (2013). *Fighting for their lives: Inside the experience of capital defense attorneys.* Nashville, TN: Vanderbilt University Press.

189   Equal Justice USA. (n.d.). Executions create more victims: The impact on those who carry them out. Retrieved April 26, 2014, from ejusa.org%2Flearn%2Fsecondary%252Btrauma

190   *Testimony of Donald Cabana before the Judiciary Committee of the Minnesota House of Representatives* [PDF]. (n.d.).http://www.theadvocatesforhumanrights.org/uploads/cabana_2.pdf

191   Equal Justice USA. (n.d.). Ron McAndrew's testimony before the Montana House judiciary committee. Retrieved April 26, 2014, from http://ejusa.org/state-leader/testimony/ron-mcandrew

192   Ault, A. (2011, October 3). In my nightmares I can see their faces. *Newsweek.* Retrieved April 26, 2014, from http://www.highbeam.com/doc/1G1-268078980.html?refid=easy_hf

193   Pickett, C., & Stowers, C. (2002). *Within these walls: Memoirs of a death house chaplain.* New York: St. Martin's Press.

194   Pickett, C., & Stowers, C. (2002). *Within these walls: Memoirs of a death house chaplain* (pp. 187-188). New York: St. Martin's Press.

195   (n.d.). Retrieved April 30, 2014, from http://ejusa.org/newsline/issue/secondary%2Btrauma

196   Dissociative symptoms in media eyewitnesses of an execution [Abstract]. (1994).*The American Journal of Psychiatry, 159*(9), 1335-1339. Retrieved April 26, 2014, from http://ajp. psychiatryonline.org/article.aspx?articleid=170547

197   Williams, N. M. (2002). *The Darkest hour: Stories and interviews from death row* (p. 76). Dallas, TX: GoodMedia Press.

198   Williams, N. M. (2002). *The Darkest hour: Stories and interviews from death row* (pp. 109-126). Dallas, TX: GoodMedia Press.

199   National Institute of Mental Health. (n.d.). Post-traumatic stress Disorder (PTSD). Retrieved April 26, 2014, from http://www.nimh.nih.gov/health/topics/post-traumatic-stress-disorder-ptsd/index.shtml?utm_campaign=Social%20%2BMedia&utm_source=Twitter&utm_medium=Main%2BTwitter%2BFeed)

200   Herman, J. P. (2013). Neural control of chronic stress adaptation. *Frontiers in Behavioral Neuroscience, 7.* doi: 10.3389/fnbeh.2013.00061

201   Johnson, R., & Toch, H. (2000). *Crime and punishment: Inside views* (p. 103). Los Angeles, CA: Roxbury Pub.

202   Information obtained through email from Public Information Office. (2012).

203   Williams, N. M. (2013). *Still Surviving* (pp. 190-191). Dallas, TX: GoodMedia Press.

204   Toch, H. (1977). *Living in prison: The ecology of survival.* New York: Free Press.

205   Toch, H. (1977). *Living in prison: The ecology of survival.* New York: Free Press.

206   Williams, N. M. (2002). *The Darkest hour: Stories and interviews from death row.* Dallas, TX: GoodMedia Press

207   Vermetten, E., & Spiegel, D. (2014). Trauma and Dissociation: Implications for borderline personality disorder. *Current Psychiatry Reports, 16*(2). doi: 10.1007/s11920-013-0434-8

208   Williams, N. M. (2013). *Still Surviving* (pp. 184-185). Dallas, TX: GoodMedia Press.

209   Williams, N. M. (2013). *Still Surviving* (pp. 213-214). Dallas, TX: GoodMedia Press.

210   Williams, N. M. (2013). *Still Surviving* (pp. 15-16). Dallas, TX: GoodMedia Press.

211   Williams, N. M. (2002). *The Darkest hour: Stories and interviews from death row* (pp. 43-60). Dallas, TX: GoodMedia Press.

212   Frankl, V. E. (2006). *Man's search for meaning.* Boston: Beacon Press.

213 Mcadams, D. P., Reynolds, J., Lewis, M., Patten, A. H., & Bowman, P. J. (2001). When bad things turn good and good things turn bad: Sequences of redemption and contamination in life narrative and their relation to psychosocial adaptation in midlife adults and in students. *Personality and Social Psychology Bulletin, 27*(4), 474-485. doi: 10.1177/0146167201274008

214 Mcadams, D. P., Reynolds, J., Lewis, M., Patten, A. H., & Bowman, P. J. (2001). When bad things turn good and good things turn bad: Sequences of redemption and contamination in life narrative and their relation to psychosocial adaptation in midlife adults and in students. *Personality and Social Psychology Bulletin, 27*(4), 474-485. doi: 10.1177/0146167201274008

215 Mcadams, D. P., & Mclean, K. C. (2013). Narrative Identity. *Current Directions in Psychological Science, 22*(3), 233-238. doi: 10.1177/0963721413475622

216 Williams, N. M. (2013). *Still Surviving* (p. 184). Dallas, TX: GoodMedia Press.

217 Guenther, L. (2013). *Solitary confinement: Social death and its afterlives* (p. 220). Minneapolic, MN: University of Minnesota Press.

218 Folkman, S. (2010). Stress, coping, and hope. *Psycho-Oncology, 19*(9), 901-908. doi: 10.1002/pon.1836

219 Minutes Before Six. (n.d.). Retrieved May 1, 2014, from http://minutesbeforesix.blogspot.com/

220 Langford, T. (2014, May 8). Lawsuits challenge transparency of Texas execution process. Retrieved June 8, 2014, from http://www.texastribune.org/2014/05/08/defense-attorneys-call-more-transparency-execution/

221 Krase, H. (2013, August 07). The solitary confinement scorecard. Retrieved June 8, 2014, from https%3A%2F%2Fwww.aclu.org%2Fblog%2Fprisoners-rights-criminal-law-reform%2Fsolitary-confinement-scorecard

222 State legislation: Examples - national religious campaign against torture. (n.d.). Retrieved June 8, 2014, from http://www.nrcat.org/torture-in-us-prisons/state-legislation-examples

223 Grissom, B. (2014, January 7). Solitary Confinement Study Approved, but Funding Remains Elusive, by Brandi Grissom. Retrieved June 8, 2014, from http://www.texastribune.org/2014/01/07/solitary-confinement-study-approved-lacks-funding/

224 Gardner, D. (2009). *The science of fear: How the culture of fear manipulates your brain* (p. 196). New York, NY: Plume.

225 Reprinted with permission of Prison Fellowship, P.O. Box 1550, Merrifield, VA 22116,www.pfm.org.

226 Reprinted with permission from Lance Lowry, AFSCME Texas Correctional Employees

227 Steeves, H. (2011, June 03). Maine state prison reduces solitary confinement. Retrieved June 8, 2014, from http://bangordailynews.com/2011/06/03/news/state/maine-state-prison-reduces-solitary-confinement/?ref=search

228 Steeves, H. (2011, June 03). Maine state prison reduces solitary confinement. Retrieved June 8, 2014, from http://bangordailynews.com/2011/06/03/news/state/maine-state-prison-reduces-solitary-confinement/?ref=search

229 Steeves, H. (2011, June 03). Maine state prison reduces solitary confinement. Retrieved June 8, 2014, from http://bangordailynews.com/2011/06/03/news/state/maine-state-prison-reduces-solitary-confinement/?ref=search

230 Bill Introduced in Colorado legislature aims to curb use of solitary confinement in prisons. (2011, February 22). *States News Service.* Retrieved June 8, 2014, from http://www.highbeam.com/doc/1G1-249710533.html?refid=easy_hf

231 Bill Introduced In Colorado Legislature Aims To Curb Use Of Solitary Confinement In Prisons. (2011, February 22). Retrieved June 8, 2014, from https://www.aclu.org/prisoners-rights/bill-introduced-colorado-legislature-aims-curb-use-solitary-confinement-prisons

232 Bill Introduced in Colorado legislature aims to curb use of solitary confinement in prisons. (2011, February 22). *States News Service.* Retrieved June 8, 2014, from http://www.highbeam.

com/doc/1G1-249710533.html?refid=easy_hf

233   Rael, A. (2012, June 04). Solitary confinement decreased by hundreds In Colorado. Retrieved June 8, 2014, from http://www.huffingtonpost.com/2012/06/04/solitary-confinement-decr_n_1571919.html

234   Haney, C., & Lynch, M. (1997). Regulating prisons of the future: A psychological analysis of supermax and solitary confinement. *New York University Review of Law and Social Change.* doi: http://www.probono.net/prisoners/stopsol-reports/416694.Regulating_Prisons_of_the_Future

235   Solitary confinement: Isolation & administrative segregation. (n.d.). Retrieved June 8, 2014, from http://www.justicefellowship.org/solitary-confinement

236   Marquart, J. W., Ekland-Olson, S., & Sorensen, J. R. (1994). *The rope, the chair, and the needle: Capital punishment in Texas, 1923-1990.* Austin: University of Texas Press.

237   Cloke, K. (2008). *Conflict revolution: Mediating evil, war, injustice and terrorism: How mediators can help save the planet* (p. 352). Calgary, B.C.: Janis Publications.

238   Cloke, K. (2008). *Conflict revolution: Mediating evil, war, injustice and terrorism: How mediators can help save the planet* (p. 360). Calgary, B.C.: Janis Publications.

239   Cloke, K. (2008). *Conflict revolution: Mediating evil, war, injustice and terrorism: How mediators can help save the planet* (pp. 357-358). Calgary, B.C.: Janis Publications.*The Darkest Hour: Stories and Interviews from Death Row*

EXPLORE OTHER BOOKS BY NANON M. WILLIAMS

www.GoodMediaPress.com

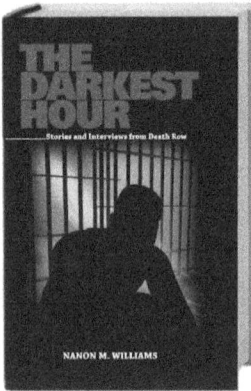

The Darkest Hour: Stories and Interviews from Death Row by Nanon M. Williams emerged from a deep and dark despair in a place where the thought of suicide often holds more appeal than the thought of living. The hopeless ones live below the line but not Nanon Williams. Williams reached high beyond despair with outstretched hands and on tiptoes. He took a firm grip on the branch of hope and hoisted himself up above the line. While on Texas' death row, Nanon was an inspirational voice. This work, now in its second edition, has expanded his inspirational influence beyond prison walls to men and women everywhere. His voice reaches others who measure their lives by an hourglass and do not see enough sand remaining to do anything of importance with their lives. We all learn from Nanon Williams that we can race against time and win.

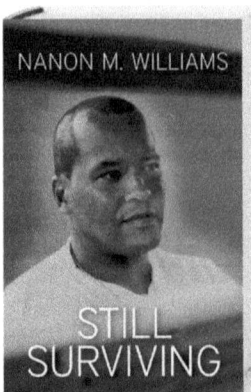

Still Surviving is the shocking account of a teenager growing up on Texas death row in one of the most brutal of prisons in the United States. Nanon Williams invites us to visit him in hell. We learn of a boy growing into manhood on his own terms while in prison and his capacity for surviving violence and racism through many devastating experiences. Nanon Williams shows us how he has managed to survive, having been falsely convicted of murder. He shows the human face of people whom society has defined as monsters and reveals shocking examples of sadistic, inhuman behavior of prison guards. Nanon Williams gives us the chance to retune our mindset when it comes to the death penalty, not as an abstract term, but as a reality for many human beings in this country.

The Ties That Bind Us is a book of poetry mixed with free verse. The poems are written from the raw feelings Nanon Williams experienced while living in solitary confinement on Texas death row. Confined to a "black out cell," Williams spent three years in total darkness with nothing but his memories and emotions to bring him solace. All of these poems describe the feelings that weighed heavy on his heart, mind and soul as he struggled to come to terms with the bleakness and despair of life in isolation. Written from a place few can imagine and even fewer will ever experience, the emotions expressed are innate to the human experience—a desire for love and human connection. Through his poetry, Williams demonstrates that there is a love that exists within us all. This love is in everything and everyone. If we choose to ignore it, the pain of separating from it remains a constant reminder of what we are missing. In the darkest, most removed prison cell in Texas' Ellis Unit, Williams reconnected with this love. This book is that expression.

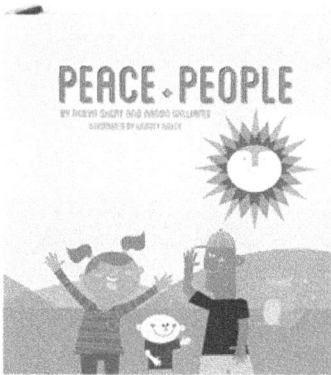

Peace People by Robyn Short and Nanon Williams is a whimsically illustrated children's book that helps young children understand the concept of peace and how to experience peace in their own lives so that they may help others to experience peace as well. *Peace People* offers a positive approach to having necessary conversations and lessons about anti-bullying at home and in school. This book helps children to understand that peace is possible when we choose to be peace. *Peace People* is perfect for children of all ages.

www.ingramcontent.com/pod-product-compliance
Lightning Source LLC
Chambersburg PA
CBHW031537260326
41914CB00032B/1844/J